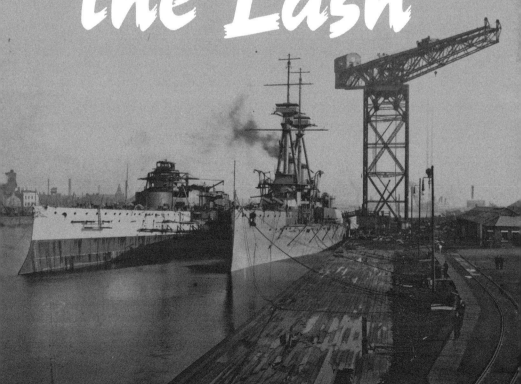

Legacy of
the Lash

BLACKS IN THE DIASPORA

Herman L. Bennett, Kim D. Butler, Judith A. Byfield,
and Tracy Sharpley-Whiting, editors

Legacy of the Lash

RACE AND CORPORAL PUNISHMENT IN THE BRAZILIAN NAVY AND THE ATLANTIC WORLD

ZACHARY R. MORGAN

INDIANA UNIVERSITY PRESS   *Bloomington & Indianapolis*

This book is a publication of

INDIANA UNIVERSITY PRESS
Office of Scholarly Publishing
Herman B Wells Library 350
1320 E. 10th Street
Bloomington, IN 47405 USA

iupress.indiana.edu

Telephone   800-842-6796
Fax   812-855-7931

♾ The paper used in this publication
meets the minimum requirements of
the American National Standard for
Information Sciences – Permanence
of Paper for Printed Library
Materials, ANSI Z39.48 – 1992.

*Manufactured in the
United States of America*

Cataloging information is available
from the Library of Congress.

ISBN 978-0-253-01420-7 (cloth)
ISBN 978-0-253-01429-0 (ebook)

1 2 3 4 5   19 18 17 16 15 14

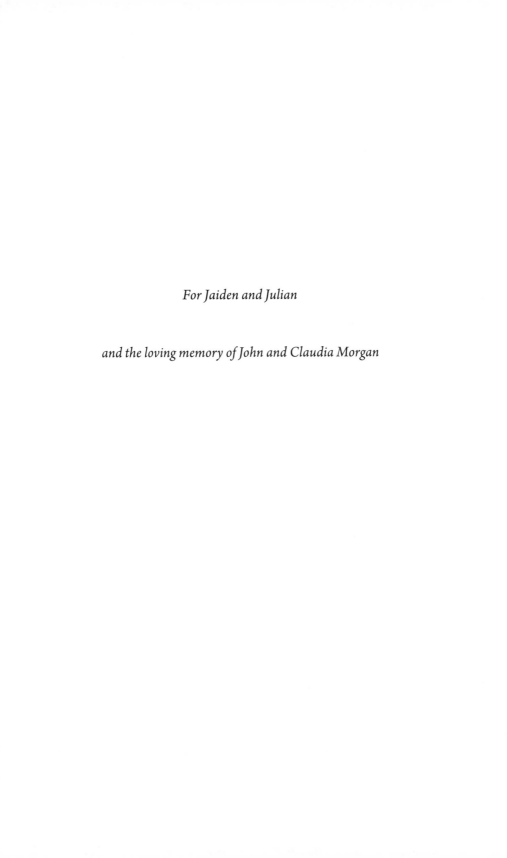

For Jaiden and Julian

and the loving memory of John and Claudia Morgan

Contents

Tables

Acknowledgments

THIS PROJECT HAS COME TOGETHER OVER MANY YEARS DURING which I have accumulated countless debts. I can only begin to thank the many friends, family members, and scholars whose inspiration, example, feedback, revisions, and support helped to make this book a reality. The credit for any success achieved herein needs to be shared widely; for its shortcomings, I beg forgiveness for not better heeding advice so generously proffered.

This project developed during a research trip to Rio de Janeiro. I arrived in Brazil with a broadly conceived project on Afro-Brazilian social mobility in the army and a consultant at the Archivo Nacional promptly introduced me to Peter Beattie, who had just concluded his outstanding work since published as *The Tribute of Blood,* on a subject similar enough to drive me screaming from the field. Peter took me to lunch and after a conversation over my interest in an institutional history of the military, he suggested the collections at the Archivo Naval on Ilha das Cobras where he had recently spent a few days conducting research. After several weeks examining their collections, *Legacy of the Lash* began to take a vague shape; for this and for Peter's support and friendship, I remain eternally grateful.

The research and writing of this book was supported by the Ford Foundation Fellowship, the Mellon Minority Undergraduate Fellowship, the David L. Boren/National Security Educational Program, the Brazil Fund, and a Nabrit Dissertation Fellowship from Brown University. More recently, a fellowship from the Woodrow Wilson National Fellowship Foundation and Faculty Research Grants from Boston College supported additional research in England and Brazil.

R. Douglas Cope, Anani Dzidzienyo, and Thomas E. Skidmore at Brown University were both supportive and critical, as the situation required. I remain deeply indebted to Thomas E. Skidmore. His encyclopedic knowledge of Brazilian history coupled with his open support for research projects far beyond his own areas and topics of historical production made him a natural mentor to students working in all regions and areas of Latin American history. Beyond that, he far exceeded the responsibilities of an advisor as he opened his home and his incomparable personal archive. He served as both mentor and friend, and he and his wife Felicity truly made me feel like family during my time in Rhode Island. This book also owes a great deal to the late Dean Bernard Bruce, who brought together a remarkable group of minority graduate students and gave us the means, the steadfast support, and the love that we needed to succeed. I know few other people who could have single-handedly succeeded in building such a nurturing community. Thanks and love to Rima Dasgupta, Gelonia Dent, Maria Elena Garcia, Rowan Ricardo Phillips, Stefan Wheelock, and all the other members of that group.

It has been my great honor and privilege to work with a gifted group of friends and colleagues who helped guide me through the process of research and writing. My heartfelt thanks for feedback and conversations go to the small group of scholars who are currently researching and publishing on various aspects of the Revolta da Chibata. For their help and camaraderie during my time in Rio's archives, as well as during conferences, panels, and papers in the U.S. and Brazil, I thank Sílvia Capanema P. de Almeida, Joseph L. Love, Álvaro Pereira do Nascimento, José Miguel Arias Neto, and Mário Maestri. In addition to those named above, over the years Sascha Auerback, Kim Butler, Amy Chazkel, Jerry Dávila, Marcela Echeverri, Ari Kelman, Deborah Levinson-Estrada, Frank McCann, Patrick McDevitt, Robert Reid-Pharr, Martin Summers Ben Vinson III, and James Woodard, read portions of the manuscript and generously shared their expertise. Along the way I also received invaluable support from many scholars. Without my undergraduate advisors at Hunter College, J. Michael Turner and Myna Bain, I suspect I would never have begun the process of becoming a historian. My deepest thanks also go to Lewis Gordon who, while I was finishing my research at Brown, offered office space, support, friendship, comments, a support staff, professional advice, and his personal network. While researching in and around Rio de Janeiro, I benefitted from advice and feedback from George Reid Andrews, Sue Ann Caufield, Todd Diacon, the late Jurgen Heye, Thomas H. Holloway, Mary Karasch, Hendrik Kraay, Jorge da Silva, Luiz Valente, Barbara Weinstein, and Erica Windler. My research on Britain and specifically on Newcastle benefitted from generous conversations with Joan Allen, John Charlton, Mary Conley, Sean Creighton, Dick Keys, and Bill Lancaster. To my friend Dona Norma Fraga de Souza, thank you for opening your home to me.

In Brazil, archivist Sátiro Ferreira Nunes and the staff at the Arquivo Nacional in Rio de Janeiro gave immeasurable assistance, suggesting collections, documents, and nearby restaurants. Many thanks also go to the staff and archivists at the Arquivo Naval and the Bibioteca da Marinha on Ilha das Cobras for their help and support, as well as to the staffs of the Biblioteca Nacional, the Arquivo do Instituto Historico e Geográfico Brasileiro, the Casa Rui Barbosa, and the Museu da Imagem e do Som.

Conducting research in England, I became deeply indebted to the staffs of the British Newspaper Library in London, the Vickers Archives held at the Cambridge University Library, the Northumbria University Library, and the University of Newcastle Library. Ian Whitehead, a maritime historian at the Tyne & Wear Archives and Museums in Newcastle, took a personal interest in my research and was particularly helpful in putting me in touch with local historians and tracking down obscure sources and images. Though images of the scale models of Newcastle-built ships didn't make it into the book, I am particularly grateful to Ian for the memorable, if dirty, tour of the nether regions of storage for a private viewing of the model of the cruiser *Bahia*.

Robert Sloan and Jenna Whittaker at Indiana University Press have worked hard to see this book through to completion. Their work, along with Carol A. Kennedy's copyediting, has made this a far better book. I thank David Marshall for his research assistance in Boston and in Rio de Janeiro.

To my friends, I owe you a great deal of gratitude for your patience, support, and friendship over these long years. Jerry Dávila, Gabi Friedman, Jessie and Julie Goff, Travis Jackson, Ari Kelman, John Laidman, Steve Wacksman, and Jordan Walker-Pearlman: you guys are truly the best.

To the historians in my family, Professors Jennifer Morgan and Herman Bennett – my sister and brother-in-law – I simply cannot begin to thank you for your patience, support, advice, love, understanding, and revisions. No one could have asked for better intellectual role models, neighbors, or family. Your loving support, for each other, for Emma and Carl, and for all those around you, should be an example to us all.

To the matriarch of our family, my grandmother Maymette Carter, thank you for your love and support over the years. You are an example to us all.

To my beautiful, brilliant, and hardworking wife Cynthia Young, I thank you for the love, friendship, support, and patience that enrich my life and helped me to finish this project. To our beautiful boys Jaiden Paul and Julian Filmore, your happiness and light make this a far better book and a far better life.

Finally, this book is dedicated in loving memory of my parents, John Paul and Claudia Burghardt Morgan. You always supported my goals in life and your strength, courage, and loving support of your friends and family continues to serve as a model for me. It saddens me that neither of you survived to see this work completed.

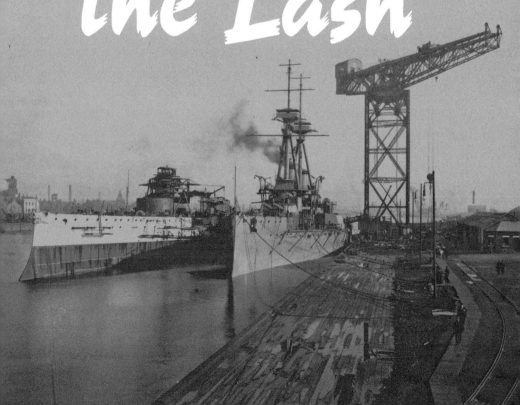

Legacy of
the Lash

Because Uncle Tom would not take vengeance into his own hands, he was not a hero for me. Heroes, as far as I could then see, were white, and not merely because of the movies but because of the land in which I lived, of which movies were simply a reflection: I despised and feared those heroes because they did take vengeance into their own hands. They thought that vengeance was theirs to take.

JAMES BALDWIN, *The Devil Finds Work*, 1976

ONE

Introduction: Race and Violence in Brazil and Its Navy

WHAT DID IT MEAN FOR BRAZIL WHEN A GROUP OF MEN, overwhelmingly poor Afro-Brazilians, violently rose up and demanded their right to citizenship? For generations, Brazilian sailors were pressed into service and forced to work under the direct threat of the lash. But then, at the end of the first decade of the twentieth century, they seized the navy's battleships and held hostage Brazil's capital city of Rio de Janeiro. These sailors, overwhelmingly Afro-Brazilians, demanded that their white officers stop "the slavery that is practiced in the Brazilian navy."[1] They staked a claim for citizenship and rights that should have resonated throughout the Atlantic; yet the story of the *Revolta da Chibata* (Revolt of the Lash) remains largely untold and has been until very recently, even for most Brazilians, forgotten.

On November 22, 1910, the Brazilian capital of Rio de Janeiro was the site of one of the great naval revolts of the twentieth century, the Revolta da Chibata. By that time, Brazilian sailors had faced nearly a century of callous and violent treatment at the hands of naval officers. In their manifesto rebelling sailors complained of poor pay, inadequate food, excessive work, and, most importantly, the ongoing application of the lash to dominate the lower ranks. In fact during the Brazilian Republic following Brazil's 1888 abolition of slavery, sailors were the only Brazilians who could be legally lashed. In the face of an aggressive policy of modernization of the Brazilian navy, sailors continued to be whipped in the traditional manner of slaves. During the first decade of the twentieth century, the Brazilian navy traded its wooden sailing vessels for modern steel battleships purchased from British shipyards.

In order to man such vessels, the navy required sailors who were at least professionalized enough to crew what have been described as factories at sea. The navy sent hundreds of sailors to the port city of Newcastle for necessary training on these new ships. Near the coast of the North Sea, these sailors freely interacted with Newcastle's radical and organized working class. Their long-standing grievance over the application of corporal punishment was exacerbated by the heightened and regimented workload on these drastically modernized ships as well as the crosscurrents of Newcastle's working-class radicalism. Together these factors motivated these sailors to execute a distinctly modern rebellion. This work tells the story of the Revolta da Chibata, its impact in Brazil, and its ties to the black Atlantic.

Approximately half of the enlisted men stationed in Rio de Janeiro – it has often been stated that the number was as high as 2,400 sailors though likely a significantly smaller number of sailors actively participated – challenged their treatment by the naval elite.[2] These men seized four warships and turned their turrets on Rio de Janeiro. Among them were three newly acquired ships from Newcastle's shipyards; two of those were new dreadnought-class battleships emblematic of Brazilian aspiration to become a "modern" nation. With guns trained on Rio's recently rebuilt downtown, and with both houses of the Brazilian National Congress (Congresso Nacional do Brasil) and the presidential palace within striking distance, the rebels demanded fundamental changes in the laws and practices governing naval service. Their actions represented both a critique of and an attack on the forced conscription of overwhelmingly black men during the nineteenth-century deterioration of Brazilian slavery. Considered through contemporary coverage in the Brazilian press, debate among politicians, and publications critical of Brazil's naval policy, this violent uprising offers a rare window into the day-to-day hardships faced by Brazilian sailors, terms of service long obscured from the world outside Brazil's navy.

During nearly a century preceding the revolt – a period also defined by Brazil's reliance on plantation slavery – the treatment of sailors at the hands of naval officers remained consistently brutal. But, in the early decades of the First Republic (1889–1930), the period that ended Brazil's monarchical governance, the social and racial strains within the navy were masked. Among the first pieces of legislation passed following the overthrow of the monarchy were reforms that trumpeted better treatment for all Brazilians; they specifically addressed improvements for those citizens serving in the navy.[3] Over time those laws were systematically ignored and later quietly overturned, allowing for the continued abuse of black men forced into naval service. In the face of this silence, the Revolta da Chibata made public, at least for a time, the brutal conditions facing sailors following the final abolition of slavery in 1888. At the very moment when Brazil's naval elite claimed a new age of military modernization based on the acquisition of modern technology, the revolt drew immeasurable shame upon them. Coverage in the local and international press garnered public sympathy for the sailors among ordinary Brazilians, the political elite, and a worldwide audience. With the very ships that substantiated the officers' claims of modernization in the hands of enlisted men, the insurgents quickly won a series of concessions from the Brazilian government.

Despite the sailors' short-term victory, the story of the Revolta da Chibata generally vanished from Brazil's historical narrative and from the general consciousness of Brazilians both black and white. It would be nearly half a century before the publication of Edmar Morel's 1959 *A Revolta da Chibata,* a popular history based largely on detailed interviews with the leader of the uprising, Seaman First Class João Cândido. Though Morel's work is credited with rekindling general interest in the revolt as a significant movement with relevance to both class and race in turn-of-the-century Brazil, during those ensuing years there was one group that retained a keen and constant interest in the revolt and the way its story was told. In 1912, José Eduardo de Macedo Soares anonymously published under the name "A Naval Officer" (*Um Official da Armada*) his book *Politica versus Marinha* (Politics versus the Navy). In it he argued that the conditions that led to the revolt were not the responsibility of naval officers; rather it was the mistreatment of the entire naval institution at the hands of the Brazilian government that created the conditions that led to the revolt. Written by an officer intimately familiar with the early-twentieth-century navy, his book blamed the circumstances that lead to the revolt on the policies of the federal government. That book drew a response from author and journalist Álvaro Bomilcar. Drawing on a series of articles he had published in 1911, he collected them into a book that challenged "A Naval Officer," arguing that the problems leading to the Revolta da Chibata were not those of politicians acting against the interests of the navy, but it was instead the racism that permeated the navy and its officers. Bomilcar, using the Brazilian army as a somewhat idealized national institution as a model, argued that the navy should allow its best apprentices into officer training to challenge the segregation that was so deeply entrenched in that institution.[4]

Also in 1912, politician and former naval officer José Carlos de Carvalho published the first volume of his autobiography *O Livro da Minha Vida: Na guerra, na paz e nas revoluções: 1847–1910.* Though Carvalho had been a high-ranking naval officer, he participated in negotiating the resolution of the Revolta da Chibata representing the interests of the government, and his portrayal of the rebel sailors was fairly sympathetic. Many naval officers felt that by negotiating with the rebel sailors, he had betrayed the interests of the officer class. He was severely criticized in several of the books produced later by naval officers. Then in the decades following the revolt several high-ranking naval officers went on to publish articles on the revolt in military journals. A series of these articles by Commander H. Pereira da Cunha was originally published serially in the *Revista Marítima Brasileira* in 1949 and was republished in book form by the Naval Press in 1953 under the title *A Revolta na Esquadra Brazileira em November e Dezembro de 1910.* Finally, in 1988 the Serviço de Documentação Geral da Marinha (an updated Naval Press) published Admiral Hélio Leôncio Martins's *A Revolta dos Marinheiros, 1910.* Martins is a well-established historian who has published widely on themes of naval history. In fact he uses his access to sources in the Brazilian navy not widely available to civilian researchers, such as João Cândido's medical records during the time he was institutionalized in a mental hospital while he awaited trail in 1911, to offer a very detailed narrative of the events surround the Revolta da Chibata.[5] Together, these works told the story of nearly incompetent rebels who were not fully in control of their ships, who were simply *incapable* of posing a serious threat to the capital, and who all but stumbled into their eventual victory because the government was invested in protecting their ships at all costs. These works shared the overall purpose to discredit the qualifications and the actions of the rebels and to critique the government for its response to the uprising.[6]

These officers, in seeking to restore the honor of a naval officer corps that lost both life and honor during the uprising, invariably claimed that their studies uncovered the "truth" that had been obscured, first by the popular press sympathetic to the goals of the revolt, and later by leftist historians. The narrative and political framing of these military scholars represented a calculated decision to present the revolt as nonpolitical rather than the critique of state-controlled naval service that it was. Journalists and contemporary scholars alike argued that the central motivation for the revolt was the low quality of the food served to sailors, making the action into a glorified food riot. Additionally, they made claims to belittle the rebels' military effectiveness: they maintain that the *reclamantes* (the aggrieved, as the rebels identified themselves to the press) would have attacked the city if they had been able to do so, that only their incapacity to hit their targets kept the city unmolested, and that they used small-caliber weapons only because of their powerlessness to fire the ships' 12-inch guns. In his 1949 study of the revolt, Comandante H. Pereira da Cunha argued that had officers been allowed to fight, the vastly outgunned ships that remained loyal to the government would have made short work of the rebel-held ships because of the officers' superior training.

It was no accident that military scholars sought to erase from Brazil's national history a story so explicitly tied to slavery, abolition, and the ongoing manipulation of freedom for black Brazilians. For the Brazilian elite at the turn of the twentieth century, a commitment to racial and cultural improvement through *branqueamento* (whitening) defined the nation. The origins and events of the Revolta da Chibata challenged the rigid racial hierarchy that privileged European culture, labor, and race over that of Brazil's existing nonwhite population. The elite – those individuals who first controlled the story of the Brazilian sailors who risked so much, and paid so dearly, for their role in ending the abuse of free Brazilian men – consciously appropriated the narrative of this national history and portrayed these enlisted men as barely competent.

These publications reconstructed the Revolta da Chibata as an event of some national significance, but as one in which the sailors who revolted played no significant role.

The publication of Morel's seminal *A Revolta da Chibata* in 1959 marked the introduction of a second wave in the historiography of the revolt. Morel sympathetically portrayed the rebels as men making justifiable claims against an abusive institution. Building off this work, most modern scholarship presents the reclamantes as unsung heroes, who successfully resisted an oppressive and manipulative state. In the decades that followed, numerous compelling works were published in Brazil. To date the most thorough is Álvaro Pereira do Nascimento's excellent 2008 *Cidadania, cor e disciplina na revolta dos marinheiros de 1910,* and several Brazilian scholars continue work on the revolt. Overall, the Brazilian scholarship focuses on the treatment of sailors within the context of the institution of the Brazilian navy and more broadly within the overarching category of military history.[7]

Joseph L. Love recently published the first English language monograph on the revolt, titled *The Revolt of the Whip.* Love's fascinating examination of the revolt through the international press looks for various motivating factors for the revolt; in this light he examines both the 1905 uprising on the Russian *Potemkin* as well as the reclamantes' understanding of European Marxism. Among the most interesting events he documents is the short time that the *São Paulo* and its crew – most of whom would participate in the Revolta da Chibata – visited the city of Lisbon while transporting the Brazilian president elect back to Rio de Janeiro from his European tour in 1910. During that stay, a republican uprising overthrew the Portuguese monarchy; within three days the Brazilian president elect received formal visits aboard the *São Paulo* from both Portugal's King Manuel and the new provisional president of the Portuguese Republic, Teófilo Braga. The Brazilian sailors witnessed this moment of political upheaval as well as the important role that naval personnel played in it. Finally, Love draws direct comparison between the Revolta da Chibata and the 1944 work stoppage among African American sailors following the naval munitions explosion at Port Chicago, California.[8]

These are interesting and necessary comparisons, but one need not go so far afield to contextualize this rebellion. The arming of slaves and free blacks in the service of the nation represents a small but growing field in Latin American, and Atlantic, history. While this uprising certainly deserves a place in our understanding of modern military history, both the revolt itself and the role of the Brazilian navy overall are better understood within the broader context of Atlantic slavery – as the sailors themselves, with their call for an end to slavery as practiced in the Brazilian navy, demanded. These events fit better into the specific context of the nineteenth-century collapse of Brazilian slavery with the obvious coming of abolition. Rather than comparison to Russian rebel sailors or African Americans rising up more than thirty years later during WWII, the more relevant context seems to be the free Afro-Cuban soldiers who fought in the Cuban Wars for independence in the second half of the nineteenth century, documented by Ada Ferrer in *Insurgent Cuba.* An understanding of the Jamaican Christmas Day Rebellion and the Morant Bay Rebellion examined by Thomas Holt in *The Problem of Freedom* and the Aponte Rebellion in Cuba examined by Matt D. Childs in *The 1812 Aponte Rebellion in Cuba and the Struggle against Atlantic Slavery* offers a better understanding of "problem" of Brazil's growing free black population and how a national policy of military recruitment helped the state control this growing crisis. More local to the site of the Revolta da Chibata, Kim Butler's *Freedoms Given, Freedoms Won* offers insight into the world that Afro-Brazilians navigated in the age of freedom, and Zephyr Frank's *Dutra's World* shows us the impact that the domestic slave trade had on the lives of both slaves and free blacks in Rio de Janeiro. Of course the Revolta da Chibata was a military revolt, but given how many of the reclamantes had been forcibly conscripted into service, examining them primarily as sailors would be like categorizing a slave revolt on a plantation as an agrarian uprising or a farmers revolt. The revolt was a movement against state policies that violently located many young black men into a state institution just as they gained their independence from slavery.[9]

But the study of the Revolta da Chibata actually demands broader historical context than the Brazilian military and its control of black bodies. What began as a research project focused on a four-day revolt in Rio de Janeiro has morphed into a project with links to the working poor, to their governments, and to industry on three continents.

Rio de Janeiro's archives fail to sufficiently address the broader context of the Atlantic World (black or otherwise). Telling the stories of these Afro-Brazilian rebels demands an understanding of elite naval policy in Brazil, England, and, to some extent, the United States. To understand Brazil's navy, it must be contextualized within the history and policies of the Newcastle shipbuilding company George W. Armstrong & Co., and to understand the radicalization of these Brazilian sailors, one must understand their contacts with worker radicalism in Newcastle and the shifting role that British sailors held as modern citizens in the British Empire. My study thus examines the 1910 Revolta da Chibata against the backdrop of nineteenth-century abolition, industry, and military modernization in the Atlantic World. This examination of the Brazilian navy goes back to its origins during the era of Brazilian independence from Portugal in the early nineteenth century, and the detailed examination of the lives and treatment of enlisted men in the Brazilian navy begins in 1860.

Although Brazil's history is spotted with military insurrections, this revolt remains unique. Enlisted men planned, implemented, and orchestrated events; they forcefully removed all officers from the ships during the initial night of the uprising. During the four-day revolt, the overall chain of military command remained intact, with the reclamantes at the helm. The enlisted men's organization and their ability to navigate ships effectively and operate armament sent a clear message to the Brazilian naval officers and to the population of Brazil. In government reports and internal documents, naval officers had long bemoaned the issue of base and untrainable sailors; officers insisted that enlisted men were incapable of obeying naval discipline without the motivational application of corporal punishment. The Revolta da Chibata shattered that misconception as enlisted men outmaneuvered and outnegotiated Brazil's naval and political elites. It was not only a violent rebellion, the reclamantes engaged in what can only be understood as a public relations campaign to show their officers and the world that they were in fact professional, trained sailors. Because men of African descent organized and carried out this military uprising, the Revolta da Chibata should stand out in both Brazil's history and the annals of the Atlantic World.

That the reclamantes themselves framed their revolt in the language of slavery cannot come as a surprise. In the decades preceding the revolt Brazilian naval officers echoed slave owners' assertions that only violence could motivate inherently lazy blacks. While the late nineteenth and early twentieth centuries saw changes in recruitment policies intended to reduce the navy's dependence on forced conscription, at the time of the revolt many of the sailors serving in the Brazilian navy had been impressed into service and were kept in line through the liberal application of the lash. These were free black men forced into service under the threat of state-sanctioned violence decades after the formal abolition of slavery in Brazil. Although corporal punishment had been practiced in all modern navies until the nineteenth century, its continued application in a Brazilian society defined by its reliance on the labor of enslaved Africans both on rural plantations and in urban centers muddies the question of how to disentangle the history of punishment of the body from the specific history of slavery. The Revolta da Chibata represented a successful military insurrection planned and overseen by black men whose origins were in Brazil's lowest socioeconomic strata. That such an action could even take place was a shock to the citizens of Rio de Janeiro and, given the response of the international press, to the world beyond. Throughout the history of the African diaspora weapons of war (the tangible manifestation of power) have all but universally been wielded by whites over blacks; in this case, however, suddenly poor Afro-Brazilians controlled the weapons of war, and thus the power.

Through their control of these battleships the reclamantes demonstrated a striking mastery over advanced technology–a phenomenon that stood at odds with the elite image of black rustics who required coercion to work. The dreadnoughts involved in the revolt were at the cutting edge of military technology. These were not just the most modern and destructive ships in Brazil's possession; they were for a time the most powerful in the world. In 1904, Brazil committed to a $31.25 million dollar contract to overhaul its navy with vessels built in the British shipyards that dominated international arms production in this era.[10] The purchase of the "all big gun" dreadnought battleships involved in the revolt briefly positioned Brazil's navy among the most powerful and most modern in the world; at the moment when Britain had just launched its first dreadnought in 1906, Brazil placed its order for three. Ironically, it was the government's acquisition of these ships that allowed the reclamantes, a small group of politically powerless men, to hold a nation hostage and dictate conditions to its federal government.

The fulfillment of this naval contract allowed for the establishment of specific ties between Brazilian enlisted men and the British shipyards of Newcastle that furthered the organization of the Revolta da Chibata. Brazilian sailors enjoyed access to these ships long before they began to arrive in Rio de Janeiro in April 1910. As many as 1,000 sailors – overwhelmingly of African descent according to British records – found themselves in the port city of Newcastle, England, training to serve as crews for the four ships either built or armed by the Newcastle shipyard, then called Sir William Armstrong, Whitworth & Co. (due to periodic name changes over the years, I will generally follow local custom and refer to the company as Armstrongs).[11] While undergoing training, hundreds of these men were housed together in hotels and boarding houses while smaller groups sought flats and rooms for rent. Most were there for several months, whereas some individual enlisted men (according to an interview with João Cândido, the leader of the Revolta da Chibata, conducted years after the fact) were there for as long as a year. There were certainly representatives of the Brazilian commission – likely both officers and enlisted men – in Newcastle from the time the keel plates of the *Minas Geraes,* one of the dreadnoughts, were laid down in the Elswick shipyards in early 1907 until the ships departed England in 1910.

Black enlisted personnel were well trained in England, as their mastery of the dreadnoughts demonstrated, but I argue that much more than technical training occurred in Newcastle. Sailors enjoyed a level of economic status and freedom of movement there generally withheld from them in Rio de Janeiro. Brazilian sailors in Newcastle received extra wages and experienced a degree of personal autonomy that placed them in contact with working people and their ideas, which, in turn, reinforced their own grievances and led, at least in part, to the outbreak of the Revolta da Chibata.

Newcastle in this era was a remarkable city, and during the months that the Brazilian sailors awaited delivery of their new ships, they were exposed to an environment radically different from Rio, and for that matter quite different from what they likely saw in other European port cities within or outside of England. Newcastle's tradition of popular radicalism throughout the nineteenth century lent broad backing to trade unions, cooperatives, friendly societies, and mechanics' institutes. Workers at Armstrongs had been central to the 1871 Nine Hour Movement, which swept the Tyneside. Once Brazilian sailors and officers began arriving in Newcastle, they witnessed two different strikes that halted work on and delayed the launch of two of the contracted Brazilian warships, including the *Minas Geraes.* The impact of organized resistance could not have been lost on these Brazilian sailors.[12]

Furthermore, Newcastle at the time enjoyed a reputation, if not quite for antiracism, at least for a certain pragmatic acceptance that Newcastle's economy flourished when foreign navies purchased their ships. With those sales came visits by hundreds of foreign crewmen, often for months at a time, and those sailors supported the merchants and businesses of greater Newcastle. The economic well-being of the entire city was linked to the regular presence of often nonwhite foreigners, and the city came to accept and welcome that truth, if at times somewhat begrudgingly. One anonymous letter to a local newspaper describes one clash between racial hostility and acceptance during the visit of a Chinese crew in the late 1880s. A group of Chinese officers were being harassed near the Central Station by some street boys who were "not conspicuous for their display of good manners." As one of the Chinese officers tried to pass, a boy repeatedly stepped in front of him to block his way. The writer "administered a sound box of the ears to the forward youth which caused him to desist." The point of the letter's publication was that good Geordies (citizens of Newcastle) had a responsibility for the protection of these exotic visitors.[13]

Additionally, in England, enlisted men in the Brazilian navy witnessed a British navy that had recently experienced its own radical transformation. During the nineteenth century, numerous reforms were implemented in the British navy, initiatives that tangibly improved the lives of British sailors and their families. Sailors received improvements in their pay, pension entitlement for their families if a seaman died in the line of duty, and professionalization of their image and appearance through the standardization of naval uniforms. These and other progressive reforms in both recruitment and the conditions under which they served transformed the image of British sailors in the national consciousness: from the drunken and dangerous lout embodied by the eighteenth-century Jack Tar to the noble hero of nation and empire embodied by the sober men of the Royal Navy.[14]

Any of the examples of modern and progressive labor policy witnessed by Brazilian sailors in Newcastle could have motivated the revolt against their officers: the effectiveness of organized labor and work stoppages in the shipbuilding industry, the general lack of racial hostility in a diverse population, the increased wages Brazilian sailors enjoyed while overseas, or the example of British sailors who successfully struggled against draconian conditions in the British navy that paralleled ongoing service in the Brazilian navy. All of these factors combined to make the idea of a return to traditional service in the Brazilian navy unacceptable, and help to explain the timing and character of the Revolta da Chibata.

That the revolt took place not immediately after the abolition of slavery in Brazil in 1888 but twenty-two years later only after the Brazilian navy was in possession of these ships and sailors had been posted to England is an important detail. In the face of an uprising among blacks against violent oppression and forced labor at the hands of a white hierarchy, it is understandable and correct to position the revolt in the context of slavery; but this revolt was as much a response to modernization as it was to the draconian traditions of exploitive and violent forced labor. Those examples of modernization, exemplified by both the acquisition of naval ships and the radicalism the reclamantes encountered during their world travel, built upon a third policy of modernization implemented by the Brazilian elite in this era: the renovation of Brazil's capital city, Rio de Janeiro, in the late nineteenth and early twentieth centuries. Those Brazilian sailors who departed for England in order to crew the new battleships departed from an urban center nearing the conclusion of a massive overhaul.

In the nineteenth century Rio de Janeiro went through a series of radical political and physical transformations. Rio started the century as the colonial capital, from 1808 it housed the Portuguese monarchy and its court after Napoleonic troops chased them from the Iberian Peninsula, from 1822 it served as the capital for the Brazilian Empire following independence, and finally, when the monarchy was overthrown, it became the capital of the Brazilian Republic in 1889. Throughout most of this period, enslaved African men and women were forced to perform the capital's physical labor. Although the impact of Brazilian abolition was arguably greatest in the rural plantation region, during the first half of the nineteenth century enslaved Africans dominated the life of Rio de Janeiro as never before. In 1821, 36,182 of the 86,323 people living in Rio de Janeiro were enslaved. Though this represented less than half of the population, nearly two-thirds of Rio's population was of African descent. According to the 1849 census, the number of enslaved Africans had ballooned to 78,855, representing 38.6 percent of the overall population of 206,000. During the 1840s the government introduced policies in favor of increased European immigration, but the booming coffee economy and the fear of an impending termination of the Atlantic slave trade into Brazil led to a "black immigration" into Rio, which peaked in 1849 as both free black and enslaved populations grew at striking rates.[15]

The census of 1849 documented a historic peak in the slave population in Rio de Janeiro; these nearly 80,000 enslaved men and women represented one of the largest urban slave populations in the Americas. In contrast, according to the *Federal Population Census,* the slave population in New Orleans peaked in 1840 with 23,448 enslaved and 19,226 free black people out of a total population of just over 102,000, whereas in 1840, Charleston had some 14,673 enslaved people and only 1,558 free blacks out of an overall population of 29,261. Only the city of Havana, with 188,929 enslaved people out of its total population of 388,073, had a higher per capita rate at over 48 percent.[16]

From 1850 until the abolition of slavery in 1888, the overall number, and the percentage of enslaved Africans to free persons in Rio de Janeiro, steadily declined.[17] Still, a declining enslaved population did not mean decline in the Afro-Brazilian population. During the second half of the nineteenth century rural lower-class men and women – overwhelmingly Afro-Brazilians – fled the plantation region for the urban centers, settling in cities up and down the coastline, and especially in the nation's capital. The promise of economic growth and employment was a magnet for former slaves from the countryside, though upon arrival most were bitterly disappointed when they found that in pursuit of "whitening," many employers withheld formal employment from free Afro-Brazilians.

With the end of the Atlantic slave trade to Brazil in 1850, money that for centuries had flowed out of the country to secure African labor instead began to flow into various area of the domestic economy. By the 1870s Rio de Janeiro was well into a program of modernization represented by newly cobbled streets, gas lighting, sewage systems, and the installation of trams in large part to replace the litters in which slaves traditionally had transported members of the city's elite. When slavery was finally abolished in 1888 Rio's renewal only accelerated. In an attempt to emulate the wide avenues and parks of modern European capitals, Rio de Janeiro's elites implemented radical changes to the landscape. This urban renewal caused considerable social and economic disruption, and went a long way toward seeding the ground for civil disorder.[18]

Brazil's capital experienced modernization as defined by advances in technology, public health, design, architecture, and the reconstruction of large parts of downtown based on a European urban model. For the elite these improvements made sense given the rapid rate at which the city was growing: between 1872 and 1890, the population nearly doubled, from 274,000 to more than 522,651, and by the time the revolt took place in 1910, the city's population had expanded by another 66 percent to 870,475.[19] The growth in Rio's population was largest among the previously mentioned former slaves fleeing the economic stagnation that settled over the agricultural northeast during the collapse of slavery, and additionally among white European immigrants who began to flood Brazil's industrial cities. These distinct populations faced very different futures in Brazil's urban centers. European immigrants were valuable to a national elite obsessed with whitening their nation; thus formal jobs that offered living wages and union protection were selectively granted to white foreign immigrants. Afro-Brazilian migrants to the city were generally forced instead to find their way in the city's informal economy. According to historian José Murilo de Carvalho, by 1890, 28.7 percent of the population of Rio de Janeiro was foreign born and another 26 percent came from other regions of Brazil; only 45 percent of the city's population was born there. In 1890, more than 100,000 people in Rio de Janeiro earned their livings on the margins between crime and legal employment, and by 1906 that population had grown to 200,000.[20] This group included "thieves, prostitutes, con-men, rogues, deserters from the army, navy and from foreign ships, vagabonds, gypsies, peddlers [and] rag pickers."[21] The city's physical changes came at a high cost to this growing population of poor blacks. In order to make Rio's downtown palatable for elites, the nonwhite informal workers were forced from their homes in the downtown area of *Centro* and into Rio's northern suburbs, which would soon house the earliest of the city's *favelas* – improvised slums. The damage to Rio's poor population was not an accidental side effect of the elite's commitment to modernization. Instead, the increased level of hardship for the Brazilian underclass was one of the essential outcomes of these "improvements"; modernization depended on the dislocation of the Afro-Brazilian poor.[22]

Understanding the significance of the Revolta da Chibata requires an appreciation of the role of the navy in Brazilian society. In contrast to the rapid and dramatic modernization of Rio de Janeiro's economy and urban landscape, the organization of the navy remained hidebound in preemancipation traditions; well into the twentieth century Brazil's navy was a highly stratified and racially segregated institution. In the nineteenth century Afro-Brazilians commonly filled the lower ranks of both the army and navy. Some won their freedom in exchange for military service for the Brazilian Empire, but in both the army and the navy, slaves freed in order to serve represented a much smaller group than those free blacks forcibly conscripted into military service. In the Brazilian navy, rank-and-file sailors, overwhelmingly of African descent, endured such harsh conditions that service was generally avoided whenever possible. In a country that relied so heavily on the labor of enslaved Africans, it followed that Afro-Brazilians were overrepresented among the men pressed into service in the lower ranks.

The racial composition of the lower ranks contrasted sharply with that of the naval officer class. As opposed to the harsh conscription and violent service faced by Brazilian enlisted men, naval officers had a long tradition of coming from an elite and genteel background. When the Royal Academy of the Navy was established in Lisbon by royal decree in December 1782, in order to qualify for admission officer candidates had either to be of nobility, to be the sons of military officers, or to receive

a dispensation from the academy itself; only elite white families qualified for consideration. Along with the monarch and the royal court, this
officer training school and its administrators shifted to Brazil, arriving
in Rio de Janeiro in January 1808, and the institution remained in Brazil
throughout the struggle for Brazilian independence. The racial origins
of enlisted men and officers were so different, and admission to officer
training was so exclusive, that the level of racial segregation of the navy
was likely as high as could be found in any Brazilian institution.[23]

In their declaration to the president of the republic, the *reclamantes*
began with the words "We, as sailors, Brazilian citizens, and supporters of the republic, can no longer accept the slavery as practiced in the
Brazilian Navy."[24] Though this was a revolt made possible by Brazilian
political and naval elites' insatiable appetite for modernity, for the reclamantes, the parallel between naval service and slavery was not empty
rhetoric. Established alongside Brazilian independence in 1822, the institution of the Brazilian navy formed as Brazil's dependence on African
slavery peaked. The lower decks were populated through various acts
of forced recruitment: lower-class men were dragooned and impressed
off the streets, orphans were placed in the naval apprentice schools, and
petty criminals were regularly turned over to the military. In the face
of coerced labor under naval officers quite similar to methods applied
by plantation owners, one sees similarity in patterns of resistance and
domination; desertion and insubordination were the most common
challenges to the institutions, and these crimes were dealt with violently, ritualistically, and publicly. In the Brazilian navy, the head officer
on board a ship traditionally dealt with most minor infractions: public
drunkenness, gambling, assault, insubordination, desertion, and acts of
sexual immorality. Rather than jailing a man and carrying out a lengthy
trial during which his labor was lost to the navy, an officer took on the
role of judge and jury. Naval punishment was immediate and violent;
there was neither defense nor appeal. In the eyes of naval officers and
slave owners alike, their institutions could not run without the liberal application of the lash. Only through a system of ritualized violence could
they retain control over the masses of Afro-Brazilians.

Men who broke the rules repeatedly *were* removed from their ships
and put on trial in front of the *Conselho de Guerra da Marinha*, Brazil's

military high court. Those found guilty – more than 96 percent of those who faced trial were eventually found guilty – were put to work without pay for the duration of their punishment, and upon completing that sentence, their term of service in the navy started over, and time served prior to their trial was lost. Depending on when they joined the ranks, minimum terms of naval service were between nine and twelve years. Therefore, there are records of men forced into service in adolescence who repeatedly deserted their ships and ended up serving well past their sixtieth birthday, and some who had been enslaved and won their "freedom" through sale into naval service who found themselves still forced to work well past abolition in 1888.

Yet those men who took their oath to serve the nation were sworn into service as citizens; neither the army nor the navy had the right to enlist enslaved men, either through impressment or as volunteers; they had to be technically freed before enlistment. Indeed, those slaves who sought to escape enslavement by enlisting into the armed services were routinely, though not universally, returned to their owners. Article 147, section 22, of the Constitution of 1824 explicitly states that if the state has a legal need to use property that belongs to a private citizen, that citizen had to be indemnified before that use takes place, and such careful language made perfect sense in a slaveholding society. The interpretation of liberalism in nineteenth-century Brazil protected slaves first as property. For enslaved men to enlist, they first had to be manumitted by their owners, though such manumission could be conditional on their actual service. Abolition in 1888 in and of itself had no direct effect on the Afro-Brazilian sailors serving in the navy. Symbolically, any group with such direct ties to African slavery must have been deeply invested in the passage of the Golden Law, but the reclamantes saw little, if any, improvement in their treatment by officers representing the interests of the state; in fact the acquisition of modern ships that functioned like factories at sea elevated enlisted men's onboard responsibilities and reportedly increased the application of corporal punishment in the decades after abolition.[25]

The contradictions of a slave society (and of a postabolition society based on racial hierarchy) that relied on black men to fulfill the basic needs of its armed forces was not lost on Brazil's military elite. These men constantly struggled with the question of how such a military could best be modernized into an honorable and ideally voluntary military institution. The service of former slaves in the nation's military was hardly a contradiction unique to Brazil; in slave societies throughout the Atlantic World the elite were not averse to having armed blacks in their midst and in institutional formations. There was a near-universal acceptance of arming and freeing slaves in the Latin American wars of independence under both Bolivar and San Martin in South America, in Mexico under Vicente Guerrero, and later during Cuba's wars for independence. Additionally, armed freed blacks played roles on both sides during the war for independence of England's North American colonies, and later in the American Civil War. For the Brazilian navy and for militaries throughout the Americas, military service served as a means to regiment black bodies, and the contradiction of armed blacks in a society predicated on white dominance was a constant source of anxiety for the political and military elite.[26]

So, the reclamantes' description of "slavery as practiced in the Brazilian Navy" need not be read metaphorically. The difference between naval service and forms of urban slavery commonly seen in Rio and other cities would have been subtle to the men forced into service; their complaint was literal. But, while sailors legitimately argued that the state treated them as slaves, it is not my intent to claim that the Brazilian elite understood these sailors to be chattel. Instead I believe that changes in recruitment pattern applied throughout the second half of the nineteenth century are evidence that beyond its primary function as a national military institution, the Brazilian navy was part of an institutional structure (which included the police, army, naval apprenticeship schools, and orphanages) that was tasked with controlling the growing free and freed black population following the abolition of the slave trade in 1850.

Understanding the turn-of-the-twentieth-century modernization of the Brazilian capital demands an appreciation of both slavery and abolition in that coastal city. The formal abolition of slavery remains a crucial benchmark in any slave state, but the experience of these particular Afro-Brazilian sailors straddled the pre- and postabolition period. Their lives illustrate the fluid relationship between slavery and freedom in

Brazil, and these sailors are best understood as part of Brazil's history of freedom in the era of abolition (from the end of the slave trade in 1850 through the wake of abolition in 1888). These sailors – free men – were part of a massive and growing population of free and freed Afro-Brazilians. To understand their service to the state and their rebellion, one must understand the state's role in controlling the labor and the movement of this growing "free" population.

Brazil throughout the nineteenth century straddled two different economies, each configured around a plantation regime; additionally it straddled two labor systems, enslaved and free workers. By 1800, the sugar plantations of the northeast had long been in decline, having been surpassed by Caribbean centers of sugar production such as Saint-Domingue and Cuba. On the other hand, the coffee plantations of the southeast were by mid-century experiencing explosive growth, which continued through the end of the century. In the decades leading up to 1850, when the importation of enslaved Africans ended – closed in large part due to long-term pressure from England – slave owners imported African men and women at the highest rate seen at any period in Brazil's history; this was because it was clear that Brazil's plantation economy would soon be forced to make the transition from slave to free labor. In the south, that fact was mitigated by the record profits enjoyed by coffee exporters; plantation owners were able to invest in labor-saving technology and could envision a future based on wage labor. In the less-profitable northeast, the transition to wage labor was much more difficult. The purchase price of slaves increased mid-century, and a domestic slave trade shifted labor from north to south.

In the face of shifting demographics in the Brazilian cities and countryside, the navy represented an important part of the modern machine developed to control the growing free black population in Brazil. As the 1850 Queiroz Law ended Brazil's slave trade and the subsequent 1871 Law of the Free Womb, 1885 Saraiva-Cotegipe Law, and the 1888 Golden Law – which respectively freed all children born to enslaved mothers, freed all existing slaves at the age of sixty, and finally abolished slavery in Brazil altogether – cash-poor northern sugar plantation owners were forced (with greater success in some regions than others) to manipulate free black workers into continuing their work on the sugar plantations.

The forced conscription of men into military service (either following arrest for trumped-up or petty criminal charges or in straightforward sweeps to dragoon men into service) was an important threat to ensure that allegedly free laborers would not leave the plantation. Alongside the navy's penal role, legislative reform expanded or created the role of naval apprenticeship schools, the police force, the army, and orphanages. Together these state institutions controlled the growing rural and urban underclass that emerged throughout the process of Brazilian abolition.

For the Brazilian elite, abolition was no shining movement focused on the rights or abuse of enslaved Africans. Instead it was a hardship mandated by British political and economic power that required a measured response in order for Brazil to become a modern nation-state. While it remains a source of pride for many Brazilians that their politicians negotiated abolition without black codes, legal segregation, or postabolition policies such as Jim Crow, Brazilian abolition actually happened in tandem with an emerging national policy designed to regulate the former slaves embodied as a growing underclass. Abolition was accompanied by elite redeployment of national institutions to control nonelites. As the Brazilian elite sought to remake Rio de Janeiro as a shiny international metropolis by building grand avenues to rival the European capitals, they also mobilized existing institutions in expanded roles designed to control the growing subaltern population. Thus the state also took on a new (or at least a greatly expanded) role in the physical and often violent control of its overall growing subaltern population. As historian of the Brazilian police Thomas Holloway argues, "state institutions assumed authority previously exercised primarily through personalistic hierarchies. Related changes included the transition . . . from public torture to disciplinary incarceration as the focus of punishment, and the development of bureaucratic institutions, such as the police, to fill public space."[27] Stated differently, under slavery, masters were responsible for controlling and disciplining enslaved Africans and Afro-Brazilians, but with the coming of abolition, the elite redirected existing state institutions (the military and the police) while creating others (naval apprenticeship schools) so as to control Brazil's growing free population. In the waning days of slavery, urban police expanded the practice of violently controlling this potentially dangerous population, and with abolition, the police became the primary defense against the impoverished masses. In fact, throughout the nineteenth century and early twentieth century, Rio's police force could better be described as controlling this potentially "dangerous" population than as responding to specific criminal acts. They regularly corralled groups of boys and men off the streets of downtown Rio. Police arrested slaves and freemen indiscriminately; slaves were returned to their masters, whereas nonslaves were kept in short-term lockup, at the *casa da guarda*. Many able-bodied men were selected as conscripts for the army or navy without further legal formalities. Crimes committed by members of the elite were not a primary concern of the police force, and for the poor, following the law offered little protection from being bound, chained, whipped, and forced into military service. As slaves became workers, vagrants, and criminals, Brazilian society created institutions to oversee them.[28]

Several histories focus on the military's role as a proto-penal institution throughout the nineteenth and early twentieth centuries in Latin America, applying Michel Foucault's definition of modern society and its basis on modern prisons and a modern police state.[29] Some prisons were built in Latin America that loosely conformed to Foucault's definition of a modern prison; that is, a facility that can "introduce in the inmate a state of conscious and permanent visibility that assures the automatic functioning of power."[30] They thereby controlled the prisoner rather than physically punishing him. These institutions, though, were few and far between and were almost always filled with "serious criminals." The vast majority of this population had committed homicide; there was simply no space for lesser criminals in the Brazilian penal system. But, a lack of space was just one shortcoming of a modern prison in Brazil. For the elite, the value of forced military conscription was an implied threat that applied not only to criminals, but also to poor laborers in both the cities and the countryside.

For much of the nineteenth century, both the army and navy played important roles in the containment of men by housing petty criminals as well as those elements that to the elite represented potential criminals; the poor, vagrants, the underemployed. Additionally, conscription threatened productive agrarian workers; free men with the right to seek higher wages either on more productive farms or in urban centers had

to break patriarchal ties with traditional landowners. These landowners were often the only men with the power to protect their workers
from random sweeps by military conscription crews. A July 1822 imperial decree clearly defined the population subject to forced recruitment,
underscoring that the draft should target those who were socially and
economically *desprotegidos:* literally, the unprotected.[31]

The army's role as a penal institution was challenged by the implementation of the 1874 Reform Laws, which attempted to remove dishonorable service such as the rank of servant to high-ranking officers,
and to abolish the practice of corporal punishment in that branch of the
military in an effort to create "honorable" service for Brazilian citizens.
In contrast, the navy is perhaps better defined not by its population of
criminals but by its population of potential criminals. Desprotegidos
acted outside of the "honorable" society and the official economy. However, in the waning years of slavery, there were many Afro-Brazilian
men – and for that matter, women – who did not or could not participate
in respectable society and economy. Officials perceived these people as
potential criminals, and they were often treated as such without actually
being suspected of any specific crime. As slavery ended, the navy was an
increasingly important tool in the control of a small but highly visible
subaltern Afro-Brazilian population throughout the country.

Systems that were originally put in place to control Brazil's transition from slavery to free labor allowed for the exploitation of black men
for decades after the passage of abolition. Brazilian sailors continued to
serve under the legitimate threat of the same ritualized and public violence that controlled enslaved men and women during centuries of Brazilian history. But in 1910, soon after returning from training in England
and empowered by dreadnought battleships that had not existed until
this time, Afro-Brazilian sailors violently revolted and demanded that
such treatment end. In part, the effectiveness of their revolt reflected the
focus of the international press, already abuzz with Brazil's possession
of the world's most powerful battleships. When Afro-Brazilian sailors
turned these ships against the nation, it unraveled the very story that this
national investment in naval technology was to tell. Brazil's possession of
a modern navy bestowed modernity; it was no accident that by drawing
attention to the draconian methods by which the nation's underclass was

controlled on those very ships, the rebels effectively shattered the goals of the Brazil elite. They dragged their mistreatment up from below deck and into the light of day. It should come as no surprise that once the story died down in the press the federal government sought to quietly claw back those accommodations the reclamantes won through their victory against the state; the government went on to exact revenge against the amnestied sailors under a fabricated state of siege. But while many individual sailors paid dearly for their actions, these sailors successfully delivered permanent changes to the institution of the Brazilian navy, and to the manner in which the state controlled its free black population. The revolt that stunned Rio de Janeiro, the story of these sailors and their trans-Atlantic ties, deserve a more prominent place in the history of Brazil, in the history of abolition, and in the history of the Atlantic World.

Yet it is said we must flog, to maintain discipline among sailors. Pshaw!! Flogging may be needful to awe a slave writhing under a sense of unmerited wrong, but never should a lash fall on a freeman's back, especially if he holds the safety and honor of his country in his keeping.

SAMUEL LEECH,
Thirty Years from Home or A Voice from the Main Deck, 1843

TWO

Legislating the Lash

THE BRAZILIAN STRUGGLE FOR INDEPENDENCE FROM
Portugal is often described as a "bloodless" transition. This is not entirely
accurate as the Brazilian army and navy fought both Portuguese troops
and Brazilian antiroyalists in Brazil from February 1822 until November
1823, and finally expelled the last Portuguese troops from Montevideo
in March 1824 when the Cisplatine Province (now Uruguay) was briefly
incorporated into the Brazilian empire. However, historians rightfully
focus on Brazil's comparative lack of violence in contrast to the Spanish
American wars of independence that shattered Spain's control over its
empire.

In the case of Brazilian independence, Portuguese Prince Pedro I
himself led the struggle against Portugal's attempts to subordinate Brazil back into the colonial position it occupied before his father João VI[1]
moved the court from Lisbon to Rio de Janeiro in 1808, and elevated
Brazil's status to that of co-kingdom with Portugal in 1815. The goal of independence envisioned by the Brazilian elite was to retain this elevated
status while at the same time conserving the socioeconomic hierarchy
that defined colonial Brazil, at the center of which was the forced labor of
enslaved Africans. Any wide scale popular mobilization of poor Brazilians – black or white – could threaten Brazil's socioeconomic hierarchy.[2]

The most direct military contribution toward Brazil's independence
took place in Europe more than a decade before the actual break between
Portugal and Brazil; Napoleon Bonaparte's 1807 invasion of the Iberian
Peninsula resulted in two models of independence in the Americas. In
the case of Spain, Napoleon's capture of the Spanish monarch created a

power vacuum in the Spanish colonies that led to their long and bloody
wars of independence. For Portugal, following the Napoleonic invasion, the prince regent packed his court, the treasury, military officers,
and many of the Portuguese archives onto ships and transferred the
monarchy, under British protection, from Lisbon to Rio de Janeiro. For
thirteen years João VI ruled the Portuguese Empire – spread across the
continents of Africa, Asia, South America, and ostensibly Europe – from
the Brazilian capital. No other European empire was ever ruled from
its colony; the impact of this transference of power on the development
of Brazil is immeasurable. In addition to promoting Brazil from colony
to co-kingdom, equal to Portugal, João VI opened the ports of Rio de
Janeiro to international trade, and he developed Rio de Janeiro as the
cultural center of Brazil by establishing theaters, a national library, an
academy of fine arts, and a botanical garden, as well as military and naval academies. The Portuguese elite, including military officers, spent
nearly a generation building ties within Brazilian society. When João
VI returned to Europe in April 1821, only twenty-seven members of the
Portuguese Naval Academy accompanied him; the vast majority of his
125 naval officers stayed in Brazil and eventually pledged their allegiance
to the independent empire.[3]

A brief comparison between the social impact of the wars of Brazilian and Spanish American independence offers insight into the contrast-
ing role of the military throughout Latin American society. Because
the Portuguese leadership arrived in Brazil intact, there was no need
for a Brazilian Simón Bolívar or José de San Martin to recruit liberation armies from all levels of society, thereby possibly redefining the
new nation. Throughout Spanish America, the Creole leadership of the
independence struggles eventually drew on free men of color as well as
slaves rewarded with their freedom in order to populate their armies.
This created routes to freedom and citizenship for large numbers of Afro-
Latin Americans and put in place an indirect path to the overall abolition
of slavery in the Spanish American states. For example, Simón Bolivar
initially envisioned an independence movement not only led, but also
fought, by free white citizens. However, early defeats by Royalist forces
led him to reconsider. In order to win the Spanish American wars of independence, military leaders were forced to free enslaved men to support

the fight for national independence. As Afro-Latin American men gained their freedom through military service they were able to pressure newly independent Latin American states to accelerate the abolition of African slavery and eliminate – at least on paper – the class hierarchy that defined the Spanish American colonies throughout their existence.[4]

However, the social equality for Latin American citizens that appeared on paper was illusory, even for those soldiers who fought in order to win national independence and personal freedom. Throughout the young Spanish American nations, rather than citizen armies that challenged social inequality, the republican elite themselves largely abandoned military service and impressed the service of the subaltern. At best, for the elite, the military represented a means to educate the masses in the ways of becoming citizens; at worst, the military became a proto-penal institution that contained the bodies of the lower classes, especially former slaves once they attained their freedom.

In comparison, while the newly independent Spanish American states rebuilt their military structures based on Creole armies largely responsible for the success of their wars of liberation, Brazil in the early nineteenth century retained much of the Portuguese infrastructure built by João VI during his rule in the Americas. But to gain independence, the Brazilian monarchy would have to quickly improve existing military institutions while building a navy almost from scratch. When the Portuguese Côrtes forced its reluctant king to return to Lisbon in April 1821, his twenty-three-year-old son, Pedro I, remained behind to rule in his stead. Once Don João returned to Portugal, the Côrtes sought to undo the improvements in Brazil's legal standing that the monarch had applied during his rule from the Americas. They denounced free trade; they demanded that military commanders in Brazil defer to the Côrtes; the armies of Portugal and Brazil were combined in order to subordinate Brazilian troops to continental officers; and finally in December 1821, they demanded that Pedro I immediately abandon Brazil and return to Portugal. He famously refused that order on January 9, 1822, stating, "If it is for the good of all, and the general felicity of the Nation, I am ready. Tell the people that I will remain." This marked the beginning of Brazilian independence, a process that required radical changes to Pedro's government and to the state-controlled institutions that no longer answered to Portugal but were not yet independent.

Pedro I mobilized the Brazilian militia in Rio de Janeiro and forced the Portuguese General Jorge de Avilez de Sousa Tavares to remove his troops from the capital and sent him, along with three battalions of Portuguese troops, back to Lisbon from Rio de Janeiro on February 15, 1822. Weeks later, a Portuguese squadron arrived in Rio de Janeiro in March 1822 but was not allowed to land. These ships were reprovisioned and forced to return to Europe, though Brazilian authorities retained the frigate *Real Carolina*. In return, the Côrtes blocked arms shipments to Brazil and demanded that Pedro I disband his government and break up the constitutional convention he called. Eventually the delivery of these orders to Pedro I on September 7, 1822, led to his famous declaration (on the Ypiranga River) of "Independence or Death."

Months earlier, in March 1822, Pedro I's government declared all of the provinces of Brazil under the control of Rio de Janeiro, but such loyalty was much easier to assert than it was to deliver. In fact, by October 1822, only Rio de Janeiro, Minas Gerais, and São Paulo immediately deferred to Pedro's rule. Portugal, as well as enjoying a strong military presence in the south (Montevideo), the north (Pará and Maranhão), and the northeast (Salvador da Bahia), retained "a powerful naval squadron well able to decide the issue by imposing a crippling blockade on Rio de Janeiro."[5] For Brazil to gain and retain its independence it would need to assert its control of the sea; thus it would need to quickly develop its navy.

Naval scholar, admiral, and baron Arthur Jaceguay, born Arthur Silveira da Motta in 1843 – son of Liberal Brazilian Senator Arthur Silveira da Motta – entered the officer training naval academy in March 1858 and spend a long and decorated career in the Brazilian navy. In his colossal memoir titled *De aspirante a almirante* [From Midshipman to Admiral], which spans the history of the Brazilian navy until his retirement in 1906, he states, "Of all of the American Colonies, the only one, on the occasion of [political] emancipation, possessing the elements to fight against the naval power of the metropole was Brazil."[6] However, the Brazilian navy was born out of necessity and did not in its earliest years represent a "national" institution populated by Brazilian, or even Portuguese, officers and enlisted men. Instead, during the brief fight for independence that began in 1822, the young Brazilian state largely populated its navy, both officers and enlisted men, with foreign mercenaries hired throughout Britain in the years following the Napoleonic Wars. One notable exception to the reliance on foreign sailors is evident in the decision first passed in February 1823, mandating that competent slaves offered to the state by their owners be purchased and admitted to the navy as sailors during the struggle for independence.[7] However, once Brazil secured its independence, the size of the Imperial Navy was drastically cut, and Brazilian citizens increasingly filled its positions.

THE NAVY IN BRAZILIAN INDEPENDENCE

Beginning in 1808, the Portuguese monarchy developed a naval infrastructure in Rio de Janeiro, which included the naval academy, naval hospital, Ministry of the Navy, naval intendants, and the arsenal and dockyards. Although many of these institutions badly needed repair after years of neglect and abuse, they offered the Brazilian state a core infrastructure around which to build their navy. Additionally, by November 1822, several Portuguese ships had fallen into the hands of the Brazilian empire, but Brazil found itself badly outgunned by Portuguese naval powers in Brazil, with only eight sizable warships carrying 200 guns, facing a Portuguese squadron of fourteen ships carrying nearly twice as much artillery as the Brazilians. Pedro I committed to the immediate purchase of suitable ships, and in early 1823 launched a national subscription specifically to pay for naval vessels. By March 1823, thanks to purchases from England and the United States and ships captured from Portugal, the number of Brazilian ships had more than tripled. Twenty-eight vessels carrying more than 600 guns were in service or were being commissioned.[8]

The imperial government also looked abroad for both naval officers and enlisted men. Although there were 160 officers in the Imperial Navy at the time of the declaration of Brazilian independence, most were Portuguese by birth; once those with loyalties to Portugal, the sick, and those considered too old to fight were removed from the list, ninety-six remained. Although this represented adequate senior officers, according to Brazilian naval scholar Brian Vale, "the number in junior grades was sufficient only to bring the vessels already in commission up to their war establishments."[9] They needed at least twenty-five new officers, and they looked to Europe and the United States to fill their roster. They also looked abroad for their leadership. In November 1822, Brazil's imperial government famously offered the command of the Brazilian navy to Lord Thomas Cochrane, an English admiral who made his name during the Napoleonic Wars and who from 1817 to 1822 successfully served the cause of Chilean independence. Under his naval leadership Brazil became independent.

Populating the lower decks also proved to be difficult. According to British travel writer Maria Graham, then living in Rio de Janeiro, "The great difficulty the navy here had to dread is the want of men. Portuguese sailors are worse than none; few Brazilians are sailors at all, and French, English, and Americans are very scarce."[10] During an early confrontation with Portuguese forces in Bahia, many Portuguese-born sailors available to the Imperial Navy demonstrated their unreliability. A national recruiting exercise was put into place, but it quickly proved to be a failure. Again, according to Brian Vale, "In spite of its extensive coastline, Brazil remained a continental country with little maritime tradition and no reserve of seamen on which to draw in time of war."[11] Instead, starting in December 1822 agents for the Brazilian navy successfully recruited among a large pool of unemployed veterans of the British Royal Navy in Liverpool and London. By the middle of 1823, 670 British sailors made up the vast majority of the enlisted men serving on the Brazilian lower decks.[12]

This Brazilian model of foreign military recruitment proved successful. Under Admiral Cochrane's leadership, the British and Brazilian officers routed the Portuguese in 1823 and consolidated Rio de Janeiro's control over the vast territory of Brazil during 1824. Cochrane then went on to fight against the Confederation of Equator, and following a second international recruitment campaign in 1825 foreign sailors eventually played a large part in the Brazilian war against Argentina from 1826 to 1828, a costly and unpopular endeavor.[13]

As the decade of the 1820s drew to a close, so too would Brazil's dependence on an expensive navy populated by foreigners. The 1828 annual report by the minister of the marines described a much-expanded navy now populated by 8,419 officers and men, of whom between one-third and one-half were foreigners; although many of these were Portuguese sailors who declared loyalty to Brazil, upward of 1,200 were natives of Britain or Ireland. The cost of supporting a national navy had tripled between 1823 and 1828, and when Pedro I abdicated the Brazilian throne in 1831 (examined in more detail in the following section), the regency that ruled in the interests of Brazil's child monarch had very different fiscal priorities than did the outgoing emperor; they supported overall political pragmatism, which included deep cuts in general spending. The massive expenditures that defined the Brazilian navy from 1822 to 1831 came to an end. Within two years, the regency had cut the navy to one-fifth of its size, to just 1,500 men; the central role of the Brazilian navy had radically changed. It had served its purpose in winning and supporting Brazilian independence against separatist uprising in the first months following the war of independence and in the Cisplatine War over the inclusion of Uruguay as Brazil's southernmost state. This smaller navy played a continued role in the suppression of the various uprisings Brazil faced during the period of Pedro II's regency while he awaited achieving the age of majority, but from the mid-1830s, Brazil took steps to shift the navy away from the recruitment of foreign sailors and toward the overall recruitment of Brazilians.[14]

As naval administrators replaced foreign sailors with Brazilian nationals, the elite held such a low opinion of the poor nonwhite men who they targeted for service that their status as Brazilian citizens was unclear. Admiral Arthur Jaceguay described this transition: "With the creation of the Imperial Navy we initiated the population of our ships' crews with a national element; but this was carried out with forced recruitment, drawing principally from vagabonds and the malevolent from the great population centers of the eastern coast."[15] Brutish sailors from urban centers defined the Brazilian navy well into the twentieth century.

THE MILITARY IN THE EARLY REPUBLIC

In the absence of a widespread and devastating war of independence, the Brazilian military played a lesser role in postindependence nation building than was common throughout Spanish America. For this reason, and also because of the presence of members of the imported Portuguese court who remained in Brazil, military service did not offer an easy entry to the established Brazilian political elite. At the moment of independence the Brazilian colonial army consisted primarily of Portuguese officers and enlisted men. Although there had been Brazilian-born men serving both as regulars in the national army and in the various regional militias, in response to a republican revolt that swept Pernambuco in 1817 an "Auxiliary Division" of 2,000 Portuguese soldiers was dispatched to Brazil, and Portuguese officers replaced Brazilians in most positions of authority. In the face of Brazil's impending struggle for independence, in May 1822 Pedro I called for the size of all royal battalions to increase from seventy-five to one hundred soldiers.[16] Given the general lack of volunteers for enlisting in the pre-expansion army, there soon followed a decree outlining Brazil's expanded recruitment policy and explicitly defining the populations subject to forced recruitment into the new national army.

The government exempted from the draft productive workers such as merchants, clerks in taverns and bars, sailors, students, employees of foreign merchants, and foremen or managers of farms and plantations employing more than six slaves. They also exempted individuals with responsibilities for others, such as married men, only children, and brothers of orphans responsible for their subsistence and education. Additionally, as long as they were actively practicing their trade and demonstrated good behavior (*bom comportamento*) muleteers, cowboys, ranchers, masons, carpenters, construction workers, and fishermen were protected from impressment. Instead the law targeted the unemployed and the dishonorable poor, the *desprotegidos*.[17] While both Portuguese soldiers and foreign mercenaries recruited from Ireland and Germany remained in service to the Brazilian nation after the conclusion of the war for Brazilian independence, in the period that followed we see the origins of the shift toward a national institution populated with Brazilian citizens. That said, in the first decades of the Brazilian Empire, the army and navy developed in strikingly different directions. Once the naval elite turned toward foreigners to populate both the lower and upper decks of their ships, it would be decades before there was any attempt by Brazil's leadership to rebuild the navy around the service of Brazilian citizens.[18]

During the Brazilian Empire, military participation in foreign wars was rare. Such conflicts were limited to the Cisplatine War (1825–28) and the Paraguayan War (also known as the War of the Triple Alliance, 1864–70).[19] The first took place in the territory that is now Uruguay (then Banda Oriental) on the northern shore of the Rio de la Plata. It had been annexed by Brazil in July 1821 as the Cisplatine Province and in August 1825 a mixture of Uruguayan and Argentine (the United Provinces of la Plata at the time) rebels called for their territory to break with Brazil and join the United Provinces. In October 1825 the congress in Buenos Aires accepted their request for annexation, and in response Brazil declared war on the United Provinces of la Plata. The Brazilian navy played a significant role in the war against Argentine interests in Brazil's southernmost territory. Though Lord Cochrane had departed for England, his foreign-staffed navy remained largely intact, making Brazil's navy larger, more modern, and better staffed than that of Buenos Aires. However, fighting dragged on for nearly three years with no clear victor. In the face of this long and costly war both Brazil and Buenos Aires faced internal threats, and eventually the British were allowed to negotiate the end of fighting. In October 1828 Brazil and the United Provinces agreed to the recognition of Oriental State of Uruguay.[20]

Brazil's second foreign war, the Paraguayan War, marked a continuation of Brazilian involvement in the Uruguayan region, but one with much greater consequences to Brazilian political and military history. In the decades after the British negotiated Uruguayan independence in 1828, Uruguay's political leadership faced competing political influence from both Argentine caudillo Juan Manuel de Rosas and the Brazilian monarchy, which represented the interests of the nearly 20,000 Brazilian residents, owners of almost a third of Uruguayan territory, who continued to reside in that country. After Rosas was overthrown in 1852 Brazilian manipulation of Uruguayan politics led to civil war between the traditional political parties of that nation, the Blancos and Colorados. When the Colorados set out to oust the Blancos from power with the combined support of the Brazilian monarchy and the new liberal president of Argentina, Justo José Urqueza, the Blancos turned to Paraguayan dictator Francisco Solano Lopéz for a pledge of military support for their rule. The end result was a war pitting Brazil, Argentina, and the Colorados leadership of Uruguay against the isolated but militarily powerful Paraguayan nation, which invaded the southern Brazilian state of Rio Grande do Sul in December 1864. Brazil cleared Paraguayan troops from Brazilian territory within the first year of the war, but as Argentina and Uruguay pulled back from their commitment, Brazil alone invaded into Paraguay with the firm commitment to remove Francisco Solano López from power. It would take five years for Pedro II's combined military forces to succeed in this goal, and Brazil's increasingly unpopular involvement in this war set events into motion that eventually undermined the Brazilian Empire. The grueling war demanded the unprecedented participation of both branches of the Brazilian military. It established the Brazilian army as a powerful national institution, the Republican Party that eventually overthrew the Brazilian monarchy had its origins in resistance to the long-fought and expensive war, and finally, army officers, whose support allowed the republicans to topple the monarchy, for the first time found themselves part of the Brazilian elite.[21]

It was much more common during the empire that the imperial government deployed the nascent military against regional threats within Brazil. In general, such threats came from the local interests of powerful landowning elite, many of whom had at their control their own provincial militias. When Brazil emerged from its war for independence the crown faced a series of uprisings in the name of regional independence. Pedro I reigned from 1822 to 1831, applying a heavy hand against those who challenged his rule – politically or militarily – striving to keep the nation united under his central authority. The monarchy attained a successful outcome against the 1824 separatist movements in the provinces of Pernambuco, Paraíba, Rio Grande do Norte, Alagoas, Piauí, and Ceará. Sparked by the emperor's dissolution of his own appointed National Constitutional Convention, the central government faced an explicit attempt to break away from the Brazilian nation; the rebels declared their territory the Confederation of the Equator. It fell largely to the navy, under the leadership of Admiral Cochrane, to quickly and successfully put down those movements.[22]

At this time, shifting the nation's fighting strength from regional militias to a national army controlled by the central government was a major focus of the monarchy. With the problem identified, shifting Brazil's fighting forces from regional authority to the Brazilian army was difficult; the change was neither immediate nor linear. As historian Hendrik Kraay documents, the consolidation of central authority over the regional garrisons of the Brazilian army and the related replacement of the various provincial militias with units of the National Guard represented an ongoing struggle that began in the colonial era and continued through the independence era. Important areas such as Salvador de Bahia did not come under central control until the 1840s, but the beginning of the consolidation of control over the regional army dates to Pedro I's rule.[23]

Although Pedro I enjoyed military victories over regional threats, he was frustrated by repeated clashes with the Brazilian legislature. After forcibly dissolving the elected Constitutional Assembly in November 1823, he drafted and promulgated his own constitution in March 1824. He delayed seating parliament as the constitution required from 1824 to 1826, and following violent demonstrations over his having replaced his popular cabinet in April 1831, Pedro I abdicated the Brazilian throne, leaving his five-year-old son in Brazil to rule.[24] A nine-year regency ruled in the name of Brazil's child monarch Pedro II, though it was to have ruled for at least three additional years until Pedro II turned eighteen in 1843. This period of regency is best defined by the backlash against the unpopular centrist policies of Pedro I. According to Latin American military historian Robert L. Scheina, the moment Pedro I set sail for Europe, "those wanting greater local autonomy, those seeking to secede from the Brazilian empire, and those desiring a republican form of government all perceived that the opportunity was now at hand."[25] The regency was marked by a renewed outbreak of violent resistance in some of the most distant provinces from the capital. Rebellions broke out in Pará (1832–36), Rio Grande do Sul (1835–42), Salvador (1837–38), and Maranhão (1839–40). Although the government succeeded in suppressing the fighting in Para, Salvador, and Maranhão, it was because of these uprisings – especially the ongoing rebellion in Rio Grande do Sul that the national government failed to subdue – that the members of the ruling Liberal Party initiated their call to have the then fifteen-year-old emperor Pedro II declared of age, thus allowing his ascent to the throne on July 23, 1840. Once Pedro II took power he and the parliament accelerated the reorganization of the army into a centralized national institution to further shift power away from regional landowners and their loyal peasant armies. Even with the Brazilian-born emperor at the helm of the nation it proved difficult for him to consolidate power. It would take most of the decade following Pedro II's ascent to the throne before the imperial authority fully overcame the armed resistance and Brazil's "Golden Age" of empire began.[26]

BRAZIL'S GROWING FREE BLACK POPULATION

Until the final year of the Brazilian Empire the economy remained dependent on agricultural exports produced by enslaved Africans on plantations; on many levels the Brazilian economy and system of labor remained tied to its colonial origins. It would be a mistake to let that consistency obscure important changes taking place during this period. For Brazil the period of empire represented political and economic independence, technological modernization, and a distancing from the colonial past; the Brazilian government, economy, and eventually labor sources would have to be reinvented. Although slavery remained central to Brazil's economy, to remain competitive in the nineteenth century, the plantation economy radically modernized. These structural modifications of traditional labor practice represented manifestations of modernization; labor – in this case slave labor – was being used in new and increasingly modern sectors of the economy. The making of the empire, and the emergence of the modern Brazilian navy, took place alongside a radical shift in the nature of where and how powerful Brazilians relied on African labor.

In the first half of the nineteenth century Brazilian agricultural exports expanded, given the 1808 suspension of Portuguese monopoly over Brazilian trade. Brazilian sugar experienced a recovery following the slave uprising in the French colony of Saint-Domingue, coffee exports began a long period of growth that drove Brazilian economic expansion throughout the nineteenth century, and cotton exports as well as agricultural production for Brazil's domestic market centered in Minas Gerais expanded. In response to this economic growth and to the enormous British pressure to end the Brazilian slave trade, the rate of importation of enslaved Africans reached a historic peak. Then, in 1850 in the midst of this growth, Brazil lost its primary source of labor as a result of the closure of the Atlantic slave trade. These events fueled an internal slave trade, as booming agriculture shifted enslaved Afro-Brazilians away from centers of less productive agriculture and from urban centers and toward dynamic areas of the Brazil's export economy.[27]

Whereas economic pressure during the mid-nineteenth century moved enslaved Africans from cities toward the countryside, to a large extent the opposite was true of the free black population in this period. As early as the eighteenth century, manumission, natural reproduction, and flight led to a well-documented and sizable free black population in colonial Brazil. According to historian Marcos Luiz Bretas's study of the relation between free blacks and the police, "Free workers – either small farmers producing for subsistence or itinerants – were present in Brazilian society from the eighteenth century. It was then that the public authorities in the mining region of Minas Gerais asked for harsher measures to deal with vagrancy."[28] The common description of these free men and women as "vagrants" during the eighteenth and nineteenth century turned out to be a dangerous irony. At the very moment that the plantation labor system that relied on the exclusive labor of slaves refused free workers sustaining employment, the nascent police forces criminalized the resultant unemployment being forced upon these free men and women. This was no coincidence; through the category of "vagrancy" the elite created value in this underclass. Bretas goes on to say, "The same authorities were . . . aware of the advantage they could gain from itinerants, either for the occupation of new territories or for recruitment as a military force."[29] The threat of forced military service was an essential motivator for these men to continue their work for landowners. Even when conditions and pay were far short of what free laborers expected to earn – short of what they needed to survive – a lack of employment meant a lack of protection from exploitative state institutions. Abandoning agricultural work made a man a vagrant, part of the growing class of desprotegidos. Even if a free man became self-employed or earned money through the informal economy away from his rural origins, he lost the protection of patriarchy. Without those ties, a worker (even one collecting a living wage) became unprotected, and when detained in recruitment sweeps, it was not a salary but the good word of a white landowner that protected a man; even an employed *desprotegido* was at great risk of being forcibly enlisted into military service.

Long before the abolition of slavery in 1888, Brazilian landowners negotiated with and relied on free labor. According to Hebe Maria Mattos de Castro's examination of labor in the second half of the nineteenth century, "whereas free and freed people composed 41 percent of the Brazilian population by 1818, [this] proportion . . . grew to 84 percent by 1874."[30] While some part of this growth can be attributed to European immigration, once African men and women were no longer imported into Brazil as of 1850, the process of nineteenth-century abolition, including the impact of manumission, natural reproduction, and escape, led to significant growth among Brazil's free black population. Again, when possible, many ex-slaves sought to escape from the limited opportunities available to them in the rural countryside in order to seek out work in the urban centers, and following abolition, urban elites increasingly meted out desirable jobs to white immigrants while forcing free blacks and former slaves into the unprotected urban underclass. This growing underemployed free nonwhite population was a concern for Brazil's urban elite. As long as people remained enslaved, their control and discipline remained the responsibility of slave owners, thus a private concern. Upon manumission, Afro-Brazilians became a problem to be administered by the state. As both Bretas and Holloway argue, throughout the nineteenth century, the role of administrator of Afro-Brazilians shifted from the private during the era of slavery to the public: the police force, prison, and military. Brazil's government had to control, rule, and (in theory) represent these black Brazilians as they struggled for citizenship and freedom. It is this growing role, this "slavery" and its violent application in the modern Brazilian state, which the *reclamantes* attacked during the Revolta da Chibata.[31]

The *Ordem e Progresso* (Order and Progress) that adorns the Brazilian national flag today has its roots in the ideology of the Brazilian elite as the twentieth century approached. The modernization of Brazil and its capital in their own eyes and in the eyes of the world was inextricably linked to the control of Afro-Brazilian bodies. Rio was the entry point for elite travelers and businessmen from around the world. It is not an overstatement to argue that only by "cleansing" the cities of their "undesirable elements" could the Brazilian elite hope to present their cities as modern metropolises comparable to their European and North American counterparts. In other words, emancipation brought no concerted effort to convey citizenship but rather brought an effort to circumscribe the possibilities for movement and freedom among a population already defined as problematic and dangerous.[32]

DIVERGENT MODERNIZATION

Throughout the empire, the branches of the Brazilian military played important roles in the formation of the modern Brazil state. In addition to the obvious role of serving the martial needs of the imperial authority and the state, the Brazilian military served a second role; according to Brazilian military historian Peter Beattie, the Brazilian military "performed seemingly contradictory functions by enforcing royal law while collecting, watching over, and employing males considered criminal, menacing, or, at best, unproductive."[33] In a similar vein, throughout the nineteenth century and well into the twentieth, the Brazilian navy served two contradictory roles: first, like the army – and this continued longer in the navy than it did in the army – the navy served as a penal institution, containing a portion of the nation's growing free and/or poor male population, especially targeting the growing urban poor, the desprotegido. This population consisted of vagrants, criminals, orphans, and the unemployed. Not surprisingly, in a society that relied on the labor of enslaved African men and women for nearly four centuries, Afro-Brazilians made up the majority of this economically underprivileged group. The political elite wished for the desprotegidos to be "controlled," and that control often took the form of widespread arrest and, for men, subsequent impressments into one of the military branches. At least initially, both the army and the navy took on this penal role as a receptacle for those who to them represented the nation's undesirables. Unlike the army, as the nineteenth century progressed the navy increasingly represented the nation's international face – warships routinely visited foreign ports; their destructive potential became symbolic of Brazil's wealth and international power.

When describing this period of nation-state formation, Brazilian historians (both in works by specialists on the military and in broader examinations of the state) use the general language of the Brazilian "military" when they are actually describing the policies of the army.[34] Thus the goals of the military elite (officers in both the army and navy) are generalized as a common interest often lumped in with those of the nation's political and economic elite, their overall goal being modernization of the state and of national institutions. At a certain level, this practice is understandable: in a nation in which the regional economies struggle against the central power of the state, both branches of the military offered the central authority, whether monarch or president, a means of policing the nation. Furthermore, forced conscription and the penal role of both branches of the military furthered the central government's control over the growing free black population by literally absorbing desprotegidos into the military's lower ranks. It also sent a clear message to the growing number of men abandoning traditional agricultural work on former plantations who thereby abandoned the protection offered by traditional patriarchal relations with powerful landowners.

These similarities between the two military branches are clear in the early empire, but they become overshadowed by significant differences by the later empire and early republic. Scholars too often present the myriad changes that affected the two branches of Brazil's armed forces in the second half of the nineteenth century as a shared single policy, folding naval policies into the changes taking place in the army. An examination of nineteenth-century military policy shows us that the military elite in each branch of service, although deeply committed to both the ideology and practice of "Order and Progress," did not share a common agenda, even if in name they shared the common goal of modernization. In fact, the means by which officers of the Brazilian army and navy conceived and implemented their goals of reform were not only distinct from one another; at their core they were at times mutually exclusive.[35]

For example, following Brazil's lackluster performance in the Paraguayan War and their officers' difficulty attracting voluntary recruits to both the army and navy, the congress took up and passed the obligatory service in 1874, though it was never applied. Politicians and army officers embraced an ideal of modernization based on the model of the French citizen army. In theory, this marked an important change to the Brazilian military, in which honorable citizens from all classes would serve the nation.[36] Although the Recruitment Laws of 1874 theoretically applied to both the army and navy, the army passed several pieces of accompanying legislation to make service in that institution more honorable, such as terminating the demeaning rank of servant required to serve officers and abrogating the use of corporal punishment (this applied only to the army; corporal punishment continued in the navy). These legislative reforms to the army continued throughout late nineteenth century and peaked with the passage of the Obligatory Military Service Law in 1908, though the government again failed to apply this law until Brazil entered w w i. In the army, the image of modernization translated to professionalization; better-trained and better-treated soldiers would make for an improved institution overall.[37]

Alternatively, when the government authorized change in the navy to modernize the institution beginning in the 1880s, a movement that peaked when congress passed the 1904 Naval Renovation Program (*Projeto de Reaparelhamento Naval*), their reforms were not in the treatment of their sailors; instead their investment was in technology. Little to no effort was made to address the conditions of service in the late nineteenth and early twentieth centuries. For the naval elite, the origin of these enlisted men was so base and dishonorable that they asserted the impossibility of their professionalization. Naval hierarchy could be enforced only with violent dehumanizing compulsion. These differences in how institutional modernization could and should be attained suggest a broad divide between the army and navy that has been largely overlooked by scholars of the Brazilian military, scholars whose focus is disproportionately – if not solely – on the army.

This disparity between the practices of army and navy elites stems in part from the racial differences between the men serving in each institution, both between soldiers and sailors and between enlisted men and officers. In general the army, which was still less white than the general population, better reflected Brazil's overall racial makeup than did the navy. Peter Beattie states that enlisted men in the Brazilian army in 1890 were about 20 percent white, while in the navy whites made up a somewhat smaller 14.5 percent. This at a time when according to the 1890 census whites represented 44 percent of Brazil's population.[38] Perhaps as important as those differences between the races of enlisted men serving in the branches of the Brazilian military was the race of the officers who ruled them. As was the case for naval officers overall, after Brazilian independence, the highest-ranking army officers began their careers as cadets who were selected from among Brazil's elite. But even in the colonial period, many army officers were promoted reflecting their service in the field, most rising from the ranks of NCOs. Again quoting Peter M. Beattie, "The army allowed men of humble background a degree of social mobility in colonial and early imperial Brazil."[39]

This mobility actually accelerated in the second half of the nineteenth century when Brazil's involvement in the Paraguayan War (1865–70) allowed increased mobility through the ranks for effective soldiers; in the army there was a real (albeit small) opportunity for good soldiers to be promoted into the officer class. Additionally, army service did not necessarily mean a complete break from a man's family and home. The army was a nation institution with bases in each region of the country; soldiers could hope for assignment at local garrisons. One can argue that in the 1870s the gap between the army as it existed and the army envisioned by the politicians seeking to legislate an improvement in military service was not so broad. Basic reforms could make army service more tolerable and could benefit poor Brazilians. In theory, as army reform took the form of a professionalization that treated its members as "honorable" citizens, the rate of volunteers would grow, and as Brazilian society became whiter through immigration and miscegenation, and thus more civilized, so too would the army.[40]

On the other hand, in addition to the segregation in the Brazilian navy, service for enlisted men was comparably harsh, with much less mobility for even the most qualified sailors. Although there were a handful of smaller naval bases and arsenals, and service regularly brought crews for service in Rio de la Plata, Salvador da Bahia, and the Amazon, the vast majority of Brazilian naval service occurred in Rio de Janeiro.[41] Unless a sailor had local origins, naval service required physical removal from one's home and family. There was also no possibility for enlisted men to be promoted past the rank of noncommissioned officer, and it was a small group of sailors who held out hope for attaining that rank. Legislation passed at the end of eighteenth century in Portugal and adopted during the Brazilian empire when the Royal Naval Academy was transferred to Rio required that officer candidates either be of nobility or be sons of other military officers.[42] While no law explicitly excluded Afro-Brazilians from the officer ranks, their path was blocked by limiting candidacy to "elite" Brazilian populations who were exclusively white. As important as that legislation may have been, which was certainly not applied universally and after the fall of the monarchy would have not been applied at all, attending the naval academy was costly. The families of officers in training paid for their sons' preparation, as well as the purchase of required materials, which restricted the pool of potential applicants. The fact that entry to the navy's officer training school was costly and prestigious led to the continued racialization and elite status of naval officers well into the twentieth century.[43]

Because in its early years the Brazilian elite looked to England for its naval officers, the Brazilian navy was modeled on British naval hierarchy, and British officers served as a model for the Brazilian officer class. But there was one important distinction between the Brazilian and the British naval hierarchy. Like British officers, Brazilian officers wished to be regarded as gentlemen. As examined immediately below, following long-established Portuguese law and tradition, Brazilian officers came from a very privileged background. In its formative years the British navy developed two very different paths to the rank of naval officer. Seamen commanders had backgrounds in actually sailing ships. As British sociologist Norbert Elias described, "They all had started as shipboys early in life; they had served their apprenticeship on board ship usually for seven years."[44] If they had money or friends, it would speed their path, but through hard work these men came to hold the same rank with and sometimes competed for positions against the second group of officers. Gentlemen commanders instead came from powerful families and initially spent little or no time at sea before earning their commissions. In the eighteenth century the post of midshipman developed as a training station for young gentlemen, but by that time the British navy was divided. An officer's origin was common knowledge; to again quote

Norbert Elias, "they differed with regards not only to their professional training but also to their social descent."[45]

The Brazilian navy, on the other hand, tracing its roots to the Portuguese navy, had no tradition of "seaman commanders." Its officer class, like the gentlemen commanders of the British navy, came to the officers' training school from Brazil's privileged families. The exclusive nature of the navy was justified by the role of the naval officials traveling to foreign ports. In his biographical essay of naval officer, and novelist Adolfo Ferreira Caminha, Peter Beattie described the military in the late nineteenth century: "Despite its vast coastline, Brazil's navy remained a small entity of some 3,000 men. While the larger army had some nonwhite junior officers, the navy's officer corps remained a more exclusive bastion of 'whiteness.' Unlike army personnel, naval officers often traveled to foreign ports where they met local dignitaries, procured supplies, and explored the sites. . . . Brazil's leaders wanted foreigners, especially Europeans, to see their nation as 'white,' even though the majority of its population was nonwhite."[46] Beattie also offers insight into the lower decks of the Brazilian navy in the period: "In contrast [to the officers], most common sailors were black or of mixed African and European heritage and were restricted to their ships or dock areas when abroad."[47]

Similarly, while no law required that enlisted men be black, in contrast with the genteel background of the naval officers, the rank-and-file servicemen were drawn from the lower classes. Brazil remained a slave society, the economic elite was negotiating abolition and the growing free black population, and the navy was a tool in carrying out the control of that population. The legacy of slavery in Brazil and the nature of its national recruitment policy created a navy that, thanks to de facto segregation, at times had nearly 85 percent nonwhite crews. As legal scholar and member of the Brazilian Academy of Letters Evaristo de Moraes Filho wrote in his preface to Edmar Morel's *A Revolta da Chibata,* "for the recruitment of marines and enlisted men, we bring aboard the dregs of our urban centers, the most worthless *lumpen,* without preparation of any sort. Ex-slaves and the sons of slaves make up our ships' crews, most of them black-skinned or dark-skinned mulattos."[48] Of course, for generations enslaved Africans had been prepared and forced to do the work required by Brazilian slave owners; this was true both on modern plantations and in urban centers where black men and women were put to work at both skilled and unskilled labor. "Ex slaves and the sons of slaves" applied these skills in the hopes of overcoming racist policies such as whitening and the related prejudiced treatment they faced from Brazilian employers. In fact, the professionalism and effectiveness of the reclamantes during the Revolta da Chibata is just one example of how well prepared the "dregs" of Brazilian society were once they achieved freedom. Nonetheless, elite perception of Brazil's navy in the nineteenth and early twentieth century was that the navy's enlisted men were racial inferiors who could not be trained to be effective sailors and had to be beaten in order to conform to military discipline. Because they were ex-slaves and the sons of slaves, officers treated them as slaves in order to retain control of their ships.

The navy's segregation during the Brazilian Empire carried over into the First Republic. A 1911 article in the *Estado de São Paulo* addressed the continued structural difference between the branches of the military in the era of the Revolta da Chibata:

> The officer had never been a sailor. The sailor could never be an officer. This point is a major difference between the organization of the [Brazilian] army and navy.
>
> In this, in order to become an officer, it is necessary to belong to the moneyed bourgeoisie, to have wealth to defray the cost of attaining one's epaulettes in the naval academy and to be as little racially mixed or as white as possible.
>
> This is the great separation: the officers, made up of white men descended from good families – or if you would – the Brazilian aristocracy (how ridiculous this aristocracy) and the sailors, in general composed of blacks, mulattoes, and cabôclos [mixed race Indian or copper-colored mulatto], were usually illiterate, and enlisted from the stratum of our nationality for whom it is believed that the constitution of the Republic does not apply.[49]

This article, published after the revolt, shows that elite perceptions of race in the navy had changed very little in the twenty-two years between the abolition of Brazilian slavery and the Revolta da Chibata.

Government attempts to indirectly professionalize the navy along with the army faced vocal resistance from naval officers. For example, the third act promulgated by the newly formed Brazilian congress on November 16, 1889, just one day after the overthrow of the monarchy, outlawed corporal punishment in the navy. Officer complaints that the navy could not be run without the lash were so vociferous and convincing that congress legally reintroduced the lash on April 12, 1890, after being outlawed for less than five months.[50] Officers and politicians instead sought to modernize the institution through the acquisition of technologically advanced warships. Anecdotal evidence suggests that once Brazil acquired these modern battleships, their crews faced more technological responsibilities for which they were insufficiently trained, their workloads increased because of the insufficient size of ships' crews, and there was a related increase in the use of regressive corporal punishment to extract more labor from the sailors. The modernization of the Brazilian navy, already violent and exploitative, made naval service even more draconian.

A number of key issues critically affected the distinct experiences of enlisted men in the Brazilian navy during the empire. Together they shed light on a policy in the Brazilian navy that stands in sharp contrast to the liberal reforms that drove the army and the government toward the Reform Laws of 1874. Both military and domestic codes impacted the lives of Brazilian enlisted men. Military codes dictated recruitment and punishment of soldiers and sailors, while at the same time civilian legislation – such as abolition laws and the legislation of orphans and foundlings under the protection of the state – diverted men and boys from civilian society into the military ranks. Structural changes completed in 1854 to some extent normalized naval recruitment and service through the establishment of naval companies and *companhias de aprendizes* (companies of apprentices), thus making the Recruitment Law of 1874 largely inapplicable to the navy. And although corporal punishment had been technically made illegal to citizens by the constitution of 1824, it remained the primary means of disciplining sailors, not soldiers, until the early twentieth century.[51] Overall, the detailed examination of each of these policies offers insight into a naval policy that is linked, through both ritualized violence and the physical control of black bodies, to the methods of domination culled from Brazil's long dependence on African slavery. However, to infer from this difference that the navy was less committed to transformation than was the army overlooks the naval elite's commitment to the acquisition of navy technology that revolutionized the navy by the first decade of the twentieth century. This simultaneity – whipping sailors onboard the world's most advanced battleships – is at the core of our understanding modernization in a postemancipation society and, more pointedly, in the critical refusal embodied by the sailors who rejected such treatment through their participation in the Revolta da Chibata.

As an insurrection against state violence, the Revolta da Chibata is rooted in Brazilian naval policy from an earlier period. The legislation that resulted in the racial hierarchy and violence evident in the turn-of-the-twentieth-century Brazilian navy was unique neither to that institution nor to Brazil. Portugal was not alone in restricting the ranks of officers to white men; naval officers across Europe and North America also restricted their membership to a racial elite. Furthermore, although Brazil was the last modern navy to ban the use of corporal punishment following the Revolta da Chibata, that practice had remained common in modern Western navies until at least the mid-nineteenth century. The sole fact that the Brazilian navy continued to lash its sailors later than other nations (the United States and Britain outlawed flogging in 1862 and 1881 respectively, whereas the Iberian powers of Spain and Portugal halted in 1823 and 1895) is not alone an important anomaly; it was, after all, also the last nation in the Americas to outlaw the enslavement of men and women of African descent, in 1888.

It is evident that the rigid racial hierarchy visible in the Brazil navy had its roots in the centuries-long history of chattel slavery, but there was no single date or event that made the continued oppression within the Brazilian navy remarkable, not even its persistence beyond the Brazilian abolition of slavery in 1888. Instead, what is remarkable is the endurance of the navy's method of internal control and the ongoing value that such treatment of enlisted men provided to the Brazilian state. From the mid-nineteenth century when the navy was reconstructed – populated for the first time by Brazilian officers and enlisted men – its methods and service to the Brazilian state have been remarkably steadfast. The navy physically confined a relatively small group of black men, while controlling the behavior of a much larger group with the same threat of confinement. It is no great surprise that such an institution formed in a slave society during a period when both slavery and manumission experienced unprecedented growth. More surprising is that as Brazil transitioned from slave to free labor, from monarchy to republic, as army officers and politicians negotiated the formation of a modern volunteer army, the methods and responsibility of the navy was so unchanged. As the state became modern around it, the naval and political elite tenaciously retained or increased both the use of the lash and the level of racial hierarchy. That Brazil's progressive reforms were supported by racially divisive oppression, by the navy and through other national institutions, is not necessarily a contradiction. Keep in mind that the modernization of plantation slavery in the mid-nineteenth century shifted the slave labor supply from the north to the south, and furthered the free black urban underclass, the "lumpen," that the state felt the need to control. The eventual abolition of slavery in no way reduced the problem of that urban underclass; in fact abolition only expanded that problem. The draconian control of that free black population through naval service was not actually the continuation of slavery that the reclamantes claimed, it was an ongoing state-sponsored response to the modern problem of Brazil's growing free black population.

LEGISLATING THE NAVY

In crown policy of 1824, some of the earliest laws of the Brazilian Empire, one finds links between race, violence, and naval service. Until the creation of Rio de Janeiro's Casa de Correção (House of Corrections) in 1835, the Arsenal de Marinha (naval arsenal) – housed partially on the Ilha das Cobras (Island of Snakes) and partially on the coastal area perpendicular to the island, near the downtown area of Centro – housed the largest prison in the city of Rio de Janeiro. In the early nineteenth century, the arsenal contained men from various nations, racial, ethnic, and socioeconomic backgrounds who were imprisoned together on the naval base; Brazilian naval men, runaway slaves, foreign sailors, merchant marines, soldiers, Afro-Brazilians, and freed Africans from many nations were held together, imprisoned for an assortment of crimes.

Among those prisoners interned on the naval arsenal, many practiced *capoeira,* an Afro-Brazilian martial art, dance, and music introduced by Angolan slaves. In Brazil's urban centers, those who studied capoeira were regularly persecuted; therefore they often practiced to musical accompaniment, so as to disguise their sparring as a form of dancing. The police believed that practitioners of capoeira – most of whom were Africans or Afro-Brazilians – were a violent threat to security in Brazil's cities, and the 1820s were marked by widespread arrest and prosecution of this population.[52]

As the number of Afro-Brazilian *capoeiristas* increased in the prison (and would have grown further), Pedro I's government introduced a policy to put them to work; on August 30, 1824, the following edict was released:

> As it is convenient to employ the greatest possible number of workers in building the docks: His Majesty the Emperor, with the Secretary of Justice [Secretaria de Estado dos Negócios da Justiça], orders that the General Superintendent of Police . . . in respect to black [negro] *capoeiristas,* remit for work on the aforementioned docks all those who are picked up causing a commotion. There they will labor as punishment for a period of three months. As a consequence of this order, the punishment of lashing – which was applied in these cases of disturbance that are frequently committed within the city – will cease.
> Palacio do Rio de Janeiro, August 20, 1824.[53]

The connection between capoeira and the Rio's maritime strength was thus established. Whether freed or enslaved, whether African or Brazilian, black men arrested for practicing capoeira were put to work building the naval docks, literally tearing into the rock on the side of Ilha das Cobras using pickaxes, hammers, and dynamite, from 1824 to 1861. Building the docks was an enormous project, and their completion would allow the Brazilian capital to carry out repairs on their merchant and military ships, and those that they would purchase in the future. The docks were a clear priority during the empire; Emperor Pedro I himself struck the first symbolic blow to the stone.[54]

Two weeks after the initial edict, a second edict was released clarifying that whites and free black men arrested for practicing capoeira were also to be sent to work on the docks alongside enslaved men. Then, in the following month, a final edict stated that in addition to the three months of work in the docks, enslaved capoeiristas should receive 200 lashes when arrested for practicing capoeira, and – in a decree unrelated to the impressment of capoeiristas on Ilha das Cobras – that certain civil-

ian prisoners, already press-ganged into service during their imprisonment, should be pardoned for their crime if they enlisted to serve in the
Brazilian navy. The emperor thus set the groundwork in the first years of
Brazilian independence for the nineteenth- and twentieth-century navy
in which Brazilians – in most cases Afro-Brazilians – who were perceived
as potential criminals populated the lower decks of the Brazilian navy.[55]

NAVAL RECRUITMENT POLICY

The shift in naval structure can be best understood through an examination of legislative changes that took place throughout the nineteenth
century. First, the Legislative Decree of October 15, 1836, established four
permanent Companhias de Marinheiros, or naval companies, which
overhauled the very structure of the Brazilian navy. The primary function of this legislation was the creation of naval companies that for the
first time remained in place in periods of both war and peace, thus preparing the nation for hostility at any time.[56] However, in the decades
that followed the passage of this legislation, a national navy staffed with
volunteers remained a wholly unattainable goal. Admiral Arthur Jaceguey stated that the forced conscription "was understood by the officers
of the [Brazilian] navy to be a necessary evil."[57] One result of this and
related legislation that followed was an indirect shift in the population
from which the navy recruited, from the "necessary evil" of the forced
conscription of men overwhelmingly recruited by force, who served
onboard ships immediately upon their being pressed into service, to
boys who underwent a period of training or apprenticeship before they
entered the naval ranks.

    The naval companies specified by the new legislation each consisted
of one hundred men, eighty-eight of whom were enlisted men. Of those
eighty-eight, sixty-two were seamen of various ranks, and twenty-six
were *aprendizes,* or seamen recruits – apprentices still receiving training in order to become effective sailors. At the time, these apprentices
consisted of boys "between 14 and 17 years old; they were orphans or
desvalidos [the worthless or unlucky]."[58] The number of companies in
the Brazilian navy would expand notably throughout the nineteenth

century, and they would go through minor structural changes, but over-all, this decree set the structure of the Brazilian navy into the twentieth century.

This restructuring represented a radical departure in the organiza-tion of the Brazilian navy. Brazilian naval historian Henrick Marques Caminha describes the enlisted men on pre-1836 warships as either "sail-ors who enlisted voluntarily or who were contracted (these were gener-ally foreigners who were paid augmented salaries) [or] sailors recruited by force from among the crew-members of merchant marine vessels, or among vagabonds, criminals, etc."[59] With this new legislation of 1836, the control and coordination of naval recruitment transitions from the hands of the individual captains of Brazilian warships into those of a national organization constructed to oversee this role. The secretary of state for the navy now oversaw both the civilian and military arms of na-val recruitment policy throughout the empire, and part of those reforms included a national policy committed to retaining a standing permanent navy made up, at least in part, of boys who would complete a term of an apprenticeship before enlisting as sailors. For naval administrators, the practice of apprenticing young men in naval service was such a success that only four years after its introduction within the naval companies it too was structured as a national model of training, and in 1840 the government created a broad institution of companies of apprentices to supervise the "training" of naval apprentices.

Throughout the Brazilian Empire, sailors entered the navy by one of three methods: The first group of Brazilian sailors (a tiny percentage of the force) volunteered for service in the navy; at least in theory these men were self-motivated to serve the nation and were inclined toward a life at sea. Alternatively, men were conscripted into service by means of forced recruitment through recruitment sweeps. Finally, young boys between the age of ten and seventeen were accepted as naval apprentices when turned over by their legal guardians; obviously a boy's parents would be the most likely guardian, but this definition also included the judge responsible for orphans (*Juiz do Órfãos*). For those who oversaw both the army and navy, true volunteers made the best soldiers and sail-ors, as they were self-motivated to serve and protect the nation and thus would respect military hierarchy and order. As incentive to join, these men were at different times offered signing bonuses or shorter terms of service than sailors forced into service.

Although all three sources of recruits do appear in naval records, in Brazil's navy the overwhelming majority of sailors in this period entered either as forced conscripts or as children. In fact, volunteering for service was all but unknown; of 16,134 who entered the navy as enlisted men between 1836 and 1888, only 460 actually volunteered, a paltry 2.85 percent of Brazilian sailors during that period.[60] This tiny number can be explained in part by the terrible reputation accorded the navy during this period; service was harsh and more often than not far from home and loved ones, punishment was brutal and violent, and overall conditions were inhumane. Anyone who could avoid naval service generally did so. In fact, the navy enjoyed such a strong reputation for violence that parents would often threaten misbehaving children with being sent off to the navy. Helio L. Martins reproduces one such threat in his book on the 1910 naval revolt: "I'll send you to the navy to be fixed, this behavior calls for the naval collar [with which a prisoner was bound in order to receive corporal punishment], with some strong lashes to the back!"[61] Indeed, although volunteer civilian service was consistently put forth as an ideal model for the Brazilian military, realistically it played a tiny role in day-to-day recruitment. As historian of the Brazilian army Hendrik Kraay states in his article "Reconsidering Recruitment in Imperial Brazil" when describing a recruiter reporting to his superior in Salvador in 1888, "[He] need not have added the adjective *forçado* [forced] to describe *recrutamento* [recruitment] for, in contemporary usage, *recrutamento* meant impressment. Indeed, the very language of recruitment emphasized its coercive nature: authorities spoke of the 'arrest' and 'imprisonment' of those whom they recruited."[62] Throughout the period of empire, police remitted sailors after arrest on petty criminal charges: drunkenness; loitering; and practicing capoeira were detainable offenses. In the latter years of the empire and well into the First Republic, it became difficult to distinguish between volunteers and impressed sailors. As Peter Beattie described, "crafty recruitment agents convinced some men they apprehended that is was better to sign on as a volunteer in order to earn an enlistment bonus that, under the empire, pressed men did not receive."[63] Also, the regular use of the broad term "recruitment" for both volunteer and forced recruits made it difficult to know exactly what percentage of sailors were coerced into service based on military documents in the late empire. Then the Republican Constitution of 1891 outlawed impressment and payments to recruitment agents. Regardless, Beattie states that "illegal impressment continued under the republic . . . [and that] [u]nder Brazil's republic (1889–1930), the cynical abuse of the term 'volunteer' became even more extreme."[64]

Still, there were tangible changes in military recruitment that targeted the navy and not the army. In the second half of the nineteenth century, there was the important shift in the source of Brazilian sailors, from men to young boys, and by the end of the Brazilian Empire, these boys had surpassed men, both conscripts and volunteers, as the primary source of sailors enrolling in the navy. In his 1859 annual report to the general assembly of the legislature, Minister of the Navy Francisco Xavier Paes Barreto proposed that the navy acquire new ships: "By adopting these measures we could have in eight to ten years a navy that, if not powerful, could at least gain us some respect as a maritime nation, and if faced with any emergency, we would have a good probability for success when our naval forces were called to intervene."[65] The minister's optimism about the future of the navy was couched in a discussion of continuing difficulties with recruitment. Listing the various problems with Brazil's options for recruitment, he described the failure of prizes and signing bonuses to attract men to volunteer for naval service, and complained that Brazil's limited maritime population preferred service in the merchant marine to military service. He goes on to say that "we retain, for now, conscription, which by the way is still used in more advanced nations, however it failed to furnish the required number of sailors."[66] Finally, complaining that even when you find individuals who are naturally called to a life at sea, and who would volunteer to serve of Brazilian ships of war instead of merchant ships, they could not get past the low pay and the "rigors of discipline." He instead puts his greatest hope in the newly organized companies of apprentices:

> The adult man, who has lived enough of his life, who above all feels an irresistible attraction to the place in which he was born, who has not already found a love of the live at sea, will never be a sailor. Orphans and the destitute, conveniently

educated from a tender age would much like adults who spontaneously enlist,
will become sailors. Created in all coastal provinces, these companies have
become necessary to the Imperial Battalion. We will have nurseries [*os viveiros*]
to produce crews as large as we need. This plan will culminate in a register of
seamen [*inscripção maritime*] . . . comprised of true men of the sea.[67]

This rare and explicit description from the highest-ranking member of
the naval elite offers insight into the manner in which he understands
that a national institution such as the company of apprentices of the Brazilian navy can take potentially dangerous and problematic young men
such as "orphans and the destitute" (a population that is overwhelmingly Afro-Brazilian) and turn them not only into functional members
of society – if not citizens – but into men who could then turn around and
improve the very institution that had produced them. It is an idea that
echoes the earliest iterations of eugenics and positivism seen in Brazil.[68]

The implementation of the first company of apprentices in 1840 and
the subsequent spread of this institution throughout the country allowed
for apprenticeship to become an increasingly important means to obtain
boys for military service. In 1841, for the first time apprentices made up a
larger portion of naval recruitment than did impressment. Of 74 sailors
recruited into the navy, 3 volunteered, 31 were impressed into service,
and 40 came from the companies of apprentices – additionally, 2 died,
2 were discharged, and 21 deserted (but 15 either returned to service or
were captured), so the overall size of the navy grew by 61 sailors to a
total of 356 enlisted men. In 1842 and 1843, apprenticeship also outnumbered conscription, but from 1844 to 1851 conscription again outpaced
apprenticeship. Between 1859 and the outbreak of the Paraguayan War in
1864, conscription represented a larger proportion of naval recruitment
policy every year except 1861, when apprentices outnumbered impressed
sailors 142 to 131. But by 1869, with the decline of the Paraguayan War,
the former minister found his wish consistently coming true. From that
year until 1873, the navy consistently admitted more apprentices than
sailors through impressment.[69]

These companies were by definition two-year schools (though some
boys remained for up to four years) into which minors were remitted by
a parent, a state judge (in the case of orphans), or the police (if the boy
was picked up on the streets engaging in criminal or suspicious behavior). Again, according to official description, boys between the ages of

ten and seventeen were to learn basic reading and writing, naval skills, and (perhaps most importantly) military discipline and subordination. Despite the letter of the law, the new national policy had little to no effect on the near-universal illiteracy rates among Brazilian sailors. Although the companies were described as "schools" in state documents, the formal education of their wards never consisted of much more than an afterthought to their design. In fact, well into the twentieth century, officers saw no need for sailors to read or write. The companies of apprentices, regardless of the rhetoric, were not institutions created to uplift the sailors. Their first function was to fill the underpopulated lower decks of the Brazilian armada; their second purpose was to get these boys acclimated to the discipline and rigors of military life and to service on ships. Although the language of the laws suggests that children would not be allowed to serve in the regular navy, the fact is that the companies of apprentices were never intended to protect the rights of children or sailors. Naval apprenticeship allowed young men to work and receive some training before being put on a boat; this was done solely for the purpose of creating heartier and more competent sailors. Boys were coerced into apprenticeship much as men were coerced into enlisting. And upon completing their apprenticeships, these sailors were expected to serve even longer terms to repay their "debt to the nation." These potential *desprotegidos* were thus contained before actually becoming threats to the state.[70]

Upon passing a physical, a boy was enlisted, and the responsible adult received a cash bonus. Although the families of a naval apprentice – or in the case of true volunteers, a recruit himself – may have received monetary rewards, the navy also kept in place a system by which the various groups involved in recruitment would be compensated for their service. Parents who "volunteered" their sons to serve in the navy received payments; as of 1866, the sum was one hundred *mil-réis*. Although complaints over the wages of sailors were chronic, significant amounts of money changed hands to further the goal of populating the lower decks, though little of it made its way into the hands of the young men who served in Brazil's navy. The state authorized the Office of the Intendant of the Navy to make direct payments to recruiters delivering men for naval service. This was well established in the earliest years of the Brazilian navy. A decision promulgated on June 10, 1833, authorized payment of four mil-réis per enlistment to naval recruiters who delivered men for service in the Brazilian navy. This decree followed up another published two days earlier calling for the use of conscription if and when naval recruiters were unable to deliver sufficient numbers of sailors to meet the crew sizes as defined by the Brazilian legislature.[71] In this case, the difference between enlistment (*engajarem*) and conscription (*recruitamento*) was a subtle one. Both likely relied on force, but the conscripts were impressed through official naval channels, whereas the authorization to pay "recruitment agents" suggests that their status was that of independent contractors. Brazilian naval scholar Álvaro Pereira do Nascimento describes three types of actors involved in the population of the navy's lower decks. "The group was composed of naval officers – subordinates of the commanders of the naval stations, to the port authorities, and the commanders of ships. Then there were agents or officials who were subordinate to the chief of police and the governor [*presidente de província*], and finally there were 'individuals' who were considered to be in the service of the navy . . . but they were neither military officer nor policemen." Nascimento argues that this type of government decree authorizing payment for enlistees represented a direct invitation from the navy to these agents "to hunt for new sailors and cabin boys."[72]

The level of payment to independent "agents" (four mil-réis per recruit) remained consistent through the early decades of the empire. Then in 1855 the government promulgated another decree that generally outlined the recruitment of volunteers and what should be done if they failed to provide sailors in a quantity "required to maintain the effectiveness of naval forces."[73] As suggested above, the Brazilian navy constantly suffered from a vast shortage of men volunteering to serve, and this annual shortfall was constant until Brazil's involvement in w w i. Thus these plans overseeing forced recruitment were being applied continuously. Included in this regulation was an explicit payment scale for the various actors employed in delivering conscripts to the navy. On top of their salaries, naval officers were paid two mil-réis for "volunteers" and five mil-réis for men captured in raids who were enlisted, whereas officers and agents reporting under the police were paid five mil-réis per recruit, and freelance "agents" received four mil-réis for foreigners and five mil-réis for nationals. Obviously profit motivated the recruitment of men and boys into the Brazilian navy. Nascimento compares these earnings through newspaper advertisements from the first half of the nineteenth century: "In 1838 each vagabond [*mendigo*] arrested represented a bonus of 10$000. A [military] recruit was worth 5$000, that is, the same value as 1855. And the capture of a fugitive slave was worth 4$000."[74] In a surprising note, the value of a military recruit was higher than that of a runaway slave.

Another important step toward the regularization of service in the Brazilian navy took place in 1854, when the passage of Decree 1,466 on October 25 normalized the length of service for naval recruits. Volunteers now served for a period of time between six and twelve years, depending on the means by which they negotiated their entry into the navy. Apprentices served the longest terms, twelve years, to repay their "debt" to the Brazilian state. Sailors who were forcibly recruited into service served ten years.[75]

All of these changes are part of the broad structural shift that took place in order to organize the nineteenth-century navy. But beyond the bonuses offered to the tiny population of actual volunteers, it is important to note that these changes were not accompanied by improvements in the treatment of individual sailors. The means by which the naval elite recruited enlisted men became far more structured and regulated, but for the men serving in the Brazilian navy, their service went through little change. Training remained rudimentary, wages were inadequate, and the application of the lash ensured order; only the methods of recruitment were by any measure modernized.

CHANGING POPULATIONS IN RIO AND NAVAL RECRUITMENT

A closer examination of shifting demographics in the face of abolition in Rio de Janeiro allows further insight into changing naval policy. Parliament passed the Rio Branco Law, or the Free Birth Law, on September 28, 1871. It stated:

> Art. 1. The children of women slaves that may be born in the Empire from the date of this Law shall be considered to be free.
> The said minors shall remain with and be under the dominion of the owners of the mother, who shall be obliged to rear and take care of them until such children have completed the age of 8 years.

On the child of the slave attaining this age, the owner of its mother shall have the option either of receiving from the State the indemnification of 600 mil-réis or of making use of the services of the minor until he shall have completed the age of 21 years.

In the former event the Government will receive the minor, and will dispose of him in conformity with the provisions of the present Law.[76]

According to common historiography, the option to turn children over to the state for money was rarely acted upon. In his *The Destruction of Brazilian Slavery,* Robert Conrad states:

Possessing the right to choose between employing the labor of the children after their eighth birthday or surrendering them for government bonds, masters overwhelmingly chose to use their labor, in part because this option required from them no action whatever. Of the more than 400,000 *ingênuos* [children born of slaves after the passage of the Rio Branco Law] registered by 1885, only 118 had been delivered to the government in exchange for the ornate certificates which the regime had printed for the purpose . . . and during the following two years only two more *ingênuos* were so exchanged.[77]

Conrad goes on to argue that many of the children who, though technically born free, grew up laboring for their former masters were sold as if still enslaved. The remaining time during which he or she could be coerced to work was transferred to a new master. The legality of such transfers was questionable and was often criticized by abolitionists in the popular press, but as evidenced by advertisements in various newspapers, the practice was common.[78] In their study of black children following the passage of the 1871 law, Lana Lage de Gama Lima and Renato Pinto Venâncio call into question Conrad's analysis of the treatment of the ingênuos – or at least its application within Rio de Janeiro.[79] Although it may have been true in the countryside that the majority of slave owners retained the children they owned until after their eighth birthday, a different situation arose in urban spaces such as Rio de Janeiro. In fact, in Rio de Janeiro at least, this law led directly to an increase in the abandonment of black children, thereby increasing Rio's black urban underclass.

The Santa Casa da Misericórdia of Rio de Janeiro was founded in 1738 to care for orphans and foundlings following the Portuguese tradition. The Santa Casa produced a detailed register of the description of the abandoned children, as well as their race (until 1896), in order to facilitate the return of these children to their families. Abandoned children stayed at the Casa da Roda until reaching the age of one or two; there the per annum infant mortality rate hovered between 50 and 70 percent. Those who survived went to the *criadeiras* (incubator) at the Santa Casa, where they stayed until the age of seven, at which time they went to adoptive families. If there was no adoptive family, boys went to the naval arsenal on the Ilha das Cobras and girls went to the Recolhimento das Órfãs. Both boys and girls were to work for seven years in exchange for room and board; at the age of fourteen, they began to earn salaries.[80]

This official link – that this population of Rio de Janeiro's male orphans and foundlings who were not adopted by families went into the unpaid service on the naval base on Ilha das Cobras for seven years – suggests the method through which many children, at the age of fourteen, entered the navy's companies of apprenticeship. In addition to police and military recruiters who turned boys and men over for service in exchange for payment, this represented an additional source of naval recruits, one that in the period marked by the passage of the Rio Branco Law in 1871 and the abolition of slavery in 1888 grew to be a sizable number of naval apprentices as the number of black orphans and foundlings in Rio increased. Between 1864 and 1881, the abandonment of *pardos* (browns) nearly doubled and that of *pretos* (blacks) nearly tripled. During the same period, the rate of abandonment of white children dropped to less than half of the 1864 figures.[81]

Additionally, on April 14, 1855, the government authorized the payment of one hundred mil-réis either to the family or guardian of a minor enlisted into the companies of apprentices.[82] These two sources of children who increasingly become the responsibility of the state are related, but their roads to state institutions are different. In the first case, these Afro-Brazilian children born to enslaved mothers are children whose labor is controlled by the owners of their mothers; children's fates were dictated not by their mothers, but by slave owners looking to maximize investment as the institution of slavery crumbled. Even as the state passed legislation that would eventually free all children born to slave mothers, it protected the rights of the slave owner over that of slave families. The second group consists of boys being turned over by their guardians to companies of apprentices in exchange for payment. Though not necessarily voluntary on the part of the individual apprentice, it was a negotiation entered into voluntarily by families. Following a pattern common in Brazilian law, the 1855 legislation authorizing payment to families who enrolled their sons as apprentices targeted poor families but it made no mention of their race. It is easy to see that this law over-whelmingly impacted Afro-Brazilian families. Of the twenty-one boys whose families received payment in exchange for their apprenticeship and who then faced charges before the navy's high court between the years 1869 and 1888, only one was white, four were *caboclo*[83] and the remaining fifteen were of African descent. Demographic growth among orphans, foundlings, and ingênuos turned over to the state between the mid-1860s and the end of slavery in 1888 resulted in an increase in the number of children under the guardianship of the Brazilian state, and Afro-Brazilian children made up an increasingly high percentage of that group.[84]

The march toward the abolition of African slavery led to the in-creased abandonment of Afro-Brazilian children in the city of Rio de Janeiro and, thus, to greater direct responsibility of the state to control these black urban bodies. Orphans were transferred into work on the naval base, where many were eventually pressured into the companies of apprentices. The control of these black boys had shifted from master to naval officers, but the method was the same, the regular and highly ritu-alized application of the lash. Even though they were not dragooned off the streets, the method of recruitment remained highly coercive. Those orphans who eventually died during their long terms of service had lived their whole lives under the violent control of Brazilian state institutions.

Brazil's free black communities have a long history dating back to the colonial period. Rural runaway-slave communities known as *quilom-bos* thrived during the late eighteenth and early nineteenth centuries, as did religious brotherhoods and mutual aid societies in cities. In the late nineteenth and early twentieth centuries, Afro-Brazilians established social and athletic clubs, newspapers, cultural groups, and cultural orga-nizations.[85] To survive the destructive nature of a slave society, free and enslaved blacks were compelled to create alternative kinship structures to protect members of the community in need, often children. This par-ticular period sees a rapid expansion of the urban underclass. Whether as the eventual result of the 1871 Rio Branco Law, the disruptive movement of slave labor from the north to the south, or the manipulation of the previously surplus free labor trying to make their way from the countryside to coastal cities seeking economic improvement, this population, the clear result of Brazilian modernization in the late empire and early republic, threatened that very modernization. In the eyes of both urban and rural elite, this group needed to be regulated by modern national institutions, the leadership of which saw coercion as the only way to regulate and control the "teeming" and unprotected urban lumpen element. The Brazilian navy thus expanded its role as a receptacle for this growing "problem" population, thereby also addressing, at least in part, the long-term shortfall in its recruitment of enlisted men.

THE LEGISLATION OF CORPORAL PUNISHMENT

For much of the life of the Brazilian Empire, men serving in the nation's military, like enslaved men and women, were subject to corporal punishment. After 1874, only sailors and slaves remained subject to the lash; this parallel was not lost on Brazilian sailors.[86] Charting the legal history of corporal punishment in the Brazilian navy is a largely academic exercise, as the illegality of the lash at times throughout the period of empire offered little protection to those Brazilian sailors still regularly subjected to corporal punishment. Still, an understanding of those rules that made it into laws offers insight into the lawmakers' values and goals, which in turn offer insight into Brazilian society. The letter of the law notwithstanding, corporal punishment remained the primary means of disciplining and controlling sailors throughout the history of the Portuguese and Brazilian navies, in periods of colony, empire, and republic, until the reclamantes who carried out the Revolta da Chibata delivered the end of the practice. The laws passed during the nineteenth century pertaining to the practice of whipping Brazilian citizens were blatantly contradictory. As the nation was reminded by the proclamation sent to the Brazilian president when the Revolta da Chibata began in 1910, the sailors involved in the revolt were citizens of Brazil. Not only could the Brazilian constitution of 1824 be interpreted to offer all citizens protection from corporal punishment, those protections from the lash were restated through the passage of legislation several times during the nineteenth century. However, until the aftermath of the sailors' revolt, the contradiction between Brazilian law and its naval policies for the control of its lower decks drew little attention. Though the use of the lash in the navy was well understood throughout Brazilian society, even its use on disorderly underage boys provoked no visible outrage except among the sailors themselves.

One reason for the contradictions in the way the state used violence to control society stemmed from the parallel contradiction of a slave society with a liberal constitution. The congressional legislation during the Brazilian Empire embodied a new juridical entity representing both the political interests of the central government and the economic interests of the Brazilian slave-owning elite. As the nation went through the process of abolition, the legislature formed national criminal codes that replaced the authority of slave owners, who had long wielded personal and political domination over their territory and the subordinates they exploited. The legislature walked a fine line between public interest and safety in the cities and the regulation of powerful land and slave owners compelled to cede their authority.

The basic regulations applicable to both sailors and officers in Brazil's navy at the time the Portuguese crown moved to Rio de Janeiro in 1808 were based on the 1796 "Provisional Rules for Service and Discipline in the Squadrons and Ships of the Royal Navy," from which most of the "decisions" promulgated as naval law throughout the period of the Brazilian Empire were taken. More important were the navy's "Articles of War" (*Artigos de Guerra*) published in 1799; whereas the Provisional Rules dictated the day-to-day regulations for the Portuguese navy, and subsequently for the Brazilian one as well, the Articles of War laid out exact punishments for specific crimes and disciplinary faults committed by enlisted men and officers in the Brazilian navy.

Similar to those of other Western navies, the Portuguese regulations of the late eighteenth century were draconian. They were written to help European powers extract fealty from men forcibly recruited into extended terms of service. Violence was central to retaining hierarchy and military service, and criminal and disciplinary faults were punished severely. According to Brazilian military historian Herick Marques Caminha, "If any institutional compromise was given in the struggle against the extremely heterogeneous population of naval enlisted men, the bulk of whom are made up of sailors recruited by force from among the dregs of society of our harbors who were then subjected to the terribly restrictive surroundings, provisions and lifestyle inherent to ships of the age, it would make it impossible for the Nation to maintain efficient operations on the ships that were to defend it, at sea, against the avarice and/or hostility of other nations."[87]

Although the 1799 Articles of War were wholly in accordance with the "brutally repressive philosophy"[88] typical of the era in which they were written, nineteenth-century Western navies uniformly shifted away from the violent control of men. The eighteenth-century origin of Brazil's twentieth-century naval legal discipline is noteworthy, because for Brazilian sailors forced to serve, international travel put them in touch with the crews of other modern navies. The lack of modern methods of discipline in a navy that had until 1888 served a slave state, and that continued to forcibly conscript black sailors into service in the twentieth century, sent the message to sailors that their treatment had less to do with Portuguese naval order, and more to do with the violent structure of chattel slavery.

Most of the 1799 Articles of War did not apply to corporal punishment administered onboard ships at all. Instead, they outlined penalties for sailors removed from their ships who faced formal courts-martial. When sailors were punished aboard ships, there was one article of that legislation invoked more than all others combined. Article 80 was a catchall ruling applied when a crime was not perceived as important enough to send a sailor off-ship for a lengthy trial. It allowed a ship's commander to call for violent punishment quickly, thus dealing with "petty" crimes in the most expedient manner available. This also sent a clear message to the ship's entire nonessential crew who were assembled to witness physical punishment. The regularity with which imperial officers invoked Article 80 shows exactly how important corporal punishment was for the day-to-day control of the Brazilian navy.[89]

The actual wording of Article 80 was purposely broad. The lash was to be applied as punishment for "all other indiscretions, such as drunkenness, gambling, and the like, that the proceeding articles did not specifically mention." Such violators "are to be punished proportionally at

the discretion of the commanding officer."[90] Any protection that the
1824 Imperial Constitution of Brazil might have offered with its statement "From this day forth the lash, torture, branding and all other cruel
punishment are abolished" was ignored, or perhaps the naval elite and
Brazilian politicians had never intended for those protections to be applied to sailors and soldiers.[91] For whatever the justification they, like
slaves, were beyond the protection of the constitution. Within a year of
the passage of the constitution, the Decision of July 23, 1825 – determined
by the Crown and transmitted by a minister – authorized the punishment of sailors who deserted the navy with one hundred lashes, applied
before the assembled crew of his ship.[92] There was no amendment to the
constitution or significant debate about this change; constitutional protection was simply set aside, and the newer regulation was implemented.

It was not only the Brazilian military that ignored the constitutional
ban on corporal punishment. In the early years of the empire, the parliament wrote and passed into law the Criminal Code of the Empire on
December 16, 1830. This legislation also authorized the application of the
lash for civilian criminal offences. In his 1834 annual written report to
parliament, Minister of the Navy Rodrigo Torres complained that the
criminal code was of no real value to the navy as it was far too "vague and
incomplete, and failed to define with precision the nature of the crimes
and punishments."[93] He announced the Decree of December 1833, which
nominated a commission to organize a new penal code specifically for
the navy, but although this commission did meet, they failed to produce
any such document.[94]

Although codes relevant to the application of corporal punishment
shifted throughout this period, there were notable attempts to ensure
that the manner in which the lash was applied remained uniform in the
Brazilian navy. On July 16, 1833, the legislature disseminated Decision no.
384, addressing patterns of physical and verbal abuse directed at sailors
in the navy. In addition to halting injurious or indecent language, the
decision demanded that no sailor be physically punished outside of the
definition of the articles of war. When corporal punishment was applied,
it could only be by order of the ship's commander. Finally, it decreed
what was already common practice: that ship's crew had to be called
to arms to witness this punishment and that the specific article of war

that was being applied be read aloud to the sailor being punished and to the crew. This legislation suggests that the naval elite wanted to halt the practice of overzealous officers and midshipmen overstepping naval hierarchy by taking upon themselves to verbally chastise, strike, and otherwise punish behavior outside of "official" military justice. Much like on a plantation, to ensure hierarchal order certain powers needed to remain in the hands of the master. Self-interested and overzealous overseers risked inviting personal retribution and thus causing insubordination. Instead, in the navy the lash was to be applied meticulously in a formal, public, and structured manner on display in front of the entire ship's crew.[95]

Twenty-eight years later, Decision 396 of September 13, 1861, repeated these concerns of the naval elite. It echoed that only a commander – of either a ship or a base – could call for the application of the lash; it had to be carried out in front of the assembled crew, including officers and the commander; and the crime for which he was being punished had to be read to the assembled crew. It also stated that the commander could not act outside of his jurisdiction or exceed regulations in carrying out such punishment. He could apply only twenty-five lashes in a day; any punishment that called for more than twenty-five lashes would be applied over several days. These protections guaranteed by the law diverted radically from naval policy. The examination of the naval court-martial records documents the fact that sailors were routinely lashed more than twenty-five times in a day, and were often lashed hundreds of times in a day; with but one exception (examined in detail in the following chapter), officers were never rebuked or put on trial for any transgression of the rights of enlisted men.[96]

As mentioned above, in 1874 the Brazilian parliament did abolish the use of corporal punishment in the army, but at the time there was no mention of its use in the navy. Decree 8,898 of March 3, 1883, regulated the punishments endured by sailors whose crimes fell under the catchall Article 80 of the Articles of War. Potential punishments were ranked from most to least grave. They were as follows: the *chibata,* from six to twenty-five lashes; solitary confinement, with or without irons, with bread and water, from three to five days; prison below deck, with single or double irons, from two to six days; *golilha* (an iron collar by which a prisoner is held against a post while standing) from two to six hours; restricted movement on board, from seven to twenty days; suspension of pay; doubled service, for two or three days; two hours of exercise; and preventative prison with irons. This structuring of penalties allowed commanders to delegate the application of all punishments, except for the chibata, to their subordinates. The commander still had to personally oversee all cases in which corporal punishment was administered.[97]

On October 15, 1886, the legislature revoked Article 60 of the Criminal Code; this ended the application of corporal punishment in the civil arena, though its legal application continued in the navy. For a short time following the passage of final abolition on May, 13 1888, in Brazil the only people who could be legally lashed were sailors enlisted in the navy. The promise of positivism and modernity finally seemed at hand in 1889 when, eighteen months after the Golden Law freed the remaining slaves, the republican congress that itself came to power through an army coup against the monarchy finally curtailed the use of the lash in the navy. On November 16, 1889, only the third law ever passed by the Brazilian congress explicitly abolished corporal punishment in the navy. Not surprisingly given the nature of the navy, this law caused so much concern among officers – and remained so widely unimplemented – that a mere five months later on April 12, 1890, that same legislature legally reintroduced the lash by creating a Companhia Correcional (correctional company) for use on board ships. Although "severe punishment" was to be applied only "within restricted limits" to seamen imprisoned within this company, in fact very little had changed. In theory, only men who had a documented history of incorrigible behavior could be whipped, and this only after a transfer to a separate naval company. In fact, these naval companies did not physically occupy separate spaces, and no physical transfer was required. This was a formal designation; any sailor could immediately be "transferred" into this "company" without any actual change in his location or service; he remained aboard his ship without physical incarceration. Once transferred, he could immediately be subjected to the lash in the same manner as it had been previously applied.[98]

Thus, the Brazilian congress allowed the application of the lash to remain the primary means of discipline onboard Brazilian warships in all sectors of the navy. Brazil experienced sweeping changes, from monarchy to republic, from slave society to democracy. As the country reformed the rights of citizens, soldiers, and slaves, applying new constitutions and legal codes that reflected the modern political age, the violent treatment of Brazilian sailors remained remarkably unchanged.

DIVERGENT PATHS: THE RECRUITMENT LAW OF 1874

Parliament began to shape the Recruitment Law in the final year of the Paraguayan War, a long, costly, and unpopular engagement. Emperor Pedro II was widely criticized for his stubborn insistence on Brazil's absolute and unconditional victory over Paraguayan dictator Francisco Solano Lopéz, choosing not to negotiate for peace once Brazil drove the fighting into Paraguay and took Asunción in August 1868. The longevity of the war had enormous political consequences for Brazil. One can for the first time trace the growth of the Brazilian army into a national institution; additionally, army officers for the first time fought their way into the political elite. Brazil was required to mobilize its army nationally for the first time, and it suffered from being undermanned and disorganized; the navy participated too, though its role would be smaller. Following a short and insufficient wave of volunteerism, in order to populate the army Brazil dragooned and armed many free Afro-Brazilians, while on a much smaller scale they negotiated with slave owners, offering compensation for slaves who enlisted in exchange for freedom at the end of their service. Some of these black soldiers experienced notable success and promotion during the war. These changes challenged the traditional hierarchy of the army. As seen during the Spanish American wars of independence, and as was occurring anew in Cuba's Ten Years' War (1868–78), it is difficult to use an integrated military to enforce the racist hierarchy of a slave society. Soon after the war's conclusion, army officers unilaterally ended the long-term practice of assigning soldiers to hunt down runaway slaves. The legislation took up the issue of recruitment in response to the difficulties the army faced recruiting soldiers in sufficient numbers during the war.[99]

Debate began in 1869, but once the war ended and recruitment became a less pressing issue for the central government, it took until 1874 for the reform to pass through the legislative process. As this procedure ground on through the early 1870s, the Brazilian army promoted its own measures toward modernization. Historically, there was a stigma attached to military service in Brazil; it was widely understood that forced recruitment impacted only Brazil's least powerful class. In order to challenge that truth, the national elite envisioned radical structural changes to military service. To make service in a modern civilian army acceptable to "honorable" Brazilians – as had occurred in Europe and the United States – the relationship between the military and its enlisted men had to undergo a radical change. Inequalities within the structure of the army became the focus of reforms. Volunteers and conscripts were for the first time to receive equal pay and status, serve the same length terms, and receive the same benefits. Among their reforms was the leveling of those ranks that tainted the institution. From the bottom, the army eliminated the lowly rank of *camarada*, a private assigned to be the personal servant of an officer. From the top they eliminated the cadet privilege, by which the sons of officers, nobles, and university graduates could not be punished by blows of the flat of a sword. This gesture of removing privilege to elite soldiers turned out in the long run to be a purely symbolic change, as article 8 of the Recruitment Law of 1874 stated, "Corporal punishment is abolished in the Army, and is hereby replaced by other disciplinary punishments as recorded in law and regulation."[100] Brazilian army officers instead appropriated European nonviolent punishments intended to reform a soldier's behavior rather than make him a violent example for others. By professionalizing service in the Brazilian army and having the legislature create a national lottery to draft young men into service, officers envisioned a national army in which the sons of the poor, the middle class, and (in theory) the wealthy could serve together, bonding and recognizing their equality before the laws of a modern Brazilian state.[101]

This suppression of corporal punishment for soldiers did not extend to sailors; from this point forward, only slaves and sailors would legally receive the ignoble application of the lash. This implementation of distinct patterns of discipline demands speculation as to why the progressive modernism so well established in European and North American militaries was taken up by the army but not the navy. This is tied to the ideas of whitening, modernization, and positivism, so central to the Brazilian elite in at the time. The army is a national institution, and after its shortcomings were so publically displayed during the Paraguayan War (and again later during difficult regional struggles in Canudos and the Contestado) these reforms become the core of a broad plan to fix the Brazilian army. Borrowing modern methods of military recruitment and discipline from powerful European states would reform the army through the public treatment of its soldiers. Once these transformations were complete, the army would play a more important role in the broader reenvisioned nation. By treating its members honorably, the army potentially becomes a viable option for the employment of all citizens, not only desprotegidos; as the nation whitens and becomes more civilized, so too will its soldiers.

During the war, naval officers also struggled with populating their lower decks. As was true in the army, Decree 3,708 of 1866 authorized the navy to compensate up to 1,600 slave owners willing to turn their slaves over for service, but for both branches of the military the relatively small number of slaves actually liberated through this legislation was of limited help in solving the overall problem.[102] Instead I refer back to statistics from the "Naval Recruitment Policy" section above. Although forced conscription represented the majority of naval recruitment during each year from 1859 to 1868 except for 1861, in general as many new apprenticeship companies had been established since the first one was opened in 1840. From the decline of the navy's role in the Paraguayan War in 1869 until 1873 when these statistics were collected, the navy recruited more apprentices into service than they did men through forced impressment. Apprentices were more valuable to the state and signed on for longer terms than sailors impressed into service; this was ostensibly a means for them to repay the state for its investment in the "education" of the apprentices. At the time the recruitment laws were being formulated, the naval elite were confident that the apprenticeship program would increasingly deliver recruits in sufficient numbers that the navy did not require the reformulation of the recruitment policies taking place in the army.[103]

For example, in his annual report to the general assembly for the years 1880 and 1881, the naval minister, Dr. José Rodrigues de Lima Duarte, described a future, premised on this shift to naval apprentices for populating the lower decks, in which the lash would no longer be necessary: "It will not be difficult to abolish corporal punishment once the composition of the ships crews' have improved, when the profession of national sailor is an honor for Brazilian citizens and it is no longer a punishment for the dregs of the army's soldiers and for those individuals for whom the police can find no other corrective."[104] It is interesting that eight years after the collection of the 1873 statistics, the minister did not feel that the apprentices had yet significantly improved the crew of Brazilian ships; the abolition of corporal punishment had to wait for this theoretical improvement. Perhaps one problem was that in his 1881 report he described the navy as serving as the institution where the army's worst soldiers and the criminals too dangerous for the police to control would be transferred, thus serving as a maximum security prison for these other oppressive institutions.

He then offered that one remedy would be the removal from the navy of those dishonorable sailors who find themselves "subject to these ignominious punishments."[105] This reads more like a threat to Brazilian society than a suggestion to improve the institution; these castoffs from the army and the most incorrigible prisoners of the police served as the ongoing justification for the harsh treatment in the navy. The minister asserted that the men they recruited were more dangerous and harder to control than the men who joined the army. The promise of honorable treatment for these base-born Afro-Brazilian men threatened naval hierarchy much more than said reforms would threaten the army, because naval officers believed that the navy simply could not function without the regular application of the lash; the navy could not reform until the dishonorable men who served on its lower decks were displaced or removed. No such purging of the navy's enlisted men was implemented until the aftermath of the Revolta da Chibata thirty years later. The navy drew on impressed labor in a slave society in which those who were not under the authority of a master were deemed simultaneously unprotected and a threat to public order and thus needed to be regimented. Racist assumptions made the application of progressive modernism an impossibility.

Following closely on the heels of the army's 1874 reforms, the government passed the Recruitment Law on September 26, 1874, calling for the adoption of a draft lottery to formalize a standing Brazilian army and navy; insufficient voluntary recruits were to trigger a draft lottery. Following the model of Prussia's peacetime draft lottery, all men between the ages of eighteen and thirty would enroll at a local parish; when necessary they would be selected randomly to serve. The law was not implemented upon its passage; too much time had passed since the embarrassment of the Paraguayan War, and there was widespread popular resistance against universal conscription. The language of that resistance showed that those reforms passed by the army were not nearly enough to convince Brazilians that army service had become honorable. According to Peter Beattie, preabolition army impressment had "reinforced sharp distinctions between law-abiding and criminal, legitimate and illegitimate, free and slave, [and] the 'honorable' and the 'dishonorable' poor . . . but conscription threatened to confuse these distinctions and inspired passionate resistance."[106] He goes on to argue that the implementation of universal conscription would require the image of soldiering being modified so that such service could be seen as "manly" rather than "emasculating punishment."[107] The reform embraced by the army in 1874 clearly had not done this.[108]

According to the letter of the law, the Brazilian army and navy would be restructured as one. This radical revision of military procedure would make military service acceptable for "honorable" men; the professionalization of soldiers and sailors meant that the Brazilian military could act as a labor market and a training ground for humble but virtuous citizens and the "dangerous" classes as well. Nonetheless, the legislation's inclusion of the navy in the restructuring of Brazil's military was curious, as it offered naval officers very little that they required to improve naval hierarchy. An 1823 law had long before separated army and navy recruitment, and the changes in naval recruitment policy examined above resulted in the two organizations recruiting from very different populations. Both the army and the navy forcibly impressed young adults, men who were ready to enter the ranks as soldiers and sailors. But in the 1830s the navy had initiated an important transformation in recruitment – the shift from men to boys. The navy increasingly preferred to recruit boys, minors who spent years in the companies of apprentices and were often sent up into official naval service well before attaining the age of majority. Officers believed that these young men would make better sailors and would eventually require less violent discipline. The expansion the companies of apprentices throughout Brazil meant that naval recruitment had already become less reliant on voluntary or forced enlistment in this period than at any previous time. In 1871, the naval minister stated, "Impressment is almost unnecessary because the Navy Apprentice Schools supply sufficient personnel each year."[109] If applied to the navy, the 1874 Recruitment Laws would have improved service for recruits that the navy was hard at work trying to replace. Any assumption among politicians that the 1874 Recruitment Law would shift the decades-old tradition of naval recruitment without any direct discussion of those changes was simply unrealistic.

In the final year of the empire, it seemed that the companies of apprentices had all but replaced forced recruitment. According to the 1888 annual report the naval minister presented to the emperor during the final year of his reign, there had been no need for forced recruits between the years 1884 and 1888. The number of apprentices who "graduated" into naval service during those four years was 1,820.[110] For the naval elite, when compared with the traditional forced recruitment of men into naval service, these boys were ideal sailors. In theory, they should have entered service better trained for life at sea than had the older forced recruits, and they served longer terms than men conscripted as adults. With the fall of the empire the naval plan seemed fortuitous as, in the heady days of the proclamation of the republic, much as congress outlawed corporal punishment, the language of the 1874 recruitment law was imported into the Republican Constitution. Article 87, section 3, called for the abolition of forced military recruitment in both the army and the navy. Should there be a shortage of volunteers, Article 87, section 4, called for the recruitment of students from the naval schools and the apprenticeship schools, and would then switch to the "previously organized draft lottery" to draw sailors from the merchant marine. This was the same lottery that had never actually been adopted.[111] Much like the quick return of corporal punishment in the republican navy, this proclamation had little immediate effect on practices in the Brazilian navy.

When available apprentices failed to meet the needs of naval recruitment, the navy fell back on old practices. While officers preferred to recruit apprentices, and the majority of sailors continued to come from what were now called the apprenticeship schools rather than companies (renamed in 1885 to improve their reputation), the republican navy retained the recruitment policies of the Brazilian empire as needed. And as naval ships became larger and more numerous, the government continued to recruit from among the nation's desprotegidos. As the republican government outlawed forced military recruitment it stopped collecting official statistics on naval recruitment. While official records on coercive conscription end after 1889, scholars of the era agree that forced conscription continued into the twentieth century. In his description of recruitment policies in the early republic, contemporary historian Marcos A. da Silva describes the ships of the Brazilian navy as being "transformed into a series of mobile prisons,"[112] while in his anonymous memoir, José Eduardo de Macedo Soares describes the Brazilian navy in the early twentieth century by saying "our navy serves as a sewer for our society."[113] In an attempt to diversify naval recruits, Minister Júlio César da Noronha in the naval minister's annual Report to the President of 1903, returned to the constitutional authorization of the navy to draft sailors from the merchant marine, and followed that up with various laws or decrees justifying the passage of Law 4901 of June 22 that allowed the navy to actively draft from the merchant marine sailors between the ages of sixteen and thirty, excluding machinists, navigators (*pilotos*), and those judged incapable of service. Such draftees would be expected to serve for terms of three years, and remain on reserve for two more. It is unclear how this draft impacted recruitment in the long term; in its first year it attracted eighty-seven sailors, sixty-seven of whom were declared unfit for service.[114]

Although the Brazilian officer corps remained unwilling to modernize the service of sailors in the Brazilian navy, it would be a massive oversight to ignore their deep commitment to modernization, a commitment rivaling that of their colleagues in the army. Officials did not cede the ground of military progress just because the navy was thoroughly dependent on the largely coerced labor of impoverished black boys; they instead embraced institutional modernization through the adoption of technological innovation. Beginning in the 1880s the government procured modern warships from abroad, and that commitment grew into the 1904 Naval Renovation Plan, which expanded again in 1906. This contract to renovate the navy's stock of warships, which eventually led to the purchase of fourteen state-of-the-art battleships from English ship-yards, including the dreadnoughts *São Paulo* and *Minas Geraes,* clearly articulates the reform naval officers sought. These ships could bestow modernity on the navy the instant they were turned over; there was no need to overhaul their internal hierarchy. As Gilberto Freyre describes this period in his *Order and Progress,* "The fact is that the Navy modern-ized its material equipment without having prepared its personnel for the technical requirements of such equipment."[115] Given the preparedness of the reclamantes during the 1910 revolt, certain enlisted men seem to have readied themselves for the requirements of the equipment. The overhaul of the armada with warships on the cutting edge of technol-ogy exacerbated the workload on what became chronically understaffed crews. This increased the application of the lash on board these ships as the ships required increasingly professional crews while officers relied on increasingly violent methods to motivate the lower decks in their increased workloads.

Let us return to the reclamantes' claim that their treatment in the navy was akin to slavery, and to Peter Beattie's quote that for Brazilian so-ciety, forced recruitment "reinforced sharp distinctions between ... free and slave, [and] the 'honorable' and the 'dishonorable' poor."[116] Orlando Patterson's definition of "enslavement" offers support for their claim. Pat-terson does not define slavery according to one person owning another and profiting from his labor. Instead of focusing on ownership, he defines "slavery" as "the permanent, violent domination of natally alienated and generally dishonored persons ... like all enduring social processes, the relation became institutionalized."[117] The majority of sailors in this era were coerced into service as children, lacking agency to resist this fate, and were motivated by the regular, systematic application of sanctioned state violence. Although sailors were not chattel, the nature of the re-lationship between sailor and officer replicated that between slave and master; the navy had its roots in slave society. To again quote Patterson, "First, in all slave societies the slave was considered a degraded person; second, the honor of the master was enhanced by the subjection of his slave; and third, wherever slavery became structurally very important, the whole tone of the slaveholders' culture tended to be highly honorific."[118] For most sailors, their lives easily fit within this definition.

It is too easy to exclude entire areas of study from their larger place in the study of Atlantic slavery by applying too narrow a definition of the term "slavery." The study of the African diaspora is enriched by broader, comparative definitions of slavery and its repercussions. Men impressed into work, who lack means to leave the service of their lords or state, who are whipped both to improve their labor output and to serve as a symbolic threat to others, are acting very much like slaves. That Brazil's sailors received meager wages and were working toward the fulfillment of the terms of a *contract* does not make them wage laborers by anyone's definition other than that of their masters and officers.

The Revolta da Chibata violently set aside these men's traditional role rooted in slavery. Patterson states, "The slave ... could have no honor because he had no power and no independent social existence, hence no public worth.... The slave, as we shall see, usually stood outside the game of honor."[119] In carrying out the 1910 revolt, these men reclaimed that honor. Twenty-two years after Brazil's Golden Law abolished slavery in 1888, sailors knew honor was something they had a right to, even if their officers did not. The coming of the dreadnought battleships – regardless of the intentions of those who authorized their purchase – delivered to these sailors the means to challenge their position. This revolt could not have occurred during the period of chattel slavery; it was only once abolition promised these men the rights to freedom and honor, and technology delivered weapons that allowed a small group to hold siege to one of the Atlantic's great cities, that they could rise up to demand their place among Brazilian citizens.

What exactly do we mean when we use the term "povo"? Certainly not this base mass of illiterate, diseased, shriveled, malaria-ridden mestizos and blacks. This cannot be called a "people," they cannot be presented to foreigners as an example of our people. The workers cannot be this example, they will never be the people. People means race, culture, civilization, affirmation, nationhood – not the dregs of a nation.

JOÃO UBALDO RIBEIRO, *Viva o povo brasileiro*

THREE

Control of the Lower Decks, 1860–1910

ACCORDING TO THE RECORDS OF THE NAVAL HIGH COURT (Conselho de Guerra da Marinha), in June 1872, cabin boy (*grumete*) Cosme Monoel do Nascimento, was found guilty of gravely wounding fellow cabin boy Francisco Palmeira d'Oliveira with a razor. He initially received a sentence of twenty years' imprisonment, though that sentence would later be reduced to ten years. Through the court records, we gain access to a laundry list of biographical detail. We learn that Nascimento was a black (preto) twenty-seven-year-old who was born in Pernambuco; his father was José Francisco das Chagas. Nascimento enrolled in the Imperial Marines (Corpo dos Imperiais Marinheiros, the more prestigious branch of the navy akin to the U.S. marines) in 1862, but in May 1871, due to dishonorable behavior, he was moved to the regular navy and demoted to the rank of cabin boy.[1]

The courts also document previous disciplinary actions, both imprisonment and corporal punishment, while in naval service. In the case of Nascimento, his trouble started soon after joining the navy. In 1863, he was whipped 50 times and chained in solitary confinement for two days as punishment for robbery, he was whipped 75 times as punishment for his first desertion, and he was whipped 300 times (in the unlikely event that the ship's officer followed the law, he would have been whipped 25 times a day for twelve days) for injuring a shipmate. In August 1867, he was again punished for injuring a shipmate, this time with 200 lashes. In April 1869, he was whipped 25 times for sleeping on the watch, and in June that year, he was whipped 100 times for "practicing immoral acts" with a shipmate. In June 1870, he was lashed 100 times for having been found with a knife, a file, and a bladder of *cachaça* (sugar cane brandy) while he was locked up in the hole. He was then imprisoned for six months on Ilha das Cobras, and in November of 1871, he gravely injured the above-mentioned cabin boy; this is the crime that brought him in front of the military high court. Though he had been imprisoned before, this seems to be the first time he faced court-martial.[2]

There is limited biographical data pertaining to enlisted men in the Brazilian navy in this era. The court-martial documents recorded under the Brazilian Empire, though incomplete, offer rare insight into the lives of the men who populated the lower decks. Not all court-martial cases contain the level of detail seen above, but most records of enlisted men's court-martial cases document their basic data (age, race, parents, physical description, region of origin, crime, sentence), while some offer impressive biographical sketches of the lives of sailors. These records document the punishment and control that remains largely invisible throughout the nation's archives. That invisibility is part of a conscious agenda of the Brazilian elite striving to civilize the history of their nation, not least by erasing the record of racist and dishonorable policies in the late nineteenth century. The obvious records of corporal punishment, the *Livros dos Castigos,* or books of punishment, from each Brazilian naval ship, have yet to be located. Thus, it is fortunate that this history can be partially reproduced based on the cases from the naval high court.

Among military court records, the statistical analysis of the legal cases of Brazil's naval high court (the Conselho de Guerra da Marinha) cannot be expected to literally apply to all Brazilian sailors. These documents record only a tiny percentage of the corporal punishment applied in the Brazilian navy. Only those men tried by the high court had their previous punishments recorded in a court-martial document. Furthermore, after the 1889 establishment of the First Republic, race and violent punishment appear with much less regularity in the official documents. But together, these cases represent the narrow end of a wedge with which we can open an investigation of practices and policies of nineteenth-century Brazil. When placed in the larger context of senate records, correspondence among and statements by the naval elite, reports in the popular press, and the contradictory laws introduced through both the federal government and the military hierarchy, we see a set of practices and policies that illuminates our understanding of Brazilian racial and military history.

These documents represent a unique and detailed source on corporal punishment and its application to enlisted men in the Brazilian navy. Of 1,860 cases tried by the military high courts throughout Brazil between 1860 and 1893, 1,163 are housed in the National Archive in Rio de Janeiro. Of those 1,163 military trials, 344 (or almost 30 percent) were trials of sailors before the naval high court in Rio de Janeiro during the empire. I focus on those cases because the revolt takes place in Rio de Janeiro among sailors stationed there. In those 344 trials, 286 individual men stood before the high court in Rio de Janeiro; some were tried more than once. In those 344 trials there was a recorded history of the application of corporal punishment in 202 cases, or in more than 58.5 percent.[3]

I do not suggest that these statistics can or should be literally applied to the general population of sailors in Rio de Janeiro, or to Brazilian sailors overall. The numbers are too small, and for reasons examined below, I suspect that the analysis of criminal cases would not exactly represent the overall body of Brazilian sailors. Rather than arguing that 58.5 of every 100 sailors were whipped during the decades preceding the Revolta da Chibata, I believe that the analysis of these numbers affirms the navy's overall reliance on corporal punishment to support military hierarchy. These cases suggest overall patterns of discipline and control, and should not be read as a method to map corporal punishment overall. That said, 58.5 percent is a high proportion of sailors to have been lashed, especially given that 286 of those 344 were being court-martialed for the first time. What's more is that there is evidence that the actual percentage of these men subjugated to corporal punishment may have been even higher. There are several cases in which the unofficial application of corporal punishment, often at the hand of a noncommissioned officer or sentry, was noted in the court-martial testimony; but that punishment had never been recorded under the victim's military record. For example, Imperial Marine Third Class Bartolomeu Antonio, a mixed-race or brown (pardo) sailor born in Rio de Janeiro, enlisted into the navy at the age of nineteen and was tried for his third desertion in 1862. When asked why he ran, he claimed that a sentry on board named Pinto had mistreated him with the chibata and with "injurious language." His assertion was that the illegal attack by the sentry on duty motivated his desertion. There is no evidence in the record that Antonio's charges against the sentry were investigated, suggesting that such abuse was not uncommon. Ignoring the justification for his crime, the court found Antonio guilty, and, according to Article 51 of the Articles of War published in 1799, he was sentenced to one year in prison while working at unpaid labor.[4]

Antonio's claim was not investigated, but there was sufficient illegal application of corporal punishment by unauthorized members of the Brazilian navy that the government addressed the problem. Decision 396, promulgated on September 13, 1861, stated: "Only those charged by the General Headquarters of the Navy: the commanders of naval stations; ships; or Marine Corps are authorized to order corporal punishment applied to naval enlisted men, within the limits of their jurisdiction, never exceeding that marked by regulations."[5] In 1864, Imperial Marine Third Class Manoel Belmiro, a pardo sailor from Porto Alegre who enlisted at the age of eighteen, also complained of an illegal assault that led to his crime. Also on charge for his third desertion from the Brazilian navy, he testified that the ship's sentry along with Seaman Manoel da Luz from the crew inappropriately lashed him, which motivated his desertion. The judge once again found his motivation neither compelling nor worthy of further investigation; he received the same sentence as had Bartolomeu Antonio two years earlier. In five additional cases, men alleged physical mistreatment by sergeants or sentries on board Brazilian warships. In none of these cases was that claim deemed significant or worthy of further investigation. As previously mentioned, during the period investigated in this study only one ship's captain was ever charged with an illegal application of corporal punishment. No petty officer, sentry, or enlisted man was ever tried for the unofficial application of corporal punishment, even though allegations of such abuses repeatedly surfaced in criminal investigations and had been absolutely prohibited by Decision 396 of 1861.[6]

Given the long history of normalizing corporal punishment into the control of Brazilian naval hierarchy, it is not surprising to find the legal system willing to overlook claims of unsanctioned corporal punishment. More surprising is the pattern of sanctioned applications of corporal punishment vanishing from official records. When the Republic was established in 1889 and immediately outlawed the application of corporal punishment in the navy, the military court often simply stopped recording corporal punishment in their records. In addition to this loss of documentation, there is evidence of a general underrecording of corporal punishment throughout the nineteenth century. There are several ways in which the use of the lash was likely to be underrepresented in these documents. For example, in the case of sailors who faced trial on multiple occasions, in more than 20 percent of records, some previous application of the lash recorded in earlier cases had been left out of the records of later trials. Of the 286 individuals who faced trial before the high court, there were forty-four cases of sailors arrested and tried on multiple occasions: thirty-two of those men were tried twice, ten were tried three times, and two men faced trial four times during the period examined. Nine of those forty-four men's records show inconsistencies in which chronologically later cases failed to record whippings that were documented in early cases. In other words, as time passed, minor infractions that had been punished with the chibata could simply drop off an enlisted man's record, thus causing corporal punishment to be underrepresented.

CONTROLLING THE NAVY

Assuming that Brazil's naval officers accepted Evaristo de Moraes Filho's assertion that the lower decks of the navy consisted of "dregs of our urban centers, the most worthless *lumpen,* without preparation of any sort" and that "ex-slaves and the sons of slaves make up our ships crews,"[7] how did they motivate these men to act as professional sailors? One conclusion we can draw from the court records is that the threat of court-martial and incarceration did not represent the central method of control or punishment in the Brazilian navy. To punish sailors with prison sentences and extended terms of service did not represent the first line of naval discipline. For a ship's captain facing the loss of a valuable crew-member for the duration of the trial and incarceration, court-martial was a last resort. Instead – as was the case during Brazilian slavery – the lash was the first and foremost measure in retaining elite dominance over a body of men who had little compulsion to offer their service and loyalty to the Brazilian military.

As ships regularly visited foreign posts far from the naval high court, the navy had a visible role in Brazil's international diplomacy. Even preceding the Brazilian acquisition of a modern fleet, such visits were an important part of how nations of this era represented their might in foreign countries. It was the officers' duty to present an orderly and structured military even though its lower decks were largely staffed with men who had often been swept off the streets by police after committing no actual crime and forced into service. Their work was grueling and underpaid, and once remitted by the police, they were responsible for a term of service to the navy that lasted – for a sailor with a perfect record – between six and twelve years. Evaristo de Moraes Filho's words draw our attention to the irony that the naval elite simultaneously had low expectations for these men but held their service to an extremely high standard. Brazilian naval officers (and this was to some extent true in all modern navies at the time) were forced into the uncomfortable system in which their competence and professionalism was judged based on their ability to control the behavior of men who they felt were unable to properly execute the tasks required for their jobs. This is one reason that officers objected so vociferously when the civilian legislators tried to take away from them the lash as a means of discipline.

To perform this difficult role, naval officers reproduced the actions and responsibilities of slave owners. Indeed, drawn as they were from the upper classes, it is highly probable that many, if not most, came from slave-owning families. Water Johnson's groundbreaking examination of the slave markets in the United States suggests parallels between these naval officers and slave owners. In an examination of the actions of slave owners who used violence to dictate the behavior of enslaved men and women, he described the manner in which slaves who broke rules or behaved badly reflected on the honorable position held by the slave owner. "By punishing slaves . . . slaveholders violently reasserted the identities they had bought their slaves to embody: they were people of refinement even if their slaves were nasty, undisciplined, or rude. . . . If they had to, they would use brutality to close the distance between the roles they imagined for themselves and the failings of the slaves they bought as props for their performance."[8] The role played by naval officers in the military hierarchy was parallel; after all, what was at stake for the naval officer trying to whip an enlisted man into submission? The literal legacy of the lash, deeply rooted in colonial slavery, continued in various aspects of this modernizing nation – notably here in its navy – as the vehicle of choice for disciplining black and other subaltern subjects; lashing itself becomes part of an attempt to enforce submission to the notion of a modern military.

Only one time, in a case unique in the Brazilian military courts, was an officer put on trial for the excessive punishment of an enlisted man. Through its analysis, we gain insight into the centrality of violence to naval hierarchy, and we see the manner in which – though the officer is put on trial for his crime – he is eventually rewarded for his behavior.

THE TRIAL OF LIEUTENANT JOSÉ CÂNDIDO GUILLOBEL

On October 18, 1873, Lieutenant José Cândido Guillobel of the Brazilian navy, the officer in charge of the warship *Bahia,* faced trial in Brazil's Conselho de Guerra da Marinha, its highest naval court. As required by military law, the officer in charge of any ship has the sole responsibility for authorizing and overseeing the application of corporal punishment. In this case, Lieutenant Guillobel faced trial for the punishment of Imperial Marine Laurentino Manoel da Silva, whom he had struck with 500 strokes of the lash in a single day. This case is unique; at no other time during the fifty-year period examined in this work was a Brazilian naval officer tried for excessively harsh punishment of an enlisted man.[9]

Returning to Decision 396 of September 13, 1861, with this law the government sought to control the application of corporal punishment in the navy. It stated that a naval commander could have a sailor whipped only 25 times in a day; should a more severe punishment be required, it would be applied over several days in limited doses of 25 lashes per day. Court-martial records show that punishment regularly exceeded the 25-lashes-per-day limits that were put in place in 1861. In scores of cases, officers ignored Decision 396 – including in the case of the whipping that eventually ignited the Revolta da Chibata – and sailors were lashed hundreds of time in a day. That an officer found himself on trial for such an offense generates unique insight into the motivation and justification that the elite used for the regular use of violence to control the lower decks. Here we uncover documentation of the process of punishment; we are essentially walked through the process of a Brazilian naval officer punishing his subordinate, and we hear his response when he is forced to justify the brutality that was so central to discipline in that institution.

On September 3, 1873, Luís de Sousa Neves served as sentry on watch aboard the warship *Bahia;* his duty was to patrol and police the actions of the enlisted men on board the ship. When a fight broke out between sailors Laurentino Manoel da Silva and Valeriano do Espirito Santo – the two were punching, kicking, and hurling insults at each other – the sentry interrupted the altercation, quickly separating the two men. In the process, Silva shifted his hostility from his shipmate to the sentry. He hurled a string of obscenities at the sentry, at which point the sentry left the deck (and Silva) in order to notify his immediate superior. That superior, an unnamed corporal of the guard (*cabo-da-guarda*) drafted a warrant for Silva's arrest and imprisonment to be delivered to the officer of the watch (*oficial de quarto*). The officer of the watch was, in turn, required to carry out the order.

The officer of the watch that night was midshipman Cândido Francisco Garrido Belas Júnior, who was thus responsible for the day-to-day running of the ship. Upon receipt of the order, he went to locate Silva. He found the sailor still berating the sentry in an extremely agitated and hostile state, and the officer of the watch ordered the sailor placed in irons. At this time, the officer of the watch, together with the sentry who originally broke up the fight and his immediate superior, the corporal of the guard, sought to manacle Silva. He wrestled free, struck a blow to the sentry's head, and pulled out his folding naval-issue pocketknife, with which he tried to stab the sentry. It was only with the intervention of several enlisted men that Silva was finally restrained, imprisoned, and placed in wrist and ankle irons.

It is only at this point the ship's head officer, Lieutenant José Cândido Guillobel, enters the story. The regular commander of the battleship *Bahia* was on shore leave, and he had Guillobel assume the post temporarily. Thus, on the day that this case made its way up the chain of command to his desk, Guillobel had not previously acted in the capacity of the ship's disciplinarian. The young officer sought to ensure that his authority was taken seriously. The ship's current commander is the final authority as to the punishment applied to enlisted men, but there is another tier above his onboard responsibility. Technically, in any instance in which a sailor stands accused of a serious crime, he should be removed from the ship and sent to face charges on the naval base on the Ilha das Cobras. That should have been the case for Laurentino Manoel da Silva; fighting with a shipmate was fairly common, but his violent resistance toward two superiors, and the attempt to stab the sentry along with his having hit the guard, should have had him removed from ship and placed in front of a court-martial. According to the 1799 Articles of War all crimes of war, injuries, homicide, high insubordination, and desertion in the Brazilian navy were to be tried by the naval high court in Rio de Janeiro. Only the punishment for lesser crimes was left to the discretion of a ship's captain, who was to refer to the laws of the nation and the military. But officers often exercised their power (or it could be argued, overreached their power) by keeping men on board the ship and punishing them as if they had committed a less serious offense, that is, through the application of the lash.[10]

According to his testimony, when midshipman Cândido Francisco brought news of these events, Lieutenant Guillobel considered the Artigos de Guerra. Overall, this volume consists of eighty articles that outlined specific punishments for any crime or transgression against military hierarchy committed by any person enlisted in the navy, whether officer or enlisted man. He claimed to focus on two specific articles when making his decision on Silva's punishment. The first was:

> Article 56: All are required to respect the sentries . . . those that do not are to be punished with six months of hard labor . . . or more rigorously, conforming with the circumstances of the case; anyone who violently attacks a sentry will be hanged, if the sentry does not kill him, an act fully within his right.[11]

The harsh punitive response laid out in Article 56 highlights the hierarchy of military discipline. Any act of insubordination should have resulted in Silva being at least jailed for six months. Had his captors not restrained Silva, and had his knife attack on the sentry succeeded, he could have been put to death – though capital punishment was actually never applied as punishment for this type of attack, regardless of legal code. However, the implementation of the applicable punishment called for a trial in front of the naval high court away from the ship; the enforcement of Article 56 would have removed Silva from Lieutenant Guillobel's authority and from his service. Instead, Lieutenant

Guillobel looked to Article 80, the final article of war – a catchall ruling applied when a crime fit no specific punishment; it was by far the most commonly invoked law by Brazilian officers punishing the enlisted men serving beneath them. The articles never authorize naval officers to selectively apply the codes they prefer. Although court documents suggest that this was quite a common practice, it had no basis in Brazilian law, maritime or otherwise:

> Article 80: All other indiscretions, such as drunkenness, gambling, and the like, which the proceeding articles did not specifically mention, are to be punished proportionally at the discretion of the commanding officer. The use of the iron collar, imprisonment in the ship's hold, and loss of rations can be applied to Officers, Noncommissioned-officers, and Skilled craftsmen. When guilt is known and there is no need for the *Conselho de Guerra* said punishments can also be applied to enlisted men, *who can further be corrected by the application of blows by the flat of a sword or the lash, not to exceed 25 strokes per day.* (italics added)[12]

It is worth repeating that there was no limit set in this article on the number of lashes that could be applied to a sailor, just a limit on how many lashes could be applied in a given day. With his decision to apply Article 80, Lieutenant Guillobel retained Silva's labor. Furthermore, he asserted his own authority by resolving this issue on his ship in front of the assembled crew in a manner not possible had he sent him off the ship for court-martial.

It is unclear whether Lieutenant Guillobel planned ahead to so violently supersede the letter of the law in applying this punishment. Corporal punishment in the navy was applied formally, publically, and ritualistically, in a manner designed to distance it both from the often violent act being punished and from the violent act of punishing. The structure and formality of naval corporal punishment had been designed to transform the lash into a rational and disinterested application of a deserved punishment. As would have been the case in any authorized application of corporal punishment, Lieutenant Guillobel first called for the assembly of his crew. Attendance of all officers and enlisted men whose service to the ship was not essential was mandatory. Only once noncommissioned officers and enlisted men were organized, the ranking officers entered. When Lieutenant Guillobel called Silva forward, the prisoner shuffled in, still shackled in chains. He was lashed to the mast with his hands over his head, immobilized but supporting his own weight.

In this case Silva wore two shirts, one of wool and one of cotton in order to protect the skin on his back. During his trial, Lieutenant Guillobel used the shirt's protection as justification for the severity of the punishment. Lieutenant Guillobel called for both Article 80 and the crime for which Silva was to be punished to be read aloud to the assembled crew. As was standard practice during the application of corporal punishment in the Brazilian navy, the number of blows that the sailor was to receive was not publicly announced. Equally true for a slave owner and naval officer, the person being punished had to be broken – physically and spiritually; only then would the whipping end. Announcing the severity of the punishment before applying the lash invited a sailor to resist by stoically enduring his beating, an unacceptable outcome given the public performance of this ritual. In his testimony to the court he stated, "I resolved to punish *imperial marinheiro* Manoel da Silva severely, that is proportionally with the transgression committed. It would be carried out in front of the ship's crew as an example [*acto de mostra*] . . . seeing the slight effect of the punishment on the delinquent, I was forced to continue the lashing until reaching the number of 500 blows." He further justified his actions by claiming, "This punishment may seem excessively rigorous by its number, but the physical effects are comparatively less than those produced by the convenient application of 100 blows with the flat of a sword, a punishment indubitably insignificant for the crime committed."[13] The whipping began and a sailor counted off the blows. The count ended only when Lieutenant Guillobel terminated the punishment after the uninterrupted application of 500 lashes. When the ship's doctor examined Silva he transferred him to the infirmary, and two days later, Guillobel transferred Silva from the *Bahia* to the battleship *Brasil*. When news of the young officer's application of corporal punishment came to the attention of the officer corps of the *Brasil*, the commanding officer of that ship brought this illegal application of corporal punishment to the attention of the naval high court. Had the transfer to the other ship for medical reasons not occurred, it is unlikely that the courts would have known of the infraction that took place, nor would the events of that September day have been recorded into the public record.

The unique event was not that a Brazilian sailor was lashed 500 times in a day. Rather, the unique event was that one officer, for whatever motivation, chose to officially report another officer's behavior to the military court. The violence applied to Laurentino Manoel da Silva was not the real source of the charges brought against Lieutenant José Cândido Guillobel. Indeed, based on the documentation at hand we know very little about Silva; we learn nothing of his race, record of service, or background as Lieutenant Guillobel's case ignores the victim of this criminal act entirely. This was the trial of a naval officer; thus, the victim's biographical information was unimportant to the court. Although we know based on the statistical evidence taken from naval court-martial records that a sailor tried by that body was nearly five times more likely to be of African descent than to be white, the race of the victim of this act of violence is not as important as the pattern of violence applied to enlisted men of both races.[14]

What this case provides is a unique window into the attitudes of officers toward enlisted men. This is the only case during the period covered in this study in which an officer stood trial for violating the rights of an enlisted man. Lieutenant Guillobel freely admitted his sanctioning of criminal behavior by calling for the application of twenty times the daily legal limit of corporal punishment to an enlisted man. He also admitted ignoring military law by overlooking Article 56 of the Articles of War, which specifically applied to an attack on sentries on board Brazilian naval vessels.

The case against Lieutenant Guillobel has been carefully analyzed by Álvaro Pereira do Nascimento in his study of the Imperial Brazilian Navy titled *A Ressaca da Marujada*.[15] Here I offer a brief analysis of the testimony in order to illuminate several points directly applicable to the overall application of corporal punishment. One could interpret the fact that such a case happened only once in the Brazilian navy as evidence that such excessive abuse of enlisted men was rare, but testimony suggests just the opposite. Several high-ranking naval officers offered testimony to defend the actions of Lieutenant Guillobel. When naval officer

Henrique Pinheiro Guedes was asked by the members of the court "if in the application of corporal punishment, Article 80 is always observed by not lashing a sailor more than twenty-five times in a day?" He responded, "If punishing a sailor with more than twenty-five lashes, and I have seen up to two hundred lashes applied, it is generally not applied according to the rules as set forth in the Articles of War." A second officer, Olímpio Inácio Cardim, replied to a similar question, "Generally the cited article is not applied. Always more than twenty-five lashes are given . . . at times more than two hundred at a time." This testimony sent a clear message: rather than being a unique situation, this level of punishment, if not typical, was certainly not that rare in the Brazilian navy.[16]

Although Lieutenant Guillobel's application of corporal punishment may have been at the upper limit of what was normal during this era – and this fact is likely what triggered the events that brought him up on trial – his behavior was interpreted by senior officers not as problematic or dangerous, but as an overzealous young officer trying to prove himself to his temporary crew. His actions belonged well within the accepted confines of naval hierarchy. The result of his court-martial by the naval high court was unanimous exoneration, although the Military Supreme Court amended his sentence to acquittal with severe admonishment. What were the long-term results of Lieutenant Guillobel's blatant failure to follow military regulation? The severe admonishment did little damage to his naval career; his rise within the naval hierarchy can be described a meteoric. In 1891, at the age of forty-six, he was promoted to the rank of rear admiral, and in 1894, he was made the minister of the very legislative body that had amended his exoneration, the Military Supreme Court.[17] During a long and distinguished career documented in the autobiographical memoirs of his son, who also enjoyed a long and distinguished career in the Brazilian navy, Guillobel was promoted to admiral, and he twice served in the office of naval chief of staff (Chefe do Estado Maior da Armada), responsible for – among other duties – the execution of the orders of the minister of the navy concerning discipline thought the Brazilian navy.[18]

The trials of enlisted men who appeared before the military high courts offer different information than the officer's case examined above. Lieutenant Guillobel's formal military record appeared in the introduction to the court case. Although the data recorded on enlisted men also included some military history – transfers, punishment, rank, promotions, and any military honors – far more interesting to the scholar of social history in Brazil's military, and especially central to this project, is that they include biographical details of these men. Although the information was not wholly standardized, most trials recorded biographical details copied out of the Brazilian navy's original enlistment books, which unfortunately are not available to the general public. The majority of naval cases tried before the naval high court were for the crime of desertion, and to facilitate the tracking and recapture of these men, general descriptions are included in biographical section of the trial documents. The biographical information for enlisted men generally consisted of the sailor's name; the name of a parent (his father if available); his rank; the city in which he was born; his age (at both the time of enlisting and the time of trial); his height when enlisted; his race; a physical description, including hair, eyes, and facial hair; the year he was remitted into service; and the sentencing. There was also a miscellaneous section where the courts recorded previous punishments, honors, desertions, and other outstanding details of a naval career.

Individually, the case of Lieutenant José Cândido Guillobel or any case of corporal punishment involving enlisted men is an anomalous anecdote – a footnote in the history of Brazil. However, a study of all of the cases tried in Rio de Janeiro under the auspices of the naval high court offers a rare insight into the workings of the institution of the Brazilian navy. The navy, a national institution with the vast majority of its manpower in Rio de Janeiro, then the nation's capital, in turn offers a view of the Brazilian government's policy toward that country's nonwhite populations during a period of vast social, political, and economic change.

Though this collection of court-martial documents offers historians rare insight into the social history of Brazil's navy and the enlisted men therein, it has limitations. Foremost among the problems inherent to a study based on these documents is the fact that a collection of criminal investigations is not representative of Brazil's naval rank and file. Men previously arrested and placed on trial – who are therefore suspected of criminal activity – likely make up a group more likely to have received corporal punishment during their naval service. Furthermore, the Brazilian navy rarely sent a man for trial the first time he committed a crime;

in the majority of cases, a sailor had been lashed on board the ship at least once before he was sent to face trial. In the case of desertion trials, the most common crime committed during this period, they often would not face the court until their third or fourth desertion.

Although the pool of men who faced criminal charges before the military high court could on the one hand be more likely than the average sailor to have been lashed in the past, hundreds of men who did not run a second or third time would have received their lashes on board but would never have appeared in court-martial documents. Naval officers were reluctant to lose their crewmembers to lengthy trials, even if their reluctance meant – as was the case for Lieutenant Guillobel – overstepping civil and military law. So officers regularly invoked the catchall clause of the Articles of War even when crimes mandated a trial.

Despite the predictable challenges of records that concern the lives of Afro-Brazilians in this time period, the information recorded in the court-martial documents allow for various analyses of the men tried in front of the Conselho de Guerra da Marinha in the second half of the nineteenth century. It has long been stated by scholars and laypeople alike that the racial demographic of the navy is far blacker than that of the army – and that of the nation as a whole. Therefore, it is instructive to have evidence that conclusively illustrates the racial makeup of Brazilian sailors. The extant records from the naval high court indicate that 14.5 percent of the sailors were white and 7.6 percent were of unknown racial origin. "Caboclos" (13.7 percent) were generally defined as mixed-race white and Indian, although the secondary definition is "a copper-colored mulatto with straight hair." I have several descriptions of caboclos with the kinky or nappy hair (*crespo* or *grenho*) generally attributed to peoples of African descent, so although I cannot go so far as to assume all caboclos are of African descent, some likely are.[19] All of the remaining categories – excluding *branco* (white), caboclo, and unknown – 64.2 percent of the sailors tried by the Brazilian courts, were men of some distinguishable African origin. Of course many of the "unknowns" would also have been of African descent, as would some of the caboclos. Surprisingly some white sailors could have found themselves in this category as well.

One example of this racial ambiguity of "white" men is found in the biographical information pertaining to Henrique Rodrigues Faqundes, tried in 1879 for his sixth desertion from the Brazilian navy. This sailor

Table 3.1. Race of Sailors Tried for Crimes in Rio de Janeiro, 1860–93

	Number	Percentage
Pardo	138	40.1
Branca	52	14.5
Caboclo	46	13.7
Preto	44	12.5
Pardo claro	11	3.2
Pardo escuro	10	2.9
Cafuz	4	1.16
Fula	4	1.16
Cabra	3	.9
Moreno	3	.9
Mameluco	2	.06
Criolo	1	.03
Escuro	1	.03
Mulato	1	.03
Unknown	24	7.6
Total	344	

Source: Records of the Conselho de Guerra da Marinha (1860–93).

was described as "branco"; he was born in Rio Grande do Sul to un-known parents and was twenty-two years of age when he entered the navy in March 1863. He was lashed fifty times on November 21 of that year for robbery and not properly caring for his uniform, and fifty times on December 7 and 9, 1863, again for robbery. Toward the end of that year, he received seventy-five lashes in a single day as punishment for desertion. In August 1868, during the Paraguayan War (1865–70), he was remitted to the jail on Ilha das Cobras to serve five years of labor for desertion during time of war. He escaped from that prison in 1870 and was captured and returned to the naval base within the year. His five-year prison term began anew for deserting, but as the war had ended, he was put back on board his ship and worked there for rations, sleeping in the ship's retaining cell. For his fourth desertion, he was tried in Febru-ary 1873 and was sentenced to an additional year of imprisonment with unpaid labor.[20]

Of the biographical information recorded into Rodrigues Faqundes's court-martial hearing, perhaps the most interesting are found in the let-ter describing his remittance into the navy in 1863:

In virtue of the government statement of March 1863, communicated by the General Headquarters of the Navy in the Order of the Day # 57 on the 13th of the same month and year, [Henrique Rodrigues Faqundes] enlisted as Seaman Apprentice and pledged to the flag of this Company on the 23 of said month and year. He was the personal slave of Dr. João Rodrigues Faqundes of the Provence of Rio Grande do Sul and was offered by him to serve the State in the Brazilian Navy, and by becoming an enlisted man he received a letter of freedom. This sailor was delivered from the House of Detention on the 21st of said month and year. On the 23 of March, 1863 he received his uniform and was enlisted.[21]

Although the presence of freed slaves in Brazil's navy was common,[22] a decision passed in 1823 guaranteed compensation for enslaved men "volunteered" by their owners for naval service; the presence of enslaved white men was unheard of. Rodrigues Faqundes could not have been an enslaved man of pure European heritage; he was likely of mixed race capable of passing. His record says that his father is unknown, but he shares a last name with his former owner, Dr. João Rodrigues Faqundes, so it is possible that he was the son of the doctor who volunteered his slave for naval service. By doing so, the doctor could have been granting his freedom while at the same time receiving compensation from the government for the boy's lost labor.[23]

It is important to recognize that the racial categorizations on which historians rely are themselves both flexible and subject to historical fluctuations. Not only was a man who was born a slave – and thus of African descent – able to claim whiteness on a document produced by a national institution, this contradictory information was recorded on numerous occasions. Both his race and his enslaved status were initially written into the navy's registration book. Subsequently this "fact" was recorded by hand on each copy of all legal and criminal proceedings (this was after all a trial for his sixth desertion from the Brazilian navy). That this detail required neither correction nor explanation suggests that "race," as it was used by the Brazilian government to categorize its sailors (and in many cases its slaves), was at times foremost descriptive and pragmatic. Its primary use was to assist in recovering deserters. The categories in these records are not set in stone; rather, the punishments meted out on the bodies of sailors reflect the debasement of certain bodies deeply rooted in the system of slavery. Whether those men's skin color was recorded as black or white, what remains at stake here is the continued definition of enlisted men as "lashable" *desprotegidos* (therefore, dishonorable, unprotected, and "slave-like") by officers who serve as extensions of the modern Brazilian state.[24]

CORPORAL PUNISHMENT IN THE
BRAZILIAN NAVY, 1860–1893

As mentioned above, of 344 criminal trials that took place during this period, 202 of the cases had a history of previous corporal punishment. Each man who had been punished by the chibata before facing trial had received a mean average of nearly 226 lashes; the median was 155 lashes. Because each man found guilty – the end result of approximately 95.5 percent of these cases – was forced to begin a new term of service, this average number of lashes applied before his first trial did not represent the violence applied over an entire military career but was more likely the measure of whatever fraction of the time he had already served in the navy, now with an additional six to twelve years added on.

During the eleven years he served in the navy, Tiberio Moreira, a sailor from Bahia designated as white in his trial records, was punished by lash more than any other sailor tried during this period. He entered the navy in the end of 1868 at the age of twenty. For showing a lack of respect to a sergeant, he received 25 lashes on both August 13 and 14, 1869. A year later, on August 24, 1870, he received an additional 25 lashes, this time for disrespecting an orderly. He deserted ship in 1874, and upon his return, he received 100 lashes on December 3. In early 1875, he received an additional 100 lashes over four days for practicing "immoral acts." Later that year, he fled the service again, and in October 1875 he received another 100 lashes over four days. In 1876, he received 50 lashes on three occasions: first for stealing a watch and some money, then for refusing an order, and finally for insulting an officer. In 1876, he deserted again and was sent to prison for two years. In prison, he was lashed 100 times for fighting with a companion, 75 times for a lack of respect, 100 times for an additional robbery, 50 times for using "injurious" language toward a soldier, and finally 75 times for refusing imprisonment. After being released back into service, he was lashed 50 times for insubordination in

1879. By August 1879, he was on trial for his fourth desertion, now having been whipped 975 times.[25]

Alexandre Menezes da Cruz, a black (preto) sailor, went on trial in October 1885 for his eighth attempt at desertion. He had been only fourteen years old when remitted by the police to the company of apprentices in Rio de Janeiro on January 7, 1865. He entered the regular service as a cabin boy on December 4, 1869, at the age of eighteen, having spent nearly five years in that company instead of the required two. It is likely that for some of that time he'd run away from the company of apprentices, but such information would not appear on his formal naval record, nor would any punishment received as an apprentice. He was whipped 25 times for eating his breakfast on duty in January and 25 times in October for fighting with a fellow crew member, both in 1871. He deserted the first time the day before Christmas 1871; he was recaptured in June 1872 and whipped 50 times for lack of respect and 75 times for deserting. In August 1872, he hit a companion and received 50 lashes. In 1873, he fought twice, receiving 50 and 100 lashes respectively; he was lashed 50 times for lack of respect and 50 more times for ripping a companion's uniform. He ran away from December 15, 1873, to February 24, 1874, again for Christmas, for which he was lashed 100 times upon his remittance to the navy. In June 1874, he was lashed 35 times for being off-ship without license. That July, he ran for a third time, and in March 1877 he ran a fourth time. After his third desertion, he was first sent before a judge, having been whipped the first two times he deserted. He spent a year in prison each time he deserted. He was lashed 50 times on three occasions in 1879 – once for robbery, once for fighting, and once for being off-ship without license. He deserted for the fifth time from October 1879 to January 1880, again enjoying Christmas as a free man. His sixth desertion was May to September 1881, and his seventh was March to April 1883. For each of the three, he was given one year in prison, and for beating a minor in 1882 he was given an additional 25 lashes. During the trial for his eighth desertion, he tried to explain how he had fallen into this pattern of violence and insubordination. He claimed that he had served ten years, four in the company of apprentices and six in the regular navy, during which he attained the rank of seaman third class and had no disciplinary problems. When he

requested a license to leave the service for six months to see his family, he
was turned down, and thus became so disgusted with the service that he
deserted for the first time, for which he was lashed 75 times. He was given
the standard sentence of one year for that eighth desertion and began his
term anew.[26] No doubt the frustration and rage that Cruz experienced
was one widely shared. For the naval elite, at least in some theoretical
future, these men's military service would become a transition into the
modern conveyance of their full freedom as citizens and protectors of
the state. In the face of that rhetoric, the refusal of the navy to recognize
their humanity or dignity in even the smallest ways – to instead increasingly rely on outdated and inhumane systems of control – must have
been the source of much "insubordination." Now thirty-four years old
and having labored in naval institutions for twenty years, Cruz's ten-year
term of service began anew. He never appeared before the courts again;
perhaps he carried out his term without committing any further crime,
or he died in service, or what would have been his ninth desertion may
have finally freed him from the control of the state.

CRIMES COMMITTED IN THE BRAZILIAN NAVY

There were two basic types of crime committed within the Brazilian
navy. Crimes committed among individuals on board the ship – robbery, fighting, rape, gambling, and drunkenness – paralleled the crimes
that took place outside of the military. These were crimes that enlisted
men generally carried out against each other; these indiscretions were
punished, but officers expected this sort of behavior to take place, and it
in no way threatened the structure or hierarchy of the navy. The second
category of crime consisted of acts against the institution of the Brazilian navy – desertion, insubordination, resisting arrest, sleeping on the
watch, or assaulting an officer. Although these crimes are expected in
any navy, the fact that they targeted the structure of naval hierarchy
meant that they were taken more seriously, and in many cases they were
punished more publicly.

Unless an act was particularly violent or an item stolen was valuable,
the commanding officer of the ship generally implemented immediate
discipline in response to crimes in the initial category. Punishments

Table 3.2. Accused Crimes of Sailors Tried by Military Courts in Rio de Janeiro

Desertion	215
Injury	47
Insubordination	32
Aggression	10
Immoral Acts	9
Unknown	6
Theft	6
Homicide	4
Attempted injury	4
Resisting arrest/imprisonment	3
Assassination	1
Drunkenness	1
Leaving ship without permission	1
Assaulting an officer	1
Attempted homicide	1
Attempted homicide of an officer	1
Total	344

Source: Records of the Conselho de Guerra da Marinha (1860–93).

were varied: double shifts; bread and water; ankle, wrist, and neck irons; and the lash were all applied liberally.

On the other hand (as categorized in table 3.2), sailors carrying out actions threatening to military hierarchy were much more likely to face trial before a military court. Although crimes against individuals were likely much more common than were crimes against the naval institution, there are few available records of the actions punished on board the ships. Unless the lost book of punishments (*livros dos castigos*) from the individual ships are located, historians interested in studying these crimes are limited to the information documented in the biographical section of these military trials.

Desertion from the military offers an obvious comparison to the act of marronage, or flight into the interior, from slave labor. In each case the act encompasses both the permanent abandonment and the temporary removal from a particular situation. Also in the case of both military desertion and the marronage of slaves, that act represented the most common infractions facing the Brazilian elite and was the most threatening crime in both institutions. Desertion was by far the most common crime for which sailors were tried, representing over 62 percent of all court cases tried during this period. However, even this impressive percentage fails to convey the significance of desertion from the Brazilian navy. Of 215 desertion cases, only 3 were for simple first-time desertion, and only 2 were for simple second-time desertion (see details in table 3.3 below). One hundred eighty-nine of these 215 cases were for a third or later successful desertion. The 88 sailors who faced trial for their third desertions alone would have been punished for a combined 176 counts of first or second desertion before their first trial, and the punishment for almost all of these first or second desertions took place on board ships without trial. It was only if a sailor continually deserted and was recaptured, or deserted during a war, that their crimes would be reflected in table 3.3.[27]

Such cases represent a sizable application of corporal punishment that never appeared in court documents. If desertion was worthy of trial only for sailors committed to fleeing repeatedly, there must have been many men who were dissuaded from abandoning service after being lashed for their first or second desertion, especially upon realizing that future attempts to run that ended with a trial would almost certainly reinitiate a full term of service. Furthermore, thirty-three of the eighty-eight men who faced trial for their third desertion had no previous record of corporal punishment in their biographies. This fact in spite of the Decision of July 23, 1825, which states, "It is mandated to punish a marine . . . for having committed the crime of desertion with one hundred *chibatadas* conforming to the practice in the army, and the punishment is to be applied in the presence of the assembled crew, with the warship at anchor in the bay."[28] This decision was not universally applied – most of the men whose punishment appeared in the court records had been lashed 50, not 100, times. But these details suggest that corporal punishment was so common in the navy that its application was overlooked in legal records. This was very likely the case for most of the thirty-three sailors tried for their third desertion who had no record of corporal punishment. It also suggests that a sizable percentage of sailors had likely been lashed for crime of desertion, but never appeared before the military courts.

The majority of criminal cases tried before the high court were for desertion, and Article 51 of the Artigos de Guerra was applied. It reads: "Sailors and Seamen Apprentices incurring the crime of desertion shall be punished with five years of prison at hard labor during times of war,

Table 3.3. Details of Desertion Cases, 1860–93

First Desertion	22
Simple	3
Aggravated	5
During Time of War	14
Second Desertion	4
Simple	2
Aggravated	1
During Time of War	1
Third Desertion	88
Fourth Desertion	43
Fifth Desertion	23
Sixth Desertion	17
Seventh Desertion	7
Eighth Desertion	3
Ninth Desertion	3
Tenth Desertion	2
Eleventh Desertion	1
Twelfth Desertion	1

Source: Records of the Conselho de Guerra da Marinha (1860–93).

and in times of peace they will serve on board ships of His Royal High-
ness for a period of one year earning only rations and the uniform cus-
tomarily given out in prison to wear; if the deserter is a Soldier, he will
be punished according to Military Regulation." The *soldados* (soldiers)
discussed served in the *Batalhão Naval* (naval battalion) on the Ilha das
Cobras and were in effect marines, though under the command of the
navy. They were generally judged by army regulations, at least until 1899,
when the army adopted the navy's reformed code and all enlisted men
were judged by the same regulations. However, although army reforms
abolished legal flogging in 1874, naval soldados were lashed until much
later, suggesting that they, unlike regular soldiers, were not protected by
reforms in the army's code. Their racial makeup was also more similar
to that of the navy than to that of the army, as can be seen in table 3.4,
which examines the soldiers tried in Rio de Janeiro through 1893. The
navy has 14.7 percent white enlistment; the marines have 13.4 percent.

Once a sailor found himself before the military high court, he had
little chance of acquittal. Of 344 cases, only 13 men were found not guilty.
Of those "not guilty" verdicts, seven were in cases of injury; four in cases

Table 3.4. Race of Marines Tried in Rio for Crimes, 1860–93

	Number	Percentage
Branco	20	13.4
Caboclo	13	9.2
Cabra	5	3.3
Moreno	8	5.3
Pardo	60	40.2
Preto	40	26.8
Total	149	

Source: Records of the Conselho de Guerra da Marinha (1860–93).

of insubordination; and one each in cases of murder, attempted murder, and immoral activity. That sailors put on trial were rarely acquitted is not surprising considering the significance of sending these men off-ship to be tried by a higher authority than the commander of their ship. To return them to service having been found not guilty would challenge the officer's decision to place the sailors on trial in the first place. To return a man to his ship undisciplined could create a potentially threatening atmosphere toward the military hierarchy, in which the captain's authority had been undermined by his superiors – an untenable situation on ships largely controlled by the threat of violence.

GEOGRAPHIC ORIGIN OF RIO'S SAILORS

There are other important details in these records. Naval recruitment did not draw evenly from across Brazil's black population; service records show a population of men almost all of whom were born in Brazil, thereby excluding the African-born population that continued to make up a large portion of the Afro-Brazilian population throughout the nineteenth century. Furthermore, even including the enslaved men who were liberated in order to be "recruited" into service during the Paraguayan War, and the much smaller number of enslaved men who might have "volunteered" for service as an act of escaping perpetual slavery in the period preceding the abolition of slavery, naval recruitment in the nineteenth century relied overwhelmingly on the service of Brazilian-born free men. This, in the face of massive increases in the importation of enslaved Africans during the final decades of the Atlantic slave trade and the fact that during the mid-nineteenth century slaves in Brazil were more likely to have been born in Africa than in Brazil. According to the 1849 census of Rio de Janeiro, 66.4 percent of enslaved men in the city were born in Africa, whereas 33.6 percent were of Brazilian descent.[29]

Brazilian naval recruitment policies – as well as broader military recruitment policies overall – excluded enslaved and African-born Brazilians. This was likely due to the wide acceptance that African-born slaves were harder to regiment and were thus more prone to rebellion. Even though the Brazilian military came to represent a state-controlled penal institution, naval ships represented Brazil's face abroad; having sailors who were born in Brazil may have been a low bar for service, but it represented a standard nonetheless. In fact, the phrasing of the law can be interpreted as excluding foreigners from both branches of military service: the Decree of the First Regent of May 31, 1822, invites "Brazilians to enlist in the Army and the Navy." However, throughout the nineteenth century, foreigners, especially European foreigners, were welcomed into the Brazilian navy, whereas Africans were not.[30]

In fact, the growing reliance on the service of young boys who entered naval service through the companies of apprentices – initiated in 1840 but rapidly expanded to a national level through the 1850s and 1860s – meant that the Brazilian navy in the later nineteenth century drew from younger recruits who, based on their youth, shifted toward being exclusively Brazilian born by the mid-1860s, even if their mothers were among the last Africans imported to Brazil. Of the 344 sailors' trials recorded between 1860 and 1894, 325 were born in Brazil. One white sailor was born in Portugal, and in the records of eighteen trials, the city of birth was not recorded. While the recruitment of sailors in the nineteenth-century was directly linked to slaves and their descendants, both freed and enslaved, these populations were far from being equally impacted.

Contemporaries described the navy as being populated by ex-slaves and the sons of slaves, but in this period during which most enslaved persons were still born outside of Brazil, we must remind ourselves that *this* group of Afro-Brazilians were just that – Brazilians; they were born in the Americas, they spoke Portuguese, and Brazil was the only land

most had known. Certainly, among the white elite (and to some extent
among Brazilian-born blacks both free and enslaved), there was an increased hostility toward and fear of foreign-born slaves in the nineteenth
century, which is evident in João José Reis's examination of the 1835 slave
rebellion in Bahia that took place among the Yoruba population of that
city. In identifying the betrayal of that African slave revolt by two creole or Brazilian-born freed slaves, Reis stresses the hierarchal distance
between African-born and Brazilian-born slaves, as well as the divisions
between the populations of slaves and free blacks.[31] At least on some
level, the historic use of corporal punishment to control enslaved Africans and Afro-descended people had been justified as a means to control
"uncivilized," foreign-born laborers. With slaves brought to Brazil in
chains, slave owners justified their actions and understood themselves
as having to force recalcitrant, potentially violent, and at times openly
hostile men and women into work. In a nation in which so much of the
population was Afro-descendent, it served the interest of the white elite
to stress divisions within the Afro-Brazilian community rather than
lumping all blacks together using segregationist policies and/or applying
a "one drop rule" to group all nonwhite together into a single community.
However, in the final decades of Brazilian slavery, it is important not to
conflate all Afro-descended people in Brazil into a single category; they
were neither all African nor all slaves; in fact, according to the nuanced
Brazilian definitions of race, they were not even all black. Regardless of
how those rights were applied, Brazilian sailors of all races were citizens;
at least technically, they enjoyed most of the rights and benefits promised
to all Brazilian citizens by the Constitution of 1824 and 1891.[32] But those
rights offered them little protection; they had neither the ability to avoid
impressment into Brazilian naval service nor the power to halt the lash
that tore the flesh of the men forced to serve.

Not surprisingly, of those men tried by the naval high court in Rio
de Janeiro, the largest group – more than one in six – was from Rio de
Janeiro. The northeastern state of Pernambuco was a close second, and
Bahia was a not distant third (see table 3.5). The Northeast of Brazil
(Alagoas, Bahia, Ceará, Maranhão, Paraíba, Pernambuco, Piauí, Rio
Grande do Norte, and Sergipe) provided over 60 percent of the enlisted
men serving in Rio de Janeiro included in this survey. This pattern of

Table 3.5. Region of Origin of Sailors Tried, 1860–93

Rio de Janeiro	61
Pernambuco	60
Bahia	50
Maranhao	22
Ceará	20
Alagoas	17
Rio Grande do Sul	16
Paraíba	15
Sergipe	12
Pará	10
Espirito Santos	7
Rio Grande do Norte	6
Santa Caterina	6
Piauí	4
São Paulo	3
Other	19
Unknown	15
Total	344

Source: Records of the Conselho de Guerra da Marinha (1860–93).

overrepresentation among northeasterners among military enlisted men is evident in both the Brazilian army and navy. One could make an argument that the Brazilian navy, an organization based overwhelmingly on coerced recruitment, had a somewhat different motivation for this disparity than did the army, which throughout the nineteenth century enjoyed a much higher percentage of volunteerism among its troops than did the navy. Indeed, in the period from 1870 to 1882, the army enjoyed an overall majority of its recruitment coming from volunteers, a trend that continued into the twentieth century.[33] However, the explanation for the northeastern origins of so many Brazilian recruits in both branches of the military is rooted in the history of slavery in northeastern Brazil, and that region's transition as the plantation economy slowed as slavery ended in the nineteenth century.

A brief analysis of the northeastern economy leading up to the nineteenth century helps explain the large presence of northeastern sailors serving in Rio de Janeiro. During the colonial period the Northeast went through a period of rapid financial growth and an influx of wealth among the sugar-producing upper class. For centuries, Brazil's enslaved population shifted with the profitable exports: during the sugar cycle, the Northeast retained the bulk of the slave populations; in the eighteenth century, populations of slaves shifted to the gold- and diamond-producing Center-South; and the growth of the coffee economy of the nineteenth century moved nearly 75 percent of the remaining enslaved population into southern Brazil by the passage of abolition in 1888. In the Northeast between 1823 and 1872, the ratio of slaves within the overall population dropped from 54 to 32 percent.[34]

When the Atlantic slave trade closed, the Northeast became a net exporter of slaves to the more profitable coffee plantations of the Southeast. By the second half of the nineteenth century, almost four-fifths of the population of Pernambuco – the region that supplied the second largest segment of sailors to Rio de Janeiro – was free. Surprisingly, during the final decades of slavery, during an overall decline in worldwide sugar prices, Pernambuco saw a rise in sugar exports. This growth was the result of the effective manipulation of free labor on sugar plantations, and forced military recruitment played a central role in that manipulation.[35]

Because there had been little development of local markets or industry in Pernambuco, the rural free found themselves dependent on landowners. The backbreaking labor of weeding, clearing land, and cutting cane that had been the work of enslaved men and women shifted to free *moradores* (tenant farmers or sharecroppers) as the enslaved population shrunk. They performed field duties for plantation owners for part of the workweek. This land-for-labor exchange provided plantation owners supplementary labor with limited out-of-pocket cost.[36]

Not all sugar regions adapted to the loss of their enslaved population as well as Pernambuco. In his comparison of Bahia to Pernambuco, B. J. Barickman states, "In Bahia, the long-term trend in the sugar trade was marked not by growth, but rather by stagnation and decline . . . at the end of the late 1880s, stagnation gave way to the nearly complete collapse of sugar exports."[37] Sugar producers in Bahia clung to slave labor until the very end, and final abolition brought economic ruin. Unlike plantation owners in Pernambuco, who enjoyed near-monopolistic control over the land and could restrict the free poor from alternative forms of work, in Bahia there was agricultural work available away from the sugar plantations, such as in coffee and tobacco production, or on farms producing food for local consumption.[38]

So, when the African slave trade ended, the economic success or failure of these sugar-producing regions was tied to their control over the existing free and freed black populations. Quoting Martha Huggins's study of vagrancy in Brazil, "so long as slaves were plentiful, there was no need to correct the undesirable qualities of the rural poor. But as the slave population declined, planters began to look upon free people's unwillingness to work at export production in an entirely new light . . . landowners could no longer afford to see free people engaging in non-wealth-producing activities."[39] An underemployed population had previously been valuable – potential labor available when needed – but the loss of slaves made free blacks who were not engaged in the production of exports for the first time a problem needing repair. It is in this context that military recruitment becomes an important way to pressure free and freed blacks into any employment situation so as to avoid impressment. This practice is directly linked to the overrepresentation of sailors from the Northeast recruited into the navy during this period.

Thus, recruitment policy throughout the Northeast did more than simply populate the branches of the Brazilian military; recruitment was linked to the control of the growing free poor in rural plantation regions, and therefore it was linked to Brazil's plantation economy as the institution of slavery unraveled between 1850 and 1888 and beyond. The role of military recruitment increased in this region during the Paraguayan War when recruitment numbers expanded radically; the army would impress more than 100,000 troops over the duration of the war. The importance of military recruitment to the rural elite was the subject of an 1871 letter to the provincial governor from plantation owner Manoel Pinto de Rocha that described the ease with which he was able to hire field hands during the war: "At that time, immense numbers of day laborers . . . subjected themselves to every sort of work, even for low wages." The threat of forced recruitment and having "to suffer the mortal fatigues of war" forced men to take on work that they avoided in times of peace.[40]

As the countryside became increasingly hostile for masterless men, displaced workers also flooded into coastal cities such as Pernambuco's capital city of Recife. The wealthy in Recife, like those Rio, had taken early steps to modernize. Much as Rio's elite had overhauled transportation and public sanitation and rebuilt the downtown area using European capitals as a model, Recife built streetcars, a technical school, a modern sewage system, and an incinerator. Although the changes to the nation's capital may have been grander, more expensive, and wider sweeping, both sets of reforms were based on similar goals and motivations. These changes were perceived and presented as examples of progress for the nation and its people, but they were never intended to benefit all of the people. As was the case in the national capital, policies of modernization were designed to benefit an idealized white Brazilian population. Urban infrastructure was transformed to benefit the city's wealthy residents and potential investors, but modernization included no space for the working poor. To the contrary, elites subsequently worried that these changes attracted a "troubling class of people who had no legitimate social place" in the modern Brazilian city.[41] Protestations aside, as the rural economies weakened, this "troubling class" created a place for itself within the cities; up to one-half of Recife's free workers made space for themselves in favelas built in the hills and swamps on the outskirts of the city. For the elite, this growing urban poor represented a threat to "civilized" Brazil, whether in the sugar-producing Northeast or the coffee-producing South. To control this urban space that attracted the free laborers unwilling to work on plantations, we see the widespread application of the vagrancy law from the 1830 Criminal Code of the Brazilian Empire, the law used to justify the dragooning of "criminals" for military service in Rio de Janeiro to round up "potential criminals" for military service.

The origins of enlisted men serving in the navy in Rio de Janeiro reflect this narrative. Although Rio de Janeiro and the Northeast had different regional histories, they underwent similar transformations during the final decades of slavery. The use of recruitment to drive workers into poor-paying jobs is repeated across the sugar-producing Northeast; thus this region comes to deliver the majority of the sailors who serve in the nation's capital. Former slaves were not offered suitable economic incentive to remain in sugar production; the desire for better-paying jobs drove them into urban centers: Salvador in Bahia, São Luís in Maranhão, Foraleza in Ceará, and Maceió in Alagoas. As Brazil navigated the shift from enslaved to paid labor, cities that benefited from export economies based on slave labor invested in modern infrastructures. The technological transformations (described in chapter 1) that swept Rio in the late nineteenth century had parallels in most Brazilian coastal cities. In each case, the cities lacked the necessary infrastructure to handle these unwelcome populations, and the political and economic elite implemented policies to control this population of desprotegidos. As took place in Rio and Recife, vagrants, criminals, and potential criminals were forcibly manipulated by various means of social control.

The methods recruiters applied when impressing men for service in either branch of the military could, at times, seem arbitrary, but the traditional patriarchy generally protected men who lived within the rules. In his examination of recruitment patterns in Imperial Brazil, Hendrik Kraay describes a recruitment raid that took place in 1888 in Salvador in which a sergeant mistakenly swept up potential recruits from too broad a populace, including men with socioeconomic connections that should have protected them from such treatment. The result was a series of rebukes and denials in the military recruitment hierarchy and the eventual loss of all those recruits from performing military service, but their connections eventually kicked in and did exactly what they were supposed to do – they protected these men from service.[42] Noteworthy is the fact that even when individual error happened, such decisions were never really in the hands of the sergeant leading the recruitment raid; the definition of those men who could be drafted was clearly laid out under both the laws and the traditions of the Brazilian Empire.

Additionally, the practice of extracting labor from a free population outlasted the institution of slavery; in 1890 the governor of Pernambuco called for the implementation of a disciplinary agricultural colony for vagrants and the unemployed. Regardless of whether their unemployment stemmed from a lack of work opportunity or from "personal vice," they were to be incarcerated. New correctional facilities were built to house idlers, and the extralegal definition of "vagrancy" was expanded among the politicians and police of Pernambuco.[43] Military coercion was just one means by which politicians and landowners sought to manipulate the labor of Brazil's free black population. Working in concert, state-run institutions controlled Brazil's poor population in the cities and the countryside: disciplinary agricultural colonies; prisons; orphanages; the police; and naval companies of apprenticeship supported the role of the army and navy. Together these institutions physically controlled large segments of the Brazilian poor, and more importantly, the threat of violence and confinement reminded a much larger population of des-protegidos of its powerlessness in the face of institutional control. There was an implied violence to their bodies, families, and communities that helped to control Brazil's poor just as effectively as had the bullwhip on the plantation.

THE AGE OF THE BRAZILIAN SAILOR IN RIO DE JANEIRO

Returning to the sailors who appeared before the Brazilian high court; the court records also record their age. Two hundred eighty-six sailors appeared in front of the Brazilian high court in Rio de Janeiro in a total of 344 cases tried between 1860 and 1893, and most were not men at all. This is another aspect of naval service that demands comparison with the labor of the enslaved. Slave owners faced no prohibitions against ex-ploiting the labor of children; be it on plantations, in mines, or in cities, masters put enslaved boys and girls to work as soon as they were deemed fit. Laws and regulations did regulate the age at which boys could enlist into naval service, but an examination of their biographical sketches shows that those protections were at best unevenly applied, and were often overlooked altogether.[44]

The mean age of the 271 enlisted men tried before the high court in Rio de Janeiro whose age was recorded during their trial (the age of 15 of the 286 men was not recorded) was just under eighteen years; the median age was also eighteen. One hundred and fifty-eight boys en-listed into the regular navy before turning eighteen. Generally, minors age fifteen and younger were submitted to the company of apprentices; most were at least ten years old when turned over for service, but several were age nine. Sixteen- and seventeen-year-olds were generally enlisted directly into regular service, but it depended on their size and "hearti-ness"; at least thirteen sixteen-year-olds spent several months or more in the company of apprentices, whereas all seventeen-year-olds appear to have been remitted directly to naval service. Approximately 60 percent of all minors "presented" to the navy were recorded as having carried out apprenticeships, though that number may have been higher as admission through the company of apprentices was fairly unremarkable and went unrecorded in several cases.

As introduced in the previous chapter, a parent who "turned over" a son to serve an apprenticeship received a cash payment. Beyond that compensation, we know nothing about Constancia Maria's motivation for turning her thirteen-year-old son, Agostinho das Neves dos Santos, over to the company of apprentices in 1871. They were from the northeastern sugar producing state of Sergipe, just north of Bahia. Her son's race was recorded as dark black (*fula*), and we do not know Constancia Maria's slave status. The fact that she was the parent noted on the naval record suggests that Neves dos Santos's father was unknown or dead as the form almost always either listed the father's name or recorded his status as an orphan. In exchange for the "voluntary presentation" (*aprezentado voluntariamente*) of her son she received a standard bonus of one hundred mil-réis, a sum greater than the annual base salary of approximately eighty-six mil-réis that he would earn only after completing his multiyear apprenticeship and entering the navy at the rank of cabin boy. In exchange for that compensation, Constancia Maria knew that her son would be required to complete a two-year apprenticeship followed by twelve years of mandatory service.[45]

There was no criminal discipline or record of corporal punishment documented until December 1876, when Neves dos Santos received a series of disciplinary actions in quick succession. He was lashed 50 times that month as punishment for his first desertion from the navy. Then just a month later in January of 1877 he received the same punishment over two days for his second desertion. Then that April he was again punished with 50 lashes over two days for having shown a lack of respect to a chief instructor. Likely as grave a punishment as the incarceration he was to receive, his term of service was extended when in August 1877 the naval high court found him guilty of committing his third desertion in times of peace and sentenced him to a year in military prison. Assuming that he survived his incarceration, when he returned to service in August 1878 he faced a new twelve-year term of service, and if he managed to serve that term without additional guilty verdicts (being lashed aboard ship did not cost a sailor his time served) he would not have been discharged from the navy until 1890, when he would be thirty-two years old.[46]

Consider the social and economic difficulty facing free black families in the northeastern sugar region. As examined above, free laborers were paid poorly; real wages for unskilled rural laborers declined throughout this period, in Pernambuco wages paid by plantation owners decreasing by more than half between 1862 and 1902.[47] Imagine the difficulty free black parents faced raising a family under these conditions, much less a single mother. For the sake of comparison, B. J. Barickman described field workers in Bahia receiving 600–640 réis for daily labor on a sugar plantation in 1874; in order to earn the navy's signing bonus, a healthy male worker would toil for 154–166 days, or 25–27 weeks working six days a week.[48] Afro-Brazilian communities were under enormous pressure, and workers were being forced into fiscally untenable positions. Once the Paraguayan War ended and sailors were less likely to see actual combat, perhaps a paying position in the Brazilian navy represented the lesser of two evils. For a parent unable to protect her child, even the uncertain future of a life in the navy may have been preferable to letting a thirteen-year-old boy grow up in the plantation economy of Sergipe. Indeed, one can envision naval service as a viable alternative to the personal domination of a violent or dangerous master or patriarch, or as a way to protect a child who found himself in trouble at home.

The navy paid parents or a guardian only in the case of "voluntary presentation"; if the police picked up "juvenile delinquents" on the street and turned them over to companies of apprentices, there was neither payment to the parents nor official notification, just the payment of four mil-réis to the officer who recruited the sailor, whether adult or child. Arrested children simply vanished, often unable to send word to their families of their whereabouts for months, if ever.[49]

Though the official language of the company of apprentices claimed that these companies (or "schools" – as they were renamed in 1885) were places of instruction, their actual role in this period was much more pragmatic. They allowed young men to work and receive some training before being put on a boat; therefore, they became heartier and more competent sailors. The use of corporal punishment in the company of apprentices was not recorded on official naval documents, nor did any criminal behavior carry over to their records as sailors. Boys judged competent were assigned to ships regardless of their age, and once they entered the service, their youth offered them little protection from harsh conditions on board.

Americo Nonato was one such sailor. He was born into slavery in Bahia in 1857 to unknown parents; his former master received payment when Nonato enlisted into the military toward the end of the Paraguayan War. He was one of 1,404 enslaved African men freed in order to serve the navy during that war.[50] Because of the war, he did not go the usual route to a company of apprentices; he enrolled into the regular navy on February 11, 1870, less than a month before the war ended when the Paraguayan president was killed on March 1, 1870. He was therefore stationed out of Rio de Janeiro at the age of thirteen, having likely avoiding combat altogether. Two months later Nonato received his first flogging because his superiors found him sleeping on duty. He received 10 lashes, the punishment for this crime probably lightened due to his youth. Six months later, the ship's officer had him whipped 25 times for fighting in the washroom, the standard sentence; he was now being punished as an adult. Over the next two years, he was whipped six more times, receiving a total of 250 lashes. In January 1874 when he deserted the first time, he was seventeen years old; he ran for twenty-one months before being remitted to the navy. At this time, in addition to any punishment that he received for this crime, he lost the time previously served in the navy and started his term anew.[51]

Imagine how little the status of this boy actually changed when he was "freed" at the age of thirteen. He, like most sailors, had been described as being unable to read or write when he enlisted; far from his family in the Northeast, his family's slave status and his own illiteracy made it unlikely that he stayed in contact with them. His transition to the navy paralleled the sale of a young slave to an unknown owner, and the decision to desert the navy at the age of seventeen paralleled that of thousands of enslaved boys and men, girls and women, who fled their forced servitude. Nonato last appears in the criminal records of the Brazilian navy in 1886; now twenty-nine years old, he deserted for a third time from February to September 1886. Since his first desertion, he had been whipped four more times, received 275 additional lashes, and spent thirty days locked in the ship's galley; on November 3, 1876, he was whipped 50 times for forcibly sodomizing his comrade. For his third desertion, he was jailed for an additional year and, as per naval law, would begin his term anew upon his release in 1887. Nonato never appeared before the court again, so we have no further record of his actions, but if he served out his term with good behavior, he would not have been discharged before 1897, nine years after the abolition of slavery from which he had been technically freed in 1870.[52]

Another example of a sailor who came to the navy very young was the Revolta da Chibata's leader João Cândido. One of eight children, he was born in the city of Rio Pardo in the state of Rio Grande do Sul in 1880 and grew up on a cattle ranch owned by João Filipe Correia where both his father, João Cándido Filisberto, and his mother, Inácia Felisberto, were once enslaved and were later – once freed – employed. Though there are no specific details as to money his parents received, we can assume they qualified and received the bonus for their son enrolling in naval service. According to Cândido, his family supported his enlisting into the naval arsenal in Porto Alegre in January 1895 at the age of fourteen. From there he was quickly transferred to the apprenticeship school in Rio de Janeiro, and once judged ready for service he was enrolled as a cabin boy (grumete) in the Brazilian navy on December 10, 1895 while he was still fifteen years old.[53]

But his enlistment into the navy was not typical of the poor sons of slaves who were routinely swept up by police and naval recruiters. He arrived to enlist with a letter of recommendation from the captain of the port in Porto Alegre, a letter requested by Alexandrino Faria de Alencar, who was at that time a frigate captain known for his service in the Paraguayan War and for his role in the Naval Revolt of 1893. He would go on to serve as naval minister under five Brazilian presidents, and he planned the 1906 naval renewal that led to Brazil's purchase of the dreadnoughts *Minas Geraes* and *São Paulo*. Alencar was also from Rio Pardo in Rio Grande do Sul, was friends with the owner of the cattle farm on which João Cândido grew up, and knew Cândido's parents. He served as João Cândido's patron as he enlisted for naval service. Unlike the powerless *desprotegidos* forced into naval service because they could not call upon a member of the elite to keep them out of service, Cândido entered the navy with a powerful patron.[54]

João Cândido's links to the powerful patronage of Alencar may have also impacted his service in the Brazilian navy before the Revolta da Chibata. According to his service record, during fifteen years of service between December 1895 and December 1910, he completed his obligatory ten-year term of service in January 1906, at which time he voluntarily re-enlisted for three-year terms in 1906 and again in 1909. During that time he was promoted from cabin boy to sailor second class in 1893, to sailor first class in 1901, and to corporal (*cabo*) in 1903. But in February 1905 he was demoted to soldier first class for sixty days for smuggling liquor on board the ship, and in June 1907 he was demoted a second time, this time indefinitely. During this period, on four occasions (November 1897, October 1898, November 1908, and July 1909) Cândido was punished, for fighting, with solitary confinement of three or four days. Once the crime was described as "assaulting a shipmate with a piece of wood" rather than "fighting." These events took place on different ships under different captains, but Cândido was never lashed, though his transgressions regularly earned other sailors punishment by the chibata.[55]

The naval ministers represented the officer class when they described the Brazilian navy's future transition away from men dragooned into service and toward boys who would be trained at an early age to be professional sailors. Their language describes a less oppressive and more honorable service that would not require violent coercion to ensure military hierarchy. In his 1859 report to the legislation, Minister of the Navy Francisco Xavier Paes Barreto stated that "orphans and the destitute, conveniently educated from a tender age would, much like adults who spontaneously enlist, become sailors."[56] Twenty-two years later in his combined report for 1880 and 1881, Naval Minister Dr. José Rodrigues de Lima Duarte described what could happen when apprentices populated the lower decks: "It will not be difficult to abolish corporal punishment once the composition of the ships' crews have improved."[57] What they failed to recognize is that the transition, begun in the 1840s and already well underway, would not change the nature of the navy. By 1875, eighteen apprenticeship companies had opened; for four years in the 1880s, apprentices met the overall needs of naval recruitment. But these boys, much like the dragooned men, were coerced, exploited, and physically abused. The Brazilian "navy of the future" had become the Brazilian navy of the present. Their biographies made clear that no steps were ever taken to make professional sailors of these boys. Worse, these unprotected children suffered the same violence and abuse as did the adult desprotegidos who continued to co-populate the navy into the twentieth century. Rather than these children making the Brazilian navy honorable, they lost their childhood and were forced into service reminiscent of slavery.

ATOS IMORAIS: SODOMY AND RAPE
IN THE BRAZILIAN NAVY

At the age of twenty, Americo Nonato, described above, was lashed 50 times on November 3, 1876, as punishment for his crime of forcibly sodomizing his comrade.[58] His background was that of an enslaved boy who was as likely to have been raised by his master or overseer as he was by his own family, assuming that his owner and his father were not the same person. At the age of thirteen he gained his freedom, at least on paper, but he was placed completely under the control of the hierarchy of the Brazilian navy. He came of age below deck on warships, likely with few opportunities to act on his sexual desire beyond the confines of the navy. Neither the sodomy nor the rape would have surprised anyone familiar with the Brazilian navy at that time. The analysis of "criminal activity" involving sodomy among Brazilian enlisted men offers insight into the world of Brazilian sailors as well as a view of a naval hierarchy often unwilling to punish certain "criminal" acts. The charge of "immoral acts" (*atos imorais*) was a blanket term applied to sexual contact among male sailors, though we also see the descriptive terms of "pederasty," "sodomy," and "libidinousness" used. The legal code called for men charged with immoral activity to be tried in front of a military court, and if found guilty they could be jailed and subsequently expelled from the navy. More specifically, the 1891 *Código penal e disciplinar da Armada* (naval disciplinary and penal code) called for one to four years of imprisonment for any sailor who used violence or the threat of violence to "satisfy lascivious passions." However, as was the case with so many naval laws, the criminal code often differed from shipboard events.[59]

An examination of the twenty naval court-martial cases in which sexual contact with another sailor appeared in a criminal record shows us that although contact between enlisted men was punished, such punishment generally took place on board the ship, not before the courts. Men were neither imprisoned nor removed from the navy as a result of sexual contact. Instead, it was understood as an infraction that fell into the category of crimes committed among individuals; like fighting, robbery, and drunkenness, homosexual contact was generally punished by lash or irons. Cases were sent to the high court only if the charge was not solely sexual contact among consenting men, but rape or statutory rape (sexual contact with a child under the age of sixteen), though more times than not, these crimes too were punished on board ships with the lash.

The punishments administered for sexual contact between sailors reflect the manner in which naval officers – as well as those members of Brazilian society who were not subject to service in the navy – understood that institution as a dishonorable location from which general society should be sheltered, a place where dishonorable men who could hardly be expected to control their base instincts could do limited damage to Brazilian society as a whole. According to Peter Beattie, "For most nineteenth-century Brazilians, individuals were neither homosexual nor heterosexual per se. Sodomy was an immoral act rather than an abstract identity shaped by sexual preference."[60] These acts were not a reflection of any personal identity so much as they were individual acts of criminal immorality that were targeted by the police in Rio de Janeiro. These sailors were already being held in one of Brazil's largest penal institutions, many after having been violently recruited into military service. Their removal from naval service only promised to place them back into respectable society, and putting them into military prisons cost commanders able-bodied sailors who were much needed at the time.

A broader historical and literary context surrounds these cases. In 1895, naval officer, author, and Naturalist Adolfo Ferreira Caminha published *Bom-Crioulo* (*crioulo* was often used as a pejorative term for black; the book can be loosely translated as "The Good Negro" or "The

Good Nigger," though it was published in English under the title *Bom-Crioulo: The Black Man and the Cabin Boy*[61]), a unique fictionalized tale of corporal punishment, racism, and homosexual love in Brazil's navy in the late decades of the nineteenth century. Because of his naval service, Caminha's work offers insight into the elite understanding of the turn-of-the-century Brazilian navy.

Through Adolfo Ferreira Caminha's 1895 *Bom-Crioulo* we are introduced to the tragic story of a romance between two men. Amaro, known as Bom-Crioulo, is a former slave who fled the plantation as a teen and was impressed as a "volunteer" and turned over to the naval company of apprentices at Fort Villegaignon in Rio de Janeiro.[62] Though forcibly recruited, Amaro is generally pleased to find himself in the navy, a much better option than his greatest fear, that of "being returned to the 'plantation' [*fazenda*] being returned to the bosom of slavery."[63] He is a dark-skinned man who, as the novel begins, is strong and healthy, an ideal specimen of masculinity, whose ability and willingness to work and natural gift as a sailor gain him the respect of both enlisted men and officers alike, as well as the nickname "Bom-Crioulo," later given to him by his ship's officers as a form of praise for both his willingness to work and his gentle demeanor. At sea, he enjoys a sense of freedom, and when he has shore leave while the ships are docked in Rio de Janeiro's Guanabara Bay, he enjoys a further sense of liberation in the city. On board during the course of a six-month deployment on an aging corvette, he falls in love with Aleixo, a delicate and feminine fifteen-year-old blue-eyed white cabin boy. Aleixo "was the son of a poor fishing family, who had enlisted him onto a ship in Santa Caterina, just as he reached adolescence."[64] After falling in love at sea, they occupy a rental room in Rio de Janeiro while on shore leave, where they are able to live out their uninhibited desires. The book chronicles Bom-Crioulo's physical and moral decline, as he grows thinner and weaker.[65] Later, when Bom-Crioulo is back at sea – now serving on a modern battleship from which he receives much less shore leave – their landlady seduces the young cabin boy Aleixo, and when Bom-Crioulo returns, he is driven by passion to kill Aleixo.

Notable for the age is the fact that, though Amaro's decline is the focus of the book, Caminha portrays romantic connections between men in the Brazilian navy in a surprisingly sympathetic light. Although the book was published during the First Republic, the romance is set during the later decades of the Brazilian empire, before the abolition of slavery. Born in 1867, Caminha entered the naval academy in 1883 and graduated in 1885. During his five-year term as a naval officer, he served on several ships and in the apprentice school in Fortaleza. His career was cut short by a combination of scandal when he moved in with the wife of an officer at the naval academy and hostility among the naval elite following his 1887 publication of an article critical of corporal punishment in the popular Rio newspaper *Gazeta de Notícias* (discussed in more detail in the following section), and he left the military for government service and a literary career in 1890. The fact that he was a naval officer during the period covered in the book offers a certain historical value and legitimacy to his descriptions of overall naval hierarchy. The book shocked Brazilian intellectuals with its presentation of homosexuality and racial transgression and hurt Caminha's reputation among this group.

The book offers rare insight into sexual contact between sailors (as well as between officers and enlisted men). It also illustrates the lives of enlisted men in the late empire, as told by an officer in that institution in ways that court-martial documents often cannot. The two main protagonists entered the navy in their teens, one a runaway slave dragooned into service as a naval apprentice, the other years later, turned over by a family who could not afford to keep him at home. Bom-Crioulo and Aleixo share a room for a year in Rio de Janeiro while their ship, the corvette sailboat, is undergoing repairs in dry dock. Bom-Crioulo is transferred onto a "new ship – one of steel. Well known for its complicated machinery and its formidable artillery capacity, a remarkable blend of naval force, which made that ship one of the most powerful in the world."[66]

Overall, Caminha's book describes a navy in which homosexual activity rarely led to expulsion; such behavior was generally acknowledged and overlooked. When it was punished, it happened on board the ship. This is certainly supported by the repeated appearance of "immoral acts" in the court-martial documents as the cause of a lashing, but never as the sole reason a sailor had been sent for trial. In fact, of the cases tried, there was only one in which men were found guilty for committing homosexual rape by the military court. This case involved navy coalman José Joaquim de Sant'Anna and Seaman First Class Antônio Ferreira da

Silva, who were accused of raping navy coalman Pedro Cavalcante in 1893. The three men got drunk while off ship and entered an abandoned house. Inside the two men fought with the weaker Cavalcante. They then "removed his clothes, forced him onto his hands and feet, and with him satiated their libidinous instincts."[67] Antônio Ferreira da Silva was already in the disciplinary company on board his ship for immoral activity, and had been previously tried and absolved for injuring a comrade while trying to forcibly practice immoral acts. The evidence was sufficient to win a conviction because the victim testified, and there were corroborating witnesses. The attackers received four years imprisonment, the maximum sentence.

Far more regularly, the punishment for such "immoral" behavior was the lash. There were twenty cases in which sailors had immoral acts in their military record. Of those, fourteen had been lashed for their crime, and one was placed in irons. Two were arrested by the police while on leave from their ships for immoral acts, and they were likely punished by the civilian court. For the remaining three the punishment was not specified, but it was likely the lash. Most received 25 lashes; three received 100 lashes. Two others received 150 and 50 lashes, respectively, for statutory rape. The final case involved Miguel José de Sauza, who stabbed Manoel Francisco Romão in 1882 in the act of forcibly sodomizing him. He received six years of prison not for rape but for injuring a comrade, and his punishment was the maximum because Miguel José de Sauza had told his victim earlier what he would do, which made the act premeditated.[68]

CORPORAL PUNISHMENT IN CAMINHA'S *BOM CRIOULO*

Caminha offers vivid accounts of corporal punishment on board Brazilian military ships. His novel is set during the initial shift from wooden to steel ships in the 1880s, and much like in the turn of the century navy, for Brazilian sailors to man modern battleships represented an entirely new skill set, one fraught with new tensions and responsibilities. Ironically, the officers overseeing these new warships often had little more technical training than the enlisted men they ruled. Such a problematic hierarchy increased tension and invited more violence. Of Bom-Crioulo's new ship the narrator stated, "On the battleship discipline was a very different thing. There the first mate, a violent individual, did nothing but talk of canings and the pillory."[69]

The novel is bookmarked by two vividly described applications of corporal punishment, and the systematized performance of the ritual is in keeping with descriptions of corporal punishment derived from historical sources. Both applications involve Bom-Crioulo. In the first, a cabin boy named Herculano, and a third-class sailor named Sant'Ana are lashed for onboard offences. The captain has the crew called on deck in formation; the officers soon follow in their dress uniforms with sword, hats, and epaulettes properly affixed: "In short order all were ready, sailors and officers – sailors in double rows on either side of the ship, the officers astern near the mainsail, all with the respectful attitude of those preparing to participate in a solemn ritual."[70] The captain makes a short speech about naval discipline, and the first mate reads the applicable rules from the naval code that apply to corporal punishment. In this case, the punishment applied to Herculano and Sant'Ana is for fighting. Herculano was found masturbating against the main rail – in the language of the Naturalist author, the sailor had "committed a real crime, but one not listed in the rule books."[71] Sant'Ana mocked the cabin boy, and the two began to fight. For this indiscretion, they each receive 25 lashes. Herculano sags into his shackles groaning inwardly throughout his punishment, while Sant'Ana writhes, weeping and tearfully calling out for mercy. In both cases, their suffering is obvious and visible.

On the other hand, when Bom-Crioulo is brought up for his punishment, his tall, proud, strong, dark body is itself understood by the officers as an act of defiance, and that defiance, in the form of his body, has to be broken by the lash. His punishment is for the crime of badly beating a second-class sailor who had "mistreated" Aleixo (the cabin boy who later became his lover). His crime was the same as the other sailors, fighting. But when then the lashes begin to fall, "the *chibata* didn't leave a mark on him; he had the back of iron":

> Bom-Crioulo had taken off his cotton shirt, and, naked from the waist up, in
> a splendid display of muscles, his pectorals rippling, his black shoulder blades

shining, a deep, smooth furrow running from top to bottom down the middle
of his back, he didn't even utter a groan, as if he were receiving the lightest of
punishments. But he'd already taken fifty strokes of the chibata! No one heard
a groan, nor seen a contraction, there was not the slightest gesture of pain. The
only thing to be seen on his black back was the scars left from the lash, one across
the other, crisscrossing like a great cobweb, red and throbbing, cutting the skin
in all directions.[72]

Finally, upon receiving a vicious blow to the kidneys he calls out and
raises a hand. Only then, when he shows some sign of suffering, of being
broken, does the captain halt the punishment after 150 blows of the chibata. In this example, art imitates life; in the case described earlier in this
chapter, when Lieutenant José Cândido Guillobel was on trial for having
a sailor lashed 500 times in a day, he justified his actions to the court as
follows: "Seeing the slight effect of the punishment on the delinquent,
I was forced to continue the lashing until reaching the number of 500
blows."[73] Although Bom-Crioulo's punishment in Caminha's novel is
nowhere near as harsh, the justification is strikingly similar – punishing
enlisted men who had the audacity to be proud before the assembled
ship's crew pressured officers to ensure that men being punished were
suitably humbled.

At the end of the novel, as Bom-Crioulo approaches his final breakdown leading him to murder the cabin-boy Aleixo, he is again the re-
cipient of a brutal lashing, this time as a punishment for "disobedience,
drunkenness, and pederasty."[74] Just as had been the case on board the
corvette, there is a general muster of the crew of the battleship; they stand
in formation on the quarterdeck. Again, he receives his lashes without
complaint or shouting out, but the months of moral and physical decline
mean that at the end of his punishment, he is in physical ruin: "At the
last blow, Bom-Crioulo writhed and fell flat on the deck, seeping blood.
There remained no skin on his back untouched by the lash. He inevitably
fell when his body had been wholly drained of strength, when his punishment reached an inhuman level and pain had conquered his willpower.
Only then appeared the ship's doctor, trembling and nervous he stated
'it's nothing, it's nothing; bring the bottle of ether and water, a little
water.'"[75] Directly following this round of punishment, Bom-Crioulo is
transferred to the naval hospital on Ilha das Cobras, where – suffering
physically and emotionally – he wastes, his body refusing to heal.

As a source, *Bom-Crioulo* offers, I believe, legitimate insight into life in the Brazilian navy, though perhaps it is better on corporal punishment than as a source on homosexuality in Brazil. As a work of fiction, Caminha's descriptions of the intimate lives of enlisted men (as opposed to officers) could be based only on his projections and imagination. After all, although the lower decks of military ships were under the direct control of the military hierarchy, they were largely unknowable to the officers; much as the intimate lives of the enslaved remained unknowable to the slave master. By the very act of entering those locations, their power and authority disrupted the space. Regardless of how compelling his description of intimate contact among enlisted men is, Caminha's understanding had to be based largely on invention.

On the other hand, his descriptions of those violent rituals in which the officers and enlisted men came together in the performative ceremony of corporal punishment not only ring true, they were based on his firsthand experience about which he has also published nonfiction. In his literary biography of Adolfo Caminha, Carlos Eduardo de Oliveira Bezerrda describes references to Caminha's 1887 publication in the *Gazeta de Notícias* of a "manifesto against corporal punishment." Although no copies of that article seem to have survived, Caminha references its publication in a later memoir. He states that the article was based on his own experiences traveling to New Orleans while serving as an officer on the Brazilian naval vessel *Almirante Barroso* in 1886. Caminha first published his memoirs of that trip in 1890 in serial format in the Fortaleza-based magazine *O Norte* under the title *"No país dos ianques"* (In the country of the Yankees). Later in 1894, the year before *Bom-Crioulo* was published, it was republished in book format under the same title.[76]

In that work, he describes corporal punishment as a "barbarous punishment" (*bárbaro castigo*) and says that watching its application was the "most revolting thing that I've ever seen." He goes on to say that "the first time that my position compelled me to witness this form of punishment, I wanted to shout out with all the force in my lungs against this attack on human nature." He describes the actual event: "The body of this poor man, a servant of the nation, stripped to the waist with hands and feet shackled, often following three days having been fed nothing but bread and water in solitary confinement. Across his shoulders, his chest, even on his face; across his body fifty, one-hundred, two-hundred lashes, in the presence of all of his companions. . . . It seems undignified behavior from gentlemen triumphantly wearing golden gallons on their uniforms – uniforms that project nobility, courage, patriotism and the honor of the nation."[77] It is clear that his novel was based on a naval hierarchy about which he had intimate knowledge, ritualized violence about which all officers and enlisted men had intimate knowledge. His descriptions offer insight into the daily life of an officer in the Brazilian navy, as well as the importance of these regular applications of the lash to overall naval hierarchy.

BRAZIL'S NAVY AT THE DAWN OF THE TWENTIETH CENTURY

On paper, the coming of the Republic in 1889 marked a period of radical change for Brazil's sailors. Yet, naval officers ignored the optimism of the republican congress; the navy never abandoned its well-established methods to recruit and control its sailors. At the turn of the twentieth century, the navy had made few changes in its treatment of its enlisted men. As it had in the nineteenth century, the naval hierarchy recruited those who lacked protection from their grasp. The shift away from forced recruitment and toward recruitment of boys through the apprenticeship schools accelerated into the twentieth century, by which time the majority of naval recruits came from these "schools."[78] But when these changes failed to deliver increases in levels of volunteerism, they quickly reverted to traditional roles of populating the lower decks. In his Ministerial Report of 1890, recently appointed Naval Minister Fortunato Foster Vidal discusses the difficulty the navy had in reaching that year's mandated target population of 4,000 sailors enlisted into the navy:

> Despite the abolition of corporal punishment and the various advantages offered [by previous legislative decree],[79] and despite the multiple notices of my predecessor regarding individuals who would enlist voluntarily as a result,[80] they have so far not only failed to attain sufficient numbers of enlisted men to meet the required crew size [4,000 enlisted men], we have failed to recruit sufficient numbers of personnel to replace the combined number of sailors who have deserted from service, who are physically incapacitated, and those who should be discharged for completion of time served. . . . The abolition of forced recruitment

and the suppression of recruitment payments, according to . . . the Constitution, made the acquisition of personnel for service all the more difficult . . . given how great is the repugnance felt by our population toward a life in naval service.

I do not think that by these methods we can count on favorable results in the near future, nor can we by drawing on the population of merchant seamen, for by doing so would for years create shortages among the crews of the commercial vessels.

On the other hand, the Schools of Naval Apprenticeship, now established in various states which annually supply the National Marine Corps with large numbers of sailors filling a great many of the vacancies that are opening, can do little to address our immediate needs, as it is largely composed of minors physically incapable of carrying out the arduous labor of the sea.

In order to mitigate the problems, Decree. 1,465 of last February 14 ordered the temporary cessation of any discharges from service.

I am forcefully requesting your attention to this important subject, and I request your advice on actions designed to prevent, for lack of crews, the paralysis of our fleet.[81]

We do not have the president's response to this plea, but as described previously, Decree 328 of April 12, 1890, reestablished the use of corporal punishment in the navy just five months after Brazilian lawmakers had explicitly abolished corporal punishment with the passage of Decree 3, passed on the second day that the Brazilian Republic existed. It is clear that the republican naval and political elite attempted to hide the fact that violence continued as an important part of naval service. The April 12, 1890, reintroduction of corporal punishment through the decree cited above happened quietly; it was one of a small number of governmental decrees that was not published in the *Diário Oficial,* the official list of federal legislation published annually by the government.

Alongside the legislative "modernization" of naval service, the new republican government did take steps to update some of the vessels in service to the Brazilian navy. They requested designs for a protected cruiser-class warship and a light cruiser in March 1890, just months after the overthrow of the monarchy. *Protected cruisers* were small, fast, armored ships that carried heavy guns; they were conceived as battleship destroyers. *Light cruiser* was a Brazilian categorization; the builders considered this design to be that of a large gunboat. In May 1891, designs were submitted by a company then named Sir W. G. Armstrong, Mitchell & Co., Ltd.[82] In July 1891, the Brazilian government accepted designs for both ships, and later that same month at Armstrongs' Els-

wick shipyards, just upriver from Newcastle, they laid down the hulls of
the protected cruiser *República* and of the light cruiser *Tiradentes*. The
República once completed displaced 1,314 tons and measured 210 feet
long; it was protected by a 3-inch plate on its hull. It carried six 4.7-inch
guns, four 6-pounders, and four 14-inch torpedo tubes. The ship was
launched in May 1892 and passed its final trials in September of that
year, reaching a speed greater than 17 knots. The matching light cruiser,
Tiradentes, was smaller, only 165 feet long and displacing 728 tons, and
was a slower class of ship protected by thinner 2-inch armor; it carried
similar-sized armament but fewer guns and torpedoes. It had four 4.7-
inch guns, three 6-pounders, and two 14-inch torpedoes. This ship was
also launched in May 1892 and passed its trials in September that year,
reaching speeds just shy of 13 knots, well under the promised 14.5 knots it
was designed for. However, the builders blamed bad weather and choppy
seas for that failure. The *Tiradentes* departed the Tyne in November 1892,
and the *República* departed in January 1893. The beginnings of the modernization of the Brazilian navy can be tied to the purchase of these two
boats, but this represented a fairly slow start. Not only were these boats
relatively small for the time, even Brazil's lukewarm commitment to the
modernization of its navy would be severely undermined by the outbreak
of the Naval Revolt in 1893, examined in the next chapter.[83]

Thus, in the decades of the early Republic leading up to the 1910
Revolta da Chibata – perhaps despite the best intentions of the political
elite – the navy continued to consist almost exclusively of white elite officers overseeing poor black sailors. It was a social institution separated
into two closed and independent units; they were physically close but
as socially as distant as they could be. In his anonymously published
book, *Politica versus Marinha* (Politics versus the Navy), naval officer
José Eduardo de Macedo Soares, writing under the title "Um Official da
Armada" (A naval officer), describes the race of the enlisted men who
populated the navy at the time of the 1910 revolt as "fifty percent black
[*negros*], thirty percent mulatto, ten percent mixed indigenous and European [*caboclos*], and ten percent white or nearly white."[84] In much of
the scholarship on this revolt, this quote (along with other anecdotal descriptions from the era) has been used to define the demographics of the
Brazilian navy. However, while researching her 2009 dissertation, Silvia

Capanema P. de Almeida first gained access to the documents of the records of the Cabinet of Naval Identification (Gabinete de Identificação da Armada, hereafter GIA), changed to the Gabinete de Identificação da Marinha, or GIM, in 1957 and the Serviço de Identificação da Marinha, or SIM, in 1973.[85] The GIA was created in January 1908 as a means to identify all personnel serving in the Brazilian navy. This was likely a response to the January 21, 1906, explosion aboard the battleship *Aquidabã* that killed 212 men, some of whom washed up on shore near Angra dos Reis, at which time the navy found itself embarrassingly unable to identify the bodies of officers and enlisted men alike. The official description of the GIA's primary justification was the recapture of deserters, a problem that plagued the Brazilian navy throughout its history. Thus notice number 853 of February 1908 called for this office to create an individual file for each sailor such that any deserter from the navy could be easily identified. Each would "examine and identify morphological traits, taking descriptive notes of coloring, distinguishing marks, scars and tattoos acquired in ordinary life or those that are congenital anomalies . . . and even the impressions of the papillary lines of the fingertips."[86]

Whereas Capanema goes on to excellent analysis of the various details included in the GIA documents, and the social meanings of scars, tattoos, and even mustaches, I here draw on the entire series of GIA files recorded in 1908 solely focusing on the race of this subset of sailors in the first decade of the twentieth century. (See table 3.6.) Note that the 750 enlisted men entered into the files of the GIA in 1908 represent less than 23 percent of the actual number of enlisted men serving in the navy that year. The records of the navy identified the effective size of the enlisted men in 1908 as 3,274 in 1908 and 4,097 in 1909 (the government had set the goal of 5,000 enlisted men for both years, up from 4,000 in 1907). Therefore, although the process of identifying enlisted men offers important insights into the sailors serving in the era of the Revolta da Chibata, this is not an exhaustive list of the race of sailors, and it is unclear how those men who were prioritized for inclusion were selected. Unfortunately, none of the future leaders of the revolt were recorded in these documents.

Although categories of race in Brazil are notoriously ambiguous, statistics on racial demographics in the early twentieth century navy are

Table 3.6. Race of Brazilian Sailors in 1908

Race	Number of files	Percentage
Pardo (brown/mixed African descent)	297	39.6%
Branco (white)	182	24.2%
Moreno (ambiguous term that translates as "brown" but often implies near-whiteness).	141	18.8%
Preto (black)	126	16.8%
Not recorded	4	0.53%
Total	750	

Source: Gabinete de Identificação da Armada (1908).

rare and valuable, even if incomplete. In contrast with the oft-cited quote from *Politica versus Marinha,* these numbers show a higher percentage of white enlisted men (24.2 percent) than does the navy that Soares portrayed as consisting of 50 percent blacks and 30 percent mulattos. Adding the catagories of preta and parda gives an Afro-descended population of 63.6 percent. As the navy does not use the category of mulatto in these files as Soares did, the ambiguity of the term morena and the likelihood of some of those sailors coming from the category of mulatto could conceivably help shift these numbers closer together. We cannot know how the completion of the identification process would have impacted the overall numbers or how the office chose to prioritize their process of identification. What we can extract from these numbers is that even with a larger "white" population than Soares described, most enlisted men serving in the Brazilian navy continued to be Afro-Brazilians, whereas the officers overseeing their discipline and control were for all intents and purposes entirely white.

Officers in the early-twentieth-century Brazilian navy allowed for the growing separation between the increasingly technological modernity of its ships and the violence and personal disregard for its naval personnel. These modern ships required sailors to take on greater responsibilities and workloads, and according to several of the rebels, they faced increasingly draconian and vicious treatment in the decade preceding the revolt. Expanding on Gilberto Freyre's previously cited groundbreaking examination of Brazilian modernization, *Order and Progress,* he stated that "the Navy had modernized its material equipment without having prepared its personnel for the technical requirements of such equipment." He then goes on to say, "[It was] the old story of the cart before the horse. And lacking this human preparation, it was necessary to follow the characteristically Brazilian procedure of improvisation, scouring the ports for instant technicians, machinists, and firemen, incorporating native thugs and foreigners with anarchistic ideas into a Navy accustomed to the old style of discipline, including that of the lash."[87] Freyre's argument in turn drew heavily on Soares's anonymously published book *Politica versus Marinha*. Soares's fifth chapter, titled "The Annihilation" (*O Aniquilamento*), which examined the impact of the Revolta da Chibata on both the Brazilian navy and the nation overall, begins:

> The Brazilian navy's situation at the end of 1910 had undergone no significant change except the considerable augmentation of new ships through the program of 1906.
> We have already seen that the crews continued to be deficient and were composed of elements that were frankly dangerous to moral and discipline on board. The professional schools slowly supplied essential contingents of specialists who then disappeared into the mass of illiterate and debased [*viciados*] sailors. By a grave administrative error, the contingent from the Apprenticeship Schools actually augmented the number of those unfortunates who could neither read nor write. Due to their desire to fill vacancies among crewmembers, ministers call for the removal of minors from their classes at Villegaignon immediately upon their attaining acceptable physical stature.[88]

Soares presents valuable descriptions of the Brazilian navy as well as the struggle between politicians and military officers, but one must keep in mind his role as an elite naval officer. Soares was a firm believer in the racist ideology so central to the Brazilian intellectual movement at the time he was writing. He, like so many officers he describes, simply could not accept a Brazilian navy that functioned without the lash. This he blames on the inherent racial flaws among the men who populate the lower decks of the Brazilian navy.

> The first impression of a Brazilian garrison is that of decay and physical disability. The blacks are underdeveloped and shifty, showing all of the signs of depravity common to the most backwards African nations. The other races submitted to the influences of the blacks who were always in the majority. . . . The entire world knows that corporal punishment has been a part of the penitentiary system of Germany, England and the United States . . . it is brutal by necessity in order to maintain order and to safeguard the life of the employees and guards of the prisons.

> In our navy, the normal framework consists of the abandonment of twelve or
> fifteen virtually defenseless officers to command four hundred to five hundred
> sailors. . . . Only one force can ensure discipline: moral force [*a forca moral*].
>   Only one element constitutes that moral force among the most backward
> and rudimentary: the fear of [physical] punishment. . . . Nearly all officers find
> the rule of the *chibata* repugnant; it is the rare commander who has not experi-
> mented with disposing of its use on his ship.[89]

He goes on to list some of the great captains and admirals who found
themselves "forced" to continue applying the lash to enlisted men, including naval ministers Jaceguay and Leão, whose annual Ministerial
Reports are cited throughout this study. He then tells the ironic story
of Commander Batista das Neves, captain of the ill-fated *Minas Geraes,*
where the Revolta da Chibata began. Neves was an idealist who committed to not use the lash on the maiden voyage from Newcastle to Rio
de Janeiro.

> At the time of his departure from Newcastle, in a sad and ironic speech that
> would be remembered in times to come, he promised a regimen of solidarity,
> mutual trust, mutual respect and discipline.
>   In no time the ship was dirty, the garrison avoided their duties, petty
> indiscipline erupted on all sides, and the commander still retained faith. . . .
> A boy of seventeen years stabbed a companion for the perverse pleasure of it,
> two days later a sailor attacked and beat a sergeant. Theft assumed staggering
> proportions. Suddenly, on board there were no guarantees, no discipline, no
> order. Only one thing was efficacious. Who dispenses with the use of the only
> force capable of ensuring discipline and lives on the ship? . . . As persistent as the
> customs and morality are that currently rein on our ships, the chibata is literally
> indispensable.[90]

Soares has praised those officers who realized that the navy required the
use of the lash, whereas he ridicules an officer – notably the first officer
killed during the Revolta da Chibata – who saw discipline crumble on
his ship but tried not to use the lash on board the newly acquired dreadnought battleship. In both cases, he presents the officers as "repulsed" by
the use of the chibata, but they were forced to do so by the base nature,
and the base race, of the Brazilian sailor.

This rhetoric is certainly not an original idea attributable to Brazilian naval officers. These civilized men, in this case naval officers, are
morally repulsed by the use of violence but are nonetheless forced to
apply it – often quite rigorously – to their subordinates who are too de-

based to participate in civilized society and represent a danger to themselves and the larger institution. As presented in the following chapter,
it was an important trope in the eighteenth-century British navy and
was echoed throughout the world's navies. However, it was an equally
common refrain among plantation owners throughout the Atlantic
World. In his now infamous *History of Jamaica,* Edward Long – once
described by Shyllon O. Folarin in his *Black People in Britain, 1555–1833*
as the "father of English racism"[91] – describes how enslaved Africans
brought to labor in Jamaica benefit from the order and civility of the
plantation:

> If they were slaves in their own country, or had forfeited their freedom by some
> crime, they have no right to repine at the want of it in the country to which they
> are driven. They were already slaves, and have only exchanged their owner and
> laws; the former, for one less arbitrary; the latter, for one more benevolent and
> gentle than they before had experience of. In general they gain life, for death,
> clemency, for barbarity; comfort and convenience, for torture and misery; food,
> for famine. Insomuch that, after some trial of their new condition, under a mas-
> ter who in fact pursues his own interest best in treating them well, they would
> account it the highest act of inhumanity to be sent back to their native country.[92]

This idea that Africans were in fact uplifted from their vile state of nature
simply because they were brought into contact with European civilization (whether British, French, Spanish, or Portuguese) was common,
and not only was applied to centuries of chattel slavery but continued
throughout the era of colonization, as whites carried their burden of
uplift into Africa and Asia.

About the violent control of men in the Brazilian navy, there has
been a recent challenge to the argument that naval service remained
largely unchanged in the years preceding the 1910 naval revolt. In several
recent articles concerning the Revolta da Chibata, Silvia Capanema P.
de Almeida has questioned the premise that the Brazilian navy turned
its back on the modernization of its sailors in the years preceding the
revolt. Although she acknowledges the continued shortcomings in the
apprenticeship schools, which include high levels of illiteracy, their ongoing use as retaining facilities for juvenile delinquents and orphans, and
the documented use of corporal punishment in these schools for children, she builds an argument based in part on various acts of legislation
and contemporary descriptions that these schools/companies indeed

represented an important shift in the populating of the Brazilian lower decks.[93] Central to her argument is the fact that during the early Republic, from a nadir in the year following the 1893 Naval Revolt (discussed below) until the year preceding the outbreak of the Revolta da Chibata, the navy came increasingly close to actually meeting the enrollment goals published annually by the federal government.

There can be little doubt that both the Brazilian federal government and the naval elite were critical of the overall method by which the lower decks were populated. Legislation against forced recruitment, corporal punishment, and the bonuses paid for the delivery of men who were more or less willing to enlist into the naval service show an overall dissatisfaction with traditional methods of recruitment and treatment. Much more important than the lip service directed by those elites toward the modernization and reform of the institution was the fact that when substantive change failed to follow on the heels of legislative reform during the early years of the First Republic, those reforms were quickly jettisoned. The naval hierarchy reverted to the violent and exploitative methods of control established alongside Brazil's reliance on the labor of enslaved African. That said, Almeida's argument that the increased reliance on the apprenticeship schools as a source for sailors in the Brazilian navy marked an important change is absolutely correct. However, the origins of the increased role for the then-named companies of apprenticeship is better understood in the context of the mid-nineteenth century and the abolition of the Brazilian slave trade than it is with the establishment of the Brazilian Republic nearly four decades later. Certainly, the companies of apprenticeship established in the 1840s and 1850s were important steps in this movement away from impressment. However, the measures taken by lawmakers during the first days of the Brazilian Republic marked their desire to complete the transition from coerced to voluntary recruitment. The overall system of apprenticeships had little to do with that particular change, and the "schools" were at that moment wholly incapable of delivering the number of sailors required to staff Brazil's increasingly modern navy.[94] (See table 3.7.)

Lacking reforms to the institution, officers at the top of the military hierarchy understood themselves as hard-pressed to enforce discipline and order among the masses, and, in the eyes of the officers, the navy

Table 3.7. Effective Population of the Corpo de Marinha Nacionais, 1892–1910

Year	Actual number of enlisted men	Mandated number of enlisted men	Number of sailors short of mandated goal	Real percentage of mandated crew size
1892	3,174	4,012	838	79
1893	916	4,012	3,096	23
1894	1,248	4,012	2,764	31
1895	1,789	4,000	2,292	43
1896	1,809	4,000	2,191	45
1897	1,792	4,000	2,208	45
1898	1,904	4,000	2,096	48
1899	1,981	4,000	2,019	50
1900	1,946	4,000	2,054	49
1901	2,091	4,000	1,909	52
1902	2,552	4,000	1,448	64
1903	3,014	4,000	986	75
1904	2,661	4,000	1,339	67
1905	2,760	4,000	1,240	69
1906	2,866	4,000	1,134	72
1907	3,120	4,000	880	78
1908	3,274	5,000	1,726	66
1909	4,097	5,000	903	82
1910	-	-	-	-

Source: Relatórios do Ministro da Marinha (1892–1910), published in Silvia Capanema P. de Almeida, "A modernização do material e do pessoal da Marinha nas vésperas da revolta dos marujos de 1910: modelos e contradições," Estudos Históricos 23, no. 45 (Jan./June 2010): 157.

could not run without the application of the lash. In a letter to the U.S. secretary of state dated soon after the revolt, Irving B. Dudley, from the office of the U.S. military attaché, wrote: "Respecting corporal punishment, [Brazilian officers] not only admit administering it but attempt to justify the practice as necessary to the maintenance of discipline and the safety of those in command. The Brazilian man-o-war's man, it would appear, is exceptionally ignorant and debased, insubordinate and prone to violence."[95] When we look at the institutional violence, lengthy terms of service, small wages, long work days, and miserable treatment applied to enlisted men, it is little wonder sailors resisted their roles at the bottom of the naval hierarchy.

PREVIOUS RESISTANCE TO CORPORAL PUNISHMENT

In fact, the Revolta de Chibata was not the first time that Brazilian enlisted men protested the structured violence under which they served;
there were at least two earlier manifestations of their opposition to the
chibata, including one that predated any significant contact between
Brazilian sailors and the British maritime world. The first followed the
April 12, 1890, passage of Decree 328, which introduced the correctional
company into the Brazilian navy, thereby ending the brief five-month
abolition of corporal punishment passed by the Republican government
in November 1889. On December 13, 1891, the crew of the *Primeiro de
Março,* a four-cannon gunship built in Brazil in 1881, revolted against
their officers, alleging maltreatment. Officers and loyal sailors rapidly put
down the rebellion, and dozens of men were imprisoned at the Fortaleza
de Santa Cruz in Rio de Janeiro.[96]

The second event, though predating the arrival of the dreadnoughts,
had clear ties to the organization of the Revolta da Chibata. In August
1910, the Brazilian government sent three warships – the scout *Bahia*
and the cruiser-torpedo boats *Tamoya* and *Timbira* – as part of a multi-
national naval presence to celebrate the centennial of Chile's independence. Serving abroad *Bahia* was Francisco Dias Martins, one of the
leaders and organizers of the upcoming revolt; he would command the
Bahia during the uprising. Martins would later claim that the Revolta da
Chibata had to be postponed until his return to Rio de Janeiro, though
subsequently he made many claims about his leadership role in the revolt
that cannot be substantiated. This voyage to Chile was infamous for the
overall insubordination of the crews and for the generous application of
the whip. Within the navy it was known as the Division of Death. Between June 16 and November 19, the 288 enlisted men on the *Bahia* alone
committed over 900 disciplinary breaches – many involved drinking on
board, and most were punished with the whip. When the ship arrived in
Buenos Aires, there were numerous desertions on the first night in port.
As the ships passed through the Straits of Magellan, someone slipped a
note under the commander of the *Bahia*'s door. It read: "I come, through
these lines, to ask that you no longer mistreat the crew of this ship who
work without stop to keep things in order. We are neither thieves nor

bandits. We want peace and love. We are not slaves to the officers, so halt the chibata. Be careful!"[97] The note was signed by the *Mão Negra*, or "Black Hand," later identified as Francisco Dias Martins.[98]

How do we understand these examples of resistance? The sailors locate the Revolta da Chibata in the context of Brazilian slavery, but why did their resistance take shape more than two decades after the abolition of African slavery? What happened in the early twentieth century that led to the Revolta da Chibata if corporal punishment had been the primary means of controlling sailors in Brazil's navy since its origins nearly a century before? Based on the December 1891 uprising against corporal punishment on the *Primeiro de Março,* the overall movement could not have its origins in the Naval Renovation Plan of 1904, or in its links with England. However, given how easily that rebellion was put down, and the somewhat limited size of the Brazilian navy in the nineteenth century, the ships built through the 1904 plan made it possible for the rebels to represent a legitimate threat to the capital and its inhabitants. In reinventing the nation and the navy, the Brazilian elite created a set of opportunities for their sailors. Although pinpointing the exact tipping point is impossible, many of those opportunities had origins in the ties between Brazil and England in the early twentieth century. Between the British dreadnoughts and the reclamantes' ability to man them, and their relatively free time among sailors of the British navy and radicals throughout Newcastle, the rebels found themselves for the first time able to challenge the conditions under which they were forced to labor. Once available the rebels seized the opportunity and changed the face of the modern Brazilian navy – and to a real extent, they changed the nature of Brazilian society.

1. The Leaders of the Revolt: João Cândido (left), sailor first class, leader of the revolt and commander of the dreadnaught *Minas Geraes*. (right) Seaman Manuel Gregório do Nascimento, by arrangement with João Cândido and unanimously supported by the rebel sailors, assumed the role of commander of the dreadnaught *São Paulo*. Source: O Malho.

2. Brazilian battleship *Minas Geraes.* Source: Tyne & Wear Archives.

3. Sir William G. Armstrong at ceremony celebrating his newest gun. Source: Tyne & Wear Archives.

BRAZILIAN BATTLESHIP "MINAS GERAES" FIRING BROADSIDE OF TEN 12" GUNS.

4. Brazilian battleship *Minas Geraes* firing broadside of ten 12-inch guns. Source: Tyne & Wear Archives.

5. "Fitting out wharf *Vanguard* and *Sao Paulo* under 150 ton crane." Reproduced by kind permission of the Syndics of Cambridge University Library, Vickers #2002.

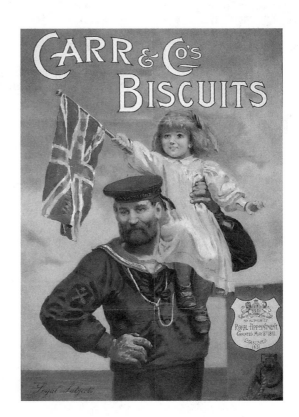

6. "Carr & Co's Biscuits: Loyal Subjects." Source: The National Archives' image library with permission from United Biscuits (UK) Limited.

7. Rowton House, Newcastle. Source: Tyne & Wear Archives.

8. Cover of the December 1, 1910, *A Ilustração Brasileira:* "The Sailors Revolt." The deck and tower of the dreadnought *Minas Geraes,* flagship of the rebel squadron. Insert photo of Captain Batista das Neves, killed during the uprising. Source: *A Ilustração Brasileira.*

9. João Cândido (center) and the crew of the *Minas Geraes* with journalist Julio de Medeiros from *Jornal do Commercio,* awaiting notification of the amnesty. Source: *O Malho.*

10. Rebel crew of the *São Paulo.* Source: *O Malho.*

11. "The Bombardment: Effect of an Imprudent Bulletin." This cartoon represents the panic initiated among Rio's population when they received news that the reclamantes were bombing the city. Source: *O Malho.*

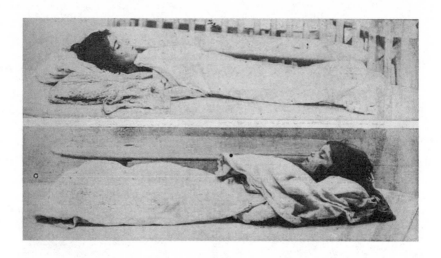

12. "Victims of the Revolt." The two civilian casualties of the Revolta da Chibata. Source: *O Malho.*

13. "Order & Progress." Racist representations of the reclamantes were common in the Brazilian press immediately following the outbreak of the revolt. Source: *O Malho.*

14. "Clearing the Waters." This cartoon represents more than one hundred reclamantes expelled from Rio following the December uprising on the *Ilha das Cobras*. They were packed onto the ship *Satélite* and were sent into forced labor in the northern state of Pará. Source: *O Malho*.

15. Cover of December 10, 1910, *Careta* magazine. Another racist depiction, this time of João Cândido, but in this case the inversion of the post–Revolta da Chibata navy includes the impossible reality of white enlisted men serving under a black admiral. Source: *Careta*.

Armstrongs wasn't just a factory in a city suburb; at its peak it *was* Newcastle. For better or worse. The story of its famous guns and ships and tanks has often been told, has become a fascinating part of British industrial history.

DAVID BEAN, *Armstrong's Men*

FOUR

Roots of a Rebellion

THE REVOLTA DA CHIBATA CAN BE BEST UNDERSTOOD IN THE
context of the broader Atlantic World. In this era, the international sale
of modern warships and the movement of the crews of naval and merchant marine vessels linked together waterfront cities throughout the
Atlantic and beyond. Too often, the end of the Atlantic slave trade has
been represented as a closing point for the comparative study of race in
the Atlantic World, limiting conceptualization of the Black Atlantic to a
colonial model. The Revolta da Chibata offers a modern example of the
complex interactions that linked the twentieth-century Atlantic World.

Events that Brazilian sailors witnessed – and those in which they
participated – during their stay in Newcastle while awaiting the delivery
of warships from Armstrongs from the summer of 1909 through the first
months of 1910 helped motivate the sailors who organized and carried
out the revolt. Not to overemphasize those British roots; resistance to
corporal punishment in the Brazilian navy clearly preceded the mass
arrival of Brazilian sailors in Newcastle over the summer of 1909. But
to overlook the impact of technological advances in Europe, the growth
of the international arms market, the naval reforms initiated by British sailors, and the radicalism of British dockworkers at the turn of the
twentieth century leaves the impression that the Revolta da Chibata
occurred in isolation. To do so ignores the experiences of foreign sailors
in Newcastle and the special nature of that city. Such neglect allows for
the harshest critics of the reclamantes to redefine the movement and, I
fear, extends the silence and mischaracterization that has for too long
defined this revolt.

Of the many changes affecting England's economic and social landscape during this period, this chapter focuses on three sets. The first is the technological advances that led to the development of the dreadnought battleships and, perhaps more importantly, the events that led to the sale of such ships to the Brazilian navy. Without these warships, any uprising against the use of corporal punishment would have necessarily taken a very different form. Equally important was the port city of Newcastle, where these Brazilian sailors were stationed for months awaiting the completion of the new ships. At a time when British cities such as Liverpool and London showed increasing hostility toward foreigners and racial outsiders, the widespread reliance of Newcastle's economy on sales to foreign navies meant that the city and its population were more tolerant of the presence of foreign sailors in their midst. Additionally, during the second half of the nineteenth century, Newcastle was a hotbed of radicalism. Workers led strikes and stoppages, and the production of the Brazilian dreadnoughts was actually halted by two different strikes. Finally, in the decades preceding the revolt, the British navy underwent a period of radical reform. Not only were laws and legal codes changed – an abrogation of corporal punishment was driven by protest on the lower decks – but the British sailors' relationship to the nation and the empire irreparably shifted. No longer viewed as a drunkard dragooned into service, the British sailors became noble warrior proudly defending the empire. Any one of the above changes could have made a deep impression on sailors arriving from Brazil. Together they suggested to Brazilian sailors that their relations with the Brazilian state – unchanged for most of a century – had to be challenged.

Additionally, the aspects of the revolt rooted in the shared history of England and Brazil are inextricably intertwined. For example, it was only because British shipyards in the decades preceding the revolt shifted sales from domestic to international markets that the modern warships used during the Revolta da Chibata were in the possession of the Brazilian navy in the first place. What impact did these new warships have on the revolt? Something as seemingly mundane as a shifting British business model allowed these Brazilian sailors to successfully execute the Revolta da Chibata. Poor black Brazilian sailors initiated the revolt because of their long-standing grievance against and the personal indignity of the use of corporal punishment, mistreatment, and forced service, but without a parallel revolution in the technology of British war ships – or what become Brazilian war ships – how effective could their movement have been? Had the Brazilian navy continued its reliance on nineteenth-century naval technology, could the reclamantes have moved against the state? They may have, as discussed above; smaller movements against corporal punishment had already twice been sparked and quickly extinguished. But could cannonballs fired from sailboats have struck terror into the heart of the population of the Brazilian capital? What percentage of the city would have been threatened? How many cariocas would have even cared?

Maritime wars during the period of Brazilian colony and empire were well known to Rio's population; nineteenth-century navies could blockade a city, but a viable threat to raze one was impossible. The 12-inch guns of the *Minas Geraes* and *São Paulo* were each capable of the near-simultaneous and accurate launch of twelve 850-pound exploding shells at targets miles away. Although the Brazilian navy had only just taken delivery of these multimillion-dollar ships, both their destructive capabilities and their symbolic value to the nation were common knowledge in Brazil and abroad. The power of their new ships had been trumpeted from the covers of Brazilian, European, and American newspapers. A photograph of the dreadnaught *Minas Geraes* appeared on the cover of the March 19, 1910, edition of the *Scientific American* under the headline "The Mighty Armament of the New Brazilian Dreadnaught 'Minas Geraes.'"[1] At the same time the local press trumpeted their acquisition: "The arrival of the *Minas Geraes* is an event for all of Brazil to celebrate. In the giant form of this seafaring colossus comes the supreme symbol of our potency . . . to hear the greetings of those mighty cannons is to hear a voice so vibrant, so full – a new voice, a new consciousness."[2] From the perspective of Brazil's naval elite, the purchase of these ships singlehandedly ushered the institution, and perhaps the nation, into the modern era.

Conversely, the control of the British-built ships would allow faceless desprotegidos to become powerful, and eventually heroic, reclamantes. And Rio's recently rebuilt downtown now provided a tempting target for such powerful ships – in the hands of those looking to threaten the nation's newly acquired sense of modernity. Without the guns of the *Minas Geraes* and *São Paulo,* there would have been no negotiation between rebels and the state, no means by which to compel amnesty from the government, and little reason to gain the attention of the international press. Thus does English shipbuilding – and specifically the policies of W. G. Armstrong's shipyard in Newcastle – play an important role in our understanding of events in Rio de Janeiro in November and December 1910.

Modernization and change did not flow only in one direction – neither solely from England to Brazil, nor only from imperial powers such as Germany or the United States to dependent economies such as those of Argentina, Chile, Japan, and China. In the years between 1890 and 1910, Brazil purchased eight warships from Armstrongs shipyards.[3] Of the foreign powers purchasing ships from Armstrongs during this period, only Japan purchased more.[4] Overall, the massive international contracts signed around the turn of the twentieth century funded by the growing economies of the former colonies made possible the international dominance that companies such as Armstrongs, Krupp, and Vickers achieved in the late nineteenth and early twentieth centuries. As had been the case during the long colonial period, the revolutionary change in modern Europe continued to reflect the economic strength of its former colonies. The societies of the modern Atlantic World were linked in subtler and more historically relevant ways than the often-repeated cause and effect of European technological modernization echoed by Latin American positivists and *científicos* (technocrats) seeking foreign investors.

The Brazilian shipbuilding contract had tangible effects on the economic strength of some of England's largest companies, and on two of England's most productive coastal cities. In Newcastle this massive flow of wealth did more than benefit Armstrong and his investments; it kept men working, it allowed pubs, restaurants, and boarding houses to thrive, it helped Newcastle to profit and expand through the early twentieth century. It may also help to explain the peaceful reception extended to these nonwhite Brazilian naval crews at a time that British port cities were not generally known for their welcoming attitudes toward black foreign visitors. Crews boarded in the city for months at a time while their ships were being built, arriving in significant numbers during the summer of 1909. The sailors had an unprecedented amount of leisure time and a great deal of freedom. While there is limited hard evidence that Newcastle was the source or incubator for their revolutionary ideas, the sailors' contact with the local population would have resulted in growing familiarity with English notions of liberty and justice, both on land and at sea.

THE NAVAL REVOLT OF 1893

Since the conclusion of the Paraguayan War (1864–70), Brazil had faced few international threats, and the navy endured a period of fiscal decline. In the final decades of the Brazilian Empire, there was little money to spend on ships or their maintenance. The navy suffered from the absence of a cohesive national policy and effective central organization. It continued to serve as the state's dumping ground for the nation's orphans, criminals, and troubled boys, and it drew free laborers from throughout the plantation regions of northeast Brazil into poorly paid jobs. The naval elite won little of the political power gained by army officers following the Paraguayan War, but with the declaration of the republic and the hurried legislation by which the new civilian government sought to modernize naval service, change seemed to be on its way. Yet by the end of the century, Brazil's navy had become a disparate collection of ships; sailboats, steamers, and early mechanized "ironsides" of various origins. One Brazilian officer and scholar describes the navy as "a shameful patchwork, and one made of rotten patches."[5] Brazil's finest ships at the time, the second-class battleships *Riachuelo* (launched in 1883) and *Aquidabã* (launched in 1885) were both built by a London-based shipyard Samuda Brothers. Impressive when launched, the ships had become dated. Brazilian naval officers – long-time supporters of the monarchy and its ties to a European tradition – disassociated themselves from the Republican government and the army, which (in the eyes of the admirals) enjoyed an enviable position of privilege in the new government. Their frustration was rooted in the central role that army officers played in the creation and governance of Brazil's early Republic.

An alliance between army officers and members of the Republican Party of São Paulo (*Partido Republicano Paulista*) toppled the Brazilian monarchy on November 15, 1889. Following the coup Marshal Manuel Deodoro da Fonseca, a popular army officer, was appointed head of the provisional government, and many of his fellow army officers were elected to the new constitutional congress. Fonseca's government called for the drafting of a new constitution and on February 24, 1891, the congressional assembly signed the document into law. The assembly then turned to the election of Brazil's first president. The army used its considerable influence to pressure the assembly to "legitimize" Fonseca's presidency. Congress indirectly elected Fonseca president of Brazil, and Marshal Floriano Peixoto as the republic's vice president. Peixoto was also an army officer, but in contrast to Fonseca's traditional support among older military veterans of the Paraguayan War, the vice president enjoyed the support of younger positivist officers who were much more committed to the overall modernization of Brazilian society.

When Fonseca led the army in surrounding the royal palace in November 1889 to expel the Brazilian monarchy from power, he declared: "The people, the army and the navy, in perfect harmony of sentiment with our fellow citizens resident in the provinces, have just decreed the dethronement of the imperial dynasty, and consequently the extinction of the representative monarchical system of government."[6] Apparently that "perfect harmony" between the army and navy was superficial. On November 23, 1891, Admiral Custódio José de Melo threatened to turn Brazil's naval warships against Rio de Janeiro based on Fonseca's arbitrary dismissal of congress on November 3, 1891, and army units in the capital came out in support of the navy. Fonseca, unwilling to give in to the admiral's demands, instead chose to remove himself from office. Vice President Peixoto stepped in and firmly took charge of the federal government, returning congress to power and removing many politicians who had supported Fonseca's attempt to seize power. As a reward for his participation, Admiral Melo was made minister of the navy.[7]

However, Peixoto favored army officials over those in the navy, which led to a split between the president and his minister of the navy. By the end of 1892, sporadic uprisings against the government had broken out in Amazonas, Maranhão, Mato Grosso, Minas Gerais, Rio de Janeiro, and São Paulo. A group of high-ranking military officers representing both the army and navy signed a public letter calling for immediate presidential elections. In response, Peixoto forced them to retire their positions. In April 1893 Admiral Melo resigned his position and publically criticized Peixoto. Criticism of the acting president escalated, and two days after Peixoto's September 4 veto of a law that would have prohibited him from participating in the upcoming presidential elections – acting in concert with a federalist uprising in the Rio Grande do Sul led by gaúcho Silveira Martins – Admiral Melo led the navy against the federal government in the Naval Revolt of 1893. He received important support from Rear Admiral Luis Philipe de Saldanha da Gama, commander of the Naval Academy at Fort Villegaignon and a well-known monarchist sympathizer who, along with his cadets, joined the revolt in December.[8]

This uprising, led by elite officers with clear political outcomes in mind, had considerable impact on the Brazilian navy. Naval historian Robert L. Scheina describes the events: "The admiral's immediate military acquisitions were all the naval units in Rio de Janeiro, many of the most experienced naval officers, and about one fourth of the navy's active-duty enlisted men."[9] The revolt is often presented as the manifestation of naval officers' desire to return to the monarchy and remake the state as an empire. Admiral Saldanha's participation in its leadership certainly lends support to that conclusion. However, the language of the leadership's published manifestos is not entirely clear on that point. It calls for the Brazilian people to hold a plebiscite and to choose what form the Brazilian government should take. Furthermore, the rebels enjoyed the support of some staunch republicans, including that of Senator Ruy Barbosa. Perhaps a more accurate description is that during the power struggle of the early Republic, the naval elite failed to gain significant power in the central government. The army dominated the political scene, and as he took office, Peixoto showed himself unwilling to relinquish his newly won power. Whereas certain naval officers were motivated by their traditional ties to the monarchy, it is likely that just as many were unwilling to sit idly by while the army elite consolidated its hold over the young republic.

Initially, the naval officers involved in the coup enjoyed an important military advantage in Rio de Janeiro. During the naval revolt, the federal government was distracted by the popular uprising in Rio Grande de Sul, where the Republic backed one side while rebel naval officers backed the other. By the end of 1893, rebel forces pushed north from Rio Grande de Sul into Santa Catarina, and in January of the following year they moved on Paraná, from where they planned to take São Paulo. However, slow movement and heavy fighting in Paraná allowed the federal government time to regroup and push the rebel forces back to the south.

With the army fighting the rebels, Rio de Janeiro lacked armed manpower and was vulnerable to the naval forces in Guanabara Bay. Still, the president refused to capitulate to the naval threat; instead, foreign powers in the area came to his defense. Commanders of naval vessels from the United States, Britain, France, Italy, and Portugal moved into defensive position to protect the city from shelling. Although these foreign powers cited humanitarian reasons to explain their actions, no one except the rebels would benefit from an interruption of Rio's commercial trade. Admiral Melo could not take advantage of the military superiority he enjoyed without risking damage to foreign naval vessels. During the seven-month rebellion, President Peixoto brought together warships commanded by loyalists that were scattered in various ports in Brazil and the Rio de la Plata region while at the same time he acquired ships in Europe and the United States. The two recently built sister ships, the *República* and the *Tiradentes,* ordered during the first months of Brazil's republican government, found themselves on opposing sides of the civil war. The *República* was commandeered by mutineers and saw action ramming and sinking the naval transport ship *Rio de Janeiro* with 1,100 men aboard. Its crew would participate in the attempted capture of Santa Catharina toward the end of the rebellion. The *Tiradentes,* at dock in Montevideo when the rebellion broke out, with a crew deemed "untrustworthy," eventually joined the government squadron though it did not participate in actual fighting.

Peixoto had also acquired another ship built in part in the shipyards of Newcastle, the deep-sea destroyer-class torpedo boat *Bueno Ventura*. When the company building it folded and the unfinished ship found its way into the hands of the Defense Vessel Construction Company, Armstrongs acquired it. Completing necessary work and adding improvements to its armor, accommodations, and speed, Armstrongs relaunched it in July 1892 as the *Aurora*. It remained unsold until agents representing the Brazilian government sought to acquire any available warships (as well as some merchant ships they could put to use) as quickly as possible. Armstrongs sold the ship to the Brazilian government in October 1893 and delivered it by steam tow to the naval base at Pernambuco in November. Renamed the *Gustavo Sampaio,* the ship participated in fighting during the revolt.[10]

By May 1894, the revolt was nearing its end, though the outcome would be determined much more by politics and international pressure than by military prowess. Ships under the control of Admiral Saldanha were unable to enforce the blockade of Rio's harbor without drawing fire from better-armed foreign vessels. When the president's fleet arrived in Rio in March 1894, Saldanha recognized that he would be unable to prevail against the combined firepower of the city's forts and the loyalist fleet. After unsuccessfully attempting to negotiate terms with Peixoto's government that would allow for the exile of his officers and spare the lives of his men, on March 12, Saldanha and his supporters abandoned their ships, seeking and receiving protection on Portuguese vessels in Guanabara Bay. To the south, on the night of April 14, the rebels' flagship, the second-class battleship *Aquidabā,* came under torpedo attack from Peixoto's newly acquired *Gustavo Sampaio* in Santa Catharina Bay. When the torpedo breached the ship's hull, the crew scuttled, beached, and abandoned the ship, after rendering its guns inoperable. On April 16, Admiral Melo and his supporters, who were in Curitiba trying to coordinate the rebellion in the south, sailed into Argentine waters and surrendered to authorities.[11]

Having failed to achieve their goals, the men who led the Naval Revolt of 1893 gave up. Their revolt badly damaged the position of the Brazilian navy. Instead of gaining power within the new republic, the navy's shortcoming resulted in a decade of isolation from Brazil's republican government. The officers' gamble cost the navy dearly; the government refused to allocate funding for purchases of new ships and neglected to maintain existing ones. Both officers and enlisted men were held suspect – whether or not they had participated in the revolt; the government simply assumed that those who had not joined lacked the opportunity to join their compatriots. As we have seen, the number of enlisted men dropped by two-thirds during the year of the Naval Revolt. The number of sailors serving in the Brazilian navy would return to the 1892 level only in 1908, two years before the Revolta da Chibata, marking more than a decade of stagnation as the navy atoned for its sins against the federal government.

THE NAVAL RENOVATION PROGRAMS

The 1904 Naval Renovation Program (Projecto de Reaparelhamento Naval) was a plan by which Brazil's national government hoped to modernize its navy. Influenced by positivism and obsessed with modernization, the Brazilian elite of the era committed to replacing the entire fleet with state-of-the-art warships to reestablish the tarnished honor of Brazil's now dilapidated navy. After a decade of isolation a new generation of ministers and politicians sought reconciliation with the naval elite. Both sides would benefit from such a rapprochement: a strong modern navy meant prestige and money for naval officers, but the state itself shared equally in the navy's prestige. At the time, nations sent naval ships to attend foreign celebrations. Those modern naval processions were in fact the single most visible evidence of a nation's standing and potential; their presence in foreign ports was a spectacle of diplomacy and nation-state during what was an era of high nationalism. Conversely, a navy suffering disrepair was a burden to the state in an international context. A 1904 U.S. Intelligence Report stated: "Neither the Army or Navy is regarded as efficient. At the time of our visit their ships appeared to be in poor condition. . . . The cruiser *Deodoro* ran out of coal while making passage from Montevideo to Rio de Janeiro recently, and succeeded with difficulty in making Santa Catherina [Island]. The enlisted force is made up almost exclusively of negroes."[12]

The program was negotiated and announced during the presidency of Rodrigues Alves in 1904 by Barão do Rio Branco (born José Maria de Silva Paranhos), a man best known for authoring the "free womb" law of 1871 and for his negotiation over Brazil's borders at the end of the nineteenth century. Rear Admiral Júlio Cesar de Norinha, then minister of the navy, championed the program, and Federal Deputy Laurindo Pita led its passage through congress. Thus it was a collaborative agreement, planned, modified, and accepted jointly by the naval elite and the federal government. The project was possible only because Brazil's exports of coffee and rubber were strong at this time, which provided capital for the purchase of the new battleships that promised to restore the domestic and international image of Brazil's navy.

That the collaboration was effective does not imply that the Brazilian political and naval elite were necessarily in agreement on how best to modernize the navy. The form that this renovated navy should take was deeply contested by two groups of Brazilian politicians and naval officers, between those who wanted a navy that better represented Brazil's domestic needs and those who wanted ships that would further Brazil's international image. Naval Minister Norinha represented the first of the two schools of thought, those who wanted to see a larger navy consisting of many smaller, faster, more navigable ships that would effectively patrol, defend, and attack throughout Brazil's vast coastal region, rivers, and estuaries. The second group pressured for a navy centered around a smaller number of battleships but ones that were much larger and more heavily armored (more impressive in foreign ports, but somewhat less useful on the Brazilian coast). With the December 14, 1904, passage of the initial decree, the first group, interested in coastal efficiency, won the day.

Initially the plan called for the purchase of as many as twenty-eight ships, including three battleships, three cruiser-class battleships, six destroyers, twelve torpedo boats, and three submarines.[13] The first contract for the construction of six of these ships went to the Newcastle shipyards of Armstrongs, which had already established a history of providing vessels for the Brazilian navy. Armstrongs had built both the protected cruiser *República* and the light cruiser *Tiradentes* between 1891 and 1893 and provided the Brazilian government with the deep-sea torpedo boat

Gustavo Sampaio in 1896, and had concluded negotiations begun during the revolt by contracting in November 1894 to build an additional three cruisers, only one of which, the *Almirante Barrosa,* ever saw duty with the Brazilian navy.[14]

The program represented a sizable investment and undertaking for the Brazilian government; the law allocated more than £4.2 million initial spending for new construction, of which two-fifths was to be spent in 1906.[15] Because of the large number of ships to be built – and to allow English firms to retain control over this segment of the developing naval market without threat from foreign firms such as Germany's Krupp – the Armstrongs shipyard shared the contract with shipyard competitor Vickers. However, in early 1906, three events took place that ensured that this contract would never be fulfilled as negotiated: an explosion on board a Brazilian battleship in January; the launch of the British HMS *Dreadnought* in February; and the election of Brazilian president Afonso Pena in March.

On the night of January 21, 1906, Naval Minister Norinha headed a commission tasked with the inspection of a proposed site for a new arsenal at Jacarepaguá near Rio de Janeiro. At 10:45 PM on January 21, 1906, the powder magazine on the second-class battleship *Aquidabã* exploded, quickly sending the ship to the bottom – reportedly within three minutes. Two hundred twelve men died and an additional thirty-six were wounded.[16] Although Norinha survived, among the dead were three admirals, two ship's captains, and Minister Norinha's son. Ideologically, the members of the naval elite killed that day were the same men who fought and won the acquisition of smaller and faster ships more suitable for coastal defense. With their death those men who challenged Norinha over the nature of the Naval Renovation Program found themselves in the ascendancy. Following the March presidential election, Alexandrino Faria de Alencar (then a senator and prominent supporter of the plan to purchase fewer, larger battleships) began campaigning against the implementation of the Norinha plan. By July Alencar pressured the Navy and War Committee of the House of Deputies to reconsider the 1904 plan in light of both the launch of the HMS *Dreadnought* and the importance of naval technology in the recent war between Russia and Japan. When in

November 1906 Alencar became minister of the navy, he pushed through congressional modifications to the Armstrongs contract, reducing the number of ships to be purchased while increasing their size in a way that was unimaginable when the original contract had been signed. This change would make the naval renewal's impact on the region and in Europe much greater.[17]

ARMSTRONGS AND ENGLISH SHIPBUILDING

Unlike the Brazilian navy's political and economic isolation in the last decades of the nineteenth century, for the maritime forces of Europe the period was one of intense growth. The wooden ships of the British navy that had sailed to the Crimean War in 1854 were outfitted with smooth-bore wrought-iron muzzle-loading guns that fired round shot, ordnance not greatly different from that used at the Battle of Trafalgar. However, it was during the Crimean War that European naval technology began to transform, both in the seaworthiness of ships and the destructive power of their weapons. Though these changes were not introduced in time to affect the outcome of the Crimean War, they are intimately linked to the growing power of England and its empire. Britain's new sense of its role in the world is captured in this editorial from an 1896 *London Quarterly Review*: "Our social progress, our international influence, our power 'to help the right and heal the wild world's wrongs,' our missions as the leaders and organizers of the backward and chaotic races that have come beneath our rule, and what is dearer to the hearts of Christian Englishmen, the opportunity to give to all the world the Gospel that has made us all free; all these, and every good we can desire ourselves or wish to share with men, depend upon our maritime supremacy."[18]

Because of its empire and global commercial interests, Britain was deeply committed to overwhelming military superiority. As ships changed from wood to steel, fewer nations were capable of producing modern weapons of war. At the turn of the nineteenth century, any state with access to timber and men educated in ship design could build warships; at the turn of the twentieth, in order to compete, a nation required iron and coal resources, manufacturing capacity, and engineering skill,

ideally all in the same place, and significant capital investment. As one
historian observes, "Naval [arms] races between Britain and foreign nations, increased fears of invasions after the 1880s, and heightened imperial anxieties over Britain's performance in the Boer War . . . led to
ever-increasing naval estimates."[19] Britain and its shipyards managed
to retain a dominant position in shipbuilding until the early twentieth
century, but doing so became increasingly difficult and expensive. By
authorizing the modernization of its navy, Brazil's naval elite found itself
in the midst of an international arms race in which the cutting edge of
both weapon and vessel design changed almost daily. Rolf Hobson suggests that "qualitative one-upmanship made it more tempting to secure
superiority by designing the fleet of the future rather than risking the
existing fleet in the destruction of its rival."[20]

Naval arms races became technological rivalries between national
ship design and construction programs. Brazil's purchase of a new navy
took place in the context of the rivalry between Britain and Germany
that was becoming monstrously expensive and had grown increasingly
unpopular among British government officials, who had difficulty justifying the nation's Two Power Standard. Instituted in 1889, this standard held that Britain should maintain superiority over the second and
third most powerful navies in the world combined. In the 1890s, facing
the fact that it could not retain numerical superiority over the rest of
the world, British policymakers opted to retain numerical superiority
where it mattered most – in the Atlantic, North Sea, and Mediterranean.
It ceded dominance in the Caribbean to the United States and, through
negotiating treaties, to Japan in the Pacific. Elsewhere, Britain had hoped
to retain qualitative superiority.

Constant technological progress became key to British naval success, but it was a commitment difficult to fund and difficult to maintain,
in large measure because, as historian Bernard Brophy observed, "progress in ordinance was the driving force – to the point that warships that
were unsinkable on the drawing board had become vulnerable by the
time they were launched three years later."[21] That need for qualitative
superiority led Britain to seek out international markets. Sales to foreign
navies kept its shipyards staffed and productive even when the British
navy would not buy all they produced.

One of the shipyards that benefited greatly from these new markets was W. G. Armstrong and Co. William Armstrong had his start in engineering in 1846 when the young lawyer resigned from his law practice, opened offices in downtown Newcastle, and purchased a seven-acre strip of land in Elswick, a mile and a half upriver due west from Newcastle. For eighteen years he enjoyed success working in the nonmilitary fields of hydraulics, cranes, and bridge building, and in 1859 he became involved with munitions production for the British government. In 1864, he and a group of investors established their privately held engine and ordnance works on his site in Elswick. In 1864 Armstrongs began building ships and quickly came to dominate the British overseas market. Between 1868 and 1927, the company became the largest producer of warships in Britain. More importantly, they built more warships for the foreign market than did the other eleven major British shipyards combined. Forty-two percent of the tonnage Armstrongs produced in this period was sold to foreign navies. William Armstrong's personal growth as an international arms dealer offers insight into British naval dominance in the early twentieth century.[22]

W. G. Armstrong's first opportunity to produce war materials for the British military had come during the Crimean War, when his company was asked to design underwater mines to assist in clearing out the hulls of sunken Russian ships that blocked access to Sevastopol harbor. Armstrong designed them with innovative electric fuses and tested them on his personal Jesmond property, where he held an afternoon tea for the principal employees from the Elswick yards: "It was a very pleasant function, and greatly enjoyed by all the guests. The mines, planted in different parts of the field, exploded in the most exhilarating manner, and after tea had been served out, the party separated, delighted with the afternoon's entertainment."[23] Once sold, the mines were never used for their original application; instead of blowing up sunken ships in Sevastopol harbor, the military unsuccessfully attempted to use them to destroy damaged docks.

Next Armstrong designed a breech-loading gun with a steel inner tube grooved to accept a fitted projectile, and, after successful testing, the design was submitted to the War Office in 1856. Armstrong recalls the origins of its development:

In the months of December, 1854, my friend Mr. [J. M.] Rendel[24]... submitted
to Sir James Graham a communication he had received from me, suggesting
the expediency of enlarging the ordinary rifle to the standard of a field gun, and
using elongated projectiles of lead instead of balls of cast iron.... I deemed it expedient to confine myself, in the first instance, to the production of a single gun,
but to make that one gun the test not only of the principles I had recommended,
but also of the feasibility of loading field pieces at the breach, and applying
certain mechanical arrangements to counteract recoil, and facilitate pointing of
the gun.[25]

This gun would change the face of modern warfare.

Best known for innovations in nursing carried out by Florence
Nightingale and for the Charge of the Light Brigade, the Crimean War
was also the last war fought with premodern weapons, and it led to a
revolution in armament. William George Armstrong made his name
at the forefront of that revolution. In a hand-typed draft of his 1905 history of Armstrongs, Alfred Cochrane (then company secretary, son-in-
law of then-chairman Andrew Noble, and former cricketer) described
Armstrong's entry into the production of weapons: "The Crimea was to
have a more important influence upon Elswick than this. At that time
the minds of men were turned towards war and war material, and not
unnaturally the active intellect of Mr. Armstrong was attracted by the
subject. More as an amusement for his leisure than for any other reason,
he began to consider the possibility of improving the heavy artillery of
the British Service, which had hardly made any advance since the time
of the Peninsula and Waterloo, forty years earlier."[26] Although there
were many innovative details to its design, two things best define the
revolutionary aspect of his new gun. Rather than round balls, it fired an
elongated shell through a rifled tube; the shell fit into the barrel of the
gun snugly, and the coiled rifling of the barrel spun the shell at it exited
the tube, greatly increasing its accuracy. A 12-pound shell fired at two
miles was more accurate than a cannonball fired at half that distance.
Armstrong's second innovation was making the gun a breach-loader.
The fit of the shell into the barrel required tight tolerances; for the rifling
to take the shell and spin it as exploding gunpowder drove it out of the
barrel, the shell (which had a soft lead coating that was forced into the
shape of the grooves of the barrel) had to be slightly larger than the inner
diameter of the barrel. Therefore it was simply impossible to drive the
shell into the front of the barrel as balls had been driven into cannons

with a damper. Instead, Armstrong designed his gun with a removable breech-screw at the rear; the shell was loaded into the gun, followed by a disk-shaped sack of gunpowder, which was then ignited.

The first gun he delivered in 1854 was small and fired a 3-pound shell. That was quickly replaced with a 5-pounder in 1856 and a 12-pounder tested in 1857. By 1858, in field tests Armstrong's upgraded 18-pounder was described by the British secretary of state for war in a report to the House of Commons: "The accuracy . . . at 3,000 yards was as seven to one compared with that of the common gun at 1,000 yards; while at 1,000 yards it would hit an object every time which was struck by the common guns only once in fifty-seven times; therefore, at equal distance, the Armstrong gun was fifty-seven times as accurate as out common artillery."[27] In comparison with the established muzzle-loading cannon, the new gun was lighter, used less powder, and had a longer range, and its initial cost was only slightly higher. Armstrong was confident that he could deliver the gun well below the cost of a traditional 12-pounder. His gun design would soon revolutionize warship armament as it had field artillery. Though not put into production in time for use in the Crimean War, it soon won Armstrong both high position in the War Office and knighthood.[28]

In February 1859, Armstrong was appointed engineer of rifled ordnance to the War Department, and the Government Ordnance Factory at Woolwich was turned over to his management in order to produce his new gun for the British military. In 1858, Armstrong and his partners built a new company specifically to produce Armstrong's gun. The Elswick Ordnance Company was located on land immediately adjoining Armstrong's Engine Works to the east, where he manufactured industrial cranes and hydraulics. In lieu of his government salary and his position overseeing the production of all guns, Armstrong gave up his financial claim in this part of the firm, though he reserved the right to rejoin it at any future moment he saw fit. According to the company history, Armstrong agreed to give the government his patents and not sell his guns to any foreign nation, in exchange for a government guarantee of his investment.[29]

Eighteen fifty-nine was a good time to open a gun manufacturing business; production at Armstrongs was unable to keep up with demand. They produced one hundred guns in 1859 and approximately three times that many the following year, but that was just a hint of what was to come, by late 1860, the government halted production of other artillery at Woolwich, and under Armstrong's leadership, both the government-owned Woolwich and the privately held Elswick were exclusively producing Armstrong's design as quickly as possible, with Elswick receiving half of the orders. Between them, the two had produced less than £8,000 worth of gun orders in fiscal year 1858–59; between 1858 and 1863, their combined production of Armstrongs breech-loading guns equaled £2,560,000. From that point forward the fortunes of Elswick were tied to the British military.[30]

INTERNATIONALIZATION OF ARMSTRONGS

Other gun manufacturers cried foul over this developing relationship between Sir George Armstrong, a private arms manufacturer, and the British government. Armstrong had not been the only engineer asked to work on a new gun design during the Crimean War. The war ministry invested tens of thousands of pounds to promote new gun technology, and the 1858 War Office field tests against their traditional field gun included a gun designed by Joseph Whitworth of Manchester, which the Armstrong gun also handedly defeated. Whitworth became Armstrong's most important, or at least most vocal, rival. Whitworth also had an established history in government-sponsored research on rifled guns, and he advised the government on rifled small arms during the Crimean War. Because his ties to government research ended when Armstrong's breech-loader gained the support of the British military, Whitworth continued a two-pronged attack on Armstrong's position. He continued developing firearms and submitting them for testing, establishing an arms career providing rifles to the French military and selling field artillery pieces to both sides during the U.S. Civil War, but his company never rose to Armstrongs' level of sales and international prestige. Whitworth and Co. did win several contracts to sell ordnance to the Brazilian government in 1862–63. The Brazilians had first come to Armstrongs to buy guns, but the British government refused to authorize this foreign sale. In the short term, Whitworth and Co. enjoyed a technological high point on September 25, 1862, when his 300-pounder became the first gun to pierce the 4.5-inch armor known as the *Warrior* target – representing the modern ironclad ships – thereby beating Armstrongs to that symbolic victory.[31]

Joseph Whitworth drew on his powerful press and government contacts to undermine Armstrong's ties to the British military. Beginning in 1861, there were parliamentary hearings looking into accusations of impropriety, government assessments of the quality of the guns being produced, and a back-and-forth between Whitworth's and Armstrong's representatives in books, magazines, and newspapers critiquing one another's gun designs. Following a protracted investigation in Parliament, and in spite of producing a better gun design and never having been found guilty of any impropriety, in the fall of 1862, Elswick Ordnance Company lost all government contracts and found itself in serious financial difficulty. Their contract prohibited them from selling to any buyer other than the British government without permission; after selling nearly £1,000,000 worth of guns in four years, the company had only just over £6,000 worth of orders in 1863–64. In December, the Elswick partners filed a claim invoking guarantees that the government was obligated to purchase the companies' assets for £137,000, which was turned down. On February 5, 1863, Armstrong resigned his government position and returned to Newcastle to negotiate the level at which Elswick investors would be reimbursed by the government, eventually agreeing on £85,000 with all movable machinery being transferred to Woolwich.[32]

Sir George Armstrong was at this time fifty-three years old and a wealthy man; at this point he seemed perfectly content to retire to his recently purchased estate in Northumberland. However, his investors and senior employees at Elswick pressured him to do otherwise. They had gambled a great deal on his eventual success, and he in turn felt some responsibility for their future wellbeing. A 1905 internal company history of the firm describes 1863 as being

> certainly the most critical in the annals of the firm. The absolute stoppage of orders threw a quantity of valuable machinery idle, and the métier of the Ordnance Company as a factory for Government supply was gone. To make matters worse, the great and unnecessary delay on the part of the Government in releasing the firm from the other side of the agreement, the side which limited their manufacture of guns to England alone, prevented Elswick accepting foreign orders. The excellent step was at once taken of amalgamating the Ordnance

and Engineering Works into one Company.... The new firm, under the title of
Sir W.G. Armstrong and Company set at once about making for themselves a
foreign connection.[33]

In his unpublished history, A. R. Fairbairn quotes a personal letter from
J. M. Rendel's son, Stuart, describing Lord Armstrong's reservations
regarding the shifting of sales into the international market:

> He had taken a knighthood . . . and a well-paid office under the War Office, and
> that therefore, he could not possibly, as soon as he had left office, start upon the
> supply of his guns to foreign powers. [Stuart Rendel] argued in rejoinder that
> his first patriotic duty was to maintain the prestige of the system he had induced
> the Government to adopt and in which he still believed; that the manufacture of
> arms for foreign powers was far from an unpatriotic act, for that the country was
> benefited to the extent to which its experience and powers of production were
> increased, whereas foreign countries were disadvantaged to the extent to which
> they were dependent on us for their munitions of war . . . to which Armstrong
> replied "If these are your opinions you are perfectly at liberty to try to give them
> effect, and if you can obtain any orders for Elswick by all means do so, and to
> make it worth your while we will give you five percent commission upon the
> orders you bring us."[34]

From the new company's earliest days its management looked beyond
the shores of Britain for their market. This event marks the origin of
international arms sales by British gun makers. It led to the Brazilian
contract to rebuild its navy, and it laid the groundwork for the Revolta
da Chibata.

International sales were not the result of some British government
policy or an agreement by the various munitions makers or shipyards
in recognition of the threat that a Krupp monopoly on foreign sales
represented to England. Instead, it was the response of an individual
disgruntled English arms manufacturer facing the looming failure of
the company he built from the ground up. Armstrong would say, "From
that time, the firm had no alternative but to commence a new career,
based on foreign support, and it was by that support – and not by government patronage – that [Sir W. G. Armstrong and Co.] was established."[35]
Armstrongs (under his control and under the helm of later leaders after his death at the age of ninety in 1900) became Britain's dominant
force in international arms trading, going head-to-head in international
sales against the German arms manufacturer Krupp, then the dominant

provider of international arms.[36] Armstrongs' shift to foreign customers would be couched in nationalism and patriotism; it was declared to be good for Britain, Britain's industrial economy, and (eventually) the British navy. Indeed, because the manufacturing of weapons for foreign markets was subject to the sanction of the government, "not a ship, not a gun, not a shell or fuze could be put in hand without the prior permission of the British authorities. That sanction was given because such work increased the capacity and efficiency of the country's armament production; it rendered the foreign country dependent on England for its naval vessels or armament, while the British Government had the advantage of every improvement and increased efficiency that was made."[37]

It did not take long for Armstrong to make his mark in international arms sales. In January 1864, Armstrong quietly negotiated the sale of five large cannons to the state of Massachusetts to be used by the Union army in the U.S. Civil War. At the same time, his agent, Stuart Rendel, the lawyer who had represented Armstrong during the inquest into his government contracts, was negotiating gun sales with representatives of the Confederate states. Soon thereafter, Rendel bought a 4 percent share of Armstrongs and became its London manager while continuing in his role as salesman. He quickly signed contracts for sales to the governments of Italy, Egypt, Turkey, and Chile. He also tried to negotiate sales to the governments of Russia, Austria, and Prussia, but Krupp took measures to retain control of those markets. By the end of the decade, Armstrongs had strong sales in Chile, Denmark, Egypt, Italy, Peru, and Turkey, while Krupp was established in Austria, Belgium, Holland, Spain, Prussia, and Russia. It was in this competitive market that the Brazilian government looked to rebuild its navy.[38]

GROWTH OF NAVAL PRODUCTION

The immediate response to Armstrong's bigger guns was a rush to develop ships capable of carrying these arms, and more importantly, outfitting such ships with armor to defend against the improved firepower. Armstrong had designed his early guns for use in the field by the British army, and as he increased their size, they were adopted for use in land fortification. The transfer of this weaponry to ships soon followed.

Armstrong now applied his experience in hydraulic engineering, acquired from his crane production, to the manipulation of the increasingly enormous guns under production. The application of technology was far more important to naval production than it could be for ground troops. "Warships are little more than floating gun platforms," writes Marshall Bastable in *Arms and the State*, "and naval architecture is determined by gun technology."[39] That technology had changed little since the sixteenth-century rise of British sea power.

Then in the late nineteenth century, all that changed. The battleships steaming from their berths at the turn of the twentieth century bore almost no resemblance to the navy that had sailed off to fight the Crimean War less than fifty years earlier. The industrial revolution drove a revolution in naval technology – a revolution in which Armstrong played no small part. As weapons and ships revolutionized, so did the industry that produced them. Western navies turned to shipyards that had previous experience with iron and steel. Several British companies – most notably Armstrongs and Whitworth and Co., and later Vickers – consolidated holdings in steel, railways, and ship production,[40] and through their control of each level of production, came to dominate the British production of armaments through the era of wwi.[41]

The first technology transformation in naval warfare took place in 1854–55 when the French and British together built what they called "floating batteries" to serve in the Crimean War. They were slow, capable only of four knots, and difficult to maneuver, but they were protected with four inches of iron plating bolted to eighteen inches of timber, and each carried sixteen 68-pounder guns. These slow, ugly batteries did exactly what they were designed for: they were impervious to the guns of Russian forts – the projectiles of the day simply bounced off them – so they roamed unfettered, destroying supply lines and forts at will. The year after their introduction, the tsar agreed to terms.[42]

A more recognizable transformation began a year later with the launch in 1856 of HMS *Terror* by Palmer Brothers in its Tyneside Jarrow shipyard. The Crimean War ended before the ship was commissioned, but this vessel marked the beginning of a revolution in warship building that far surpassed simple armor plating. *Terror*'s hull was protected by 4-inch iron plate and carried sixteen 300-pounder guns. But the real innovation was that steam power had replaced sail.

Armstrong saw the writing on the wall. However, it was impossible at the time to build ships of any significant size at Elswick; the river Tyne upriver from Newcastle was shallow, and the dredging technology that would eventually deepen the river was not yet available. Rather than starting from scratch acquiring a shipyard, Armstrong sought a partnership with an existing firm for the production of ships and signed an agreement with Charles Mitchell, who owned the Low Walker yard. As of 1867, Mitchell's firm would build the ships, and Armstrongs would build and install the weaponry. Their first ship, HMS *Staunch*, was completed in 1867 and was contracted for the British admiralty. As described by Armstrong in a letter to the *Times* of London, *Staunch* was a weapon "necessary for defense of our seaports" against the intrusion of a heavily armed warship.

> This vessel, though a mere barge in point of size, carries a 12½-ton gun, the movements of which are effected by steam power, so that a very small crew suffices to working it. The boat is propelled by twin screws, which give her such a power of turning that she can change the direction of her large gun as easily and quickly as if it were mounted on a turntable. She is encumbered with no armour, because her safety lies in her smallness, which renders her difficult to hit. . . . Finally she is cheap. The cost of a couple of ironclad frigates would furnish a hundred Staunches.[43]

Given such access to the press, Armstrongs was able to advertise to the world how their inexpensive new gunship could make the modern navies of the world suddenly obsolete. Expensive and vulnerable coastal batteries were no longer necessary; any navy that purchased these light, fast, cheap, destructive gunships could face off against a modern invading army.

Armstrongs fueled the naval race that would preoccupy modern states, their naval officers, and eventually their citizens well into the twentieth century. Never again would weapons technology remain as unchanged as it had during the classic age of sail. New guns and technologies were constantly introduced, and from this point on all modern navies were at risk of overnight obsolescence. If gunships such as *Staunch*

could sink any modern warship, then all warships would have to be rede-
signed with protective armor. The obvious response to improved armor
was building larger gunships capable of penetrating the hulls of the new
warships. The obsolescence brought about by each of these technological
advances was a costly development for the governments and navies of
the world, but it was also an opportunity for a nation like Brazil, with its
booming foreign trade providing the cash by which to acquire a competitive modern navy.

As soon as Armstrong had the prototype of HMS *Staunch,* he built
twenty-seven additional ships at Mitchell's Low Walker yard based more
or less on this design. Five were sold to the British admiralty, but the
majority found markets abroad: two went to Holland, eleven to China,
five to the Australian colonies, and two to Italy. Later two more were sold
to Argentina and one to Siam. In actuality, the design of the unarmored
gunship suffered serious flaws; the ships were too heavily gunned for
their size, and due to their lightness and lack of turrets, they were hard to
fire accurately from any significant distance. Their lack of armor quickly
made them vulnerable to even smaller ships armed with lightweight
rapid-firing weapons such as the Gatling gun, a gun Armstrongs won
the license to produce in Britain in 1870. *Staunch*'s actual military importance was limited, but it marked Armstrongs' entrance into shipbuilding
and international sales.[44]

As orders increased in the first years of the 1880s, Armstrong acted
to formally introduce naval architecture and the direct manufacturing
of warships by his company through a merger with Mitchell, and in November 1882 a new limited company was formed: Sir W. G. Armstrong,
Mitchell and Co. It was announced that engineering and munitions
would occur at Elswick whereas shipbuilding would continue at the
Low Walker yard. However, by early 1883, the partners began work on
a freestanding shipyard at Elswick, and eventually agreed that military
vessels would be produced at Elswick. Though there was criticism of the
merger from partners – especially from George Rendel, who would soon
leave the company for a position in the admiralty – Armstrongs had absorbed a competitor and radically expanded the company's shipbuilding
potential output just as the market for maritime production was set to
explode. Between 1881 and 1900, employment at Armstrongs grew from

Table 4.1. Brazilian Ships Built by Armstrongs

Ship	Year	Type	Weight (tons)
Pará	1891	Launch	29
Tiradentes	1892	Cruiser	728
República	1893	Cruiser	1,260
Gustavo Sampaio	1893	Gunboat	465
Almirante Barroso	1897	Cruiser	3,437
Amazonas (sold to USA)	1898	Cruiser	3,457
Minas Geraes	1910	Battleship	19,281
Bahia	1910	Scout	3,100
Rio Grande de Sul	1910	Scout	3,100

Source: "Ships built at Elswick & Walker, notes on," Doc. No. 811, Vickers Archive, Cambridge University Library.

approximately 4,000 to nearly 23,000 men; profits in 1883 were £144,000, whereas in 1900 they had grown to £664,000. In 1897, following Joseph Whitworth's death, Armstrong absorbed his former competitor's arms company. By the turn of the twentieth century, Armstrongs had moved to the forefront of the British shipbuilding industry.[45]

In the years following the merger of Elswick and the Low Walker yards, the patterns of international sale expanded. Between 1885 and 1914, Elswick launched eighty-one ships, as well as several ships and submarines that were completed at the Walker yards. The British admiralty contracted for thirty-two; the remainder were sold to Austria, Italy, China, Spain, Romania, Argentina, Japan, Chile, Portugal, the United States, Norway, Turkey, and Brazil.[46] (See table 4.1.)

A modern navy was more than a symbolic expression of wartime power. Naval strength was the primary means by which to demonstrate a nation's ability to influence distant nations, diplomatically or militarily. It would become a great source of pride for Brazilians that theirs was the only Latin American nation to participate in both of the twentieth century's great wars. Brazil's investment in a professional navy demonstrated to the world that it wished to be considered among the great nations of the world. It also had a tangible impact on British shipping, as noted in a July 1904 article in the *Newcastle Daily Journal:* "At a time when the shipbuilding industry is very quiet, it is interesting to know that a Brazilian commission is in this country with the object of placing

orders for the Brazilian Navy. These offers will include three battleships
... of 13,000 tons each, three armoured cruisers ... of 9,500 tons each;
six destroyers of 400 tons; six torpedo boats, 130 tons; six torpedo boats
50 tons; three submarines; and one transporter, 6,000 tons. The majority
of these orders will be placed in Great Britain."[47]

Even though the original plan to buy as many as twenty-eight new
ships, at a potential cost of $31.5 million, was never implemented, the re-
vised contract of 1906 was even more striking for the British shipyards.[48]
Initially, the largest ships would have been three 13,000-ton battleships.
As impressive as that order was, the completion of the 18,000-ton HMS
Dreadnought in 1906 led to a radical change, not only to the Brazilian
naval contract, but to the production of warships in general. HMS
Dreadnought, with its battery of ten 12-inch guns and maximum speed
of twenty-one knots, so changed naval design that all subsequent battleships took on the name of "dreadnought," whereas all previous ships
were dismissed as "pre-dreadnought." Brazilian officers and political
officials modified the contract to include three 20,000-ton dreadnought-
type battleships (at £2M each) along with two cruiser-type ships of 3,100
tons apiece (about £1M for the pair).[49] This would mean that at a time
when England had only one dreadnought of 18,000-tons, Brazil placed
an order – the first order anywhere – for three.

It was orders of this size and scope that gave Armstrongs its dominance during this period, and it was due in no small part to the role of
such privately owned shipyards that England enjoyed such maritime
supremacy. Brazil, along with other developing nations with pretensions
to international military power, helped assure Britain's rule of the seas.
In a private letter dated October 2, 1908, that J.M. Falkner, Esq., wrote
to Lord Stuart Rendel – both men were members of the board of directors of Armstrongs – Falkner made note of that fact even when, after
the completion of the first two dreadnoughts, Brazil sought to delay or
cancel the purchase of the third: "I feel a distinct and probably foolishly
quixotic, sympathy with these people who have given us an order at
which the world of business stood stupefied – who by this order have im-
mensely strengthened our prestige – who have out-Heroded Herod and
by these gigantic ships have set all the other navies hard at work to follow
Elswick's lead."[50] The impact of Brazil's contract arguably challenges the

traditional neocolonial interpretation of the balance of economic relations between Britain and Brazil.

Two of the dreadnoughts, as well as two cruiser-class battleships, were to be built at the Armstrongs yard in Elswick. Through a somewhat murky profit-sharing agreement between Armstrongs and its greatest British rival, Vickers, an additional dreadnought was to be built with Vickers providing the basic shell of the ship and the engines and Armstrongs all guns, ordnance, and armor. Vickers would also supply the engines for the ships being built at Armstrongs. The method by which profits would be divided was unclear and would be debated for years. The contract for the third dreadnought, originally called the *Rio de Janeiro*, was never fulfilled. It was instead sold to Turkey; though when WWI began, the British Royal Navy retained the rights to that ship, which was renamed the *HMS Agincourt*.[51]

Across the Atlantic, the contract led the nations of South America into a local arms race of their own, which echoed the one that raged between England and Germany. European governments had long subsidized their "private" shipyards by inviting Latin American officers for instruction and training in their naval facilities. These sales benefited European (especially British) interests, both political and commercial, and until this time, Europeans had cornered the market on the production of warships, excluding the fledgling North American shipyards from any international sales. However, the 1904 contract touched off a skirmish between Brazil, Argentina, and Chile that would result in massive contracts being signed and in the United States entering the international arms market with its first successful contract to produce warships.

For a short time following the struggle for independence, thanks to the aggressive leadership of Admiral Thomas Cochrane, Brazil had the largest and most modern fleet in South America, but during the first decade of the First Republic, Argentina and Chile outspent Brazil; this was in large part related to the Brazilian republican government's withdrawal of economic support following the navy's involvement in the Anti-Republican Revolt of 1893.[52] When the massiveness of the 1904 project became public, Chile and Argentina canceled a 1902 nonaggression pact by which they had agreed to limit naval armament for five years. In September 1907, the Argentine cabinet announced they would put

forward a naval armaments appropriations bill of $35 million – this from
a government that faced a $7 million deficit and that would be forced
to take out foreign loans to float the debt. By the time the chamber of
deputies worked through their issues in August 1908, the appropriation
had ballooned to $55 million.

The representatives of international arms concerns swarmed to Buenos Aires like mosquitoes. Argentina initially made an offer to purchase
the contract for one of Brazil's battleships, thus achieving parity without
actually having to buy two ships, but when this offer was rejected, Argentina made an offer for tenders. For the first time, under William Howard
Taft's leadership and financial backing, the United States entered the
fray. Argentina eventually ordered two dreadnought battleships from
the United States, each with a full armament of 12-inch guns. Chile in
response ordered two dreadnoughts from Armstrongs, but these were
to have 14-inch guns. Once Brazil saw that their third dreadnaught, the
Rio de Janeiro, would be obsolete by the time they took delivery, they
sold that contract to Turkey and instead placed an order for the *Riachuelo,* with massive (though impractical) 15-inch guns. The only thing
that stopped all of this from a continuing escalation was the start of the
World War, and the depression that followed the war kept it from resum-
ing. Argentina did take delivery of two ships as w w i broke out, but the
rest of the contracts remained unfulfilled.[53]

BUILDING A DREADNOUGHT

Brazil just happened to have an open contract with Armstrongs at the
right time, putting them first on the list to purchase dreadnoughts.
The shipwrights had in fact already begun executing Brazil's original
1904 contract. The naval architect responsible for their design and the
management of the Elswick yard at the time was J. R. Perrett. In his
November 15, 1906, Report to the Meeting of Directors in London, he
explained that both of the smaller battleships had been laid down, and
that the "framing in the shops for the first vessel is well advanced, whilst
about 7,000 tons of material have been delivered," while "corresponding
progress has been made with the work on the Brazilian Battleship at Barrow."[54] In the following report two months later, he described stopping

all work on the ships until January 7, 1907, when the revised design had been accepted and construction on the new design "re-commenced" when the new keel was relaid in May of that year.[55]

According to Perrett, work proceeded smoothly on the ship through the first report of 1908, at which time framing and plating to the height of the main deck was largely complete, and they were about to start "fixing armour plates." His prediction to the directors was for an initial launch in April 1908. Additionally, they laid the hull for the cruiser *Bahia* and hoped to move those ships along quickly as well. But his next report, dated March 19, 1908, begins:

> The work generally in the Shipyard has been very seriously interfered with by the strike of Shipwrights, Joiners and Drillers ... and the stoppage of these trades has made it so difficult to carry on the work of other trades, that, whilst the men actually on strike number some 700 only, the total number of men who have had to be discharged or suspended, including those on strike, now exceeds 2,500. ... [T]he work of the Engineers on some of the vessels in hand has also been brought up by the Engineers Strike; thus the work on the machinery of HMS "Superb" is at a standstill, and the trials of HMS Afridi cannot at present be completed.[56]

Work on both the *Bahia* and the *Rio Grande do Sul* also came to a standstill awaiting the resolution of the strike. The stoppage among the shipwrights, joiners, and drillers would eventually drag out from January 24 until the return of the workers June 1, 1908. The number of available men working in the Elswick yard dropped from 4,998 at the time of Perret's January report to a mere 1,255 men, comprising 716 men and 539 apprentices. Rather than April, the *Minas Geraes* would not launch until September 10, 1908.[57]

J. M. Falkner described the launch of the Brazilian battleship in a letter to Rendel: "The launch of the *Minas Geraes* went off with great precision and éclat. She is the largest ship of war ever launched in English waters. There is now a very large permanent Brazilian colony in Newcastle – and a great many more Brazilians came for the occasion, from all parts. At a dinner which Admiral Bacellar (Chief of Commission) gave, we sat down one-hundred thirty people."[58] Launches were symbolically important to both the shipyards and the nations buying the ships, and hundreds of emissaries representing Brazil and England, as well as various other states, viewed the launch along with thousands of spectators. Senhora F. Regis de Oliveira, the wife of the Brazilian minister, performed the naming ceremony for the ship, and Minister R. Regis de Oliveira, speaking for his nation, said:

> Allow me to express here the feelings that are overflowing my own heart, as well as those of all Brazilians at this moment, when the *Minas Geraes,* ploughing her first furrow in her element, is getting ready to be an emissary of peace and civilization on behalf of a nation determined to grow strong and prosperous under a flag which means progress and freedom. Let me lift my glass to the firm of Sir W. G. Armstrong, Whitworth and Co., Limited. . . . It would be preposterous to expatiate on the praise of this firm; it is known all over the world. The future will prove once more that we have been right in trusting it and the *Minas Geraes* will be the glory not only of the Brazilian Navy, but also of the Elswick Shipyard.[59]

The impact of the Brazilian acquisition was felt far and wide. The cover story of the March 19, 1910, issue of *Scientific American* ran under the headline "The Mighty Armament of the New Brazilian Dreadnought '*Minas Geraes,*'" and the photo was a huge picture taken down the front of the deck with eight 12-inch and four 4.7-inch guns trained directly toward the camera. The article described the colossus: 543 feet in length, 83 feet in breadth, with a top speed of twenty-one knots. It was the first ship in the world to carry twelve 12-inch guns and was "the most powerful vessel in commission at the present time."[60]

Regardless of the pomp and circumstance of the launch, it was largely symbolic. Although the ship was afloat, it was essentially an empty shell; there remained a great deal of work to be done: installing armor, engine, and boilers, and welding on the deck. There were some further delays due to the Brazilian Commission's slow turnaround in their approval of any changes to the build plans. By spring 1909, the hydraulic for the guns and the gun housing was being installed, and electrical work was done, as were cabins, pumps, drainage, and ventilation. The ship steamed to a mooring away from the dock under its own power on May 19, 1909, and on August 16, 1909, it passed through Newcastle's swing bridge and was moored at the Walker yard for examination and testing of underwater fittings. The *Minas Geraes* passed its time trials in early October 1909, and its completion trials of guns and electronics on November 30, 1909. Workers withdrew from the ship on December 11, 1909, and the ship was taken over by its Brazilian crew on January 5, 1910. After a month of training, the ship sailed from the Tyne on February 5, 1910. Throughout this time, the scouts *Bahia* and *Rio Grande do Sul* went through the same process of launch and completion. The *Bahia* sailed from the Tyne on April 16, 1910, and the *Rio Grande do Sul* was turned over to its Brazilian crew on July 19 and departed the Tyne for Brazil on August 17, 1910.

BRAZILIAN SAILORS IN NEWCASTLE

The Brazilian navy had previously received several modern warships from Newcastle shipyards in the 1890s, but little had been done in this period to transition enlisted men overall to the rigors of modern naval responsibilities.[61] In 1909, as the majority of Brazilian sailors suddenly prepared for service on modern ships, their officers faced the fact that preparing crews was not as simple as demanding more and better work from the enlisted men. In the staffing of the four new battleships, and especially for the two new dreadnoughts, officers and enlisted men alike needed basic training in the technical servicing of the ships before they could even move the ships from the shipyards of Newcastle to Rio's Guanabara Bay. Eventually Brazilian naval administrators contracted a small group of British engineers to accompany the ships back and to help train their crews. But in the short term, Brazilian sailors went to England in order to receive training.

Before the overhaul of Brazil's navy, officers oversaw ships sufficiently small in size and simple in function they could be personally managed by their commanders. Both the mechanical details of the ship and the mood of the crew were in plain sight, if not obvious. Officers had innumerable responsibilities, but the roles of *contra-mestres,* or petty officers, were not yet well defined. In fact it was only in 1910 that the navy opened its first Escola de Contra-Mestres within the naval college to retrain petty officers for their increasingly significant role on Brazilian warships. But before the Brazilian navy could teach these responsibilities officers had to learn them. To effectively manage these 19,000-ton battleships, naval officers had to professionalize, thereby relearning the basics of naval navigation and warfare. This expertise was imported from the same place as the ships themselves: the naval coast of Newcastle.[62]

During the three-year period of construction of the ships at Armstrongs, Brazil sent numerous officers and enlisted men to England to accompany the work and study the ships' protocol. Men from all levels of the Brazilian naval hierarchy spent months housed in various dormitories in Newcastle. Officers and enlisted men alike received the technological training needed to crew the ships. But for the Brazilian enlisted men, there turned out to be far more to learn in turn-of-the-century industrial England than naval training.[63]

A small contingent of Brazilian naval officers arrived in Newcastle in late 1906 or early 1907 to deal with the revised plans for the dreadnought battleships. In his March 1907 report to Armstrongs' board of directors, the chief naval architect, Josiah Perrett, described tearing up the vertical keels of the smaller battleships Brazil had originally contracted for after Brazilian representatives in Newcastle had accepted the new designs.[64] During this period there would have been Brazilian enlisted men accompanying and transporting the Brazilian officers. But it was not until the launch of the dreadnought *Minas Geraes* on September 10, 1908, and then the smaller cruisers *Bahia* on January 20, 1909, and the *Rio Grande do Sul* on April 20, 1909, that there would have been a regular need for Brazilian officers and sailors. And it was not until that summer, in August 1909, that by the hundreds the men needed to staff each of these ships arrived in Newcastle, where they would stay for months.

The Brazilian sailors' time in Newcastle, though much longer than other stays abroad, was not unique in terms of travel and contact in foreign ports. Like all sailors in modern navies, they experienced domestic and international travel at a sometimes-dizzying pace. According to João Cândido's service record, he had seen a great deal of the world before arriving in Newcastle. After joining the navy in 1895, he traveled extensively around Brazil, training several times at Ilha Grande in 1896, and then to Angra dos Reis, Santa Catarina, Salvador da Bahia, Pernambuco, Ceará, Itaparica, and Santos in 1897. In October 1900 his ship carried newly elected Brazilian president Manuel Ferraz de Campos Sales on a visit to Buenos Aires. In December 1902 he entered the naval hospital on Ilha das Cobras with pulmonary tuberculosis; he would suffer with recurring episodes throughout his life. When he was released in February 1903 he was assigned to work as an onboard instructor at the apprenticeship school in Pernambuco. In June 1903 he was assigned to the crew of the *Andrada* in the city of Recife, and he had soon traveled to Pará, Paraiba, Ceara, Maranhão, and Rio Grande do Norte, as well as returning to Pernambuco and Bahia before returning to Rio de Janeiro in August 1903. There he switched ships, now crewing the small unarmored messenger ship *Jutahy*. He returned to the Amazon, first to the city of Belem in Pará; he then spent nearly a year assigned to the flotilla on the Amazon River and traveled as far as Manáos (renamed Manaus in 1939) mapping Brazil's land in its northwestern territory. Brazil was in conflict with Bolivia over land in Acre as rubber had become extremely profitable. He returned to Rio de Janeiro in June 1904.[65]

In terms of international travel, he was in Rio de Janeiro for nearly a year before transferring ships and departing for Montevideo in March 1905. In 1906 he traveled to Europe for the first time, serving as a crewmember on the *Benjamin Constant*. They departed from Bahia in March, and his ship stopped in Ponta Delgada on the Portuguese territory Ilha de São Miguel, Copenhagen, Stockholm, Kiel, Amsterdam, Dover, Lisbon, and Las Palmas before returning to Rio de Janeiro in December. Then after serving on the *Benjamin Constant,* which had been converted into a teaching ship, in and around Rio de Janeiro with trips to Montevideo and cities throughout Brazil, on May 1909 he was dispatched from Rio de Janeiro to Europe, this time for training and transfer to the first of Brazil's new dreadnought battleships then in production in Newcastle. They departed from Pernambuco on July 22, and again stopped on the Atlantic Island of Ilha San Miguel August 15–23. They reached Plymouth on August 28 and departed on September 5 for Newcastle, arriving on September 14. There he spent more than a month in training as helmsman of the *Minas Geraes*. The *Benjamin Constant* later traveled in Europe with stops in Lisbon and Toulan before returning and discharging its remaining crew in Newcastle on November 15. The *Minas Geraes* departed February 5, 1910.[66]

Although Newcastle's history is deeply associated with the production of both warships and merchant vessels, it housed no military naval base. It is a city much more associated with its population of shipbuilders than it is with actual sailors, and its history has generally been told through the lens of labor and social history rather than through that of naval or military history. However, as ships for foreign navies were completed, it repeatedly became the short-term home for large populations of foreign sailors, and even as Newcastle took on its role as the preeminent producer for foreign naval markets, the owners of the shipyards never built barracks or formal group housing for these visiting crews. In fact, though Armstrongs factories were primarily in Elswick, its workers were overwhelmingly housed miles away, in Newcastle. From the time of William G. Armstrong's initial success in the mid-nineteenth century, there were calls in the local papers for him to establish on-site housing for his employees there in Elswick. An article in the *Northern Examiner* stated: "He should build cottages for his men. . . . His workmen are either scattered throughout the town [of Newcastle], from which they come in swarms, along the road in the darkness of the wintery morning or they are forced to inhabit the pestilential cribs of such places as Greenhow Terrace – a place from its nastiness and filth, fatal to many a man and woman."[67] Armstrong ignored such requests. Rather than building a self-contained community at Elswick for his workers, Armstrong retained his ties to the city of Newcastle, and as his business grew throughout the nineteenth and early twentieth centuries, the economic health of Armstrongs was closely associated with that of Newcastle. Decades later, when Brazilian sailors arrived to await the production of ships from the Elswick yards, there was still no housing available near the factory site; men were housed at a distance, informally spread throughout the city of Newcastle.

As Brazilian sailors arrived in significant numbers during the summer of 1909, the older naval vessels on which they arrived went in for repair and overhaul of weaponry. Sailors were housed informally in inexpensive hotels, in a newly established men's home called the Rowton house similar to the YMCA, and in short-term rental apartments. They were distanced from the naval hierarchy, and they enjoyed a great deal of freedom during their stay. Although the Brazilian officers were suitably entertained by representatives of Armstrongs (along with the Brazilian delegation that had been overseeing the implementation of the contract for some time), until the ships were ready to take on crews some months after those crews arrived, Brazilian enlisted men had autonomy and an unprecedented amount of leisure time. As becomes clear, they had a great deal of freedom during their time in Newcastle, and although there is a lacuna of documentation pertaining directly to their planning of the revolt, a population of hundreds of overwhelmingly black sailors left with a relatively free reign over a coastal British city leaves a trail through the archives. Since these sailors were young they had been confined and regimented. While Caminha's *Bom Crioulo* describes the waterfront bars and brothels sailors frequented in Rio, the desprotegidos lacked the time and money to experience leisure and recreation. To put it bluntly, sailors who were accustomed to masturbating at the edge of the ship and engaging in sodomy as both a release and an enactment of their sexual desire now found themselves in an exotic locale with unprecedented freedom.

For sailors from Rio, their time in Newcastle must have been eye opening. From the early nineteenth century, Newcastle's politicians and newspapers supported the international abolitionist movement, though it would be asking too much of the available sources to link that abolitionist drive to a tangible antiracist movement on the Tyneside.[68] Like all active port cities, Newcastle and its surrounding towns attracted foreign sailors, many of whom were racially distinct from the local population. Unlike other active port cities in the United Kingdom, Geordies (a term for people from Tyneside) have earned a reputation for accepting racially diverse populations in the area. There is a sizable Yemeni community in South Shields (a neighboring town to Newcastle) that dates back to the 1890s. Sydney Collins describes Newcastle's white population as "generally accepting of the community of black sailors, which dates back to the first decade of the twentieth century."[69] But racial diversity in and of itself does not necessarily lead to racial acceptance, and the racial violence that swept port cities in the UK following WWI in 1919 did not spare the Arab community of Tyneside.[70]

Although black seamen could not expect to be welcomed with open arms by Newcastle's population, Geordies seemed to employ a grudging pragmatism that created space for these visitors; a response defined by a mixture of racism and accommodation. One example of this inherent tension appears in Joe Robinson's autobiographic interview with Francie Nichol, the owner of a Tyneside lodging house who was born April 18, 1889. She describes the arrival of black sailors looking for a place to stay in the time period just preceding 1913. "We didn't have many coloured

fellers in because of the trouble ye always got, but at one time I had these
coal black darkies for a few days. They seemed quiet and well-mannered
enough. They had come off a ship and wanted somewhere to stay. No-
body else would take them so I said I would as long as it was only for a
little while."[71] Nichol describes the orderly behavior of these foreign
guests alongside a detailed description of their meticulous bathing hab-
its; both details that obviously surprised her.

Beyond the diverse body of foreign merchant mariners living in
Newcastle at the turn of the century, there was a particular aspect to
Newcastle's race relations that was exceptional. One result of shipbuilding and weapon sales for international markets on the Tyneside communities was a direct link between Newcastle's economic success at
any given moment and the presence of the crews of foreign navies, both
officers and enlisted men. In contrast to those later violent xenophobic
outbreaks against ethnic minorities that reached a high point in British
port cities in 1919, from the time Armstrongs began catering to foreign
navies in the late nineteenth century the presence of initially Japanese,
then Chinese, and finally Afro-Brazilian enlisted men in Newcastle was
a sign of the area's economic well-being. These foreign sailors did not
threaten British jobs in Newcastle; instead they ensured the economic
well-being of the community. By the turn of the twentieth century, Armstrongs employed more than 25,000 laborers when orders were good,
but when production slacked off, those numbers plummeted. Orders for
dreadnought battleships signaled unprecedented stability in employment for years at a time. Furthermore, cafes, bars, grocery stores, and,
perhaps above all, lodging houses faced times of plenty when these foreigners arrived. In *The Big Battleship,* a history of the Tyneside construction of the dreadnought *Rio de Janeiro,* Richard Hough describes the
positive responses of the various workers across Newcastle's community
to the arrival of "these dark-skinned Brazilians."[72] Rather than feeling
threatened by nonwhite foreigners competing for jobs, it was actually
when foreign sailors left that Geordies faced layoffs and hardship.

Although the men at the bottom of a socioeconomic system do not
leave the same trail of documents as those who run corporations and
state institutions, it is possible to trace the activities of approximately
1,000 overwhelmingly black non–English speakers. The crew of the *Bar-*

roso arrived on the Tyne on August 12, 1909, while the crew of the *Benjamin Constant* arrived in Tyneside on the same day that the *Minas Geraes* passed its speed trials, on September 14, 1909.[73]

For Brazilian sailors, the contrast between naval service in Brazil and England – and the contrast between service in the Brazilian navy and their time in Newcastle – was vast. For example, the 434-man crew of the *Almirante Barroso* departed Rio de Janeiro on July 3, 1909, and after a forty-day crossing with stops in Cape Verde and the Canary Islands, the ship arrived in Plymouth. The *Almirante Barroso* was built in Armstrongs' Elswick yards. Its hull was laid down in August 1895, and Brazil took delivery of the vessel in April 1897. It weighed 3,400 tons, had 2-inch thick armor, and carried six 6-inch and four 4.7-inch guns. Although it remained quite a modern build compared to most of the Brazilian fleet, the ship was scheduled for maintenance and rearmament. Upon arrival in Plymouth, two crewmen were diagnosed with beriberi, an acute vitamin deficiency caused by a lack of thiamine (vitamin B1). Like scurvy, it was common on board ships in the nineteenth century, but by the early twentieth century it was unheard of in European navies. Beriberi had been wiped out in the British navy by improvements in rations for sailors. By the time the ship landed in Newcastle on August 12, 1909, three more sailors had been diagnosed, and by September 22, nineteen additional cases had been diagnosed.[74] Due to the inhumane treatment of slaves in the northeast, beriberi was still prevalent there, and at the time, the disease was still believed to be transferrable from man to man; this reasoning helped doctors justify breakouts often occurring on a single ship. Eventually forty men from the Brazilian crew came down with the disease, notably all officers were spared. Beriberi, if untreated, is often fatal, but once the sick men were transferred to the floating hospital at the Jarrow Slakes near Newcastle, nearly all quickly responded to the improved diet, and all but one sailor soon recovered. Certainly, these events support the reclamantes' claims of insufficient and substandard rations in the Brazilian navy. Like the lash, beriberi was exclusively found in the population of Brazilian slaves and sailors. The crew of the *Almirante Barroso* enjoyed health benefits the instant they landed Tyneside.

What can be pieced together from Brazilian and British sources is that overall these Brazilian sailors had unprecedented freedom in Newcastle. The two largest of the Brazilian ships, the *Almirante Barroso* and the *Benjamin Constant,* dropped their crews in order to await the completion of their new ships in August and September 1909, respectively. Those ships were then turned over for inspection, overhaul, and rearmament. Additionally, in this same period other naval ships simply dropped off crew members before returning to Brazil. Because Brazilian sailors stayed in hotels and guesthouses and were responsible for their own meals, their meager wages were doubled while serving abroad, and (perhaps in contrast to their service at home) they were paid on time with hard currency.[75] For months, except for basic training, men were free to fill their days as they saw fit while they waited for their new commissions.

While in Newcastle, many sailors stayed at Rowton House, an artisan men's hostel that was opened on Christmas Day 1907 and could house 500 men. It had modern amenities – laundry, steam heat, electric light – and each man had a private sleeping cubicle and an individual locker to stow his things. According to newspaper reports many others stayed at private boarding houses throughout the city. Housed miles from the shipyard with no officers assigned to stay with them at Rowton House, some saw it as an opportunity to cut loose.[76] According to the local papers there was a lot of drinking, and there were many fights (among the Brazilians and with Britons), several robberies, and a handful of shootings.

On January 6, 1910, the *Newcastle Daily Journal* covered the investigation of a shooting that had occurred the night before; both the victim and the shooter were crewmen on the *Minas Geraes.* The shooting took place at a party in a private home where a group consisting of Brazilian sailors and young girls were drinking. A sailor who was being forcibly removed from the party drew a gun and shot randomly, striking a member of his ship's crew in the jaw with the bullet. While questioning the arresting officer, the court clerk asked, "There are [hundreds] of these men quartered in Rowton House, and hardly a day goes by but we have some case here, and they are getting more and more serious. Is there no officer, no superior person, in charge of these men?" When he was told that the highest-ranking officer in the guest house was a sergeant, he replied, "There might be some proper person in charge . . . [as] a heterogeneous collection of men such as they are ought to be under the strictest supervision."[77]

In the days following this shooting, there was further criticism of the Brazilian sailors in the local papers. One editorial noted the concern of the Newcastle community due to the "presence of the Brazilian sailors belonging to the crew of the *Minas Geraes*. The danger is not confined to the free use of revolvers: the evidence reveals a danger not small on the score of immorality. These men, mostly half-breeds, seem to lodge where they like, go where they like, and do pretty much what they like."[78] On January 10, in that same column, an anonymous respondent stated that "the Chinese and Japanese sailors are heathens, but that when sojourning in Newcastle they behaved like gentlemen; whereas the Brazilian sailors now with us are Christians, some of them are not behaving well."[79]

The sailors exercised their newfound freedom in a number of ways. Ernest Hambloch, who served in the British consul's office in Brazil, describes an interaction with three young women who came to his office. They were from Newcastle and had all three married Brazilian sailors whom they met there:

> I think my most unexpected visitors were three white girls whom I found sitting in the waiting-room nursing snuff-and-butter babies.... They were Englishwomen ... married to firemen on a Brazilian man-of-war. I had them in to see me. Their story, a true one, was that they had been married by a parson at Newcastle. Their husbands were negro firemen, part of a nucleus crew sent to Newcastle to bring to Brazil the new dreadnought, *Minas Geraes*. They wanted me to send them home. Their husbands, whom I sent for, were willing that they should go, because they could not afford to keep them.[80]

He goes on to explain that due to the sailors' elevated pay in Newcastle, these women assumed they would be well cared for in Rio, not realizing what the conditions would be like for their husbands when they arrived home. Hambloch sent these girls home as "distressed British citizens."[81]

Brazilian sailors could not have overlooked the significance of the radical unions, whose strikes had at one point stopped the construction of the very ships they were then waiting to crew back to Brazil. During the period when Armstrongs became established in the late nineteenth century, unions had little power in Newcastle. Working for Armstrongs carried prestige and was seen as a passport to skilled engineering work around the world. When the Nine Hour Movement began in Sunderland in northeast England in 1871, the majority of its supporters were not union workers. The same was true in Newcastle; the men who came out in sympathy with the Sunderland movement were nonunion, but they would not stay that way for long.

When Armstrong refused to meet or recognize the delegation pushing for the nine-hour day, almost 7,000 men came out on strike in Newcastle. They enjoyed support from the *Times* and from other members of trade unions across the nation. Armstrong sought scabs in Scotland, Belgium, and Germany, but according to an article in the *Times* dated September 11, 1871, "If Sir William Armstrong could have retained his Prussian and Danish labourers, he might have laughed at the strike; but Prussians, Danes and English have all succumbed to the pressures of working class opinion in the North."[82] Eventually the strikers were successful; after almost five months, they won their nine-hour day. When the strike began, only 800 of the 7,000 men at the Elswick yards were union members; at its completion, most all of them were, and they remained so.[83]

When the Brazilian sailors arrived at the end of the first decade of the twentieth century, their schedule was already disrupted by the organization of Armstrongs' workers. From January 24, 1908, until June 1, 1908, the strike of shipwrights, joiners, and drillers halted construction on the *Minas Geraes,* the *Bahia,* and the *Rio Grande do Sul.* Seven hundred men were out on strike, but it led to the discharge of 2,500 men out of a workforce of 5,000.[84] A concurrent strike among Armstrongs' engineers halted machinery work and trials on other ships. Eventually Armstrongs was driven to negotiate and accept terms. For the Brazilian sailors arriving in Newcastle in the year following this strike, the ability of the British unions to shape the policies of Armstongs – a shipyard producing warships for nations spanning the globe – could only have served as a model to men already laying plans to reshape the Brazilian navy.

A TALE OF TWO NAVIES

As the ties between the British and Brazilian navies were reestablished and strengthened, the glaring differences between naval service for British and Brazilian enlisted men became all the more apparent. For the British navy, the nineteenth century represented a period of notable social reform. According to one social historian of the British navy, as

British imperial and naval power grew, British sailors became aligned with imperial manliness and the British sailor became a model of respectability. "Naval men came to be represented as defenders not only of British interests abroad but also of Britishness."[85] The image of the British sailor as Jack Tar, the drunken lout, kidnapped into naval service, as much criminal as sailor, was gradually replaced in the public mind by the proud, heroic Blue Jacket. Additionally, this symbol of the new professionalism of the British navy was marketed to the British public in advertisements, theater, children's literature, and imperial ephemera.[86]

Another British naval historian claimed that before the mid-nineteenth-century reforms in the British navy, to the extent that the British public knew sailors at all, it "knew him only on land, out of his element. The sailor on the run ashore, probably drunk and riotous."[87] Civilian concerns during the eighteenth and early nineteenth centuries bemoan the need to control these base and dangerous men through forced recruitment and the application of the lash. These complaints echo – or, better yet, herald – those made by Brazilian navy officers almost a century later to justify their policies of impressment and corporal punishment. For example, in his 1777 treatise "On the Legality of Impressing Seamen," lawyer and legal scholar Charles Butler described sailors in the Royal Navy "as individuals [who] seldom possess the ethereal spirit of patriotism in a sufficient degree to make them seek [such service] by their own choice . . . it is absolutely necessary that government should have recourse to compulsory methods."[88] But in justifying the practice of forced conscription, Butler minimizes the toll it takes on young sailors, arguing instead that men generally benefit from the service. "Ninety-nine times out of an hundred," he argues, "[that call] snatches him from disease, from misery, or perhaps an ignominious death; the inseparable attendants of idleness, intemperance, and bad company." These were men incapable of "reasoning seriously upon their real interest": "What makes seamen so averse to the king's service? The answer is, the strict discipline kept on board the king's ships, thereby they are prevented from running into those irregularities and debaucheries, of which seamen are so particularly fond, and which prove so fatal to them"[89] Men incapable of understanding or protecting their best interests, men hardly different from children who needed to be "strictly disciplined" to be saved from their own base nature: this replicates the language used by Brazilian naval officers, and that of plantation owners throughout the Atlantic World, to defend the violent control of their laborers.

For both British and Brazilian officers, forced recruitment and physical mistreatment was justified by a sailor's inability to act honorably; he had not earned rights of citizenship. As historian Isaac Land describes these British sailors in his groundbreaking 2001 article "Customs of the Sea," "this meant that a slave in Jamaica and a [British] sailor aboard a ship both inhabited peripheral, non-British space and had no claim to British liberties."[90] When British sailors targeted abolishing the use of the lash, Land compellingly argues, they did so not by taking on the morality of flogging men, but by attacking the definition of seamen as "non-British." If sailors could be seen as part of the Protestant majority in England, they could push for reforms based on the fact that white British citizens should not be subject to the same discipline as plantation slaves. Their agitation was against the practice of flogging the "true British seaman" because "this individual experienced flogging *differently* from a non-British individual such as a black slave."[91] As sailors asserted their status as citizens and the image of the noble Blue Jacket took hold, sailors became proud Englishmen who bravely served their country throughout England's massive empire.

During the second half of the nineteenth century, British sailors won radical improvement in the nature of their service. In the year after its initial passage in 1860, the Naval Discipline Act was repealed, modified, and reenacted in 1861, then for five additional years the British legislature continued to amend this piece of legislation. What resulted was a comprehensive reform to British navel service, which led to – among other protections – the cessation of corporal punishment in the British navy. The act formally established a monthly leave policy as well as distinguishing between overstaying a leave and the act of desertion; it limited the crimes that called for the death penalty, as well as crimes that could be punished onboard a ship at the discretion of the ships captain without formal court martial. Then, in the 1860s the admiralty urged that even when officers were within their right to use the lash, they should apply the penalty of confinement rather than corporal punishment. They also limited the number of lashes that could be legally applied to a sailor to

48, following the lead of the British army. This all culminated with the December 18, 1871, suspension of corporal punishment during times of peace and the 1879 suspension of the lash during times of war.[92] It is worth noting that, as stated by Eugene Rasor, social historian of the British navy "suspended did not mean abolished. In the Royal Navy, corporal punishment could still be awarded for mutiny and gross personal violence to and officer until after the end of World War II."[93]

Additional reforms to the British navy in this period include improvement in pay, pensions, death benefits, and promotion, as well as improvements in the physical well-being of British sailors, symbolized by the introduction of physical training and gymnastics. All of these reforms culminated with the intended outcome of increasing voluntary recruitment levels as called for by the 1889 Defense Act. What British sailors had won from their government was not merely a refurbished image, but real reforms in the nature of their service. These gains stood in stark and powerful contrast to the lives of sailors in the Brazilian navy, which had changed so little during their country's century-long struggle for modernization.[94]

By the turn of the twentieth century, when Brazilian sailors found themselves in England's port cities, the British sailor was no longer an object of scorn. In fact, he had become the subject of popular musical theater as in Gilbert and Sullivan's 1878 smash hit *H.M.S. Pinafore; or, The Lass That Loved a Sailor* (1878), and his image was used in magazines and on billboards to sell sundries such as tea and soap. Even for a Brazilian sailor who spoke no English, it was easy to see how radically the status of the British sailor differed from his own. Their ongoing service in the Brazilian navy put Brazilian sailors much closer to the century-old stereotype of Jack Tar than the clean and fresh-faced Blue Jacket.

Brazilian seamen had come to England to learn how to crew the new ships, but their trip to Europe marked a further step toward a nascent political consciousness. Interviewed in secrecy in 1968 during Brazil's military dictatorship, João Cândido, the leader of the Revolta da Chibata, was asked whether the revolt had been a spontaneous occurrence. Cândido responded, "It was a conspiracy, we conspired to protest. [Brazilian] sailors knew, all sailors knew." When asked how it was to happen, were they awaiting a special date, Cândido responded, "We were waiting for a date and for power, we were waiting for the construction of the new ships in Europe, having been there for two years in contact with sailors from other nations."[95] He described how the organizers met at several locations in Rio de Janeiro, including at João Cândido's apartment, in the years preceding the revolt. This discussion continued in Newcastle: "[In Brazil] we had a committee of conspirators at *Vila Rio Barbosa,* under the nose of the police. We had a shelter there, we rented a floor and met there. ... In England, we maintained the committees in the very hotels where we were residing, awaiting the construction of the ships. Almost two years paid by the Brazilian government, we sent messengers to sound out the situation here [in Brazil]. We did this so that when we arrived, we would be prepared to act."[96]

Corporal punishment had been suspended in the British navy in 1879, so one can only imagine how jarring it was when each group of sailors, both British and Brazilian, suddenly in the same cities found themselves in part defined by the other. Brazilians saw sailors who were no longer impressed, no longer lashed, who were accepted as citizens – as proud representatives of their nation and empire – at home and abroad. On the other hand, British sailors saw thousands of men, brothers in service, who were still recruited and controlled by the same violence that British sailors had only recently shed. Cândido clearly states that British sailors interacted with their Brazilian colleagues. We can't know which aspect of Brazilian character was more important in defining them and their rights, their blackness or their status as sailors, but the struggle against corporal punishment was rooted in a struggle against being treated as slaves. Is it any wonder that such a social space as Newcastle in the early twentieth century would contribute to an event such as the Revolta da Chibata?

What was the exact event that led them to carry out the Revolta da Chibata? What convinced them to risk their lives and futures in order to stop use of the lash and other draconian punishment by the Brazilian navy? When asked to specifically locate the origin of the revolt, Cândido replied: "The movement was born of the sailors themselves to combat their poor treatment, the insufficient and low quality rations, and to finally and definitively end the use of the lash in the navy. It was the case that those of us coming from Europe who were in contact with other sailors, we were unwilling to admit that in the Brazilian Navy men still had their shirts removed so that they could be whipped by other men."[97] A former sailor named Eurico Fogo, who served in Europe with João Cândido, said that when Cândido was in Europe he "took it upon himself to seek out foreign mechanics, establishing intimate relations with them in order to learn about naval technology."[98] While certain links between the sailors and British culture are better documented than others, it is clear that although the Revolta da Chibata cannot trace its origins solely to the time the reclamantes spent in Newcastle, the movement was profoundly shaped by their experiences in England.

The torturer took up a stiff, medium weight hemp cord, pierced with small steel needles. In order to make it swell, he soaked it in salt water, until just the tips of the needles protruded from the cord. The ship's crew was ordered on deck to view the shackled prisoner. The *comandante,* after a moment of silence, read a proclamation of the sailor's crime. The shackles were removed from his wrists and he was suspended – stripped from the waist up – from the iron structure that secured the ships ballast. Then . . . the master of the tragic ceremony began to apply the blows. The blood ran. The beaten man moaned, pleading, as the torturer continued, enthusiastically, with his inhumane task. The drummers played with fervor, drowning out the man's screams. Many officers averted their faces; each [officer] was properly uniformed, gloved and armed with a sword. The enlisted men dispersed, repulsed and profoundly indignant.

EURICO FOGO, petty officer second class, served 1898–1910

FIVE

The Revolt of the Lash

AS THE SUN ROSE OVER GUANABARA BAY ON NOVEMBER 16, 1910, guards led a shackled Marcelino Rodrigues Menezes, a sailor from Bahia, onto the deck of the battleship *Minas Geraes*. All nonessential members of the ship's crew were assembled on deck and the charges against the seaman were read publically, as was the specific article of the Articles of War being invoked in the punishment of the sailor. Only when each of the steps in this ritual of violence were carried out did Captain (*Capitão-de-Mar-e-Guerra*) João Pereira Leite order that Menezes's flogging begin. He was being punished for the crime of injuring seaman Waldemar Rodrigues de Souza, whom he had attacked with a shaving razor four days prior. According to most sources, his punishment was 250 lashes,[1] though following naval tradition that number would not have been announced before Menezes's lashing commenced so as to not challenge the sailor to resist authority by stoically accepting his punishment without being broken. As a crewmember counted out the number of lashes the assembled crew took some solace that if their two years of preparation played out as planned, this egregious act of state violence could be the last sanctioned flogging in the Brazilian navy. The reclamantes later met with the government negotiator, Captain José Carlos de Carvalho, aboard the *Minas Geraes*. To confirm the legitimacy of their claims, the mutineers requested that he examine Marcelino Rodrigues Menezes, the sailor whose whipping had sparked the revolt. At the end of the examination, the man was taken ashore for treatment in the Naval Hospital. Carvalho later reported: "Mr. President, the back of this sailor resembles a mullet sliced open for salting."[2]

Menezes's lashing signaled the start of the Revolta da Chibata, the unprecedented mutiny that reverberated far beyond the confines of the *Minas Geraes;* in fact, it echoed from Rio de Janeiro across the Atlantic. A group of sailors drawn from the crews of various ships in Guanabara Bay organized this uprising in both Rio de Janeiro and Newcastle. They originally planned the start of the insurrection to follow the inauguration of Brazil's new president on or around November 15, 1910, but they chose not to revolt too near to the presidential inauguration. They were committed to revolting against general mistreatment and poor conditions in the navy, and they consciously wanted to avoid conflating their cause with the presidential politics. So, when Captain Pereira Leite of the *Minas Geraes* presented them a perfect opportunity by lashing Menezes the day after the inauguration on November 16, the reclamantes opted to delay their actions. In order to allow sufficient time to organize and plan the mutiny and distance it from the inauguration, the leaders waited until November 22, at which time approximately half of the men stationed in Rio de Janeiro joined in the uprising.[3]

The revolt played out with clocklike precision. Nearly simultaneously, the crews of four warships revolted: hundreds of men on the battleships *Minas Geraes* and *São Paulo* (19,821 tons each), the older coastal defense vessel *Deodoro* (3,150 tons), and the light cruiser *Bahia* (3,150 tons) threw in their lots with the leadership of the Revolta da Chibata. The crews of several other ships abandoned service, as did many sailors serving on shore; some joined the crews of the rebellious boats while others simply avoided service during the revolt. It is difficult to know which were in sympathy with the reclamantes and which were simply protecting themselves from the violent and dangerous uprising. By all accounts the revolt actively involved somewhat less that half of the enlisted men on duty in and around the Brazilian capital; the numbers most cited are that 2,379 out of 5,009 enlisted men in and around Rio de Janeiro participated. In fact, both numbers are based on the projected or estimated size of crews. It is difficult to confirm the exact number of sailors involved, but if patterns of desertion and general short staffing are taken into account, the actual number of men in service in the capital on the night the revolt broke out was likely closer to 4,000 than 5,000, and the number of men involved is probably 1,500–2,000 rather that the often cited 2,379.[4]

On the night of November 22, fifty-four-year-old Captain João Batista das Neves of the *Minas Geraes* attended a celebratory dinner with both Brazilian and foreign naval officers in attendance onboard the French cruiser *Duguay Trouin* at anchor in Guanabara Bay. The French ship was named for the famous corsair Rene Duguay Trouin, best known for his 1711 capture of the port of Rio de Janeiro, during which he successfully held the Portuguese governor hostage for ransom. When the festivities ended, Captain Batista das Neves and his second lieutenant, Armando Trompowsky de Almeida, made their way back to the *Minas Geraes* aboard a small launch; the lieutenant dropped the captain and departed for shore. As he had been attending a formal event, the captain wore a dress uniform with a sword on his belt. He arrived at his ship that evening soon after 10:00 PM, and, according to Edmar Morel's description of the revolt, "noticing something unusual, did not go directly to his cabin, instead remaining on deck in conversation with a young officer. Ten minutes later the revolt exploded."[5] That young officer was Second Lieutenant Álvaro Alberto da Mota e Silva. Just as his conversation ended with the captain:

> Lieutenant Alberto went down the interior steps of the ship. At the exact moment that he called back "Until tomorrow, commander," he was struck a powerful blow to the chest. It was the stroke of a bayonet swung full force by a sailor. The lieutenant, having stumbled, leaned with his left hand on the gun of the offender, while with his right he drew his sword, with which he slashed the stomach of the sailor who attacked him.
>
> In response to the shouting, as the wounded sailor fell down the final meters of the staircase, officers and rebels rushed on deck.[6]

The insurgents confronted a group of officers led by Captain Batista das Neves; he tried to calm the situation, but fighting soon broke out. Shouting, "End the chibata!" and "Long live liberty!" the *reclamantes* proceeded against the officers; rebellious seamen rushed the deck. In the melee that followed, a sailor struck and injured Captain Batista das Neves with a length of iron. Fellow officer Captain-Lieutenant José Cláudio da Silva Jr., along with a loyal sailor named Eugênio Alves de Assis

Bulhões and a cabin boy named Joviniano de Oliveira, protected the captain and briefly pushed the rebels back, but the captain-lieutenant was cut down by a bayonet-wielding sailor. While Joviniano tried to carry the officer to safety, both the captain-lieutenant and the cabin boy were shot and killed by a reclamante named Vitorino Nicássio de Oliveira. Additionally, the ship's quartermaster, Sargent Francisco Monteiro de Albuquerque, was fatally stabbed during this melee, and First-Lieutenant Mário Lahmayer was moments later shot and killed while trying to escape the *Minas Geraes* with a group of loyal sailors. Another rebel sailor named João José do Nascimento shot and killed the badly wounded Captain Batista das Neves.[7]

According to naval historian Vice-Admiral H. L. Martins, several of the reclamantes then dishonored the body of their captain. Seemingly in response to Batista das Neves having mandated an unpopular daily calisthenic program aboard the *Minas Geraes* – likely adopted from British naval officers – several sailors broke out in gymnastics around his corpse. One sailor slapped the captain's head, shouting, "You want a cup of water, old woman?"[8] Then, as a final insult, Aristides Pereira a sailor known by the nickname Chimney (*Chaminé*) urinated on the corpse.[9]

It was Lieutenant Trompowsky who, before the outbreak, delivered Captain Batista das Neves to the *Minas Geraes* and subsequently departed. As he sailed away from the dreadnaught the sound of gunfire alerted him that the ship was in revolt. He rushed to the home of the minister of the navy, Joaquim Marques Baptista de Leão, and notified him by 10:30 PM that members of the navy were in revolt. He then set out to return to the *Minas Geraes* with another officer. Before he was killed, Captain Batista das Neves had ordered the gravely wounded Lieutenant Álvaro Alberto da Mota e Silva to retire from the melee. The lieutenant and a group of loyal sailors had successfully departed from the *Minas Geraes* in a small launch. Lieutenant Trompowsky's boat met the one transporting Lieutenant Álvaro Alberto da Mota e Silva from the *Minas Geraes,* and they accompanied him back to Ilha das Cobras to seek medical attention. Once the *Minas Geraes* was in the hands of the reclamantes, the mutiny's leader, thirty-year-old Afro-Brazilian João Cândido, seaman first class of the 40th Company of the Brazilian navy (who avoided the initial violence on board), moved the ships through Guanabara Bay, periodically discharging the battleships' 4.7-inch guns, announcing to waiting seamen on board other ships that the revolt had begun.[10]

Nearby in the harbor, Afro-Brazilian sailor Manuel Gregório do Nascimento led a similarly well organized contingent of reclamantes to inform First Lieutenant Salustiano Lessa that the crew was in revolt, and that the officers of the *São Paulo* should not fight. He requested that all officers withdraw and ensured that if they followed orders, the rebels would commit no violence against them. The chief officer and most of his staff agreed. The rebels rounded up the other officers, loaded them aboard a small boat, and sent them toward shore. In an act of resistance to both the reclamantes and the officers who had agreed to their terms, the *São Paulo*'s only casualty, First Lieutenant Americo Sales de Carvalho, stayed behind hidden in the armory, hoping to later disrupt the rebellion. Frustrated, rather than confronting the sailors, he eventually shot himself. He was still alive when he was transported from the ship, but he later died of his self-inflicted wounds. By 2:00 AM on November 23, the two most powerful battleships in the Americas were under the direct control of the overwhelmingly Afro-Brazilian men who populated their lower decks.

On both dreadnaught battleships, the rebels did not grant the machinists, the telegraph operators, and the noncommissioned officers (NCOs, or *oficiais inferiors*) permission to disembark. This group included the British technicians who were contracted to the Brazilian navy to keep the electrical systems operating. According to Vice Admiral H. L. Martin, their contracts linked them to the running of the ships, and by remaining onboard they were not necessarily making common cause with the rebels, though he acknowledges that their interests likely were closer to those of the rebels than of the officers.[11]

The British Consul assigned to Brazil told a different story in his memoir:

> The British guarantee engineers caught on board on the outbreak of the mutiny were not turned adrift with the Brazilian officers, for though the sailors could maneuver the ships – and, indeed, did so with great skill – they could not work the engines without expert aid. The British engineers had to work them under

threat of loaded revolvers. One of them who showed signs of resistance was
swung to and fro by two negroes in front of an open furnace – a threat of the fate
which awaited him and others who attempted to disobey orders.[12]

When the rebels took over the scout *Bahia,* under the leadership of
Chief Steward Francisco Dias Martins, First Lieutenant Mario Alves de
Sousa was the only officer on board. When he heard the uprising on the
other ships he armed himself with pistol and sword, and finding his crew
armed with rifles and pistols, he fired on them, injuring several mutinous
sailors and killing one. The rebellious crew turned on the lieutenant
and killed him. There were no casualties on the older coastal battleship
Deodoro. Upon hearing the shots fired on the *Minas Geraes,* the officers
attempted to contact naval leadership on land. In the confusion, as the
breadth of the rebellion became clear, reclamantes allowed the chief officer on board to negotiate their peaceful departure; they left the ship in
the hands of the rebels.

Before midnight the rebels had taken control of three of the most
powerful ships in the Brazilian navy as well as the older *Deodoro;* only
one of the newly acquired ships remained under the control of its officers,
the scout *Rio Grande do Sul.* The ships central to the revolt came under
the control of enlisted men who conspired in the uprising. Seaman First
Class João Cândido commanded the 20,000-ton dreadnaught battleship
Minas Geraes while twenty-four-year-old Manuel Gregório do Nascimento, seaman first class from Alagoas, commanded the sister ship to
the *Minas Geraes,* the dreadnaught *São Paulo.* Francisco Dias Martins,
thirty-one-year-old chief steward from the city of Fortaleza in Ceará,
commanded the 3,150-ton light cruiser *Bahia,* and finally twenty-year-old
Seaman First Class André Avelino de Santana from Bahia initially commanded the 3,150-ton coastal battleship *Deodoro* though he would later
transfer to the *São Paulo,* replaced by José Alves da Silva. For the first
time in the history of the Brazilian navy, there was the realization of elite
racial anxiety, the desprotegidos – those lumpen who could only be coerced, beaten, and broken – had risen to challenge the authority and the
power of regulation that mediated the relationship between master and
slave, between white officers and black sailors. To rebuild that system of
racial hierarchy would be among the officer class's greatest challenges.

Additionally, most of the crew of the protected cruiser *República* – an older vessel purchased from Armstrongs in 1893 – abandoned their ship to support the revolt. Thirty-two members of that crew joined the crew of the *Deodoro,* and the remaining men who supported the revolt joined with the crew of the *São Paulo.*[13] The crews of six additional ships abandoned their ships and either fled to the safety of land or joined with the rebels. An article in *O Estado de São Paulo* described it: "At the moment at least, we can report that the crews of cruisers *República* and *Tirandentes,* training ships *Benjamin Constant* and *Primeiro de Março* battleships *Florino* and *Deodoro* and steamer *Carlos Gomesa* have abandoned their ships and fled to land."[14]

The crews of twelve vessels in Guanabara Bay remained loyal to the government, though throughout the revolt, the naval hierarchy had difficulty assessing exactly how deeply the uprising had impacted those crews. Minister Leão later stated in a report to the president, "At that moment, it was not possible to say with absolute certainty which ships were revolting."[15]

That night the rebels attempted to open a line of communication with the president. When President Fonseca arrived at the presidential mansion (the Palácio do Catete) from a dinner party he attended at the Club Tijuca on the night of November 22, he was notified that the radio-telegraph station had received the following statement from the crews of *Minas Geraes, São Paulo,* and *Bahia:* "We do not want the return of the *chibata.* This we ask the President of the republic and the Minister of the Navy. We want an immediate response. If we do not receive such a response, we will destroy the city and the ships that are not revolting."[16] The president offered no response to the rebels' demands – in fact, he personally refused to enter into any direct communication with the rebels during the four-day revolt. He had occupied the office of the president for only seven days, and in 1910, he had won the presidential election in a close campaign against Rui Barbosa, the senator from Bahia who would play a critical role in the resolution of the revolt. The outbreak of a military revolt in the opening days of his presidency had to be treated cautiously. After receiving the first telegram from the *reclamantes* on the night of November 22, he ordered that all further rebel communications be withheld from the press. Therefore, the first night of the Revolta da Chibata ended with the reclamantes awaiting a response from officers, congress, and/or Brazil's new president.[17]

João Cândido later claimed that it was at this moment, when the president refused to negotiate with the sailors, that he decided to take the ships to the open sea and wait for the government to change its attitude. He felt as the standoff extended and their story reached the world, the reclamantes would likely gain more options.[18] Living up to their threat, when the reclamantes received no response from their telegram to the president, João Cândido called for his ships to commence a periodic shelling of the city, though populated areas of the city were avoided. Throughout the revolt, the four ships involved each flew a red flag to signify they were in a state of rebellion, but they each additionally flew Brazil's national flag emblazoned with the positivist motto "Order and Progress." As was reported widely in the local press, by retaining their national flags, they sent the message that they were not in revolt against the state; rather they had been forced into action as a response to the slavelike treatment they faced while serving the Brazilian state, albeit overwhelmingly by force. The second flag was flown to signal that their revolt was not targeting the nation or its government; it instead targeted their condition. Their desire to couch their revolt as nonpolitical seemed effective; the first edition of the Rio daily, the *Correio da Manhã,* cited the 1:20 AM radiogram sent to the radio-telegraph station on the *Morro da Babilônia,* stating that the motivation of the action was solely the end of corporal punishment and the inhumane treatment of sailors in the Brazilian navy.[19]

Like the reclamantes, the government was deeply invested in the claim that this revolt was not a political action, though arguably for quite different reasons. Their claim is documented repeatedly in both the domestic and international press, in the Brazilian government reports such as the naval minister's report to the president on the Revolta da Chibata, and in the reports submitted to the U.S. Department of State by military intelligence officers in South America. Newspapers as far away as the *New York Times* led their first coverage of the Revolta da Chibata with this claim: "The movement was declared to be *without political significance.* The mutineers sent a message by radiograph to President Fonseca setting forth their claims for the immediate abolition of corporal punishment on board ship, an increase in their pay according to the programme submitted to Congress some time ago, and diminution to the work with which they are burdened owing to the maintenance of incomplete crews" (italics added).[20] The sailors' claim that their actions had no political significance – that taking over a well-funded and prestigious national institution so as to hold hostage the population of the nation's capital in an attempt to radically alter the working conditions of said institution – may be difficult to accept, but it can be understood as an act of self-preservation. By identifying their movement as nonpolitical the reclamantes offered the government a way out; if the uprising is wholly about conditions within the navy and not a critique of any aspect of government policy, the government could theoretically resolve these events by simply improving food and service, and abolishing the lash. On the other hand, the government's latching on to this justification can be better understood in the broader context of elite response to subaltern violence. Scholar of subaltern studies Ranajit Guha argued that if subalterns are denied a political vision, their actions can be presented as being spontaneous, base, and disorganized. He states that "this, too, amounts to an act of appropriation which excludes the rebel as the conscious subject of his own history."[21] Instead of describing the revolt as a well-organized and well-executed military exercise against the Brazilian state, the government's interpretation allowed the Revolta da Chibata to be lumped into a long list of similar acts of violent resistance to the modernizing authority of the Brazilian Republic. A partial list of such events includes the anti-vaccination riots in Rio de Janeiro in 1904, the war waged against the Bahian settlement of Canudos in 1897, and the civil war fought in the southern state of Paraná region of the Contestado from October 1912 until August 1916. Although each was a widespread, costly, and effective uprising against the state, together they could easily be categorized as backward and even confused responses to the progress of the modern Brazilian state. In fact, each fits neatly into the categorization of backward, racially heterogeneous, and uncivilized resistance to Brazilian progress made famous by Euclides da Cunha in his firsthand account of the war against Canudos. Cunha is credited in this work with modeling Brazil as a struggle between the modern urban coast and the primitive interior. In fact, the model need not be overly reliant on geography; urban movements such as the anti-vaccination riots or the Revolta da Chibata still fit into this paradigm based on the overall racial heterogeneity of the participants and their violent resistance to the often painful "modernization" forced on them by the republican state.[22]

THE SAILORS' MANIFESTO

According to Minister Leão, in the early morning of November 23 a merchant ship arrived on Ilha das Cobras carrying the bodies of Captain João Batista das Neves and Captain-Lieutenant José Cláudio da Silva Junior, the officers killed on the *Minas Geraes*. A gravely injured Sergeant Francisco Monteiro de Albuquerque, who was stabbed by a bayonet, was aboard the same vessel. Albuquerque had in his possession a manifesto from the reclamantes to be delivered to President Fonseca.[23] I quote the entire document:

> We, as sailors, Brazilian citizens, and supporters of the republic, can no longer accept the slavery as practiced in the Brazilian Navy, we do not receive – and have never received – the protection guaranteed us by this Nation, we are tearing away the black veil which covers the eyes of this patriotic but misled population. With all the ships under our control, with the officers prisoners, those same officers who made the Brazilian Navy weak by continuing, twenty years after the founding of the Republic, to withhold the treatment we have earned, that of citizens working in defense of our country. We are sending this message in order that his honor the president can grant Brazilian sailors the sacred rights guaranteed us by the laws of the Republic, end the disorder, and grant us some favors to better our Brazilian Navy: such as, to remove incompetent and indignant officers from serving the Brazilian nation. Reform the immoral and shameful code under which we serve, end the use of the whip, the *bôlo* [the beating of the hand with a ferule] and other similar punishments, raise our pay according to the plan of Dep. José Carlos de Carvalho, educate those seamen who lack the competence to wear our proud uniform, and put a limit on our daily service and see that it is respected. Your Excellency has the pleasure of 12 hours in order to send us a satisfactory response, or else you will see the Nation annihilated.
>
> Sent from the Battleship *São Paulo* on November 22, 1910
>
> Note: The comings and goings of the messengers shall not be interrupted.
>
> *Marinheiros*[24]

This document is a remarkable statement, which defines the very essence of the revolt. It is an extraordinary example of the ability of the recently emancipated to articulate a discussion and a critique of freedom and citizenship in the face of institutional abuse and organized state violence. In this document, the reclamantes convincingly present the moral justification of their entire movement to President Fonseca and to the nation in turn. Their demand to be seen as citizens and to no longer be treated as slaves shapes the congressional debates over the next two days.

DAWN OF THE REVOLTA DA CHIBATA

As dawn turned to daylight on November 23 the rebel-held armada performed exercises in Guanabara Bay; the reclamantes circled their ships throughout the harbor in neat formation and discharged small-caliber guns over Rio de Janeiro and the city of Niterói on the opposite side of the bay. The only response they received to their demands since the previous night was a telegraph from Minister Leão: "The Minister of the Navy, on behalf of the president of the Republic, declares that the demands, while just and based in the law, can only be addressed when made with deference and respect to the constitutional powers."[25] As their demands were unaddressed, the reclamantes made plans for a lengthy siege of Rio de Janeiro. They were, in their own words, prepared to annihilate the nation's capitol. Under threat of attack, they demanded provisions and ammunition, as well as requisitioning coal from a private supply depot on Vianna Island, and seized barges carrying coal to the French and British ships in Guanabara Bay. By the morning of November 23, they were in possession of supplies to see them through a long uprising if necessary.[26]

At 7:00 AM on November 23 the rebel ships passed Ilha das Cobras and fired light-caliber shells at the army forts of Lage, Santa Cruz, and São João; the bases did not return fire. The insurgents also controlled the movement of vessels in the harbor, stopping passenger ships and occasionally firing on ships loyal to the government. Loyal torpedo boats took up position at the eastern end of the bay behind the Ilha da Mocangue near Niterói and awaited command. The naval arsenal,

the islands of Villegagnon and of Cobras, and the ships anchored in
São Bento drew heavier fire from the rebel ships, but suffered no direct
hits. The population took note of their skills, according to the *Times*
(London): "Crowds of sightseers gathered on the quays and heights,
and expressed their wonderment at the dexterity with which the huge
vessels were handled, and it was difficult to believe that there was not a
single officer on board. As soon as they were over the bar the mutineers
put about and re-entered the bay, taking up positions commanding the
city, and firing their guns at various points."[27] Observers were surprised
by the seamanship of the mutineers. Beyond fulfilling their basic neces-
sities, the reclamantes were putting on a show. Throughout the revolt,
and in the decades that followed, Brazilian officers and those scholars
sympathetic to those officers have repeatedly made the argument that
the rebels were unable to deliver on their threats against the capital city,
that the rebels were simply incapable of unleashing the potential destruction that these battleships offered. As the rebels were in touch with
journalists throughout the revolt, these statements certainly made their
way to the reclamantes. Throughout the four-day revolt, they reveled
in their ability to control these ships, and they broadcast in clear terms
their skill and power.

A report by the U.S. military attaché, John S. Hammond, addressed
the common belief held by the Brazilian elite

> that the great Dreadnaught *Minas Geraes* could not be handled by the Brazilians.
> There were reports, that when the firing tests of the *Minas Geraes* took place, that
> the Brazilian crew went below, and that the guns were entirely handled by the
> employees of the Armstrong Co [the ships' builders]. It was further understood,
> that this ship had not lifted anchor since she had been placed in the harbor of
> Rio de Janeiro by the Armstrong people. The fact that these vessels have been
> ably handled by seamen has lead to the knowledge, that they are capable of being
> used. It also has shown that the sailors have been well instructed.[28]

In describing the specific actions of the mutineers he goes on to say:

> On the morning of the 23rd the squadron passed out of the harbor of Rio (a very
> difficult channel) and at sea the squadron passed in review before João Cândido
> and executed some battle manouvers. . . .
>   About noon the ships returned to the harbor. They were handled in a manner
> that was nothing short of wonderful considering that the commanders, in every
> case were seamen, (no officers were among the mutineers). After entering the

harbor, the loyal torpedo boats started to attack the squadron, but upon seeing the large guns of the *Minas Geraes* being trained upon them they gave up the attempt.[29]

Another eyewitness to the revolt, this one a British citizen with extensive experience in the Royal Navy, stated:

> The handling of the Brazilian warships sans officers was a novel sight to us. I confess that I never saw evolutions performed in a smarter style than those undergone by the mutinous warships. . . . All day long the mutinous ships performed evolutions in the bay and at night retired in perfect order to the anchorage grounds outside, signaling all the time. I doubt whether a flag officer of rank would have done any better.[30]

These sources show that not only were the reclamantes capable, they were also quite restrained in the way they used the weapons under their control. In fact, one can argue that even when violence was applied, it was restrained. At the time the revolt began, according to naval records, there were nearly 270 officers onboard the four ships they seized. During the melee of the night of November 22, six officers were killed, whereas twenty enlisted men died; some were reclamantes while others fought to defend the officers. Throughout the revolt, the rebels restricted themselves to the use of the small-caliber guns, and they fired into largely unpopulated areas of the city. They did not, however, avoid all civilian casualties. On the morning of November 23, a shot fired from the *Minas Geraes* struck a home at 16 Misericórdia (Mercy) Street in the Castello neighborhood in Centro where two children were killed. Although there were allegations of other civilian casualties throughout the revolt, these killings in particular weighed on João Cândido. In an interview with Edmar Morel, he told the author, "from the miserable pay we received, we collected 200 *mil-reis* and sent it to the family to help bury those children."[31] Then, in 1919, while he was living in Santos, he gave an interview that appeared in *O Combate* in which he said that regarding the Revolta da Chibata, "I only have one regret: the death of the two innocents and nothing else."[32]

The limited loss of life among civilian and military populations, as well as the controlled damage to property throughout Rio de Janeiro, has resulted in a division among scholars of the Revolta da Chibata. Their dispute is over the level of mastery that these sailors attained over the warships that they briefly commanded. Their crisp execution of maneuvers surprised and impressed civilian and military eyewitnesses to the four-day revolt. However, supporters and detractors of the reclamantes have built arguments based on the fact that the uprising did so little damage to the nation's capital and its population. Those historians who portray the mutineers as heroes struggling for the rights of Brazil's underclass generally argue that the reclamantes purposely avoided harming Rio, its population, and the ships and sailors that remained loyal to the government. Much of the available evidence supports this conclusion. An article in the *Times* (London) states: "The urban station has intercepted a wireless telegram from the bluejacket João Cândido, the leader of the mutineers on board the *Minas Geraes,* addressed to his comrades on board the *São Paulo,* whom he advises to act with great coolness and not to fire any guns without orders from the *Minas Geraes.*"[33] If it was not a show of humanitarian restraint, by shelling over the city and around the bases and the warships that did not hoist the red flag of rebellion they made a pragmatic decision to consciously avoid unnecessary destruction; such action would gain them support among the politicians negotiating the conclusion of the revolt, with the press, and with the population of Rio. Such destruction would therefore remain their last resort.

Evidence certainly suggests that if they found it to be necessary, the mutineers could have fired their guns, at least most of them. One of several reports sent from the office of the military attaché in Buenos Aires to the U.S. Office of Naval Intelligence stated: "The chief features of the mutiny were the skillful handling of the ships by the mutineers and their ability to send and receive signals, including wireless. Of the handling of the guns they knew nothing. Not having the keys to the magazine, they broke into them with axes. On the *São Paulo* the [sic] filled the hydraulic system with salt water and the turret guns would not work."[34] That the turret guns onboard the *São Paulo* were disabled is not contested, but the reclamantes fired smaller shells throughout the four-day rebellion. There is good reason to believe that had they so chosen, the mutineers could have posed a violent threat to the city and an effective challenge to the loyal naval forces.

When the reclamantes took over, João Cândido assigned all sailors to their previous tasks, with the exception of those coconspirators who took over in the role of officers. A group of eighteen British engineers stayed on the dreadnoughts throughout the revolt and were given the responsibility to fire the boilers and work the engines. Several weeks after the resolution of hostilities, in a letter dated December 19, 1910, one of these engineers who worked on board the *Minas Geraes* during the revolt reported on conditions in the two battleships:

> You may be interested to know about these two Dreadnoughts. There are all sorts of stories about their not being able to fire their guns etc. The *Minas Geraes* is in perfect order, the *São Paulo* cannot fire her guns at present as the mutineers the other day ran salt water into all the hydraulic turning gear for the turrets. The English engineers are at work putting that to rights now. As a matter of fact the big guns have not been fired yet on board either ship. The contract of the guarantee men belonging to the English builders expires next month and they all leave then and the ships will probably deteriorate rapidly, as the Brazilians have neither the will nor the power to keep them efficient.[35]

Whether coerced or voluntarily, the engineers gave assistance that was essential to the effectiveness of the revolt. Their familiarity with the workings of the dreadnoughts supports the argument that the 12-inch guns could have been used if the leaders of the revolt deemed it necessary, though it is possible that these engineers would have refused to fire the guns if asked.

RIO HELD HOSTAGE

As for the civilian response to the actions playing out in Guanabara Bay, most *Cariocas* (residents of Rio de Janeiro), lacking means of communication, were ignorant of the night's events and the significance of the gunfire. Many, like the president, likely assumed that among the many festivities held in the Guanabara Bay following the inauguration, there were celebratory fireworks being set off. However, at dawn the news flooded the city's neighborhoods, and the populace grasped that the nation's most powerful warships were now under the control of the predominantly Afro-Brazilian enlisted men who crewed them. The city was explicitly threatened with bombardment if the government failed to accede to their demands. All citizens of the city – elite, workers, and the sizable underclass – suddenly found themselves hostage to the nation's "basest" underclass.

Thus, the immediate sense of panic that swept the city of Rio de Janeiro when its population awoke on November 23, 1910, was overwhelming. Cariocas found a naval revolt underway and the nation's most powerful warships firing on their city. The crews of the two foreign-built dreadnoughts hailed as invincible upon their arrival in Rio only a month earlier had inexplicably risen against the city. Ships with the capacity to accurately launch tons of projectile explosives at targets miles away had fallen into the hands of one of Brazil's most oppressed populations. Under the leadership of Seaman First Class João Cândido, these men betrayed their officers, killing several of them, and demanded humane treatment. Afro-Brazilians, who had expected freedom and opportunity with the passage of abolition in 1888, instead had found themselves unemployed, harassed by police, pressed into military service, and lashed as if still enslaved. With their newfound power these men demanded a radical change in Brazil's military, and thus a change in the very nature of twentieth-century Brazilian culture. The Brazilian elite quickly understood the violent repercussions they potentially faced.

The local press initially fanned the flames of panic. The headline of the *Correio da Manhã* on the morning of November 23 proclaimed: "Various Ships of the Squadron have Revolted: Rio and Nictheroy [Niterói] are attacked by gun and cannonball!" A reporter stated that at 1:00 AM, one of the revolting sailors had shouted to a neighboring vessel, "Yes we shoot to kill, we will kill everyone!" Contradicting the headline, the article went on to state that the shots were fired over, not at, the city, and as early as 2:00 AM, reporters stated, "It is clear that the revolting sailors do not wish to destroy the population of the city."[36] The headlines left Rio de Janeiro's population fearful of widespread destruction; a particular sense of panic swept the city's elite. Under the threat of the great guns targeting their homes, those who could afford to do so fled the nation's capital; on November 23 alone, over 3,000 people left by private railroad cars to the mountain city of Petrópolis. The population of the Zona Sul bolted by the thousand for the suburbs, jamming all means of available transportation.[37]

In fact, the reclamantes had followed up their original threat to the city with another less inflammatory telegram to Minister Leão. It arrived at 7:30 AM on November 23, stating, "We do not wish to harm anyone. We only request an increase in salary and no further use of the *chibata*. In the name of the dead, we request that a commission come speak with us before midday."[38] Their reassurance did little to quell the growing panic in the city, but along with fear, there was a growing curiosity about the four warships flying their red flags of revolution. At the time, the capital city had an estimated population of 870,475, and though thousands who could afford to do so fled, that left hundreds of thousands who remained.[39]

Brazil's press response followed an interesting trajectory; the presentation of the reclamantes shifted over the coming days: first they were criminals, then men wronged by an institution, and eventually, especially for the city's largely Afro-descended underclass, they became heroes. People who had continually suffered reprehensible treatment at the hands of government institutions in the name of "progress" could not help savoring the irony of the current situation. Once it was clear that the rebels were not going to immediately attack the city, large crowds swept to the waterfront to witness events.[40]

President Fonseca and his minister of the navy Joaquim Marques Batista de Leão were suddenly confronted by an impossible decision with few palatable outcomes. The officers, supported by enlisted men who were trusted to remain loyal, could attack the reclamantes using loyal ships not involved in the uprising. If the officers persevered, the naval elite would save face and preserve their honor, but at what cost? Their success would realistically mean destroying the very vessels that promised to deliver Brazil an image of a powerful navy; Brazil's purchase of these ships had gained worldwide recognition and prestige, and having to destroy them would be a costly and public humiliation. The alternative was arguably even worse; acquiescing to the rebels' demands might have physically saved Brazil's new *Esquadra Branca* (White Squadron), but it would allow racial inferiors to dictate terms to Fonseca's newly installed government, to undermine the progress of the modern Brazilian state. This outcome acknowledged that their costly "New Navy" was incompetent, and bending to the reclamantes' demands would be to publically admit that their naval hierarchy was built on an outdated and shameful system of labor extraction. What's worse, the elite would have allowed these aggrieved enlisted men to violently wipe out measures of social controls over Brazil's visibly racialized lower decks. A third (almost unspoken) scenario was equally terrible in the minds of the military elite. If the officers, with the support of those sailors who had remained loyal to the government (but whose loyalty was deeply suspect in the eyes of the military elite) attempted to retake these battleships in open combat, the likely outcome was the defeat of the loyal officers and the physical loss of the now outdated portion of the Brazil navy. Their loyal ships were much smaller than the dreadnoughts, and most were also quite old; they had little in the way of weaponry that could challenge a dreadnaught battleship. As well as their utter humiliation at the hands of men whom they regularly described as incapable of performing as sailors in the first place, it would have been hard to imagine rebuilding a navy after such a catastrophic outcome.

CIVILIAN VS. THE MILITARY RESPONSE

In the face of these choices, during the four-day uprising, Fonseca hedged his bet through the pursuit of two simultaneous, though in many ways contradictory, responses to the revolt. The first was a negotiated settlement with the rebels spearheaded by the Brazilian legislation embodied by senator Rui Barbosa and negotiated by congressional deputy and former naval commander José Carlos de Carvalho. On the other hand, President Fonseca and Minister of the Navy Leão invested in the pursuit of a military counteroffensive, though the plan faced repeated obstacles to its implementation.

On November 23 the reclamantes received a response from the government, though it did not yet meet their demands. Congress summoned federal deputy and retired naval officer José Carlos de Carvalho to represent the government in their negotiations with the rebels. At around 1:00 PM on November 23, dressed in his formal uniform and flying the white flag of peace from the mast, he approached the *São Paulo*. When he asked who was responsible for this revolt, the rebels called back as one: "We all are!" He approached each ship speaking with rebel representatives and noted the level of order and competence on each boat. He later told congress that the boats were being moved with precision and – much to their dismay – "that all their artillery is functioning well."[41] Carvalho was received on the rebellious ships with all appropriate military honors. When the political emissary interviewed the rebel sailors on the *São Paulo,* they said to him: "Powerful ships such as these can be neither overseen nor kept up by the half dozen marines who are on board; the work has doubled, the rations are inadequate and badly prepared and our punishments have been indecently increased. We are in a true moment of desperation: without food, overworked, and with our skin shredded by corporal punishment, it has reached the point of cruelty. We are not concerned with a raise in wages because a Brazilian sailor never trades the fulfillment of his debt and service to the fatherland for money."[42] He examined the ships to see that all was in proper order and that these jewels of the Brazilian fleet were being properly cared for.

In his 1988 study, naval historian and former vice admiral Hélio Leôncio Martins charged that Carvalho made explicit promises to the mutineers during his meeting with them. "With this," he charged, "the expectation of victory took form."[43] This is not supported by the testimony Carvalho offered to congress and the president of Brazil on November 24. Carvalho apparently did contact the rebels to inform them that the senate was debating the amnesty and to warn them to avoid any action that might prejudice their demands, but there is no evidence that he made any promises during his initial meeting with the mutineers, which would have exceeded the commission granted to him by congress.[44]

In his report to President Fonseca and his ministers and then to the national congress, Carvalho described a well-organized, effective, and militarized operation that had gained control over most of the naval power in Guanabara Bay. The naval officers enjoyed the continued loyalty of about half of Rio de Janeiro's enlisted men, and they controlled the navy's torpedo boats; this represented the government's only military option against the reclamantes. Although Carvalho refrained from assessing the government's ability to challenge the revolt militarily, he described the situation as extremely grave. He told them, "the people on board are capable of anything."[45] Many feel that by confirming and thus legitimizing their complaints and by describing the effectiveness of the rebel command, he pushed the government toward a negotiated settlement. Once congress officially considered these men citizens with legitimate complaints, it became harder to deal with them through military methods alone. By the afternoon of November 23, congress began discussing the passage of a general amnesty for the sailors.

Tremendous pressure came from all sides to free Rio de Janeiro from the threat of destruction, but not everyone accepted that an amnesty was the government's best action. Minister Leão, along with the vast majority of naval officers, was angry that Carvalho had agreed even to meet with the mutineers. By holding civilized negotiations with men who had murdered naval officers the previous night and by publicly accepting the validity of their claims, he opened himself and his reputation as a naval officer to violent criticism from the military elite. The anger directed at Carvalho did not quickly pass. In his 1953 study of the revolt (initially published in a magazine in 1949), Commander H. Pereira da Cunha states, "He should have been ashamed to shake the hands of the assassins of his colleagues, and even more repulsive, in order to demonstrate the barbarity [the mutineers] used to justify the revolt, he brought ashore the sailor who had been lashed."[46] Clearly for the military, the impact of these events was long-lived.

The naval minister pressed the president to defeat the sailors on the high sea using the troops and ships still loyal to the government. The president was clear: he refused to participate in any negotiation or communication with the rebel sailors as long as they held the city of Rio de Janeiro under siege. Loath to limit his choices prematurely, the president would rule out neither a military nor a negotiated settlement, and while congress moved toward an amnesty, naval officers made plans for a military confrontation.

That afternoon the rebel ships received a telegram from the torpedo boat destroyer *Paraíba,* a ship allegedly loyal to the government, claiming that loyal destroyers in the area were preparing an attack. Perhaps leery of such an attack, the rebels resolved to pass the night of November 23 (the second night of the revolt) outside of Guanabara Bay. They gave wide berth to the army *fortalezas* and passed without incident from the bay to the ocean, where they were far less susceptible to torpedo attack. The night was spent at a safe distance beyond the islands of Maricás, Redonda, and Cagarras. On the morning of November 24, they returned to the bay at 10:00 A M in tight formation. The rebel ships resumed patrol of the bay but discharged fewer shells and on the whole were less aggressive. The reclamantes, hopeful that their movement could end through negotiation, carefully avoided measures that might lead to confrontation.

NOVEMBER 24, 1910

By all accounts, on November 24, both mutineers and the press knew that Congress was preparing a decree of amnesty. The city remained tense, but there was a gradual shift – especially among the member of the press – from panic to curiosity. On that day, many members of the press became openly sympathetic toward the mutiny, as is evident in the front-page article in *Diário de Notícias:*

> What are the revolting sailors asking for? Simply this: that corporal punishment be abolished, the infamous lashings [*chibatadas*] that are in vogue in the national navy. Commander José Carlos de Carvalho, Federal Deputy and parliamentarian, who was on board the two dreadnoughts, had the opportunity to verify the torture inflicted on the flesh of a Brazilian dressed in the glorious uniform of the Brazilian navy. But long ago both the laws of the old regime and of the provisional government of the Republic extinguished from the national legislation the lines that authorized this degradation of a person's character.... The Constitution of February 24 abolished those infamous punishments, making impossible their application in all of the national territory. And after 20 years of republican regime, Brazilian sailors ... have to prosecute a truly low military to defend the respect of the nation's laws, their human dignity and that of the uniform.[47]

Another Rio daily, the *Correio da Manhã,* noted that it had

> become evident that, in express opposition to the determination of Brazil's highest law, the general use and abuse of corporal punishment continues aboard our ships.
> That, as in the time of the slave quarters and the plantation overseer, the *chibata* cuts the skin of our sailors, consonant with the whims of more or less vitriolic officers.
> It is also verified, by the laments of the revolting men, that the meals offered in the sailors mess halls are pernicious, prepared with adulterated and rotten

produce, not suitable for dogs. These facts constitute abundant motivation for the government to energetically and firmly proceed in establishing a respect for the equity and justice that is now demanded.[48]

This shift is also evident in the way that João Cândido himself was portrayed. In an article in the November 24 *O Correio da Manhã* titled "*O Almirante João Cândido*" (The Admiral João Cândido), he was described as follows: "João Cândido is a dark-skinned guy, tall, nice, and brave . . . full of ardor and courage, as soon as the movement began, he assumed leadership of the revolt, serving as the head of the rebellious fleet."[49] This type of description was soon taken up by the Brazilian press; João Cândido became "*O Almirante Negro*" (The Black Admiral).

Additionally, Lieutenant John S. Hammond, 3rd Field Artillery, American military attaché, Buenos Aires, Argentina, had positive words about João Cândido in the days following the revolt: "The course pursued by Joao Candido, has excited universal respect for this man. He lead a revolt for a purpose and accomplished it. He asked no favors for himself, and has proved that there is excellent ability in the Brazilian ranks, even though his success will be an everlasting humiliation to Brazil."[50] Sympathy and support came from much broader circles than the national press. Among politicians, the reclamantes found a powerful ally in Senator Rui Barbosa of the northern state of Bahia. The language he used on the floor of the Brazilian senate during the amnesty debate offers insight into the way the Brazilian elite perceived citizenship, race, slavery, and nation in the early twentieth century. Barbosa stressed the need to resolve the issue quickly. He exalted the cause for which the sailors were fighting, and he praised both the efficiency with which the sailors maneuvered the ships and the good faith they showed by not attacking the city.

Whereas Senator Barbosa's role as supporter and champion for the reclamantes is clear from the documents, his motivations are more opaque. According to some members of the naval elite, Rui Barbosa's "civilian campaign" for the presidency of the republic in 1910 was at least partially to blame for the Revolta da Chibata. The campaign of 1910 was the first hotly contested presidential election of the First Republic. It was an ugly fight, and it drove a wedge between pro- and antimilitary supporters. When Hermes da Fonseca won office, those who supported Rui Barbosa – especially the men within the federal government – remained hostile to the nation's new president. Thus, according to Commander H. Pereira da Cunha, "The amnesty of the revolting sailors among the ships in our armada, the shameful and unpatriotic amnesty, was the truly rotten fruit of the resentments of those politicians who put their personal interests, their resentment and hate, above the justice and the interest of this nation."[51]

Whatever his initial motivation, Senator Barbosa came out in firm support of the reclamantes. On the first day of the uprising, November 23, 1910, he addressed the senate chambers as follows: "It is important however, that we not forget the truth and justice that lay deep in the heart of these complaints; we must not fail to recognize that these masses rise up for the principle of a human right, an important principle of humanity and of law."[52] On Thursday, November 24, Senator Barbosa introduced his various reasons – an ideological platform of sorts – for supporting the reclamantes. The first was that the uprising was an "honest revolt," neither political nor antigovernment. Because it was nonpolitical, he cast them as honorable men fighting for their rights as Brazilian citizens. He stressed that their actions had been neither violent nor disorganized:

> They have cast into the sea all the liquor that was on board so that no-one can become drunk; they have placed sentries to guard the chests where the valuables are stored, they have ordered that sentries block the entrance to the officers quarters so that they will not be violated . . . they have been faithful to their ideas; they have been loyal to each other. . . . Men of this order cannot be discarded. Mourn their subterfuge, but recognize the human valor that they represent.[53]

He went on to say:

> I am intimately persuaded that a great part, the greatest part perhaps, of social ills which grieve Brazil today, are due to the moral influence of slavery, which has already been extinct for many years. We extinguished slavery over the black [*negra*] race: however, we maintain slavery over the white race in the Army and the Navy, the servants of the Nation who have gained the sympathy of all Brazilians.
> 　　It is necessary that we do not continue to forget that the sailor and solder are men. . . . The civilization of our country demands another system of education for our men of war . . . and the extinction of corporal punishment.[54]

His description of the slavery of white men in the military is particularly interesting because, as I argued in chapter 3, whites were underrepresented in the lower ranks of both the army and navy. It seems that his protest was over the fact that whites in these institutions were treated in a manner in which Brazilians had long since grown accustomed to treating Afro-Brazilians. White and black men had both been "enslaved" in Brazil's military, but the powerful rhetoric that he applied was to focus on whites who, according to Brazil's elites, should have been better treated. Thus the true "wrong" committed was toward the white minority who were unfortunate enough to find themselves in the Brazilian military in the first place.

To bolster his argument for a diplomatic rather than a military solution, Barbosa utilized the same language the military elite previously had used to justify the purchase of the "New Navy." He stated that if the dreadnoughts were unsinkable – as the naval elite had claimed – then the handful of destroyers that remained loyal to the government could not be a viable threat against them. He then argued that even if the naval officers could defeat the rebels, "they did not have the right to sink ships that represent a considerable part of the public fortune."[55] Nor, he went on, did they have any more right to take the lives of the citizens aboard the ships than did those citizens have a right to destroy the nation's capital and its million inhabitants. Barbosa's argument – that if a naval attack took place with the support of congress, the responsibility for the possible destruction of Brazil's capital city would be theirs – carried enough of a threat to win overwhelming support in the senate.

By the afternoon of November 24, the federal senate began to push through a bill of amnesty toward all persons involved with the insurrection once the ships were submitted to the constitutional authorities. The senator from Rio Grande do Sul, José Gomes de Pinheiro Machado, led the opposition to the amnesty's passage, but his was not a strong ideological disagreement. He agreed that it was incontestable that the insurrection was the result of criminal and moral abuses at the hands of naval officers. However, he argued that as hostages, the senate could not offer a magnanimous act to those men holding them hostage: clemency could only be granted, never seized. Furthermore, he feared that such a show of weakness would lead only to further armed uprising among the Brazilian population. Pinheiro Machado argued that the sailors had to first turn themselves in; only then could an amnesty be passed. Were the reclamantes unwilling to do so, a military attack should not be ruled out.

The two senators also debated whether the mutineers could fight the loyal warships. Men supporting each opinion had presented compelling arguments to the senate body. Although the viability of a military challenge remained an unknown variable, both politicians and military officers pressed to fight the insurgents.

Senator Barbosa argued compellingly:

> Granted that their munitions may not be sufficient to carry out a battle for months, they are certainly sufficient for a resolute and decisive attack in which the insurgents can win immediate victory by disastrously turning their artillery against our shores, the Capital of Brazil.
>
> The destruction of the Capital of the Republic is a hypothesis naturally figured into the material situation that we are planning for, and the destruction of the Capital of the Republic would be sufficiently calamitous to determine and manifest our utter defeat.[56]

Although the debate dragged on for hours, it was soon clear that Barbosa had won. The senate voted unanimously to pass the legislation late in the afternoon of November 24 and sent it to the chamber of deputies for debate the following day.

While congress attempted to negotiate an end to the crisis, naval officers (with the president's support) had different plans. It was well known that congress was in the process of passing the amnesty; if the senate served as any indication of the bill's future in the chamber of deputies, it would pass by a large enough margin to easily override any potential presidential veto. That said, the reclamantes not only had to remain free until the official implementation of any amnesty, they could ill afford an armed confrontation with the loyal warships before they returned the ships to Brazilian naval officers. Even if the sailors were victorious in an altercation, sympathy for the mutineers depended largely on the continued absence of bloodshed. A battle with loyal troops would jeopardize their positive position with the press, in the congress, and among the population of Rio de Janeiro.

THE MILITARY RESPONSE

The reclamantes had delivered a humiliating attack to the naval elite by expelling them from the warships under their command. Then congress responded to that attack by embracing the sailors' demands, and finally the popular press – in need of a scapegoat – vilified the officers as inhumane, incompetent criminals. Naval leaders believed that only a military confrontation with the rebels would restore their lost honor. They also knew that an amnesty was in the congressional pipeline and that any action against the mutineers would therefore have to take place before the measure cleared congress, and it was increasingly apparent that this might occur as early as November 25.

Of the fleet's newest and most technologically advanced ships acquired through the Naval Renovation of 1906, Brazilian naval officers retained control of only the light cruiser *Rio Grande do Sul* and the division of eight smaller *Pará*-class destroyers produced by the Yarrow shipyards of Glasgow, Scotland. The *Rio Grande do Sul* displaced 3,100 tons and carried ten 4.7-inch guns. The destroyers, each named after a Brazilian state, were the *Alagoas, Amazonas, Mato Grosso, Pará, Paraíba, Piauhi, Rio Grande do Norte,* and *Santa Catarina.* They were designed for river and coastal defense. Each displaced 570 tons and was armed with two 4-inch guns and two 3-pounders. They were lightly armored but they were fast, and each had two torpedo tubes. Additionally, officers retained control of the cruiser *Almirante Barroso,* outfitted with 6-inch guns. Like the dreadnoughts, Armstrongs' shipyards in Newcastle built the *Almirante Barroso,* but the Brazilian navy took delivery of this ship in 1897. The loyal fleet would be at a severe disadvantage against the brand-new dreadnoughts, each of which – carrying twenty-two 4.7-inch guns in addition to their twelve 12-inch guns – outgunned the officers' combined flotilla. But if there was to be a military challenge to the revolt, these ships would play an important role. The new ships were extremely efficient, and officers believed that if crewed by loyal and competent men, these ships could challenge the insurgents.[57]

With 1,500–2,000 of 4,000 enlisted men in Rio involved in the revolt, there were therefore upwards of 2,000 troops whom the admiralty considered loyal to the state. However, naval officers lacked confidence in these troops' allegiance. When hostilities broke out on November 22, there had been insurgent activity on board five ships. In addition, the crews on board an additional seven ships had immediately abandoned their posts for land. Therefore, as officers arrived at the naval base throughout the day of November 23, they were assigned to personally crew all combat positions on the boats likely to be called into action during the revolt. As much as possible, officers removed the enlisted men from positions from which they could pose a threat, and many were sent off altogether.[58]

Though they succeeded in manning the government ships, arming them turned out to be a far more difficult problem. As Commander Pereira da Cunha self-consciously noted in his history of the revolt, "in times of peace torpedo war-heads (which are loaded with explosives) are always guarded on land, in a storage magazine; they leave on board the adapted torpedoes that are non-explosive. This is true in all the world's navies."[59] During the first night of the revolt, the minister of the navy ordered an officer to procure warheads for the loyal ships from the munitions depot on the Island of Boqueirão. The necessary warheads could not be located, however, and were eventually found stored nearby at an islet called Paiol near Niterói on the far side of Guanabara Bay. However, the mutineers' active patrol of the bay separated the loyal ships from their ordnance and thus made it impossible to requisition and deliver the needed warheads.[60]

The army bases had already received orders to stand down; the forts' officers realized that antagonizing the reclamantes and facing their twenty-four 12-inch guns at point blank range was not in their best interest. The destroyers in Guanabara Bay remained ready to procure their warheads, but the vigilant patrol of the revolting ships allowed no opening. In fact, two destroyers on a reconnaissance mission were driven back by shots fired from the *Deodoro,* though these shots did not strike their targets.[61]

Once the insurgents left the bay on the night of November 23 for reasons of security, the radio station at Ilha das Cobras repeatedly attempted to contact the division of destroyers. The officers had sailed their ships to safety at the eastern end of Guanabara Bay, and although the departure of the mutineers to the high seas could have allowed the officers an opportunity to arm the destroyers, the signals from the radio tower failed to reach them. A transport ship loaded with warheads planned to meet the destroyers just to the north of the Ilha do Engenho, but after waiting all night for the destroyers to arrive, that ship finally returned the ordnance to the magazine at Niterói. It would be nearly forty-eight hours before the officers managed to deliver and distribute torpedoes to the division of destroyers and the *Rio Grande do Sul*. When that shipment finally occurred, the officers received fewer than one dozen torpedoes.[62]

On the afternoon of November 24, the reclamantes – preoccupied with the possible actions of the loyal ships in the bay – requisitioned and received water from Ilha das Cobras and received ammunition, coal, and other stores from Vianna Island. They then returned to the relative safety of the high seas, where they had more space to maneuver and could better defend against a surprise torpedo attack.[63] That night, President Fonseca gave his officers the order to attack. In his annual report to the president, the minister of the navy stated:

> It was resolved by you to attack the rebels with all the forces on land or sea at the disposal of the Government, at 2:00 AM I received order to arrange everything toward that objective.
>
> The attack was to have been carried out by the scout *Rio Grande do Sul* and the Division of Destroyers, and instructions to that end were circulated, at the same time, in a telegram to the commander of the forces in Nictheroy, I ordered that the cruiser torpedo-boat *Tymbira* and the torpedo-boat *Goyaz* to load the necessary munitions, and crew and attack the rebel ships, as soon as the attack is initiated by the other ships.[64]

According to Edmar Morel, the telegraph operator on the *Timbira* was leaking information to the reclamantes.[65] Either because they received information about a planned attack or as part of their general defensive measures, the rebels simply did not return to Guanabara Bay on the morning of November 25, thereby thwarting the plans of the president and the naval officers. The rebels stayed at sea until receiving concrete news of the passage of their amnesty. The minister's report continued: "The rebel ships did not enter port that morning, and when they did pass the *Fortalezas* of [Santa Cruz da] Barra that afternoon, there was already activity in the passage of the project of amnesty and the order to attack was revoked."[66]

THE AMNESTY

As the amnesty that released Rio de Janeiro from its state of siege was announced, a final conflict erupted that threatened to undermine all of the negotiations. On November 23, before Deputy José Carlos de Carvalho met with the president – in fact while he was on board the *Minas Geraes* and *São Paulo* meeting with the insurgents – the president called a meeting with leading members of his cabinet. The mayor of Rio de Janeiro, General Bento Ribeiro, and the chief of police, Belisário Távora, were also in attendance. Based on discussions held at that meeting, on the morning of November 25, Ribeiro and Távora distributed the following statement to the press:

> That the authorities not allow sailors to disembark on land, except on the Arsenal de Marinha.
> Do not respond to any radio transmission the rebels make.
> If the rebels do not give themselves up immediately, their ships will be torpedoed.[67]

The message was widely distributed and covered in the press. The local government's hostile and threatening tone came as a shock to Rio de Janeiro's population. Cariocas who believed that the uprising was about to end suddenly faced the possibility that this release could aggravate the rebels and thus cause an attack on the city. A general panic ensued, and people once again sought to flee the city in case fighting broke out.

Immediately the rebels broadcast the message, "We do not wish to hurt anyone, but we cannot accept the chibata!" The crew of the *São Paulo,* sharing the fears of the population of Rio de Janeiro that the announcement could foment violence, and perhaps cause division among the insurgents, radioed to the *Minas Geraes, "Não se afobem!"* (Take it easy!).[68]

That afternoon the president forced the chief of police to revoke his morning's statement and issue the following:

> The government has absolutely no intention to start bombing against the revolting ships, nor does it authorize the statements made in the bulletins distributed this morning....
> Thus there is no reason for the unusual panic that alarmed the population with the fear of eminent and grave danger.
> We are doing everything in the hope of avoiding the bombing of the city and to normalize within a short time the situation created by the uprising among our naval troops.[69]

With this dispatch, the revolt drew to a close. That afternoon the battle was waged solely through communications. The mutineers, distrustful of the military, stayed at sea until they received news that the amnesty had cleared the chamber of deputies. They received near-constant notice of the progress toward the amnesty project, and it passed by a vote of 125 to 23. The president signed the amnesty – as a veto could have been easily overruled be the near-unanimity with which congress passed the project.

Once the demands of the reclamantes were met, and they received word that Barbosa would submit a bill to congress abolishing corporal punishment in the army and navy within days, the revolt approached its conclusion. The leaders of the revolt asked for no special treatment or privileges, but they did request that all ships involved in the revolt come under the command of new officers. Also at the request of the mutineers, the *Minas Geraes* would be commanded by Captain João Pereira Leite, and they would turn all of their ships over to his command.

On that final night, the reclamantes again opted for the relative safety of the high seas so that they could proudly enter the bay one last time in charge of their ships and officially receive their amnesty from the naval official to whom they returned the ships. Throughout the night and into the early morning, the telegraph machines on the rebel ships remained active as the reclamantes discussed the conditions for the return of the ships, using code among themselves and on open channels with government and naval officials.

On the night of Friday, November 25, the insurgents, led by João Cândido, were confident that their movement had been a success, but they had a final hurdle to clear. That afternoon and evening, the telegraph machines on the four rebel ships were consistently in use, as the ships exchanged coded messages, exchanging opinions and suggestions as to their actions. For the first time, there seem to have been serious questions among the sailors about the decisions of the insurgent leaders. According to José Alves da Silva, who took command of the *Deodoro* during the revolt, "the sailors could not understand the resistance among their leaders, when the government seemed willing to give them anything being that they still had the guns under their control."[70]

José Alves da Silva was a caboclo of barely twenty years at the time of the revolt. He asked why they would turn over the ships while they enjoyed the upper hand and had not yet received all of their demands.

João Cândido replied from the *Minas Geraes* that as the government had granted the amnesty and assured them that the chibata would be considered extinct; to continue resisting would turn public opinion against them, as had already begun to happen.

Alves de Silva responded with the following manifesto, which was turned over to the government representative when the ship was surrendered:

> The Comandante of the *Deodoro,* and its small crew . . . at the risk of our very lives, never faulted support for our companions from the other revolting boats from [November] 22 to 25. And this has been done with splendor, good feeling and love. But on the night of [November] 25 we became intensely disgusted with those companions to whom we have given so much support. All of this disgust is directed toward Comandante João Cândido for having accepted the amnesty, made on land, without the presence on board of the President of the Republic and the Minister of the Navy.
>
> Even though the Comandante of the revolted division attempted to convince us of the impossibility of the government's representatives coming to sign the bill in our presence, we still had discordance, it was not only this, but the fact that our salaries had not been augmented by law. . . .
>
> We should not have been rushed by the amnesty. We should have waited several more days. Didn't they say our salaries would be discussed in Congress? We should have awaited that discussion. We had the key in our hands to a better nation. We had the power. The people were conscious of what was happening. He should have helped to force the Government to give us what we all wanted.[71]

Again, we have here an extraordinary moment in which the terms of citizenship and freedom are being argued among men who have traditionally fallen outside the story of politics in Brazil and the Atlantic World. These statements produced by the sailors themselves, in this case a twenty-year-old sailor catapulted onto the world stage by these events, offer a rare insight into the potential of the desprotegidos not as sailors but as men who were targeted and repressed by the Brazilian state. This rare clear articulation by a young non-white man in 1910 of his desire for freedom and citizenship suggests that the motivation for the Revolta da Chibata was much more than the simple cessation of corporal punishment. Their movement represented a struggle to gain the honor of citizenship that the state had systematically refused them. It was withheld not only from sailors, but from all poor Afro-Brazilians, who were forced to live outside the formal economy and away from respected society while the country's elite fabricated a fragile "civilization" and "modernization" that did little to shift the nation toward any real progress.

THE CONCLUSION OF THE REVOLTA DA CHIBATA

The turning over of the ships was marked for 12:00 noon on Saturday, November 26. That morning, the *São Paulo* and the *Bahia* entered Guanabara Bay to requisition water in order that the crew members could bathe. At that time, they still flew the red flag of rebellion. According to José Alves da Silva's description cited above, the sailors and the common men on the wharf chanted together, "Viva a liberdade! Viva a liberdade!" After filling the tanks of the *São Paulo,* the two ships returned to the protection of the open sea.

The appointed hour passed, and the ships did not reappear. Rumors abounded: some said the bay had been mined and the ships had fled; others said that the red flags flown that day meant that the insurgents would not turn in the ships as agreed. Though the formal complaint of José Alves da Silva of the *Deodoro* would not be turned over to the government officials until the ships were surrendered, his strong reservations about when and if the ships should be returned to the government likely initiated intense debate among the *reclamantes.* Finally, more than an hour late – with the *Minas Geraes* leading, flanked by the *Deodoro* and *Bahia,* and the *São Paulo* in the rear – the ships entered the bay with the rebel commanders at their helms for the last time.

When the government's representative, Captain Pereira Leite, came aboard the *Minas Geraes* to meet with João Cândido, the rebel leader stated: "It is not only I who will resolve this. Wait for the commissioners of all the ships involved."[72] The leaders of the four insurgent ships – Manuel Gregorío de Nascimento of the *São Paulo,* Francisco Dias Martins of the *Bahia,* and José Alves de Silva of the *Deodoro* – met, together with Captain Pereira Leite and João Cândido of the *Minas Geraes,* for the first time since the outbreak of the Revolta da Chibata. The following discussion took place when the government delegate asked,

The amnesty has already been conceded. There is no more corporal punishment [in Brazil's military]. Your wages are going to be augmented. What more do you want?

– We want guarantees! We want that none of us will be persecuted. We want the rights for which we rebelled, when these promises were not being observed.

– Not promises, the law!

– For many years the law stated you could not beat sailors, yet officers cudgeled us indiscriminately.

– The government has power, officers are not free to act in such a manner. He who is disposed to resist will be considered a pirate and will be exterminated.[73]

The argument went back and forth throughout the afternoon. The government agent assured the insurgents that the law of November 16, 1889, had abolished corporal punishment, and thus rendered further legislation unnecessary. It was clear that the reclamantes feared that the government would not uphold its end of the bargain, but at 7:00 PM on Saturday, November 26, 1910, the insurgents accepted the amnesty. The red flags of rebellion were lowered, and the sailors returned the ships to the officers of the Brazilian navy.

In fact, it was almost impossible with them on board, to maintain discipline. To the eyes of the people, the newspapers had presented João Cândido, a black man, as a national hero and had attributed to him the capacity of a great seaman, purposely treating him as an admiral.

FELIPE MOREIRA LIMA, tenente in the Brazilian army, 1910

The terrible feature of the revolt is the apathy of the officers under this crushing indictment of inefficiency, and incompetence. The modern powerful battleships, scouts, and torpedo boats are useless in the hands of Brazilian naval officers and men. Without preliminary training they are not experienced enough to handle them and the navy is disorganized, disoriented, and a navy in name only.

IRVING B. DUDLEY, Memo to the U.S. Secretary of State

SIX

Betrayal and Revenge

BRAZIL'S CONGRESS AND PRESIDENT ENDED THE REVOLTA DA Chibata through the passage and ratification of the general amnesty of the insurgent sailors on November 26, 1910. Following its negotiated conclusion, the repercussions of this armed uprising resonated throughout Brazil. The divisions that formed between naval elites and members of the Brazilian government during the revolt – rooted in the struggle over the implementation of either a military or diplomatic solution in ending the uprising – reignited into long-term hostility over this issue. For decades, partisans blamed each other for the circumstances that culminated in the Revolta da Chibata.

Once the threat of immediate violence toward Rio de Janeiro and its population passed, there was much criticism of the government's handling of the situation. Although the amnesty saved Brazil's sizable investments in these modern tools of naval warfare, many now questioned the price paid for such a rescue. For the elite, the intention of the naval renovation itself was to fix their institution, propelling Brazil to the front of a South American arms race, and to make their navy competitive with that of any Western nation. Instead, enlisted men had used those very ships to humiliate the naval elite. The ships were saved, but at what cost? The Brazilian elite, military and civilian alike, saw themselves broken by men they defined as Brazil's basest class. For the officers, the reclamantes were dishonored men, overwhelmingly descended from slaves who through their rebellion demanded that naval officers no longer treat them as slaves. These sailors forced the state to make good on the promises of honor and citizenship written into the Republican Constitution of 1891 – promises that the government and naval officers alike had by then made clear, in the more than two decades since the promulgation of that constitution, that they never intended to deliver. In demanding their own honor, the reclamantes had effectively stripped it from these naval officers, and what good were the ships if the men who commanded them had been stripped of their honor? Through their revolt, the reclamantes had inverted the very nature of military hierarchy. For the officer class, the only short-term way to win back their position was to tear down this inverted naval hierarchy with their own show of crushing violence. Given time, they spent generations manipulating how the story of the Revolta da Chibata was told.

Members of the political and naval elite, each independently of the other, began pragmatic defensive maneuvering in order to avert or avoid blame and dishonor for themselves and their institutions for the conditions that led to the revolt. In several cases, each group absolved its own branch of government from blame by scapegoating the other; Congress pointed its finger at the naval elite and vice versa. There has been some question whether, while the revolt was under way, government agents fabricated communications from the rebels to make them appear more sympathetic and less hostile so as to better justify the passage of the amnesty on November 26. In part, this chapter focuses on the interactions between the men and the Brazilian elite; it offers insight into the power the reclamantes retained in the Brazilian navy and how far naval officers would go to wrest back their position of dominance over the sailors serving in the Brazilian navy.

THE QUESTION OF GOVERNMENT
MANIPULATIONS AND MISINFORMATION

In his 1959 book *A Revolta da Chibata* Edmar Morel claimed that in the process of resolving the revolt the government initiated a campaign of manipulation to improve public opinion of their actions. He speculates that the office of President Hermes de Fonseca fabricated messages from the insurgents in order to justify his government's negotiation with the reclamantes. Historians on both sides of the revolt, that of the reclamantes and that of the officers, have accepted that there were probably forged messages on two occasions, but this claim has not been confirmed.

The first instance concerns two messages received on Friday, November 25. The first came from the *Minas Geraes* and was addressed to "the *povo* and to the President of the Nation." It was eloquently written, and it basically laid out the insurgents' motivations for revolting. It read:

> From the Chief of the Nation, the illustrious Marechal Hermes da Fonseca, whose government we sailors hope is crowned with peace and inexceedable brilliance, we *reclamantes* only want a general amnesty, and the complete abolition of corporal punishment in order to better our armed classes.
>
> We sailors lament that these occurrences have taken place at the beginning of the presidency of Your Exellency, Sr. Marechal Hermes da Fonseca, to whom the crew of the *São Paulo* is especially sympathetic.
>
> To the Brazilian people, the sailors ask that you look upon our cause with the sympathy that it deserves, for it was never our intent to act against the lives of the hard working population of Rio de Janeiro.
>
> Only in a final emergency, if attacked or if all was lost, would we sailors fight in our own defense.
>
> [Signed] The Sailors of the Brazilian Armada[1]

The second was addressed to the minister of the navy from aboard the *São Paulo*. Its tone is far less deferential to the president or to any other symbol of authority.

> For this we ask Your Excellency, to abolish the use of the *chibata* and of other barbarous punishments by the right of our freedom, with the end results that the Brazilian Navy would be an Armada of citizens and not a plantation of slaves who only receive from the masters the right to be beaten. . . .
>
> We are obliged to tell Your Excellency, that the Brazilian Navy can only hope to accept the offer of peace in the following manner: the President of the Republic must come in person, with a commission of Senators and Deputies, along with Your Honor [the Minister of the Navy] and with this commission resolve the terms of peace in the following manner: by decree of the President of the Republic corporal punishment must be abolished in the navy, also the officers and petty-officers do not have the right to verbally mistreat *praças* [a term for low-ranking soldiers and sailors with roots in the Brazilian colonial era.] with aggressive words, along with the decree of Sr. President the all sailors who were involved in this uprising are pardoned.[2]

The two messages effectively ask the same things, but in starkly different tones. According to Retired Vice-Admiral Hélio Leôncio Martins, "The first letter clearly could not have been written by the sailors. The style of the letter was not consistent with the initial letter of the revolt, nor with the known letters written by Francisco Dias Martins. The refined style of the document is far beyond his literary possibilities, even though he was the official scribe of the revolt."[3] Martins describes the second message as the authentic one. It matched the style of the other communiqués, and, like the other messages, it was sent from the *São Paulo.* Few men could read and write well – João Cândido could read but left writing to other men – and this letter was clearly written by an educated person. If he had written it, the "official scribe" for the revolt, Francisco Dias Martins, would have been onboard not the *Minas Geraes* (the ship from which it was allegedly sent), but rather the *Bahia.*

That said, we have already seen disagreement among the sailors on different ships, so the mere fact that their messages were not exactly in agreement or that they did not share a tone is not enough to state that either was not produced by the reclamantes. Even if Martins is correct that this letter was not written by Francisco Dias Martins – a hard conclusion to support based on his further statement that he does not believe that F. D. Martins was the author of the original manifesto either – the fact that we don't know who penned the telegraph is not enough to define it as a fabrication. Historians Marco Morel and Sílvia Capanema P. de Almeida make a compelling argument that two other sailors involved in the organization of the uprising – Adalberto Ferreira Ribas and Ricardo de Freitas (who were both trained as telegraph operators) – could have written the original manifesto and, being that the messages arrived by telegraph, could have also produced these letters.[4]

The author of the first message and the reason it was written become more interesting when we put it into the context of a third message received from the insurgents. Just before Senator Rui Barbosa presented the amnesty for a vote by the senate, a telephone call announced that the president had just received the following message:

> His Excellency, Marechal Hermes da Fonseca
> President of the Republic
> Having repented of the action we took in our defense, for love of order, of justice and of liberty, we lay down our arms, confident that amnesty will be

> granted us by the National Congress, abolishing, as the law commands, corporal
> punishment, increasing our pay – and the members of the crew have no care – so
> that the work may be performed without our sacrifice. We will remain on board,
> obedient to the orders of Your Excellency, in whom we have great confidence.
>   [Signed] The "Reclamantes"[5]

The content of this telegram had no basis in fact: at no time did the sailors plan on turning over their weapons until the amnesty was signed, but does that mean that the message was false? Certainly, for many scholars it seems extremely unlikely that such a message originated from the reclamantes at all. According to Edmar Morel, "This telegram was forged in order to ease the task of the Federal Senate, which needed an honest way out."[6] Regardless of its origins, the message certainly served that purpose; immediately after receiving the news of the statement the senate halted debate and passed the amnesty bill unanimously. The president also cited the importance of this telegraph, which he received several hours before signing the amnesty bill into law. Although his veto would have done nothing but delay the bill by some hours, he had pledged that he would not sign the amnesty until the insurgents had laid down their arms, and Minister Leão responded to their initial demand by stating that their demands "can only be addressed when made with deference and respect to the constitutional powers."[7] Although this message certainly contradicts their initial demands sent on the morning of November 22, in which they said if demands were not met in twelve hours it would lead to the bombardment of the city and loyal ships, a great deal had changed in that time. On November 24, it was widely understood that congress was working on the passage of the amnesty bill, and they had met with Deputy Carvalho, who certainly would have made them aware of the need for the reclamantes to remain conciliatory as the conclusion of negotiations approached.

The argument that these sailors were incapable of producing eloquent prose falls into the general racist assumptions that the officer class repeatedly made about the skills of their enlisted men. To dismiss them because they were contradictory to earlier statements from the reclamantes assumes a unanimity of purpose already undermined by José Alves da Silva's manifesto from on board the *Deodoro*. While the legitimacy of these documents cannot be conclusively proven, dismissing them as forgeries plays into the historical narrative of those scholars seeking to undermine the qualification and legitimacy of these sailors.[8]

DIFFICULTIES IN REBUILDING NAVAL HIERARCHY

In the aftermath of the revolt, the popular support that the reclamantes enjoyed days earlier rapidly evaporated. A letter to the U.S. secretary of state from the American Embassy in Petrópolis described the situation:

> I may add that since the danger has passed, much criticism is freely expressed by civilians, also; some taking the position that the offer of amnesty, which induced the surrender, should not now be observed, because made under duress of the appalling threats of a band of outlaws.
>
> The European press quoted in the Rio papers, notably that of France, severely criticizes the course of this Government in yielding. Yet few newspapers of Brazil, and none at Rio de Janeiro, opposed the action while under discussion in Congress and none at Rio has since criticized it. The feeling now prevalent at the national capital is one of humiliation. It is also realized that the future may demonstrate how dearly bought has been the deliverance of to-day, should the seeds now sown bring forth their natural fruit in the army, the navy, and the ranks of lawless labor. The leaders of the revolt are popular heroes.[9]

To end the threat of Rio de Janeiro being bombarded, the government had passed an amnesty and the cessation of the application of corporal punishment. But those concessions did little to reimplement an effective military hierarchy. As the soldiers used the language of "slavery as practiced in the Brazilian navy," let me again extend that metaphor. Naval service and hierarchy in the period leading up to the revolt was based on the same code of violent hierarchal control that regulated slavery. For plantation owners throughout the Atlantic World, the reintroduction of order following a violent insurrection was a vicious and public ceremony to show the men and women who were returning to slavery that any attempt at such a dangerous transgression to society would be punished exponentially. However, in this case, officers who traditionally believed the day-to-day running of the navy demanded the draconian control offered by the lash suddenly found themselves in a navy, overseeing men who had just overturned naval hierarchy with their rebellion, now with none of the tools by which white elite retained control over the bodies of poor black men. Unfortunately for the sailors involved in the revolt, white elites were consistent in their methods of reprisal after removing the immediate threat of violence – in responding to both slave and military uprisings.

Conditions on one of the ships were described in a report sent to the U.S. Office of Naval Intelligence: "Since the Amnesty, things had gone from bad to worse on the *Minas Geraes*. In the first place the crew had asked for a certain officer to be ordered in command, and he had been detailed. They asked to have all the officers changed and that was done. Whenever the officers gave orders, the men passed the orders forward and after approval by Cândido, they were issued by the petty officers."[10] In the aftermath of the revolt, the sailors feared government retaliation, and with good reason. This left the sailors suspicious of all requests from officers, which in turn made military hierarchy of any form all but impossible to enforce. Once the amnesty was signed into law, popular opinion turned against civilian and military leaders, and officers were unable to run their ships effectively. The frustration on board was clear to the former rebels, and in the days following the revolt, a sense of panic grew among them. According to Edmar Morel, a commission of ex-rebels sought a hearing from both Rui Barbosa and Pinheiro Machado but were turned away. André Avelino, the initial leader of the *Deodoro*, fled Rio de Janeiro for the north of Brazil due to his fear of government reprisals. It would not take long for the suspicions of the amnestied sailors to be proven correct and for the government to go back on its agreement.[11]

GOVERNMENT RETALIATION

Naval officers began to implement changes that would remove the potential threat of the warships crewed by the men who revolted against the government. On the day the revolt ended, Saturday, November 26, 1910, many of the amnestied men were given license to go ashore, and on November 27 the ships were disarmed. Again, the report to the U.S. Office of Naval Intelligence described the event:

> It may be asked what assurance the Government can feel that these same sea-
> men will not rise again, destroy their officers and once more threaten Rio de
> Janeiro with bombardment if new demands are not complied with. The answer
> undoubtedly is that the Government is laboring under no delusion, for as soon
> as the ships were delivered up, the work at once began of removing from them to
> the land all munitions of war and the breech block of the principal guns. While
> manned by such a crew, it was deemed advisable that the dreadnoughts should
> be rendered as harmless as steamboats.[12]

The following Monday, November 28, the president announced his
Decree 8,400: "In support of the Minister of the State of Affairs of the
Navy, it is resolved to discharge and exclude from service of the Brazilian Navy any man who has become inappropriate to discipline. They
will be dispensed of using Art. 150 do *Regulamento anexo ao Decreto*
N°. 7,124 of Sept. 24 1908 and any orders to the contrary are revoked."[13]
When it was introduced and passed, the justification offered for such
a ruling was that the navy could no longer discipline insubordinate or
violent recruits by applying the lash; therefore, officials needed a way to
remove from service men who represented a threat to discipline. Again,
nineteenth-century modernization had called on state-run institutions
such as the army, navy, and police to take on the authority previously
held by slave owners for the regulation and regimentation of the undisciplined, violent, urban and rural menace. Without the ability to control
these populations with violence, naval officers opted to simply remove
those elements from their institution. They further argued that because
the men were not being tried for crimes, they were not going against
the nature of the amnesty. However, the reclamantes' demands were
not that they be excluded from criminal charges, but rather that they be
excluded from any persecution. Again, Rui Barbosa eloquently argued
in front of the senate:

> The captive, the servile property among us was a social flagellation of a fellow
> creature, an institution that disregarded and abolished human nature, a social
> interest that disrespected in man the sentiment of honor and of his native
> dignity.
>   The evil of slavery among us brought on the first rebellion of the military
> forces against the constitutional authorities. That it did not assume another form
> was due to the unanimous sentiment toward this reaction. And they were able
> to act with such immediacy and with such force in the balance that the question
> found itself immediately resolved, the resolution was not however without its

cost; perhaps the acknowledgment of a form of government below the level that we maintain to have.

Today the captives of the *chibata* and the *açoite* [the whip used on slaves] in the military service are clamoring for their privileges as free men.

It has been 20 years that the Republic granted those rights, it has been 20 years that they have continuously been unrecognized.... Once there was adopted by Congress and sanctioned by this Government an amnesty; it was a definite, irreparable and irretraceable act.

If I am not mistaken however, Sr. President, it was this act that was annulled by decree yesterday, in which the President of the Republic, heeding the Minister of the Navy, invoked art. 150 of the regiments of 1908, thus dispensing with the guarantees established in said [amnesty].[14]

Again, we find Barbosa defending these sailors and the justness of their revolt. He reminded the senators how the reclamantes had been treated, now adopting their language critiquing the "evil of slavery" that brought on the first rebellion. If the cause of their revolt was just, then how could the nation justify their betrayal? He went on to analyze the language of the bill being invoked. It was not only a betrayal of their word and as such an immoral act; it was illegal according to military law. No one could legally be excluded from the Corps of National Marines without first receiving a regular trial in front of a military tribunal. The president and minister of the navy were overstepping their boundaries. He closed by stating, "Few times in our political history have we proceeded with such imprudence, thoughtlessness, and offense to previous acts of our own Government."[15]

Barbosa argued that sooner or later all people will inevitably act against the agents of their mistreatment, and the greater the abuse, the greater the repercussions. The insurgents had the law on their side, and soldiers and sailors in service of the nation deserved (regardless of their color) to be treated as citizens; therefore, they should not be punished for their actions. This time, however, Rui Barbosa's impassioned appeals fell on deaf ears. Without popular support, the senators were pleased to follow the president of the Republic in his steps toward a reconsolidating of power over the navy and toward revenge on those men who took part in the government's humiliation.[16]

According to the minister of the navy, by the end of December, 900 men were removed from the navy, and by the first months of 1911, that number had gone up to 1,216. Eventually his report claimed that the government purchased tickets from the Lloyd Brasileiro shipping line to send 1,078 of these men back to their home states in an attempt to disperse this unwelcome element out of Rio de Janeiro. The policy was successful; there was so drastic an emptying of Rio de Janeiro's naval forces that the ships lacked crew members to carry out basic services and maintenance. It was necessary to contract Portuguese merchant sailors from all over the city to work the ships until the admission of new sailors from the apprenticeship schools scattered around Brazil.[17]

In fact, those numbers reported in Minister Leão's report were lower than the actual list of the names of excluded sailors that the navy published in 1912. This document, by which one could verify if a man had been excluded from the navy, listed 1,292 actual names under the title "*Praças* excluded from the Navy as a consequence of the movements of November and December of 1910," but those 1,292 names of enlisted men were only those removed by Decree 8,400 of November 28. Men excluded based on events in December 1910 were covered by a separate law, 1708 of April 28.[18]

When the policy was first implemented after the disarming of the ships on November 27 and 28 and the initial dismissal of men began on December 3, officers regained effective control over their ships' day-to-day operations – though by no means were conditions wholly normalized. On December 7, the chief of staff of the navy met with a group of officers to plan for the gradual removal of additional enlisted men whose presence on board was "inconvenient." They were first to be transferred to Ilha de Villegagnon and then to be dismissed from service. The following day, eight sailors were removed from the *Minas Geraes,* including João José do Nascimento, the man who shot and killed the wounded Captain João Pereira Leite, the officer in charge when the revolt broke out. Eight men were also from the scout *Bahia,* including its rebel leader Francisco Dias Martins, the notorious "Black Hand"; his name appeared on page 10 of the excluded sailors.[19]

Although officers attempted to reintroduce normality to their ships, the changes caused relations to become progressively more strained and tenuous. Enlisted men were increasingly nervous as they watched officers go back on the guarantees they has won through the revolt. According to historian Hélio Leôncio Martins, men hoarded what weapons they could find – rifles, portable munitions, and swords vanished. Rumors of new revolts began to circulate. On December 2, eight sailors were arrested in Lapa, and early in the morning on December 4, in the neighborhood of Piedade, twenty-two more were taken. All were accused of conspiring to foment a new rebellion. They were taken to the small, overcrowded prisons of Ilha das Cobras, the site of the marine infantry.[20]

THE DECEMBER REVOLTS

On the night of December 9, 1910 two events led to renewed violence in the capital once again. The first was the uprising of the crew of the scout *Rio Grande do Sul,* the Armstongs-made scout that avoided involvement in the Revolta da Chibata; the second was the near simultaneous uprising on Ilha das Cobras of the marine infantry battalion. It seems that the two events took place independently of one another, though the men involved in the second uprising seem to have had news of the outbreak of the first. The government would use these uprisings as a means to exact their revenge on those reclamantes who had not yet been removed from their ships and forced out of the capital. The origins of both revolts are difficult to confirm, but João Cândido is not alone in his belief that "the government, for vengeance, fabricated another revolution in order to storm the ships and kill the sailors who took part in the *Revolta* [*da Chibata*]."[21] In any event, both seemed spontaneous and poorly (if at all) organized. In neither case were demands made of the government – or if there were such demands, they were not made public. Both revolts were put down quickly and completely. By December 10 at 3 PM, the rebellions were over, but as soon as they had broken out, the congress began to legislate the passage of a state of siege for President Fonseca, which would allow for wide-sweeping retaliation against the sailors involved. The state of siege allowed for the silencing of newspaper coverage, and no participants in the December revolts were interviewed. One source detailing the December revolts is the collection of documents produced by American correspondents reporting to the U.S. Office of Naval Intelligence (ONI) who were in Rio de Janeiro at the time. The result is detailed eyewitness reports of many of these events:

> Earlier in the evening, and apparently as a disconnected act [from the later revolt at the Marine Infantry Battalion described below] the crew of the *Rio Grande del* [*sic*] *Sul* the new scout cruiser had revolted. The captain had announced about

9 PM that the ship would sail next morning for Santos to assist the shore forces in restoring order among a lot of immigrants that were revolting aboard an Italian immigrant ship there. This seemed to dissatisfy the crew and they became very disorderly and riotous whereupon the captain sounded to quarters, but the crew did not fall in promptly. Lieutenant da Cunha, the officer on duty, who had only joined the ship a few weeks before . . . attempted to co-erce [sic] the crew to fall in at quarters and was bayoneted and shot. One man was killed and [another] officer wounded. The captain got the crew under control, but the ringleaders deserted in a boat and were captured by a destroyer. The news of the revolt on the *Rio Grande do Sul* somehow reached Cobras Island, probably by wireless but some say by boat. It is thought that the Marine Battalion expected the other ships to again revolt. At any rate they revolted and during the night made preparations to defend the island.[22]

An hour later, another uprising broke out, this one at the Marine Infantry Battalion on Ilha das Cobras. It was described for the Office of Naval Intelligence in the same document:

At about 10 PM, December 9th, the Commanding Officer Marquis de Rocha, and what few officers there were on duty on the Island of Cobras, were warned that the Marine Infantry Battalion was in revolt, and that their lives were in danger unless they escaped from the island by a boat that was waiting for them. They took to the boat and de Rocha proceeded to the Naval Arsenal and Ministry of Marine [minister of the navy] to notify them that his men were in revolt.[23]

It is the revolt of the marine infantry battalion, or naval battalion, that is most curious. The naval battalion was a different institution than the traditional navy. It was populated by soldiers assigned to land duties on naval bases, and they did not face the same type of violent control as did sailors in the navy. According to the U.S. naval document, the American officer was allowed to visit the barracks on December 6 at 2 PM, just days before the uprising:

There was every reason to believe that the Marine Infantry Battalion on Cobras Island, five companies of about 600 men in all, were faithful and reliable. . . . The Marine Infantry corresponds to our U.S. Marine Corps, except that its officers are regular line officers of the Navy. . . . A great deal of money had been spent on the Marine Infantry Barracks and Naval Prison, and it was certainly well spent. The barracks were spotlessly clean. The men were in neat Kahki [sic] uniforms with leather leggings, were smart in appearance . . . and had the appearance of being well disciplined. The hammocks in which they swung in the barrack rooms were very white and very neat, and the bedding clean . . . the men were contented, the discipline excellent, and the battalion faithful and loyal to its officers. . . .

> During my visit I had seen in the armory six Armstrong 12 pounder landing
> guns and four Hotchkiss automatics and in another room 250 Brazilian Mauser
> Rifles in racks in reserve. These were all used by the mutineers as I saw later [he
> returned to visit again on December 12]. All during the night they kept up a des-
> ultory rifle firing on the Naval Arsenal and at this time the army was distributing
> its forces along the shore and mounting field guns.[24]

It is important to note here that there was no connection between the
amnestied sailors and either of the groups that revolted on December 9.
In the first uprising of that night, when the *Rio Grande do Sul* revolted,
they sent false notice to the *Minas Geraes* and the *São Paulo* to motivate
them to join in the new uprising. They stated that army soldiers and officers had attacked them and that many sailors were dead or wounded.
There was much confusion, and some insubordination – including men
who disobeyed direct orders – but the sailors did not again turn on
their officers. A letter sent by Irving B. Dudley to the U.S. secretary of
state described the circumstances: "The seamen of [the *Minas Geraes*
and *São Paulo*] assured the President by wireless of their loyalty to the
Government, adding that they had been abandoned by their officers."[25]
Throughout the new uprising, the amnestied sailors remained loyal to
the government.[26]

Their loyalty is especially interesting considering that once the
trouble started, João Cândido once again found himself in charge of the
Minas Geraes. With panic and confusion on board, First Mate Sadock de
Sá, the ranking officer at the time, resolved to abandon the ship along
with all other officers. João Cândido, who was asleep in the quarterdeck,
came on deck. He, with several other sailors, requested that the officers
not leave (they were in no danger) and that they await commands. Regardless of the promises offered by the former insurgents, the officers fled
to Niterói, where they were, much later, ordered to return to their ships.[27]

João Cândido contacted the authorities by radio and informed them
that the ship's officers had abandoned their posts and that he had been
left in charge and was awaiting orders. Both the *Minas Geraes* and the
São Paulo received a message from the presidential palace stating that
the president recommended that the crews of these ships should remain
loyal to the government. The situation on the *São Paulo* was similar;
confusion ruled. The crew feared they would be attacked, and they had
no means of defending themselves, as they and their ship had previously

been disarmed. Alarmed by the insubordination, the officers abandoned their posts. The sailors moved the ship away from the revolt on Ilha das Cobras to await orders.[28]

The revolt on Ilha das Cobras is difficult to describe in detail. There is no good narrative of the events that took place after the officers fled the island. It is clear that members of the naval battalion rose up and released the prisoners detained on the island, many of whom had been recently arrested for conspiracy to revolt. Their complaints were not made clear, and their demands were never heard. We do know that there was little organized corporal punishment among these companies, and according to descriptions by foreign officers who visited the island, conditions were better than in most other naval posts.

Members of two companies, the 1st and 5th, revolted at 10:30 on the night of December 9, 1910. They streamed into the central patio, shouting, "Long live liberty, death to *carrancismo!*"[29] They fired rifles into rooms, broke the telephone, and doused the lights on the base. They broke into the weapon magazine, brought artillery and machine guns onto the patio, and freed the prisoners. This all happened quickly while officers made their escape. Soldiers and sailors who were not involved in the revolt were confused and unarmed. Many locked themselves in the hospital, only to escape by boat later to the naval arsenal on the mainland. An officer led most of the 3rd Company in a bayonet attack on the patio. One sergeant was killed, and many men were wounded on both sides of the melee.[30]

Remember that rumors of an uprising had been circulating for days and that the government made arrests of people conspiring to revolt. Edmar Morel argues that the government knew precise details, including the day it was to occur. Whether they knew the specifics of the uprising or not, they were ready to put it down, and this time there would be no negotiations.

At 5:15 AM the following morning, the government's forces opened fire on the island, first with field artillery, and then from the ships *Deodora*, *Almirante Barosso*, *Rio Grande do Sul* (after its officers regained control of that ship), and the *Floriano*. According to eyewitnesses, the loyal ships fired erratically, whereas the marine infantry fired well: "The firing from the *Rio Grande do Sul* was so bad that many people thought she was firing on the city on purpose."[31] Much to everyone's surprise, at approximately 7:00 AM, the *Minas Geraes* opened fire with a 4.7-inch gun.

At 4:30 AM, the minister of the navy had given orders to fire on Ilha das Cobras. As the *Minas Geraes* was previously disarmed, it was considered excluded from this order. When the other ships opened fire, João Cândido "located" a gun-breech that must have been previously hidden. Though they had only one working gun, they fired it continuously until the cease-fire order was given at 10:00 AM.[32] Throughout the morning several messages were radioed to the government assuring their fidelity and requesting that all gun-breeches be returned aboard so that they might more effectively defend their government.[33]

At 10:00 AM the government suspended fire in order to transfer the sick and injured from the naval hospital. The rebels folded quickly and hoisted a white flag, requesting that they be put on the *Minas Geraes*. The army did not accept the surrender and instead ordered further bombing of the island. From 10:30 AM until 3:00 PM, the government continued to bomb the insurgents. During this period of bombing, João Cândido pulled the *Minas Geraes* out of the range of the rebels' artillery, as that ship had drawn significant fire. Throughout the day, they continued to send messages asserting their fidelity and requesting munitions to help put down the revolt.

Throughout the night of December 10, the ships patrolled the water surrounding Ilha das Cobras with searchlights. Over 200 mutineers were captured while trying to escape the island in boats. The following morning, December 11, the army faced no opposition in taking the island. The army reported twenty-three killed and eighteen wounded, but some believe the numbers were much higher. In a brief to the U.S. secretary of state from the embassy at Petrópolis, Irving B. Dudley (U.S. ambassador to Brazil) claimed that there were "nine dead and three hundred wounded on the shore, and eleven dead with the number of wounded on the island not ascertained."[34] In his book, Edmar Morel claims that the emergency room at the naval hospital received 132 wounded by bullets or shrapnel. He claims that hundreds of men were missing who might have been killed.[35]

THE STATE OF SIEGE

Why did the Brazilian government refuse to accept the surrender of the soldiers of the naval battalion in the morning of December 10? One reason is obvious; after their inability to deal effectively with the first revolt, all of Rio de Janeiro's elite relished the glory of the moment as honor was reclaimed through military might. A second potential justification, though perhaps less obvious, was no less important: on the afternoon of December 10, the president of the Republic requested that congress pass a thirty-day state of siege – a declaration of martial law from which, of course, all members of congress would be immune. U.S. Ambassador Dudley stated that the state of siege was problematic: "It has been suggested that the necessity for this law has passed. This is controverted upon several grounds. The loyalty of the seamen in control of the two dreadnoughts was wholly distrusted. No credit was given to their good faith."[36] On December 12 the army moved in and imprisoned all rebels but declared the site to be under control only after the congress agreed to declare the state of siege. With such an allowance, the government could easily clean the slate of the foul memories left by the Revolta da Chibata.

Perhaps not surprisingly, Senator Rui Barbosa was the lone voice of opposition in the senate. He argued:

> It was one more method to show off the strength of the government, it was necessary to show off our military valor. But what of the victims who lost life; men, women and children, people's sons, paid with their lives to exhibit this farce. When the President of the Republic acts within the limits of the law and of the Constitution, he will have all of my support. But in this case I see no reason for a State of Siege. Vote against it. For if it is approved, all parliamentary guarantees end . . . in a regime of liberty and equality, it is not possible to shield the members of Congress with immunity, while you tear away all rights and freedoms from the people.[37]

The measure passed unanimously in the house; in the senate, Rui Barbosa was the lone voice of opposition on December 12, 1910. The president immediately issued his state of siege, and at 3:00 PM, the president gave the order to the crews of all the ships involved in the Revolta da Chibata to disembark:

> The crews of the Brazilian ships were sent to the prison in the island and fortress of Villagagnon. Juan [sic] Cândido was captured trying to escape from the *Minas Gerais* [sic]. About 100 men on the latter ship refused to surrender, and it took

two days of "blockade" to get them out. Volunteer firemen and machinists from the commercial steamers of the Lloyd Brasilero Company were put on board all the ships to assist the contract engineers, and officers were detailed for service on them to put them in reserve....

The following five days the government discharged most of the crews as "services no longer required" and paid their passage to their homes. Those against whom there were any charges were held for trial. Juan [*sic*] Cândido is in jail on several charges....

The *Minas Geraes* is to go into the new floating dock on December 26. All the ships are to be kept in reserve except the destroyers, until such time as the service can be reorganized.[38]

The cells of the central police were crammed full. Almost 600 amnestied men were rounded up in the streets and transferred to Ilha das Cobras. João Cândido and several companions were imprisoned for several days in the general quarters of the army in the Praça da Republica. According to Edmar Morel, Major Estanislau Vieira Pamplona attempted to force him at gunpoint to say that Rui Barbosa had plotted the entire revolt.[39]

REVENGE

In the early morning on December 24, 1910, João Cândido and seventeen of his comrades were transferred from the army quarters to Ilha das Cobras. He was charged with disobeying orders during the second revolt – despite the fact that he had vocally and publically remained loyal to his government – but many of the reclamantes were thus rounded up. There were already over 600 prisoners being held on the Ilha das Cobras, where there was only one available cell according to Assistant General Anthero José Marques.[40] This cell, number five, was for solitary confinement. In his history of the Revolta da Chibata, Edmar Morel described the cell:

There is a tunnel 180 meters in length, three meters wide, which connects the patio of the Ilha das Cobras to the penitentiary. 30 meters from the tunnel's entrance, on the left side, there is a hole in the wall. To enter, one must descend seven steps carved into the rock. At the foot of the stairs is the first door to the cell, made of iron, 90 centimeters away stood another door of wood.

The solitary cell is carved from the rock, like a shaft. It does not receive the slightest light from sun. Ventilation is provided by minuscule holes made in the iron plate of the metal door and in the wooden door. The floor and walls are made of rock.[41]

The prisoners arrived with a recommendation that they be separated from other prisoners, as they were extremely dangerous. Captain Marques de Rocha, in charge of the Ilha das Cobras, ordered that all eighteen men be placed in the solitary cell and that the keys be given to him for safe-keeping. Late that night, the guard sent word to Marques de Rocha that there was screaming coming from the cell, but a message returned that he was spending the night at the Clube Naval. It was not until the following morning that he returned to the island. Upon opening the cell, he made the grisly discovery that sixteen of the eighteen men therein had died of asphyxiation. Apparently they were killed by asphyxiation and high temperature, primarily the result of the guards throwing buckets of quicklime in with the sailors, allegedly to disinfect the cell. Quicklime (calcium oxide or CaO) is a strong corrosive that when mixed with CO_2 gives off heat. Of the sailors who entered the cell, only João Cândido and a soldier named João Avelino survived the night.[42]

João Cândido described that night during an interview with Edmar Morel:

> The cell was small and the walls were sealed with pitch. We felt a splitting heat. The air was stifling. The sensation was of being cooked in a huge pot. Some, driven by their thirst, drank their own urine. We carried out our human necessities in a barrel that became so full of waste, that it tipped and flooded a corner of the cell. In order to disinfect the cubicle, they threw a mixture of water and lime. The floor was slanted and the liquid, having flowed to the lowest part of the cell, evaporated leaving only the lime. We become very still, so as to not stir up dust. We thought we would last six days, with bread and water, but within 10 hours, the heat was suffocating. We cry out. . . . Clouds of lime come up from the floor and invade our lungs, suffocating us. . . . The moans diminished, until a silence fell over that inferno where the Federal Government, in which we blindly trusted, threw 18 Brazilians with their political rights guaranteed by the Constitution and by a law passed by the National Congress.[43]

When they were released in the morning, the bodies were removed, the cell was washed with clean water, and the two survivors were returned to the cell. João Cândido remained a prisoner on Ilha das Cobras until April 18, 1911. When the press asked Captain Marques de Rocha how the men had died, his response was "I don't know . . . the heat . . . the weather was hot."[44] The naval doctor declared their death the result of sunstroke, and although Captain Marques da Rocha was charged with the men's deaths, he was absolved of any wrongdoing by the Conselho de Guerra in June of 1911; according to Hélio Leôncio Martins, he went on to enjoy a successful career in the Brazilian military.[45]

SATÉLITE

Other sailors involved in the Revolta da Chibata faced equally draconian and illegal measures at the hand of the government. Two days after João Cândido was locked into a cell with seventeen other men, on Christmas night of 1910, the cargo ship the *Satélite* slipped out of its berth en route to Acre, far up the Amazon. The ship was commissioned under Lloyd Brasileiro, the same company that organized the extraction of 1,078 former sailors from Rio de Janeiro. Aboard the ship were hundreds of desprotegidos; the ship was transporting "105 ex-sailors, 292 vagabonds, 44 women [presumably prostitutes], and 50 soldiers [acting as guards]."[46] They were under the command of Captain Carlos Brandão Storry and three second lieutenants. Ex-sailors, vagrants, radicals, and prostitutes being removed from the nation's capital to be put to work in laying telegraph lines and in rubber collection in the Amazon, the 292 "vagabonds" on board had been removed from the house of detention and forced below deck onto this makeshift prison ship. Many were not criminals but had been picked up during the state of siege for the fact that they had expressed sympathies toward the sailors involved in the Revolta da Chibata. Vice-Admiral Hélio Leôncio Martins described the Amazon as Brazil's "equatorial Siberia" for the more than 400 men and women sent there in this period.[47]

One prisoner was recruited to replace an infirm stoker, and that man informed the captain that there was a revolt being planned among the prisoners to take over the ship on Christmas night. It was being led by a sailor named Hernâni Pereira dos Santos, who went by the nickname "Sete" (Seven). He and his six coconspirators were all sailors who participated in the Revolta da Chibata. Vitalino José Ferreira was a member of the planning committee for the Revolta da Chibata, the second in command behind João Cândido on the *Minas Geraes*; he had been accused of participating in the death of Captain Batista das Neves, the injured commander of the dreadnought killed during the first night of the revolt.[48]

Aristides Pereira was the sailor known as Chimney who had urinated on the corpse of Captain Batista das Neves that night.[49]

According to Edmar Morel, the uprising and the officers' exposure of it was a complete fabrication. He argues that those seven men "had been condemned to death before the ship even left port, their names had been marked with a red X."[50] Captain Carlos Brandão Storry's logbook helps describe the federal government's revenge on the sailors who challenged the use of the lash in the Brazilian navy:

> Following various inquiries, it was proved that a revolt was planned and that "Sete" was its leader. The revolt was to happen as follows: The seven sailors being transported, while moving about the ship, would procure ammunition for weapons, knives, etc., and according to the deportees, at midnight [on Christmas] they would attack the guards and seize their weapons. Then the prisoners would rise, the officers and the guards would be killed and the ship would come under the command of former sailor "Sete."[51]

On the night of January 26, near Rio Doce in Espírito Santo, Sete was shot, while Chimney "threw himself" into the sea, though he was bound in handcuffs. In the coming days, as his "investigation" uncovered that more of the men whose names had been marked in red were part of the plot, they met similar fates. Captain Storry's logbook continues:

> January 1. – As we enter the New-Year of 1911, we are already outside of the bay and I have moved away from the coast in order to shoot six men, which was to be done at 2:00 AM, however, two . . . threw themselves into the sea, before they could be executed, and died of drowning, seeing as they were tied by their hands and feet.
>
> January 2. – At 11:00 PM two more sailors were shot. In all 9 of the bandits that we are transporting are dead.[52]

When they reached the Amazon, the prisoners were split onto two groups. Described again in the captains logbook: "February 3. – Two hundred men have been delivered to the Commission of Colonel Cândido Rondon,[53] conforming to government orders. The rest have to disembark with them and abandon them on the riverside. The rubber trees along the river need men. Thus, in one day, we are free of the talons of the perverse bandits."[54] Upon arrival in the Amazon, they would work either on the telegraph line or in the production of rubber. Labor in the jungles, on Rondon's telegraph line or in the rubber trees, was infamously unhealthy, and worker numbers quickly would have dwindled. Together, the events that took place in the prison cell on the Ilha das Cobras and on board the ship *O Satélite* reveal a pattern of President Fonseca and Minister Leão's willingness to retaliate against the reclamantes using any methods, both legal and illegal, to strike back at the men involved in the Revolta da Chibata. Predictably, Senator Rui Barbosa again attacked the Brazilian president, for the death of the sailors and for the prisoners aboard the *Satélite*. He described the area to which they were sent as "a place where one only dies; one does not live, one is not born – one dies,"[55] and in the senate he attacked the government for resorting to violence against the sailors, given that the government had passed the state of siege, thus legalizing taking nonviolent action against the sailors.[56]

THE TRIAL OF JOÃO CÂNDIDO

João Candido was imprisoned on Ilha das Cobras until April 1911. During this time, he began to suffer recurring hallucinations of the night he spent with sixteen dying men in a cell. After an examination on April 7 by the medical team on the Ilha das Cobras, he was transferred to the Hospital National do Alienados at Praia Vermelha, a mental hospital, where he was treated for these visions. According to Vice-Admiral Hélio Leôncio Martins, who enjoyed unique access to Cândido's medical records through the Naval Archive, Cándido was very confused. "He said he was born in Argentina, that he was sleeping when Comandante Batista das Neves was killed . . . that he was kept in a cell on Ilha das Corbas for four days without food and water."[57] Once transferred, he received a sunny room and was regularly examined by a team of doctors and nurses, with many of whom he made friends. He read the newspapers each day – a fact that confirms his literacy – and for several months, he lived comfortably. He had numerous opportunities to run if he wished, as he was allowed to leave the facility, but he always returned. Eventually, his symptoms subsided, and after receiving a clean bill of mental health, he was returned to the prison at Ilha das Cobras to await trial for the crime of participation in the revolt of December 1910.[58]

And wait he did; he was imprisoned for almost eighteen months in full before he and his comrades stood trial. They were represented by three lawyers contracted by the Irmandade da Igreja Nossa Senhora do

Rosário (The Brotherhood of the Church of Our Lady of the Rosary). The Brotherhood was established in 1640 and was known for its part in the fight for the abolition of slavery and for the defense of Afro-Brazilians. It hired three prestigious lawyers to argue the case of "João Cândido e outros." One was Evaristo de Morais, a famous criminal defense attorney known for his role defending the Afro-Brazilian dockworkers during their strike in Rio de Janeiro in 1906.[59] He, Jônimo de Carvalho, and Caio Monteiro de Barros represented the sailors on a pro bono basis.[60]

The forty-eight-hour trial began on June 25, 1912, eighteen months after the Revolta da Chibata, an act for which they had already been amnestied. Charges were leveled against sixty-eight former sailors, but only João Cândido and nine fellow reclamantes faced charges; the others had been returned to their home states or had fled. Among them were Francisco Dias Martins and Manuel Gregório do Nascimento, leaders of the *Bahia* and *São Paulo* respectively during the Revolta da Chibata. As the trial was solely for their actions during the revolt of December 10, 1910, the fact that they had remained loyal to the government was taken into consideration. The judges recognized that "it would be unfair and absurd to attribute to their actions [reestablishing order, pledging loyalty to the government, and firing on the rebels] the character of seditious acts in order to punish these individuals as accomplices to a revolt . . . which they fought to put down."[61] Marking the Fonseca government's only real failure in their actions against the reclamantes, Cándido and his codefendants were unanimously absolved of any role in that revolt. After eighteen months, João Cândido was formally discharged from the navy, along with the other leaders of the Revolta da Chibata.[62]

THE BLACK ADMIRAL

A long time ago in the waters of Guanabara Bay
The Dragon of the Sea reappeared
In the Figure of the brave sailor
Who history has not forgotten

He was known as the Black Admiral
He had the dignity of a master-of-ceremony
And when navigating the seas
With his assembly of frigates
He was hailed in port
By the French and Polish girls
And a battalion of mulattas

Crimson cascades gushed from the backs
Of blacks struck by the tip of the lash
Flooding the hearts of every crew
With the example of the sailors' screams.

SEVEN

Conclusion: The Measure of a Revolt

AT LEFT ARE THE ORIGINAL TITLE AND FIRST VERSES OF A SONG by João Bosco and Aldir Blanc, written about João Cândido and his revolt during the Brazilian military dictatorship in 1975.[1] The military government censured the song for supporting antimilitarism; the title was changed from "The Black Admiral" to "O Mestre-Sala Dos Mares" (The master-of-ceremony of the sea), and the lyrics were rewritten. The whipped "sailor" became a "sorcerer," and the "crimson cascades that gushed from the backs of *negros* [blacks]" would instead flow from the backs of *santos* (saints). "Hail the black admiral," which ended the song, was changed to "Hail the black navigator." The censured song went on to become a hit and has since been sung by some of Brazil's biggest stars.

ERASING THE RECLAMANTES

Through the president's passage of Decree 8,400 on November 28 1910, 1,292 men were discharged from the Brazilian navy for the role they played in the Revolta da Chibata. Of those men, 1,068 were forcibly removed from Rio de Janeiro on Lloyd Brasileiro ships (the same company that owned the *Satélite*) and were sent back to their home states.[2] One hundred five sailors had been packed into the hold of the *Satélite;* upon arrival in the Amazon they were forced into labor either on Rondon's telegraph line or in the production of rubber. Most of these reclamantes, many while still children, had been coerced into the Brazilian navy as a solution to the problem of free labor in the countryside and the growing "dangerous" underclass in Rio and other coastal cities. Though they were absolved of any wrongdoing by the government's passage of amnesty on

November 26, 1910, the naval elite once again targeted and victimized these men who represented a threat to their institutional hierarchy. Their actions represent an extension of the government policy that forced desprotegidos out of the "modernized" parts of the city of Rio de Janeiro during the first decade of the twentieth century. The reclamantes, along with any other sailors who threatened naval hierarchy, as was allowed by decree 8,400, were removed from the navy because without the violent control over their bodies naval officers believed that the Brazilian navy could no longer perform the penal role it had served since its establishment in the early nineteenth century. The government took steps to remove these former sailors not only from the navy but also from the capital city because upon removal from the navy they were again desprotegidos; they were neither useful for the elites' plans for modernization, nor could they be easily contained. Instead, those from outside Rio de Janeiro, the majority being from the Northeast, were returned to the regions they once called home.[3]

This transformation was not unique to the Brazilian navy. Institutions that formed or adapted in the mid-nineteenth century in response to Brazil's transition through the abolition of the slave trade and then of slavery itself had changed over time. The role of the orphanage and the judges in charge of those children's "protection" that developed following the passage of the 1871 Rio Branco law was a direct response to specific conditions between 1871 and 1888. Following the abolition of slavery in 1888, Brazil would of course still need orphanages, but their role in controlling a population of abandoned children would lessen. Similarly, the army served a similar penal role to the navy before the Paraguayan War. Because of changes during that war, the institutional penal role of the army shifted; at the end of the war army officers refused to hunt down runaway slaves. Not, I assume, because they had a group realization that such service was wrong, but because allowing former slaves to fight alongside free citizens and allowing for their promotion in reflection of their service changes the nature of the military hierarchy; the army broke from its traditional role. The internal reforms to make the army a space for honorable men (such as the abrogation of corporal punishment and the termination of the servant rank) put in place during the negotiation of the Recruitment Law of 1874 improved the lives of enlisted men, even if popular protest forestalled the implementation of the legislation and conscription. The question of a civilian draft lottery was taken up again in 1908, and a draft was implemented only with Brazil's participation in WWI, but the 1874 reforms remained; the institution had changed.[4]

By most accounts of the time, the treatment of Brazilian sailors until the 1910 Revolta da Chibata had not changed notably since the nineteenth century; impressment and flogging continued to define naval service. According to José Eduardo de Macedo Soares's anonymously written *Politica versus Marinha* (Politics versus the navy), "The situation for sailors in the end of 1910 had suffered no notable alteration except the considerable augmentation of new ships though the program of 1906."[5] He describes apprenticeship schools that "graduate" illiterate sailors who cannot effectively learn the operations of these technologically advanced ships. He then gives an example of the racism facing these sailors by blaming the lack of progress on the race of the sailors themselves: "The first impression that is produced by a Brazilian crew is decay and physical incapacity. Blacks are stunted, barely visible, with all the depressing signs of the backward African nations. The other races are subject to the influence the environment created by blacks [*negro*] who are always in the majority. Profoundly distant from any notion of comfort, our sailors dress badly, do not know how to eat, do not know how to sleep. Improvident and lazy, they weigh down the race with their inability to progress."[6] The actions of the reclamantes between November 22 and 26 challenged those assertions of racialized incompetence.

In many ways the navy had already begun to change by 1910, beyond the technological modernization associated with acquiring these new ships, it needed to change *because* of these ships. For decades officers and ministers had bemoaned the quality of their sailors, and their difficulty in finding boys or men who would serve the navy well. As Brazilian naval historian José Miguel Arias Neto pointed out, one of the four basic points of the Naval Renovation Plan Minister Júlio César de Noronha announced in 1904 was the improved instruction and training of incoming naval personnel. To better run these powerful ships the naval authority planned to reform the naval apprenticeship schools. The minister proposed that the naval school would become school in more than just name – would begin training in technical areas such as electricity, telegraph operation, and submarine theory. The apprenticeship schools would, after boys spent a year studying basic literacy, start advanced students in defined areas of specialty. This type of reform was proposed several times during the ships' production, and as examined below, one additional time by the then naval minister Leão, in his report to the Brazilian president immediately following the Revolta da Chibata.[7]

And though Soares bemoaned the illiteracy of the apprentices, Brazilian naval historian Silvia Capanema P. de Almeida argues for a navy that in the era of the Revolta da Chibata had already begun making the necessary changes to modernize. She documents a 1910 naval report that trumpets the apprenticeship schools graduating 700 cabin boys in 1908, and 905 in 1909. Reportedly, all could read and write, and they were familiar with modern specialties. Almeida admits that these figures are certainly exaggerated, but these examples represent actual reforms, an attempt to finally professionalize incoming sailors who will spend their naval careers on modern battleships.[8]

The Ministerial Report of 1909 additionally identified those areas of specialty being offered in each naval company, mandated by Decree 7,124 on September 24, 1908. He presents the necessary number of sailors in each specialty in each fifty-man company; among others they included artillery (10), navigation (2), stokers (8), and torpedo-men (5). It is always hard to measure exactly how successful the navy's mandated reforms were, especially given that the following year, the Revolta da Chibata disrupted all of the above-mentioned modification. Regardless, even with specialists, the work was no less difficult on undermanned ships, and that same September 24, 1908, decree addressed the problem of undermanned ships by extending terms of service for all enlisted men: the terms for boys who enter as apprentices changes to fifteen years, for volunteers ten years, for contractors at least five years, and for those who reenlist three years.[9]

The problem with these reforms is that for the sailors who conspired to take over the naval ships and hold the city hostage, even if the navy was changing around them, those reforms would have no impact on their service. There was no plan to retrain existing sailors or improve their wages, food, or types of punishment. Coffee plantation owners experimenting with mixed labor in the late nineteenth century were frustrated by European immigrants who refused to work alongside slaves who were still being lashed in the fields. It took the abolition of slavery before the desired floodgates of white immigration really took hold in Brazil. Similarly, naval officers recognized the futility of building a navy populated in part by modern sailors incentivized by honorable and humane service while at the same time the remaining enlisted men are violently lashed into compliance with naval hierarchy. Technical training, literacy, areas of specialization, were to benefit a hypothetical future body of sailors, but the sailors who organized, participated in, and supported the Revolta da Chibata were linked to the navy's past, not its future. By all accounts this age of the technological modernization of the Brazilian navy through the acquisition of modern dreadnoughts actually represented increased hardship for its enlisted men, who were forced to take on more responsibilities without proper training. The work became harder; if levels of violence changed with the arrival of the dreadnoughts, they were augmented. The officers under whom they served – who were themselves not technologically capable of running these ships – held deeply racist ideas about the ability of these sailors to serve, and that racism drove them to retain brutal methods to enforce naval hierarchy long after they had been abandoned by all other modern Western navies. Even when the reclamantes' skill and ability played out for the world to see, contradicting the racist claims made by Brazilian officers over a decades-long period, the humiliated officers ignored legislation amnestying the reclamantes and drove them out of the navy. The Revolta da Chibata allowed officers to do more than persecute the reclamantes. Decree 8,400 also allowed them to remove any of the other premodern sailors who represented the dregs of Brazilian society from their institution. In theory the Revolta da Chibata allowed the naval elite a complete break with the past, a chance to create a modern navy that no longer served the role of the Brazilian prison.

In a report Rear Admiral Raymundo de Mello Furtado de Mendonça, chairman of the Joint Chiefs of Staff of the Armada, prepared in 1911 for the minister of the navy, he presented a plan for the overhaul of the Brazilian navy following the Revolta da Chibata that would radically reform its nature. The lives, training, and health of both officers and enlisted men would finally be modernized to reflect the technological assets of the Brazilian navy.[10] Minister Leão was in complete agreement; in his report to the president sent in the same month of May 1911, after acknowledging that "the majority of our recruits are from the refuse of vagrants and criminals, and as if that were not enough, the origins of naval apprentices are no better, they are prematurely removed from schools to meet the needs [of the navy] without the preparation required to prepare a person for naval service,"[11] he goes on to argue that the navy requires a complete overhaul. He argues for a new penal code that would no longer restart a sailor's terms of service when he was found guilty of a crime; he would revise recruitment policies, update apprenticeship schools, initiate promotion for both officers and enlisted men based on merit rather than time served. He offers a detailed plan rooted in the historical problems of the institution, and he recommends that it be initiated immediately.[12] Though his proposal was initially accepted and was passed by congress, and in June of 1911 he signed new contract with Armstrongs to increase the size of the third dreadnought, *Rio de Janeiro*, and to increase the size of her guns from 12 to 15 inches, by January 1912 Leão had been replaced as minister of the navy and his plan for a naval renovation was abandoned. By September 1913 the Brazilian admiralty contacted their creditors at Rothschild and informed them the *Rio de Janeiro* was for sale. The contract was transferred to Turkey in December of that month at a sizable loss, and the ship was renamed *Sultan Osman I*. When World War I broke out the British navy claimed the ship, and it fought under the name HMS *Agincourt*. At the end of the war, in 1921, England offered to sell the dreadnought back to Brazil at the reduced price of £1 million, but at the time Brazilian president Epitácio da Silva Pessoa declined.[13]

Paralleling the period following the Naval Revolt of 1893, the navy entered a period of contraction and neglect. A letter written to the secretary of state dated December 8, 1910, likely written by the U.S. military attaché in Buenos Aires, John S. Hammond, states: "The terrible feature of the revolt is that apathy of the officers under this crushing indictment of inefficiency, and incompetence. The modern powerful battleships, scouts, and torpedo boats are useless in the hands of Brazilian naval officers and men . . . the navy is disorganized, discredited, and a navy in name alone."[14] The same author followed up in another letter dated

December 24, this time describing the December Revolt on Ilha das Cobras in even bleaker terms: "Brazil has no navy and in order to get one, must start all over."[15] Rather than starting over by raising the level of sailors and officers to that of their technically advanced warships, the ships that offered the promise of modernity to the Brazilian nation were allowed to deteriorate – as did the navy alongside them. Although Brazil joined the Allies and participated against Germany in w w i, neither the *Minas Geraes* nor the *São Paulo* was fit for service during the war. Both ships were sent to the United States for refitting, and the work was not completed in time for the ships to see action.[16]

How does one take the measure of a revolt? In much of the modern scholarship on the Revolta da Chibata the measure of its effectiveness is caught up in either the decline of the Brazilian navy or the frustrations that João Cândido experienced in his life after the revolt. For João Cândido, the last day of his trial was also the last day that he would wear his uniform, and for the remainder of his life he was bitter that he had been cashiered from service following the December 1910 state of siege. He worked for several years in the merchant marine, but according to his 1968 interview, he was harassed for his participation in the Revolta da Chibata. He found work on a Greek boat, but missed Brazil. He made his way back to Rio de Janeiro and found work fishing and as a fishmonger in the market at Praça XV. He worked selling fish for forty years, he had three wives and five sons, and he died in 1969. But as important as João Cândido's role was in the planning, leadership, and implementation of the Revolta da Chibata, his relationship with the Brazilian navy stands in sharp contrast to that of most of his fellow reclamantes. He was not really one of the desprotegidos because though poor and black, he enjoyed patriarchal ties to the elite. Rather than using those connections to keep himself out of the navy, he used them to his benefit while in the navy. Even after his discharge from the navy he was able to draw on those connections. While Cândido was in the merchant marine, on a return trip from Argentina to Rio Grande do Sul, upon his arrival the captain of the port recognized Cândido as a former reclamante and promptly had his travel papers seized. Cândido returned to Rio de Janeiro and went to the house of his patron Alexandrino Faria de Alencar, who was by now an admiral and the minister of the navy. According to Cândido, Alencar telephoned the captain of the port of Rio Grande do Sul and demanded, "Return João Cândido's papers immediately, I was also a rebel and now I am the minister of the navy!!"[17] It seems unlikely that any other of the reclamantes could have appealed to the minister of the navy in such circumstance. The men for whom he fought, many of whom had been dragooned into service or had joined as young as 10 years old, may have responded much more positively to being expelled from the Brazilian navy.[18]

To assess the success of the Revolta da Chibata one must identify the reclamantes' goals. Did these men expect their actions to transform the navy into a modern and honorable institution in which they could continue to serve? If yes, than the revolt was a failure by any measure. The actions of the officers and politicians in the weeks following the Revolta da Chibata can be correctly interpreted as a vengeful elite seeking retribution for the public humiliation they suffered at the hands of men they defined as their social and racial inferiors. Their navy had no place for these insurgents, and without corporal punishment it no longer had a place for the desprotegidos who largely populated their navy's lower decks; they used the state of siege as an opportunity to remove the "dangerous class" from their ships.

If, however, the reclamantes' goal was to challenge the naval elite's ability to trammel the rights of poor, black, unprotected citizens, if their critique was less centered around the abuse individual sailors suffered in the Brazilian navy, but instead targeted the damage that the institution did to their communities, than perhaps the answer is that it met those goals. Remember their manifesto: "We, as sailors, Brazilian citizens, and supporters of the republic, can no longer accept the slavery as practiced in the Brazilian Navy." The navy had curtailed the rights of free Brazilian citizens within and outside of that institution for generations. To successfully take away naval officers' ability to violently enforce naval hierarchy, the reclamantes undermined the navy's penal role in Brazilian society; the reclamantes not only successfully changed the nature of the Brazilian navy, these men challenged the control that the Brazilian government had over the lives of poor Brazilian men in both cities and the countryside.

Notes

1. INTRODUCTION

1. Original letter housed at the Arquivo Naval, Ilha das Cobras, Rio de Janeiro. Facsimile reprinted in Edmar Morel, *A Revolta da Chibata*, 5th ed. (São Paulo: Paz e Terra, 2010), 98–99.

2. I analyze the reported number of sailors involved in the revolt in chapter 5, note 4, but I believe that between 1,500 and 2,000 men were active participants in the revolt.

3. Decreto 328 de 12.04.1890. In the forty-volume collection of materials pertaining to the overall legislation and administration of Brazil in both the colonial and national periods, *História Administrativa do Brasil,* Herick Marques Caminha published two volumes that focus on the Brazilian navy. Volume 15, *História Administrativa do Brasil; organização e administração do Ministério da Marinha no Império* covers the period of Brazilian Empire (1821–1889). Its chapter 8, "Resenha cronológica e analítica dos principais atos da legislação naval brasileira no período imperial (1821–1889)," 227–360, lists naval codes and decrees, as well as state legislation pertaining to the navy in this period. Volume 36, *História Administrativa do Brasil; organização e administração do Ministério da Marinha na República,* covers the national period

through 1983, and its chapter 8, "Resenha cronológica e analítica dos principais atos da legislação naval brasileira no período republicano (1889–1983)," similarly lists codes, decrees and state legislation pertaining to the navy in the national period. My analysis of Brazilian naval codes and national legislation as it applies to the navy draws on these collections, and unless otherwise cited, all references to naval laws, acts, decisions, or decrees from October 26, 1889, or earlier draw on Herick Marques Caminha, *História Administrativa do Brasil; organização e administração do Ministério da Marinha no Império,* vol. 15 (Brasília and Rio de Janeiro, RJ: Fundação Centro de Formação do Servidor Público; Serviço de Documentação Geral da Marinha, 1986), and will be cited as "Legislação naval Brasileira no período imperial," while all such references from November 16, 1889, and later draw on Herick Marques Caminha *História Administrativa do Brasil; organização e administração do Ministério da Marinha na República,* vol. 36 (Brasília and Rio de Janeiro, RJ: Fundação Centro de Formação do Servidor Público; Serviço de Documentação Geral da Marinha, 1989), and will be cited as "Legislação naval Brasileira no período republicano."

4. Morel, *A Revolta da Chibata;* Um Official da Armada [José Eduardo de Macedo Soares], *Politica versus Marinha* (Rio de Janeiro: Á venda na Livraria H. Garnier, n.d.), 85. In his book, *Cidadania, cor e disciplina na revolta dos marinheiros de 1910* (Rio de Janeiro: Mauad X: FAPERJ, 2008), Álvaro Pereira do Nascimento convincingly argues that "A Naval Officer" was José Eduardo de Macedo Soares. He was best known as a journalist and for his later support of the *Tenentismo* movement (from *tenente* or lieutenant, a movement among young idealistic army officers who pressed for social reforms during the 1920s), but he attained the rank of first lieutenant in the navy before leaving naval service in 1912, and he was part of the Naval Commission in Europe that oversaw the construction of the battleships *Minas Geraes* and *São Paulo.* After returning to Rio de Janeiro from Newcastle on the inaugural voyage of the *Minas Geraes* he returned to Europe in November 29, 1910, immediately after the revolt, where he almost certainly penned *Política versus Marinha.* See ch. 2, "Das ruas ao conves," 74–75. Álvaro Bomilcar, *O preconceito de raça no Brazil* (Rio de Janeiro: Typ. Aurora, 1916), 35, 95–98.

5. Hélio Leôncio Martins, *A Revolta dos Marinheiros, 1910* (São Paulo: Editora Nacional; Rio de Janeiro: Serviço de Documentação Geral da Marinha, 1988), 193.

6. José Carlos de Carvalho, *O Livro da Minha Vida: Na guerra, na paz e nas revoluções: 1847–1910,* vol. 1. (Rio de Janeiro: Typo do Jornal do Commercio, 1912). No fewer than three high-ranking naval officers published essays to polish the tarnished reputation of the officers involved in the revolt. Comandante H. Pereira da Cunha, *A Revolta na Esquadra Brazileira em November e Dezembro de 1910* (Rio de

Janeiro: Imprensa Naval, 1953), published originally in *Revista Marítima Brasileira* (Oct., Nov., and Dec. 1949); Almirante Antão Alveres Barata, "Revolta dos Marinheiros em 1910," *Revista Maritima Brasileira* (Feb. 1962), 10317, originally presented at "UNITER," November 20, 1961; Martins. *A Revolta dos Marinheiros, 1910.*

7. Morel, *A Revolta da Chibata;* Nascimento *Cidadania.*

8. Joseph L. Love, *The Revolt of the Whip* (Stanford, Calif.: Stanford University Press, 2012).

9. Ada Ferrer, *Insurgent Cuba: Race, Nation, and Revolution, 1868–1898* (Chapel Hill: University of North Carolina Press, 1999), Thomas C. Holt, *The Problem of Freedom: Race, Labor, and Politics in Jamaica and Britain, 1832–1938* (Baltimore, Md.: John Hopkins University Press, 1992); Matt D. Childs, *The 1812 Aponte Rebellion in Cuba and the Struggle Against Atlantic Slavery* (Chapel Hill: University of North Carolina Press, 2006); Kim D. Butler, *Freedoms Given Freedoms Won: Afro-Brazilians in Post-Abolition Sao Paulo and Salvador* (New Brunswick, N.J.: Rutgers University Press, 1998); Zephyr L. Frank, *Dutra's World: Wealth and Family in Nineteenth-Century Rio de Janeiro* (Albuquerque: University of New Mexico Press, 2004).

10. The specific costs to the Brazilian government in British pounds sterling of each ship are recorded in the records of W. G. Armstrong & Co. in Newcastle and appear in chapter 3. The preauthorization number shifts around throughout the primary and secondary material, and given that the contract goes through various changes between 1904 and 1913, including the cancellation of the third dreadnought *Rio de Janeiro,* the overall cost of the contract is smaller than this number. This

value comes from "Information on file concerning the Brazilian battleships," Mar. 16, 1907, U.S. Navy Department Archives, General correspondence, Office of Naval Intelligence, case 8079, as cited in Seward W. Livermore "Battleship Diplomacy in South America: 1905–1925," *Journal of Modern History* 16, no. 1 (March 1944): 31–48.

11. See my examination of the changing name of Armstrong in chapter 3, note 1.

12. On the Nine Hour Campaign and dockworkers' strikes see David Bean, *Armstrong's Men: The Story of the Shop Stewards Movement in the Tyneside Works* (Newcastle: Vicker Limited, 1967)

13. Anonymous letter quoted in Dick Keys and Ken Smith, *Down Elswick Spillways: Armstrong's Ships and People, 1884–1918* (Newcastle: Newcastle City Libraries, 1996), 19.

14. Mary Conley, *From Jack Tar to Union Jack: Representing Naval Manhood in the British Empire: 1870–1918* (Manchester, UK: Manchester University Press, 2009).

15. Mary C. Karasch, *Slave Life in Rio de Janeiro, 1808–1850* (Princeton, N.J.: Princeton University Press, 1987), 61–65.

16. Demographic data pertaining to Havana is drawn from Cuba's 1841 census compiled in the index of Kenneth F. Kiple in his *Blacks in Colonial Cuba, 1774–1899* (Gainesville: University Presses of Florida, 1976), titled "Census of 1841." The demographic data from New Orleans and Charleston is based on the U. S. *Federal Population Census* from 1860 and was compiled from Claudia Dale Goldin's *Urban Slavery in the American South: A Quantitative History* (Chicago: University of Chicago Press, 1976), table 13, "Population Data for Ten Southern Cities, 1820–60."

17. The 1849 census also marked a high point for enslaved Africans, as 66 percent of Rio's slave population was African born. When the slave trade was abolished the following years, without a source for foreign slaves those percentages dropped quickly. The low reproductive rate among enslaved women; early death for various reasons, including yellow fever and cholera; and the sale of slaves from the city to rural coffee plantations led to the slow reversal in the growth of Rio's slave population. Karasch, *Slave Life in Rio de Janeiro*, 64–65.

18. Teresa Meade, *"Civilizing" Rio: Reform and Resistance in a Brazilian City 1889–1930* (University Park: Penn State Press, 1997).

19. Table "População do Brazil por Estados (1872, 1890, 1900 e 1910)," in Ministério da Agricultura, Industria e Commercio, Directoria Geral de Estatistica *Annuario Estatistico do Brazil 1908–1912*, vol. 1: *Territorio e População* (Rio de Janeiro: Typographia da Estatistica, 1916), 252.

20. José Murilho de Carvalho, *Os Bestializados: O Rio de Janeiro e a república que não foi*, 3rd ed. (São Paulo: Companhia Das Letras, 2005), 17.

21. Ibid., 18.

22. Among the most striking attacks on the lives of Rio de Janeiro's poor who lived downtown was the construction of the Avenida Central (renamed Avenida Rio Branco in 1912 after Brazil's famous diplomat) between 1904 and 1905. It was a broad 1.1-mile road placed directly through Centro, and Rio's Mayor Pereira Passos authorized the destruction of hundreds of homes, many that were tenement housing occupied by the poor. This project and similar ones that followed – to build docks, roads, and the famous opera house the *Theatro Municipal*, inaugurated by President Nilo Peçanha in 1909 – would eventually destroy upward of 2,700 homes.

Glória Kok, *Rio de Janeiro na época da Av. Central* (São Paulo: Bei Comunicação, 2005).

23. The history of the Naval Academy (Academia Real de Guardas-Marinha) is presented in Antonio Luiz Porto e Albuquerque's *Da Companhia de Guardas-Marinhas e sua Real Academia aÃ Escola Naval, 1782–1982* (Rio de Janeiro: Escola Naval, 1982), and a copy of Queen Maria I's December 14, 1782, decree that created the officer training school and limited the background of those admitted therein appears on 24–26 of that work: the original is housed in the Arquivo Nacional da Torre do Tomba (Lisbon).

24. Original letter housed at the Arquivo Naval, Ilha das Cobras, Rio de Janeiro. Facsimile reprinted in Morel, *A Revolta da Chibata*, 98–99.

25. For a discussion of the legality of military service for slaves in both the army and the navy, see Hendrik Kraay, "Slavery, Citizenship and Military Service in Brazil's Mobilization for the Paraguayan War," *Slavery and Abolition: A Journal of Slave and Post-Slave Studies* 18, no. 3 (1997): 228–56, whereas Manuela Cameiro da Cunha's "Silences of the Law: Customary Law and Positive Law on the Manumission of Slaves in 19th Century Brazil," *History and Anthropology* 1, no. 2 (1985): 427–43, addresses the negotiation between states and individual rights throughout the movement toward the abolition of slavery.

26. The impact of the role of slaves in the Spanish American wars of independence is the focus of Peter Blanchard's *Under the Flags of Freedom* (Pittsburgh, Pa.: University of Pittsburgh Press, 2008).

27. Thomas H. Holloway, *Policing Rio de Janeiro: Repression and Resistance in a 19th-Century City* (Stanford, Calif.: Stanford Univ. Press, 1993), 3–4.

28. This role of police in postabolition slave societies is not unique to Brazil. Khalil Muhammad's *The Condemnation of Blackness* (Cambridge, Mass.: Harvard University Press, 2010), examines the way that in the urban north of the Unites States, social scientists linked race and crime through their study of criminality, whereas Bryan Wagner's *Disturbing the Peace: Black Culture and the Police Power after Slavery* (Cambridge, Mass.: Harvard University Press, 2009), examines the place of blackness in U.S. law and the role of police and police power in the lives of African Americans.

29. I refer to Thomas Holloway's previously cited work, Ricardo Salvatore and Carlos Aguirre's *The Birth of the Penitentiary in Latin America: Essays on Criminology, Prison Reform, and Social Control, 1830–1940* (Austin: University of Texas Press, 1996), and Peter M. Beattie's works, "Conscription versus Penal Servitude: Army Reform's Influence on the Brazilian States' Management of Social Control, 1870–1930," *Journal of Social History* 32, no. 4 (Summer 1999): 847–78, and *The Tribute of Blood: Army, Honor, Race, and Nation in Brazil, 1864–1945* (Durham, N.C.: Duke University Press, 2001).

30. Michel Foucault, *Discipline and Punish: The Birth of the Prison* (New York: Vintage Books, 1995 [1975]), 201.

31. Decisão N. 67, "Marca o modo por que se deve fazer o Recrutamento," *Collecção das decisões do império do Brazil de 1822* (Rio de Janeiro: Imprensa Nacional, 1887), 56–58.

2. LEGISLATING THE LASH

1. At the time of the move to Brazil in 1807, he retained the title of prince regent; he received the title João VI only in 1816.

2. For a clear narrative of Brazilian independence see Leslie Bethell, "The Independence of Brazil" in *Brazil: Empire and Republic, 1822–1930*, ed. Leslie Bethell (Cambridge: Cambridge University Press, 1989), 3–45.

3. José Muriho de Carvalho, "As Forcas Armadas na Primeira República: O Poder Desestabilizador," in *História Geral da Civilização Brasileira, O Brasil Republicano*, book 3 of *Sociedade e Instituições*, ed. Boris Fausto (São Paulo: Bertrand Brasil, 1977), 188–89.

4. See Blanchard, *Under the Flags of Freedom*, for a broad examination of the motivations and benefits for free and freed slaves involved in the Spanish American wars of independence. Chapter 2, "Serving the King in Venezuela and New Granada," addresses Bolivar's initial resistance to arming slaves in the struggle for independence. Also on this topic see Marcela Echeverri "Popular Royalists, Empire, and Politics in Southwestern New Granada, 1809–1819," *Hispanic American Historical Review* 91, no. 2 (May 2011): 237–69. The broader impact of arming slaves is the focus of Christopher Leslie Brown and Philip D. Morgan, eds., *Arming Slaves: From Classical Times to the Modern Age* (New Haven, Conn.: Yale University Press, 2006), and the role of both enslaved Africans and indigenous populations in pre-independent Spanish America are the focus of Ben Vinson III and Matthew Restall, "Black Soldiers, Native Soldiers: Meanings of Military Service in the Spanish American Colonies," in Restall, *Beyond Black and Red*, 15–52

5. Brian Vale, "British Sailors and the Brazilian Navy, 1822–1850," *Mariner's Mirror* 80, no. 3 (August 1994): 312.

6. Almirante Arthur Jaceguay, *De aspirante a almirante: minha fé de ofício documentada*, vol. 2: *1870–1900*, 2nd ed. (Rio de

Janeiro: Serviço de Documentação Geral da Marinha, 1984), 664.

7. Decisão de 25.02.1823, Legislação naval Brasileira no período imperial, 231.

8. For a detailed examination of the role of the navy in gaining Brazilian independence, see Brian Vale, *Independence or Death: British Sailors and Brazilian Independence, 1822–1825* (London: Tauris Academic Studies, 1996), which the following description draws from 14–15, 37–39.

9. Ibid., 17.

10. Maria Graham, *Journal of a Voyage to Brazil and Residence There during Part of the Years 1821, 1822 and 1823* (London: Longman, Hurst, Rees, Orme, Brown, and Green, 1824), 218–19.

11. Vale, *Independence or Death,* 22–23.

12. Vale, "British Sailors and the Brazilian Navy" 319–20.

13. See Brian Vale, "Lord Cochrane in Brazil: The Naval War of Independence 1823," *Mariners Mirror* 57, no. 4 (1971): 415–42.

14. Relatório da Repartição dos Negócios da Marinha, Rio, 1828 & Relatório da Repartição dos Negócios da Marinha, Rio, 1832 as cited by Brian Vale, *Independence or Death,* 173–74n2–3.

15. Almirante Arthur Jaceguey, *De aspirante a almirante 1860–1902, Minha fé de officio documentada*, vol. 5: *1895–1900* (Rio de Janeiro: Typographia Leuzinger, 1907), 47–48.

16. Decree, May 8, 1822, "Eleva o numero de praças de cada uma das companies dos Batalhões de 1a Linha desta Côrte," in *Collecção das Leis do Imperio do Brazil de 1822*, 2nd part (Rio de Janeiro, Imprensa Nacional, 1887), 15–16.

17. Government Decision, *Guerra*, No. 67, July 10, 1882, "Marca o modo por que se deve fazer o Recrutamento," in *Collecçao das decisions do império do Brazil de 1822*

(Rio de Janeiro: Imprensa Nacional, 1887), 56–58.

18. For a brief discussion of the early years of the Brazilian army see chs. 6 and 7 of Robert L. Scheina, *Latin America's Wars: The Age of the Caudillo, 1791–1899,* vol. 1 (Dulles, Va.: Brassey's, 2003).

19. Some define Brazil's military support for the anti-Rosas alliance of the Argentine provinces of Entre Ríos and Correintes with the Colorados of Uruguay in the 1851–52 Platine War against the Rosas's Argentine Confederation as a third foreign war. Brazil's role in the civil wars in Uruguay and Argentina after the Cisplatine War and their participation in the Battle of Caseros in December 1851 are better understood in the broad history of the Paraguayan War, not as a separate war. See John Lynch, *Argentine Caudillo: Juan Manuel de Rosas* (Lanham, Md.: SR Books, 2001), for analysis of Rosas's role in in the Rio de la Plata.

20. On the 1825–28 Cisplatine War, see ch. 7 of Scheina, *Latin America's Wars,* vol. 1.

21. On the Paraguayan War see Richard Graham's ch. 3, "Empire (1822–1889), 1850–1870," in Bethell, *Brazil: Empire and Republic.*

22. On the separatist uprisings of 1824 see ch. 13 of Scheina, *Latin America's Wars,* vol. 1.

23. For a detailed examination of the Brazilian army's slow transition from a regional to national institution see Hendrick Kraay, *Race, State, and Armed Forces in Independence-Era Brazil: Bahia, 1790s–1840s* (Stanford, Calif.: Stanford University Press, 2004).

24. See ch. 1 in Roderick J. Barman, *Citizen Emperor: Pedro II and the Making of Brazil, 1825–91* (Stanford, Calif.: Stanford University Press, 1999), and ch. 3 in Emilia Viotti da Costa, *The Brazilian*

Empire: Myths and Histories (Chapel Hill: University of North Carolina Press, 2000).

25. Scheina, *Latin America's Wars,* 1:149.

26. On the period of regency see Barman, *Citizen Emperor,* ch. 2, and chs. 3 and 4 on the period of political and military consolidation; Scheina's *Latin America's Wars,* vol. 1, ch. 13, covers the period of insurrection from 1831 to 1849.

27. See Robin Blackburn, "Cuba and Brazil: The Abolitionist Impasse," in *The Overthrow of Colonial Slavery* (London: Verso, 1988), 381–418. Zephyr L. Frank's *Dutra's World* does an excellent job examining the impact of the abolition of the African slave trade on the urban slave population of Rio de Janeiro and its lost socioeconomic mobility in the face of economic pressure to sell enslaved Africans to plantation owners.

28. Marcos Luiz Bretas, "Slaves, Free Poor, and Policemen: Brazil," in *Crime History and Histories of Crime: Studies in the Historiography of Crime and Criminal Justice in Modern History,* ed. Clive Emsley and Louis A. Knafla (Westport, Conn.: Greenwood Press, 1996), 258.

29. Ibid.

30. Hebe Maria Mattos de Castro, "Beyond Masters and Slaves: Subsistence Agriculture as a Survival Strategy in Brazil during the Second Half of the Nineteenth Century," in *The Abolition of Slavery and the Aftermath of Emancipation in Brazil,* ed. Rebecca J. Scott et al. (Durham, N.C.: Duke University Press, 1988), 55.

31. An important study of Brazil's colonial free black population is A. J. R. Russell-Wood's *The Black Man in Slavery and Freedom in Colonial Brazil* (New York: St. Martin's Press, 1982). On the role of the police in the nineteenth century, see Holloway, *Policing Rio de Janeiro de Janeiro,* and Bretas, "Slaves, Free Poor, and

Policemen: Brazil." Alternatively, an examination of Brazil's urban poor in the late nineteenth and early twentieth centuries is Martha Knisely Huggins, *From Slavery to Vagrancy in Brazil* (New Brunswick, N.J.: Rutgers University Press, 1985).

32. This is clearly argued in Celia Maria Marinho de Azevado's *Onda negra, Medo branco: o negro no imaginário das elites, século XIX* [Black wave, White fear: The black in the imagination of the elites in the nineteenth century] (Rio de Janeiro: Paz e Terra, 1987).

33. Beattie, *The Tribute of Blood*, 17.

34. Just one example of this is seen in Peter Beattie's excellent examination of the Brazilian army between 1864 and 1945. Beattie slips into the language of change in "military service" when he describes that the "draft transformed enlisted military service from a punitive to a preventative institution of social reform" as it took steps to become more honorable. This is true in the army but not in the navy. Beattie, *The Tribute of Blood*, 13.

35. We can see the different directions "modernity" takes in studies focused on the army, such as Beattie, *The Tribute of Blood*, and Shawn C. Smallman, *Fear and Memory in the Brazilian Army and Society* (Chapel Hill: University of North Carolina Press, 2002), as well as in studies of modernization such as Richard Graham, *Britain and the Onset of Modernization in Brazil 1850–1914* (Cambridge: Cambridge University Press, 1972), and Roberto da Matta, *A casa e a rua: Espaço cidadania, mulher, e morte no Brasil* (Rio de Janeiro: Ed. Guanabara, 1987).

36. One central theme in this era of warfare was the new role of the citizen soldier as defined by the republicanism so central to France's Revolutionary and Napoleonic periods. With France's August 1793 declaration of the *levee en masse,* the idea of compulsory military service regardless of a man's income or status redefined military service and readiness throughout Europe and eventually across much of the world, and this was true even in nations that never applied compulsory service. It is generally accepted that the fairness of the application of the *levée* reduced resistance to the draft among citizens and allowed France to raise its 600,000-man army, an unprecedented number. Furthermore, these soldiers, understood to be motivated by patriotism and their love of liberty, defeated the royalist army. The idea of citizens willing to fight for the modern republican goals impacted the development of modern militaries throughout the nineteenth century. Daniel Moran and Arthur Waldron, eds., *The People in Arms: Military Myth and National Mobilization Since the French Revolution* (Cambridge: Cambridge University Press, 2003).

37. Although the Reform Laws of 1874 were passed in parliament, they were nowhere effectively implemented. The structural changes meant to improve service in the Brazilian army did happen. I am deeply indebted to, and this chapter greatly benefits from, Peter Beattie's groundbreaking work on the Recruitment Laws of 1874 in *The Tribute of Blood*, chs. 3–4.

38. For the statistics of enlisted men see Beattie, *The Tribute of Blood*, 155, and for the navy see table 5 in ch. 3 below.

39. Beattie *The Tribute of Blood*, 25.

40. I have addressed parts of this argument in "Legislating the Lash: Race and the Conflicting Modernities of Enlistment and Corporal Punishment in the Military of the Brazilian Empire," *Journal of Colonialism and Colonial History* 5, no. 2 (2004): n.p. See also Thomas E Skidmore,

Black into White: Race and Nationality in Brazilian Thought, 2nd ed. (Durham, N.C.: Duke University Press, 1993 [1974]), for an excellent analysis of the "whitening" process in Brazil.

41. The true center of the Brazilian navy was established in Rio de Janeiro, where the bulk of training, administration, and shipbuilding took place. Much smaller bases were established in the colonial period and during the nineteenth century. The Arsenal de Marinha do Pará was established in 1761, the Flotillha do Amazonas was first established in Manaus in 1868, the Arsenal de Marinha da Província de Mato Grosso was established in Cuiabá in 1827, and the Base Fluvial de Ladário in Mato Grosso do Sul was established in 1873.

42. A copy of Queen Maria I's December 14, 1782, decree that created the officer training school and limited the background of those admitted therein appears in Antonio Luiz Porto e Albuquerque's *Da Companhia de Guardas-Marinhas e sua Real Academia à Escola Naval, 1782–1982* (Rio de Janeiro: Escola Naval, 1982), 24–26. The original is housed in the Arquivo Nacional da Torre do Tomba (Lisbon).

43. Carvalho, "As Forcas Armadas na Primeira República," 188–89.

44. Norbert Elias, "Studies in the Genesis of the Naval Profession," *British Journal of Sociology* 1, no. 4 (Dec. 1950): 298.

45. Ibid. Elias's article on the naval profession that first appeared in 1950 has recently been republished along with his other published and previously unpublished work on the British navy in Norbert Elias, *The Genesis of the Naval Profession* (Dublin: University College of Dublin Press, 2007).

46. Peter M. Beattie, "Adolfo Ferreira Caminha: Officer, Ardent Republican,

and Naturalist Novelist," in *The Human Tradition in Modern Brazil,* ed. Peter M. Beattie (Wilmington, Del.: SR Books, 2004), 91.

47. Ibid.

48. Morel, *A Revolta da Chibata,* 32.

49. *O Estado de São Paulo,* June 5, 1911, quoted by Álvaro Bomilcar, *O preconceito de raça no Brasil* (Rio de Janeiro: [Typ. Aurora], 1916), 27–28.

50. Corporal punishment was outlawed by Decreto 3 de 16.11.1889, "Legislação naval Brasileira no período republicano," 321, and was reintroduced by Decreto 327 de 12.04.1890, ibid., 323.

51. The protections of many constitutions are not necessarily applied to members of the armed forces, and the fact that the Crown would authorize the lash as punishment for deserters in 1825 suggests that those protections may have never been intended to apply to men in the armed forces.

52. For an examination of police response to capoeiristas and slaves in nineteenth century Rio de Janeiro, see Carlos Eugênio Libano Soares, *A capoeira escrava e outras tradiçofies rebeldes no Rio de Janeiro, 1808–1850* (Campinas, Brazil: Universidade Estadual de Campinas, 2001), and Thomas H. Holloway, "'A Healthy Terror': Police Repression of Capoeiras in Nineteenth-Century Rio de Janeiro," *Hispanic American Historical Review* 69, no. 4 (Nov. 1989): 637–76.

53. *Colleção das desisões do Governo do Império do Brazil,* #182, Justiça, "Manda empregar nas obras do dique os negros capoeiras presos em desordem, cessando a pena dos açoites" (Rio de Janeiro, 1886), 87.

54. Juvenal Greenhalg, *O Arsenal de Marinha do Rio de Janeiro na História, 1822–1889,* vol. 2 (Rio de Janeiro: Arsenal de Marinha, 1965), 73.

55. Ibid., 193. Justiça, "Declara que a Portaria de 30 do mês passado compreende somente os escravos capoeiras," 129, 215. Justiça, "Declara que os escravos presos por capoeira devem sofrer, além da pena de três meses de trabalho, o castigo de duzentos açoites" 153. "Decisão de 12.03.1823" and "Decreto de 21.03.1823," "Legislação naval Brasileira no período imperial," 231–32.

56. Decreto de 22.10.1836, "Legislação naval Brasileira no período imperial," 277.

57. Jaceguey, *De aspirante a almirante*, 5:48.

58. Caminha, *História Administrativa do Brasil*, vol. 15, ch. 4, "Quadros de Pessoal," 104.

59. Ibid., 101–102.

60. *Reletório do Ministerio de Marinha*, 1888, "Mappa estatistico do Corpo de Imperiaes Marinheiros desde o anno de 1836 a 1888" (Rio de Janeiro: Imprensa Nacional, 1889).

61. Martins, *A Revolta dos Marinheiros*, 124.

62. Hendrik Kraay, "Reconsidering Recruitment in Imperial Brazil," *Americas*, 55, no. 1 (July 1998): 2.

63. Beattie, *The Tribute of Blood*, 133.

64. Ibid., 134.

65. *Reletório do Ministerio de Marinha*, 1859, 20.

66. Ibid., 21.

67. Ibid.

68. For an analysis of the origins of eugenics throughout Latin America see Nancy Leys Stepan, *"The Hour of Eugenics": Race, Gender and Nation in Latin America* (Ithaca, N.Y.: Cornell University Press, 1991), and for an examination focused on Brazil see Lilia Moritz Schwarcz's *The Spectacle of the Races: Scientists, Institutions, and the Race Question in Brazil, 1870–1930*, trans. Leland Guyer (New York: Hill and Wang, 1999),

first published as *Brazil, as Espetáculo das Raças: Cientistas, Instituções e Questão Racial no Brasil 1870–1930* (São Paulo: Companhia das Letras, 1993).

69. *Reletório do Ministerio de Marinha*, 1873, table 5, "Mappa estatistico do corpo de imperiaes marinheiros desde o anno de 1836 a 1873" (Rio de Janeiro: Typographia Nacional, 1874).

70. Law nº. 148 of August 27, 1840, changed the structure of the Brazilian navy to include the first Companhia de Aprendezes on the *fortaleza* [fortress] *de Boa Viagem* (Niterói, RJ), to better prepare youths who "wanted" to pursue naval careers. In 1841, because of the superiority of sailors with training through apprenticeships over those taken off the street, the Crown expanded the decree to create Companhias de Aprendezes throughout Brazil. Those institutions opened in the following order: Para and Bahia (1855); Mato Grosso, Pernambuco, and Santa Catarina (1857); Maranhão and Rio Grande do Sul (city of São Pedro) (1861); Espírito Santo (1862); Ceará and Paraná (1864); São Paulo (city of Santos) and Sergipe (1868); Paraíba and Amazonas (1871); Rio Grande do Norte (1872); Piauí (city of Parnaíba) (1873); and Alagoas (1875). Caminha, *História Administrativa do Brazil*, vol. 15, ch. 4, 105.

71. That year the Imperial Navy was to have 1,800 men and was to be able to get to 3,000 quickly in the face of an emergency, as required by a law passed on August 26, 1833, as stated in *Reletório do Ministerio de Marinha*, 1833, 32. "Decreto N° 309, de Junho 1833," and "Decreto N° 302, de Junho, 1833."

72. Álvaro Pereira do Nascimento, *A Ressaca da Marujada: Recrutamento e disciplina na Armada Imperial* (Rio de Janeiro: Arquivo Nacional, 1999), 69.

73. "Decreto N°. 1,591, 14 April, 1855," article 1.

74. Nascimento, *A Ressaca da Marujada*, 70; "Decreto N°. 1,591, de 14 Abril de 1855," articles 6–8.

75. Decreto 1,466, 10 October, 1854, "Legislação naval Brasileira no período imperial," 299. In 1908 the term for apprentices was extended to fifteen years. See chapter 7, note 9.

76. The Rio Branco Law, 28 September 1871, as quoted and translated by Robert Conrad, *The Destruction of Brazilian Slavery, 1850–1888* (Berkeley: University of California Press, 1972), appendix II, 305.

77. Ibid., 116.

78. Ibid., 114.

79. They argue that his analysis pushes aside regional variations and the differing impact that the law had in the cities and in the countryside. Lana Lage da Gama Lima and Renato Pinto Venâncio, "O abandono de crianças negras no Rio de Janeiro" [The abandonment of black children in Rio de Janeiro], in *História da Criança no Brasil*, ed. Mary Del Priore (São Paolo: Contexto, 1996), 61–75.

80. Ibid., 66–67; *Regimento da Casa dos Expositos* (Rio de Janeiro, 1840), 23.

81. Lima and Venâncio link this change to the profitability of renting out female slaves without child as wet nurses in Rio, which paid ten times what the government offered for slaves turned over to the state. With child mortality rates as high as they were at the time, the rent of an enslaved woman was a far surer source of income than was the sum that could eventually come in from her child's labor. "O abandono de crianças negras no Rio de Janeiro," 68–70.

82. Decreto No. 1,591, 14 April 1855, "Manda observar as instruções por que deve ser feito o alistamento de voluntários e de recrutas para o Serviço da Armada," "Legislação naval Brasileira no período

imperial," 301. Full text of this legislation appears under Document No. 18 in the appendix to Camina, *História Administrativa do Brasil*, 15:431– 39. The naval minister stressed the ongoing importance of this legislation in his anual report to the General Assembly in 1867, in *Relatorio do Ministério da Marinha*, 1867, 9.

83. *Caboclo* generally means mixed-race white and Indian, although its secondary definition is "a copper-colored mulatto with straight hair." I have several descriptions of caboclos with the kinky or nappy hair generally attributed to peoples of African descent, so although I cannot go so far as to assume all caboclos are of African descent, some clearly are. Regardless, they are being defined as non-white. *A Portuguese-English Dictionary*, ed. James L. Taylor (Stanford, Calif.: Stanford University Press 1989).

84. Based on the court martial documents of the Conselho de Guerra da Marinha (1860–93), Arquivo Nacional, Rio de Janeiro.

85. See Butler, *Freedoms Given, Freedoms Won*.

86. *Codigo Criminal do Imperio do Brazil* (Criminal Code of the Brazilian Empire), promulgated on December 16, 1830, allowed for the limited use of corporal punishment on civilian prisoners and suspects. This practice ended on October 15, 1886, when the legislature revoked Article 60 of the civilian Criminal Code with the passage of Law 3,310.

87. Caminha, *História Administrativa do Brazil*, vol. 15, ch. 4, 112.

88. Ibid.

89. Court-martial documents 1860–93 show that more than 58 percent of sailors who were tried for a crime had been previously flogged; on average, these men had been lashed 226 times.

90. Artigos de Guerra para manter na sua devida ordem o Serviçoe Disciplina

das Minhas Esquadras e Armada Real, Art 80 (1799). The Articles of War are reproduced as Document No. 2 in the appendix to Camina, *História Administrativa do Brasil*, 15:393–401.

91. Brazilian Const. Art 179, sec. 19 (1824).

92. "Legislação naval Brasileira no período imperial," 240.

93. *Reletório do Ministério da Marinha*, 1833, 16.

94. Ibid.; *Código criminal do Império*, Art. 60.

95. Decisão N. 384, 16 July 1833, *Collecção das Decisões do Governo do Imperio do Brasil de 1833* (Rio de Janeiro: Imprensa Nacional, 1908), 220.

96. One officer was put on trial in 1873 for whipping a sailor 500 times in one day. After he was exonerated from all charges he went on to enjoy a meteoric rise through the ranks of the Brazilian navy, eventually serving as minister to the Supremo Tribunal Militar, the very court that adjudicated the highest level of his trial. His case is discussed in detail in the following chapter. Archivo Nacional, Conselho de Guerra da Marinha, proceso n°. 695, October 1873, caixa 13170, galaria 508. Decisão 396 de 13.09.1861, Caminha, *História Administrativa do Brasil*, vol. 15, ch. 8, 314.

97. Decreto 8.898 de 03.03.1883, ibid.

98. Lei 3.310 de 15.10.1886, ibid., 355, Decreto 3 de 16.11.1889, and Decreto 328 de 12.04.1890, in "Legislação naval Brasileira no período republicano," 321, 323.

99. Additionally, political infighting within the national legislation and the emperor's cabinet led to the establishment of Brazil's first republican opposition party. Though it took some time, it was a combination of that republican opposition and those army officers who had joined the political elite that toppled the monarchy

in 1889. On the use of enslaved Brazilians in the Paraguayan War see Jorge Prata de Sousa, *Escravidão ou morte: Os escravos brasileiros na Guerra do Paraguai* (Rio de Janeiro: Mauad Editora Ltda, 1996.

100. Lei 2,556 de 26.09.1874, "Legislação naval Brasileira no período imperial," 338–39.

101. Beattie, *The Tribute of Blood*, 67–68. Soldiers could also in fact still be transferred to disciplinary detachments in which corporal punishment was still practiced. However, for the overwhelming majority of soldiers, the army was free from the arbitrary violence that had been traditionally practiced in the Brazilian military.

102. Sausa, *Escravidão ou morte*, 73.

103. *Reletório do Ministerio de Marinha*, 1873, table 5, "Mappa estatistico do corpo de imperiaes marinheiros desde o anno de 1836 a 1873."

104. *Reletório do Ministério da Marinha*, *1880 & 1881* (Rio de Janeiro: Typographia Nacional, 1882).

105. Ibid.

106. Peter Beattie, "The House, the Street, and the Barracks: Reform and Honorable Masculine Social Space in Brazil, 1864–1945," *Hispanic American Historical Review* 76, no. 3 (Aug. 1996): 439–40.

107. Ibid., 443.

108. Lei 2,556 de 26.09.1874, "Legislação naval Brasileira no período imperial," 338–39. For a detailed discussion of the debate surrounding the Recruitment Law and Brazilian conscription in general see ch. 3 of Beattie, *The Tribute of Blood*; his "The House, the Street, and the Barracks," 439–73; and Frank D. McCann, "The Nation in Arms: Obligatory Military Service During the Old Republic," in *Essays Concerning the Socioeconomic History of Brazil and Portuguese India*, ed. Dauril Alden and

Warren Dean (Gainesville: University
Press of Florida, 1977), 211–43. Only after
passage of the Obligatory Military Service
Law, introduced in 1908 (replacing the
1874 Recruitment Law) would the army
see the "modernization" that it had hoped
for. That draft was implemented only in
1916, when volunteers failed to fill the
army's roster.

109. Letter from the Barão de Angra
Chefe do Quartel Gerald a Marinha to
the Navy Ministry, June 19, 1871, Arquivo
Nacional, RJ, xm 268, no. fo. nos., as cited
in Beattie, *The Tribute of Blood*, 327.

110. *Reletório do Ministerio de Marinha*,
1888, "Mappa estatístico do Corpo de
Imperíaes Marinheiros."

111. Brazilian Constitution, 1891, Art. 87,
§ 3.

112. Marcos A. da Silva, *Contra a chibata: marinheiros brasileiros em 1910* (São
Paulo: Brasiliense, 1982), 24.

113. Um Official da Armada, *Política
Versus Marinha*.

114. Ministerio da Marinha, "Sorteio
Naval" in *Relatório do Ministério da
Marinha*, 1903 (Rio de Janeiro: Imprensa
Nacional, 1904), 42–51.

115. Gilberto Freyre, *Order and Progress:
Brazil from Monarchy to Republic*, (New
York: Knopf, 1970), 400.

116. Beattie, "The House, the Street, and
the Barracks," 439–40.

117. Orlando Patterson, *Slavery and
Social Death: A Comparative Study*
(Cambridge, Mass.; Harvard University
Press, 1982), 13.

118. Ibid., 79.

119. Ibid., 10.

3. CONTROL OF THE LOWER
DECKS, 1860–1910

1. Archivo Nacional (hereafter
AN), Conselho de Guerra da Marinha

(hereafter CGM), Proceso n°. 687, June
1872, caixa, 13170, galaria 508.

2. Ibid.

3. According to holes in the case file
numbers, 698 cases from the naval high
court have never been archived into the
collection and are presumed lost. The
lost cases represent whole years during
which records are missing, not random
individual cases. The missing years are
1867 to 1869, 1878, and 1888 to 1892 following the establishment of the Brazilian
Republic. An officers' rebellion against
the republican government breaks out in
in the navy in 1893–94, which increases
and disrupts the court cases, so I use the
rebellion as the end point of my analysis
of these cases. Both Álvaro Pereira do
Nascimento and Peter M. Beattie have
published works drawing on their analysis
of some of these cases. To date, mine is the
only work that amalgamates the data from
all of the court-martial cases available that
were tried in Rio de Janeiro during this
time period.

4. AN, CGM, Proceso n°. 140, April
1862, caixa 13158, galaria 508; Article 51,
Articles of War, Lisbon, September 18,
1799.

5. Government decisions were
determined by the emperor and were
transmitted through a communication or
edict from a minister, in this case by the
minister of the navy. "Legislação naval
Brasileira no período imperial," 314.

6. AN, CGM, Proceso n°. 242, August
1864, caixa, 13161, galaria 508; Proceso n°.
227, March 1864, caixa 13160, galaria 508;
Proceso n°. 263, June 1865, caixa 13162,
galaria 508; Proceso n°. 277, November
1865, caixa 13162, galaria 508; Proceso n°.
254, July 1864, caixa 13161, galaria 508;
Proceso n°. 307, May 1866, caixa 13164,
galaria 508.

7. Evaristo de Moraes Filho, preface to Morel, *A Revolta da Chibata*, 13.

8. Walter Johnson, *Soul by Soul: Life Inside the Antebellum Slave Market* (Cambridge, Mass.: Harvard University Press, 1999), 206.

9. AN, CGM, Proceso n°. 695, October 1873, caixa 13170, galaria 508. All specific references to Lieutenant José Cândido Guillobel's case in the following pages drew on this trial record.

10. The Artigos de Guerra were adopted in Lisbon, September 25, 1799.

11. Ibid., Art. 56.

12. Ibid., Art. 80.

13. From the letter addressed to "Snrs. Presidente e Vogáes do Conselho de Guerra," dated November 22, 1873, found within Lieutenant Guillobel's trial record.

14. At least 14.5 percent of the sailors tried by the court between 1860 and 1893 were described as white, whereas more than 64.2 percent were of notable African descent. A detailed breakdown of the races of the men tried appears in table 3.1.

15. Álvaro Pereira do Nascimento, *A Ressaca da Marujada: recruitamento e disciplina na Armada Imperial* (Rio de Janeiro: Arquivo Nacional, 2001).

16. As stated above, all of this testimony draws on the trial records of Lieutenant Guillobel, but much of it has been reprinted in Nascimento, *A Ressaca da Marujada*, ch. 1, 31–66.

17. In 1893 the naval high court (Conselho de Guerra da Marinha) was absorbed into a single military court, the military supreme court (Supremo Tribunal Militar).

18. Renato de Almeida Guillobel, *Memórias* (Rio de Janeiro: Livraria F. Alves Editora, 1973), 11.

19. Taylor, *A Portuguese-English dictionary*.

20. AN, CGM, Proceso n°. 710 & 1091, February 1873 and November 1879, caixa 13171 and 13175, galaria 508.

21. AN, CGM, Proceso n°. 1091, November 1879, caixa, 13175, galaria 508.

22. Jorge Prata de Sousa addresses the role of slaves fighting in the Brazilian military in his *Esravidão ou Morte*. He focuses on the Brazilian navy in the section "Recrutamento na Marinha," 73–78.

23. The text of the decision is as follows: "The Decision of February 13, 1823 orders the acceptance as sailors and seaman apprentices in the National and Imperial Navy, those slaves who have been offered by their masters, who will be credited suitable compensation." "Legislação naval Brasileira no período imperial," 231.

24. In this era of whitening, the fact that enlisted men were so overwhelmingly of African descent, whereas officers were exclusively white, could reasonably lead to an expectation that white men in the lower ranks could have enjoyed protection from the harsh treatment applied to Afro-Brazilians. In fact, the statistical evidence shows that on the whole, whites were convicted of crimes at the same rate as Afro-Brazilians, and they have similar histories in the application of corporal punishment for their criminal activities. While the documents analyzed in this project cannot tell us if whites were arrested and tried less often, or whether they were disciplined on board with less regularity, neither the trial records nor the naval documents of the time suggest any great discrepancy among the men who faced the naval high court in Rio de Janeiro.

25. AN, CGM, Proceso n°. 1100, August 1879, caixa, 13176, galaria 508.

26. AN, CGM, Proceso n°. 1395, October 1885, caixa, 13184, galaria 508.

27. This excludes the two cases each of first desertion that were tried by the court.

Desertion during time of war drew a penalty of five years in prison at labor instead of the one year associated with desertion during peacetime. Aggravated desertion generally involved violence or a threat of violence to another sailor in fleeing service and often drew harsher punishment at the discretion of the court.

28. Caminha, *História Administrativa do Brazil,* vol. 15, ch. 8, 240.

29. Karasch, *Slave Life in Rio de Janeiro,* 8, table 1.1, "Comparative Percentages of African and Brazilian Slaves in the City of Rio de Janeiro, 1832–1849."

30. "Legislação naval Brasileira no período imperial," 230.

31. João José Reis, *Slave Rebellion in Brazil* (Baltimore, Md.: Johns Hopkins University Press, 1995), 73–74.

32. Enlisted men were excluded from voting during the period of both empire and republic, and as most sailors were reported to be illiterate they would have been excluded from the vote for this reason as well.

33. Beattie, *The Tribute of Blood,* table B.8, "Percentages of Pressed Troops (P), Volunteers (V), Reenlistments* and Others (O) by Region 1850–61 and 1870–82," 294.

34. Huggins, *From Slavery to Vagrancy in Brazil,* 19.

35. Peter L. Eisenburg, *The Sugar Industry in Pernambuco: Modernization without Change, 1840–1910* (Berkeley: University of California Press, 1974), 183 and "Abolishing Slavery," 588.

36. This actually caused real wages for unskilled rural laborers to fall markedly, decreasing by more than half between 1862 and 1902. Eisenburg, *The Sugar Industry in Pernambuco,* 190.

37. B. J. Barickman, "Persistence and Decline: Slave Labour and Sugar Production in the Bahian Reconcavo,

1850–1888," *Journal of Latin American Studies* 28, no. 3 (Oct.1996): 589.

38. Ibid., 614–17.

39. Huggins, *From Slavery to Vagrancy in Brazil,* 56–57.

40. Manoel Pinto da Rocha to the President, Sept. 28, 1871, cited in Barickman, "Persistence and Decline," 607.

41. Sandra Lauderdale Graham, *House and Street: The Domestic World of Servants and Masters in Nineteenth-Century Rio de Janeiro* (Cambridge: Cambridge University Press, 1988), 132.

42. Kraay, "Reconsidering Recruitment in Imperial Brazil," 133.

43. Huggins, *From Slavery to Vagrancy in Brazil,* 72–73.

44. Unfortunately, those who documented the age of sailors in the navy were not entirely consistent. At times, a boy's age was recorded on the date on which he enrolled into the navy as an enlisted man, usually at the rank of cabin boy (grumete). At other times, when recording the age of minors, they instead wrote the age at which a boy entered the company of apprentices, where he was to receive two years of "training" before enlisting. Not all minors went to the company of apprentices before enlistment, and not all of the boys remained apprentices for the prescribed two years. It is therefore sometimes difficult to confirm a sailor's age, though in most cases there is sufficient information available to estimate or triangulate age. Ages discussed in this section, unless otherwise noted, are their ages when a sailor enlisted into naval service with the rank of cabin boy or seaman third class, not the time they entered the company of apprentices.

45. AN, CGM, Proceso n°. 923, August 1877, caixa, 13174, galaria 508.

46. Ibid.

47. Eisenburg, *The Sugar Industry in Pernambuco,* 190

48. Barickman, "Persistence and Decline," 610.

49. The level of payment given to different recruiters was made into law by an 1855 decree that outlined the recruitment of volunteers and what should be done if sufficient volunteers for service were not available; this shortage of volunteers occurred every year until Brazil became involved in WWI. Caminha, *História Administrativa do Brazil,* appendix, "Documento n°. 18, Decreto N°. 1,591, de Abril de 1855," 431–39; The salary of enlisted men between 1872 and 1880 appears in the text of AN, CGM, Proceso n°. 1339, March 1884, caixa, 13181, galaria 508.

50. Sousa, *Escravidão ou morte,* 79.

51. AN, CGM, Proceso n°. 1570, December 1886, caixa, 13189, galaria 508.

52. Ibid.

53. João Cândido's biographical details are based his service record, "Da caderneta subsidiara do livro de socorros pertenecente ao Mirinheiro nacional da 16ª Companha 1ª classe, no 85 João Cândido." In Proc. 565/1910, "Processo-crime em que João Cândido e outros são acusados de sublevação após anistia ("Revolta da Chibata")," 344–55, and on the interview Cândido did with historian Hélio Silva on March 29, 1968, at the Museu da Imagem e do Som. The full text of this recording was printed in Museu da Imagem e do Som, *João Cândido, o almirante negro* (Rio de Janeiro: Gryphus, 1999).

54. Cândido, "Depoimento," 76; Silvia Capanema P. de Almeida, "Vidas de Marainheiro no Brasil Republicano: identidades, corpos e lideranças da revolta de 1910," *Antíteses* 3, n. esp. (Dec. 2010): 104, and Love, *The Revolt of the Whip,* 68–69.

55. "Caderneta" of João Cândido, 344–52.

56. *Reletório do Ministerio de Marinha,* 1859, 20.

57. *Reletório do Ministério da Marinha,* 1880 & 1881, Terceira Parte, "Dos castigos" 93.

58. Cosme Monoel do Nascimento, the sailor whose biography opened the chapter, was also lashed for the crime of "practicing immoral acts" with a shipmate. He was whipped 100 times in June 1869 at the age of twenty-four. He entered the military at the age of eighteen. AN, CGM, Proceso n°. 687, June 1872, caixa, 13170, galaria 508.

59. There are two examinations of male sexuality that were essential to my understanding and analysis of these documents. James N. Green's *Beyond Carnival: Male Homosexuality in Twentieth-Century Brazil* (Chicago: University of Chicago Press, 1999), and Peter Beattie's chapter "Conflicting Penal Codes: Modern Masculinity and Sodomy in the Brazilian Military, 1860–1916," in *Sex and Sexuality in Latin America,* ed. Daniel Balderston and Donna J. Guy (New York: New York University Press, 1997), as well as his expanded version of this chapter: "Ser homem pobre, livre e honrado: a sodomia e os praças nas Forças Armadas brasileiras (1860–1930)," in *Nova História Militar Brasileira,* ed. Celso Castro, Vitor Izecksohn, and Hendrik Karaay (Rio de Janeiro, Editora FGV/Editora Bom Texto, 2004). Although Beattie's work certainly includes an examination of the navy, its focus is a much broader examination of the military in general, focusing on the army.

60. Beattie "Conflicting Penal Codes," 66. James Green makes this argument as well, but his focus is on a later historical period. See his chapter "Control and Cure: The Medicolegal Responses," in *Beyond Carnival,* 107–46.

61. The English version of the book, translated by E. A. Lacey under the title *Bom-Crioulo: The Black Man and the Cabin Boy* (San Francisco: Gay Sunshine Press, 1982).

62. The site of the Naval College, Villegaignon Island, has since been joined to downtown Rio de Janeiro (Centro) by landfill.

63. Adolfo Caminha, *Bom-Crioulo* (New York: Luso-Brazilian Books, 2006 [1895]), 11. Both Beattie and Green offer excellent overall analyses of Caminha's novel. See Beattie's "Conflicting Penal Codes," 70–72, and Green in *Beyond Carnival*, 35–38.

64. Caminha, *Bom-Crioulo*, 16.

65. Reflecting the Naturalist beliefs of the author, very common in nineteenth-century Brazil, that the loss of semen in any form, whether by sexual contact or masturbation, was deleterious to a man's health.

66. Caminha, *Bom-Crioulo*, 41–42.

67. AN, CGM, Proceso n°. 1922, July 1893, caixa, 13191, galaria 508. My thanks to Peter Beattie for generously drawing my attention to this citation that initially fell outside of my dates of research.

68. AN., CGM, Proceso n°. 1227, May 1882, caixa, 13180, galaria 508.

69. Caminha, *Bom-Crioulo*, 43.

70. Ibid., 3.

71. Ibid., 6.

72. Ibid., 9.

73. AN, CGM, Proceso n°. 695, October 1873, caixa 13170, galaria 508., From the letter addressed to "Snrs. Presidente e Vogáes do Conselho de Guerra," dated November 22, 1873, within Lieutenant Guillobel's trial record.

74. Though he had been arrested for fighting on shore. Caminha, *Bom-Crioulo*, 62.

75. Ibid., 63.

76. Bazzerda was unable to locate a surviving copy or microfilm of the article, though it has been described in various literary works. It was cited by Caminha biographer Sânzio de Azevedo in his *Adolfo Caminha (Vida e obra)* (Fortaleza: UFC Ediçoes, 1999), 22, and it was referenced, though not formally cited, in Peter Beattie's biography of Caminha titled "Afolfo Ferreira Caminha: Navy Officer, Ardent Republican, and Naturalist Novelist," 96.

77. This book is very rare, but a copy of its first edition was digitized on January 7, 2008, by Project Gutenberg (Ebook #24190) under the incorrect title *No Paiz dos Yankees*, and it is freely available to download. The format has chapter headers but no page numbers; all of the above quotes are from ch. 5, the focus of which is corporal punishment. Adolfo Caminha, *No país dos ianques* (Rio de Janeiro: Livraria Moderna, 1894).

78. The companies of apprenticeship were renamed schools of apprenticeship by Decreto 9,371 of 02–14–1885.

79. One example of the sort of reforms offered to retain and attract qualified sailors was Decision 6 of January 14, 1890, which authorized the payment of ten milréis per year for up to two years for sailors who voluntarily reenlisted at the end of their term of service. In fact, many sailors accepted these signing bonuses because the navy often did not allow sailors to be discharged when they completed their required period of service. Such refusals are addressed in this quote of Vidal's report in the text.

80. Minister Vidal had recently replaced Eduardo Wandenkolk as naval minister, and for the first time, two Ministerial Reports were prepared in 1890 and published in 1891. Wandenkolk's was addressed to the head

of the provisional government (Chefe do Governo Provisorio), whereas Vidal's was addressed to the president (Presidente da Republica dos Estados Unidos do Brazil). This was clearly a critique (by Minister Vidal) of promises made by the outgoing naval minister of the effectiveness of volunteerism in the navy.

81. *Relatório do Ministro da Marinha, 1890* (Rio de Janeiro: Imprensa Nacional, 1891).

82. To avoid any confusion based on the frequent name changes at the company between 1863 and 1927, I will hereafter follow tradition and simply refer to the company as "Armstrongs."

83. For information pertaining to specific ships built by Armstrongs, see Peter Brook, *Warships for Export: Armstrong Warships, 1867–1927* (Gravesend, Kent, UK: World Ship Society, 1999), 77–78, 216–17

84. Official da Armada [José Eduardo de Macedo Soares], *Politica versus Marinha,* 85.

85. Silvia Capanema P. de Almeida, "Nous, marins, citoyens brésiliens et républicains: identités, modernité et mémoire de la révolte des matelots de 1910" [We are sailors and citizens of the republic of Brazil: identities, modernization and the record of the past in the Mutiny of 1910], PhD diss., l'École des Hautes Études en Sciences Sociales, 2009), 154–63. She has subsequently published work based on this material in several articles. See Silvia Capanema P. de Almeida, "A modernização do material e do pessoal da Marinha nas vésperas da revolta dos marujos de 1910: modelos e contradições," *Estudos Históricos* 23, no. 45 (Jan./June 2010): 147–69, and "Vidas de marinheiro no Brasil Republicano: identidades, corpos e lideranças da revolta de 1910," *Antíteses* 3 (Dec. 2010): 90–114. She drew on 250

files on sailors in 1908 (of 750 available) and came up with the following: 56.4% parda (mixed black), 20% white, 11.6% preta (black), 10.4% morena ("brown"), 1.2% branco corado (literally "colored or tinted white"), and 0.4% parda clara (light-skinned black).

86. Annex to the *Relatório do Ministro da Marinha, 1908* (Rio de Janeiro: Imprensa Nacional, 1909), 260.

87. Freyre, *Order and Progress,* 400.

88. Official da Armada, *Politica versus Marinha,* 84–85.

89. Ibid., 87–88.

90. Ibid., 89.

91. Shyllon O. Folarin, *Black People in Britain, 1555–1833* (London: Oxford University Press, 1977), 98.

92. Edward Long, *A History of Jamaica,* Vol. II (London: T. Lownes, 1774), 403.

93. See Silvia Capanema P. de Almeida's recent articles "A modernização do material e do pessoal da Marinha nas vésperas da revolta dos marujos de 1910," and "Vidas de marinheiro no Brasil Republicano."

94. For an earlier discussion of recruitment in the Brazilian navy, see Morgan, "Legislating the Lash."

95. U.S. Office of Naval Intelligence (ONI), Reg. # 799, no. 70, "Brazilian Naval Revolt. 1910" [various sources and dates, 1910–11]. Signed Irving B. Dudley, Petrópolis, November 29, 1910, NARA.

96. These events are briefly described by Glauco Carneiro as a direct response to the reintroduction of corporal punishment to the Brazilian navy in his examination of the Revolta da Chibata, titled "A Revolta dos Marinheiros," *O Cruzeiro* (June 27, 1964): 105.

97. Morel, *A Revolta da Chibata,* 60

98. An "anonymous" letter was sent to Comandante Luiz de Alencastro Graça on September 5, 1949, describing how

Francisco Dias Martins not only commanded the *Bahia* but was the mastermind
and sole leader of the entire revolt. The
letter is replete with inaccuracies and
contradictions pertaining to the revolt
itself, as well as racist slurs toward João
Cândido, the "illiterate, negro, 'Admiral.'"
It is broadly accepted that the letter was
written by Francisco Dias Martins himself
in an attempt to carve himself a more
favorable position as a Brazilian revolutionary. Comandante H. Pereira da Cunha
accepts Francisco Dias Martins's claims
at face value in his *A Revolta da Esquadra
Brasileira em Novembro e Dezembro de 1910.*

4. ROOTS OF A REBELLION

1. "The Brazilian Battleship '*Minas
Geraes,*'" *Scientific American* 102 (March 19,
1910): 240.

2. *Correio de Manhã,* April 19, 1910.

3. The actual name of the company
went through many changes, and there
is some disagreement among secondary sources as to how and when that
company's title changed. According
to an in-house history dated 27/10/27
that was produced for the Encyclopedia
Britannica (though a different draft was
eventually used) W. G. Armstrong and
Company was established as a privately
held firm in 1847 as an engineering firm
focusing on the production of hydraulic
cranes. When Armstrong took a job for
the British government, W. G. Armstrong
and Co. became the Elswick Engine
Works. When he resigned his government
position in 1864, two firms (the Elswick
Engine Works and the Elswick Ordnance
Company) were amalgamated under the
title Sir W. G. Armstrong and Company.
After eighteen years of existence as a
privately held firm, Armstrongs became
a limited liability company under the
title of Sir W. G. Armstrong, Mitchell

and Company, with capital of £2 million
in 1882. In 1896, the name "Mitchell"
was dropped from the title after Charles
Mitchell's death in 1895. In 1897, the
company purchased Whitworth Works
at Openshaw in Manchester, where they
installed an armor plate plant, at which
time the name changed to Sir William
Armstrong, Whitworth and Company.
Finally, in 1927, the company was acquired
by Vickers at Barrow, and became part of
the new firm Vickers-Armstrong. Locally,
regardless of the era, the company is generally referred to simply as Armstrongs.
The first of three typed documents in
Document 590 "Armstrong, Whitworth
and Co. Ltd., (W.G.) and (Sir W.G.),
History 1886–1926," Cambridge University
Library, Department of Manuscripts and
University Archives, Vickers Ltd: Records,
MS Vickers.

4. Japan acquired ten warships, its
last purchased in 1905. Chile's navy made
the third highest number of purchases,
with seven warships in this period. Based
on "List of War Vessels etc., Launched
from Elswick and Walker Shipyards
from 1883 to 1913." From A. R. Fairbane's
unpublished history of the Elswick's works
catalogued as "Unpublished History,"
Document # 593, Cambridge University
Library, Department of Manuscripts and
University Archives, Vickers Ltd: Records,
MS Vickers, 38–40.

5. H. Pereira da Cunha, *A Revolta
na Esquadra Brasileira em November e
Dezembro de 1910,* 21.

6. Proclamation of November 15, 1889,
printed in translation in U.S. Department
of State, *Papers Relating to the Foreign
Relations of the United States, Transmitted
to Congress, with the Annual Message of the
President, December 3, 1889* (Washington
D. C.: U.S. Government Printing Office,
1890), 61.

7. June E. Hahner's "The Brazilian Armed Forces and the Overthrow of the Monarchy: Another Perspective," *Americas* 26, no. 2 (October 1969): 171–82, offers excellent analysis of the negotiations facing the various leadership groups in the Brazilian military – including members of the navy – in the period leading up to the 1893 naval revolt.

8. For a contemporary overview of the revolt and its political context, see Felisbelo Freire's *História da Revolta de 6 de Setembro de 1893* (Rio de Janeiro: Cunha and Irmãos, 1896). For a recent analysis see "Political Intervention During the Era of Gun and Longboat" in Robert L. Scheina's *Latin America: A Naval History: 1810–1987* (Annapolis, Md.: Naval Institute Press, 1987), 53–79.

9. Scheina, *Latin America: A Naval History*, 68.

10. The *Gustavo Sampaio* is best known for firing the torpedo that sunk the second-class battleship *Aquidabá* in April 1894, effectively ending the uprising, but the ship also acquired infamy for accidentally ramming and sinking one of the five newly purchased German-built torpedo boats that the Brazilian government acquired to assist in putting down the rebellion. For information on the *Gustavo Sampaio*, see United States, Office of Naval Intelligence, "General Information Series, No. VII, "Information from Abroad" (Washington, DC: Government Printing Office, 1888), 399, as well as references to that ships and the other Armstrongs-built ships in Brook, *Warships for Export*, 76–77, 166–67, 216–17.

11. "The Sea Fight at Desterro," *New York Times*, May 30, 1894, 2.

12. ONI, "Brazilian Naval Personnel, 1910–12, Extract from an Intelligence Report on Rio Janeiro [*sic*], Brazil, by Lieut. C.L. Hussey, Fleet Intelligence

Officer, South Atlantic Squadron, November 24, 1904," Reg. 423.

13. The text of the decree is reprinted in Cunha, *A revolta na esquadra brasileira*, 22.

14. "Ships built at Elswick and Walker, notes on," Doc. No. 811, Vickers Archive, Cambridge University Library, and Brook, *Warships for Export*, 85–87.

15. Scheina, *Latin America: A Naval History*, 80.

16. "Warship Blown Up, 212 Lost," *New York Times*, January 23, 1906, 1.

17. Changes to the Brazilian naval contracted are examined in Robert L. Scheina's "The Dreadnaught Race," in *Latin America: A Naval History*.

18. *London Quarterly Review*, January 1896, originally quoted in Arthur J. Marder, *The Anatomy of British Sea Power* (New York: Alfred A. Knopf, 1940), 15.

19. Conley, *From Jack Tar to Union Jack*, 6.

20. Rolf Hobson, *Imperialism at Sea: Naval Strategic Thought, the Ideology of Sea Power and the Tirpitz Plan, 1875–1914* (Boston: Brill Academic Press, 2002), 12.

21. Bernard Brodie, *Sea Power in the Machine Age*, (Princeton, N.J.: Princeton University Press, 1941), 119.

22. Table 1/5, "Warship Output of Major Shipyards, 188[missing digit]–1927," in Brook, *Warships for Export*, 19.

23. There are several drafts and unpublished articles in this folder; many include quotes from the upper management at Armstrongs. The third unnumbered article, dated 11-5-1905, is by Alfred Cochrane and is titled "ELSWICK," 5–6. "Armstrong, Whitworth and Co. Ltd., (W. G.) and (Sir W. G.), History 1886–1926," Document 590, Cambridge University Library, Department of Manuscripts and University Archives, Vickers LTD: Records, MS Vickers.

24. J. M. Rendel was a civil engineer associated with marine design for the admiralty who supported Armstrong's ordinance design. His sons were central to Armstrongs. His eldest, George, was partner and head of ordnance operation from 1858 until 1882 while Stuart, a politician and lawyer, was a director until his death in 1913.

25. Sir W. G. Armstrong, "Report on the Construction of Wrought-iron Rifled Field Guns, Adapted for Elongated Projectiles," *The Industrial Resources of the District of the Three Northern Rivers, the Tyne, Wear and Tees, including The Report on the Local Manufactures, read before The British Association in 1863*, 2nd ed., ed. W. G. Armstrong et al. (Newcastle-Upon-Tyne: A. Reid, Printing Court Buildings, 1864), 309–10.

26. Alfred Cochrane, "ELSWICK," 6–7. Doc. 590, Vickers Archive, Cambridge University Library.

27. House of Commons Debate, 152, 3s., 1859, col. 1319, as quoted in David Dougan, *The Great Gun-Maker: The Life of Lord Armstrong* (Northumberland, UK: Sandhill Press, 1991 [1st ed. 1970]), 63.

28. For a detailed history of the revolution of British armament, see J. D. Scott's *Vickers: A History* (London: Weidenfeld and Nicolson, 1962), ch. 4, "British Armaments and Their Makers from the Crimea to 1888."

29. Marshall J. Bastable, *Arms and the State: Sir William Armstrong and the Remaking of British Naval Power, 1854–1914* (Aldershot, UK: Ashgate, 2004), 60.

30. Ibid., 63. Of that number (£1,525,000), the value of the contracts for breech-loading guns alone between 1858 and 1863 was just under £1 million, £800,000 of which came in the two years 1860–62. Ibid., 100.

31. Dougan, *The Great Gun-Maker,* 99–101, and Bastable, *Arms and the State,* 75–77.

32. For a descriptions of these negotiations, see Scott's ch. 4, "British Armaments from the Crimea to 1888," in *Vickers,* 23–39, and Bastable's "Defending England: Monster Guns or Iron Ships," in *Arms and the State,* 67–106. Armstrong would enjoy the final victory. Following Whitworth's death in 1887, Armstrong purchased his company to acquire its armored plate production.

33. Alfred Cochrane, "ELSWICK," 9–10. Doc. 590, Vickers Archive, Cambridge University Library.

34. "A.R. Fairbairn's Unpublished History," Doc. 593, Vickers Archive, 69–70. A. R. Fairbairn was commissioned by Vickers-Armstrong to write a history of the company, but he died before he could finish. The title page bears the note, "This copy was photographed from Elswick's carbon copy of Fairbairn's final draft of his history of Armstrongs. Twelve copies were made of the draft, but only this one of Elswick's and this photographed copy are known to exist." His collected documents and the copy of the manuscript were loaned to J. D. Scott while he was researching and writing his 1962 book, *Vickers: A History.*

35. Quoted in Scott's *Vickers: A History,* 31.

36. Dougan, *The Great Gun Maker,* 103.

37. "A. R. Fairbairn's Unpublished History," 94. Doc. No. 593 Vickers Archive, Cambridge University Library, 94.

38. Dougan, *The Great Gun-Maker,* 104–108.

39. Bastable, *Arms and the State,* 47.

40. Armstrong absorbed Joseph Whitworth and Co. in a merger in 1897, just as Vickers would eventually merge with Armstrongs in 1927.

41. Armstrongs' greatest competition, as it turned toward the international markets, came from the French company Le Creucet and from the German firm Krupp. Indeed, Armstrongs and Krupp would dominate the international trade from the 1860s. In 1898 and 1900, Germany made political and economic commitments to produce a fleet to challenge even the strongest naval power – that of England. See Lieutenant-Commander P. K. Kemp's "The Royal Navy," ch. 13 in Simon Nowell-Smith's *Edwardian England, 1901–1914* (Oxford: Oxford University Press, 1964). Until WWI, approximately two-thirds of the world's fleet was produced in Great Britain. During the war, the seafaring nations of the world, with the United States and Japan leading the way, expanded their annual output by up to eight times. By the end of the war, the British, though still dominant, produced less than half of the world's fleet. For further details, see "The End of Disarmament," ch. 17 of Scott's *Vickers*.

42. Bastable, *Arms and the State,* 52–53.

43. Ibid.

44. "Gunboats," in Brook, *Warships for Export,* 22–23.

45. Kenneth Warren, *Armstrongs of Elswick: Growth in Engineering and Armaments to the Merger with Vickers* (London: MacMillan, 1989), 24–25.

46. "Ships built at Elswick and Walker, notes on," Doc. No. 811, Vickers Archive, Cambridge University Library.

47. "Important Shipbuilding Orders for British Builders," *Newcastle Daily Journal,* July 11, 1904, in "Elswick Yards, Warships, press cuttings 1904–1911," Doc. No. 641, Vickers Archive, Cambridge University Library.

48. Livermore, "Battleship Diplomacy in South America," 31.

49. "Letters Concerning Board Affairs: March 1896–December 1912 including papers concerning orders from Brazil, Portugal and Russia; also memoranda on Turkish and Balkan business and on armour plate production," Ref. No. 31/7595, Tyne and Wear Archives.

50. Herod was the king of the small Jewish state in the final decades before the Common Era. He is best known for the biblical tale of the slaughter of the infants of Bethlehem, but this mention was a reference to the fact that he ruled with the foreign support of Mark Anthony and weapons made available to him from the foreign power of Rome. "Letters Concerning Board Affairs: March 1896–December 1912 including papers concerning orders from Brazil, Portugal and Russia; also memoranda on Turkish and Balkan business and on armour plate production," Ref. No. 31/7595, Tyne and Wear Archives.

51. For a detailed study of that particular ship, see Richard Hough's *The Big Battleship* (Penzance, UK: Periscope, 2003 [1966]).

52. Almirante Hélio Leoncio Martins, "A revolta da Armada-1893," in *História naval brasileira* (Rio de Janeiro: Serviço de Documentação da Marinha, 1995).

53. Seward W. Livermore, "Battleship Diplomacy in South America: 1905–1925," *The Journal of Modern History* 16, No. 1 (Mar. 1944) 31–33.

54. "Elswick Shipyard Reports Books Nos. 1 and 2, 1883–1913," "Report to Meeting of Directors to be held in London on Thursday, November 15, 1906," J. R. Perrett, 166, Doc. No. 1158, Vickers Archive, Cambridge University Library.

55. Ibid.

56. Ibid.

57. Ibid.

58. "31/3700–3733 Elswick papers 18. Letters, January–December 1908," Ref. No. 31/3727, Tyne and Wear Archives.

59. "Progress of Brazil: Big Battleship Launched at Elswick," *Newcastle Daily Journal,* September 11, 1908, 4.

60. "The Brazilian Battleship 'Minas Geraes,'" *Scientific American,* issue 102 (March 19, 1910): 240.

61. Brazilian sailors would have been dispatched to Newcastle to pick up the smaller ships acquired in the late nineteenth century, but never in the number or for as long as the sailors who arrived in the summer of 1909. Although sailors had been assigned to modern warships, as depicted by Adolfo Caminha when Bom-Crioulo was transferred to a modern steel ship, this represented a small portion of Brazilian sailors; most enlisted men remained unaffected by these earlier acquisitions, though they likely dreaded transfer to one of those ships.

62. Cunha, *A Revolta na Esquadra Brasileira em Novembro e Dezembro de 1910,* 25–26.

63. João Cândido Felisberto, *"Depoimento" de João Cândido,* in Museu da Imagem e do Som, *João Cândido, o almirante negro* (Rio de Janeiro: Gryphus, 1999), 65–101.

64. "Elswick Shipyard Reports Books Nos. 1 and 2, 1883–1913," Doc. No. 1158, Vickers Archive, Cambridge University Library.

65. João Cândido's service record was reproduced in the court transcripts during his trial for participation in a second naval revolt in December 1910. Proc. 565/1910, "Processo-crime em que João Cândido e outros são acusados de sublevação após anistia ("Revolta da Chibata)," vol. 2, Supremo Tribunal Military, 1910–12, AN. 344–49.

66. Ibid., 349–55, and Love, *The Revolt of the Whip,* 70.

67. As quoted in Dougan, *The Great Gun-Maker,* 51.

68. Joan Allen, *Joseph Cowen and Popular Radicalism on Tyneside* (Monmouth, Wales: Merlin Press, 2007), 23 and 142.

69. Looking back to an earlier era, a 1961 article in the *Guardian* examining the origins of the sizable Yemeni community in South Shields (a neighboring town to Newcastle) dating back to the 1890s described the Tyneside area as "a study in integration: a place where racial prejudice died years ago." In fact, the reputation Tyneside enjoys for racial exceptionalism is likely only in part deserved. Yemeni firemen (the men who shoveled coal into a ship's engine) established their generally peaceful enclave in South Shields only after years of difficulty finding accommodations in the area. The Arab Seaman's Boarding House was established in 1909 to help mitigate these difficulties. See David Bean "Islam-on-Tyne," *Guardian,* March 17, 1961, 9.

70. See section titled "A Negro Community on Tyneside" in Sydney Collins's *Coloured Minorities in Britain* (London: Lutterworth Press, 1957), 35–116. Barry Carr addressed the issue of racial tolerance in Newcastle in "Black Geordies," in Robert Colls and Bill Lancaster, *Geordies: Roots of Regionalism,* 2nd ed. (Newcstle, UK: Northumbria University Press, 2005), 133–48. Additionally Sascha Auerbach examines hostility toward Chinese labor in the British empire in the period 1903–1906 in the chapter "'Chinese Labour' and the Imperial Dimensions of British Racial Discourse," opposition and violence against Chinese workers in London in his chapter "The Dragon and Saint George, 1910–14," and the origins of the race riots that swept British cities in 1919 with a focus on both anti-Chinese and antiblack sentiment in the chapter "'This Plague

Spot of the Metropolis,' 1919–21," in *Race, Law, and "The Chinese Puzzle" in Imperial Britain* (New York: Palgrave Macmillan, 2009), 15–50, 51–88 and 151–84.

71. Joe Robinson, *The Life and Times of Francie Nichol of South Shields* (London: Futura Publications Ltd., 1777), 59–60.

72. Hough, *The Big Battleship,* 43.

73. "Brazil's New Battleship," *Newcastle Daily Chronicle,* Sept. 15, 1909, 3, and "Beri-Beri," *Newcastle Daily Journal,* February 5, 1910, 10.

74. "Beri-Beri in the Tyne," *Newcastle Evening Chronicle,* Sept. 22, 1909, 4, col. 2.

75. The British consul to Brazil, Ernest Hambloch, describes some of the effects of the increased pay scale on the sailors while posted to Newcastle in his book *British Consul: Memories of Thirty Years' Service in Europe and Brazil* (London: George G. Harrap, 1938). 127–28.

76. "A Local Rowton House," *Newcastle Daily Journal,* Aug. 8, 1906, 6, col. 4–5.

77. "A Brazilian in Custody: Another Shooting Case in Newcastle," *Newcastle Daily Journal,* Jan. 6, 1910, 7, col. 2.

78. "The Brazilian Sailors," signed Whist, *Newcastle Daily Journal,* Jan. 7, 1910, 4, col. 5.

79. "Brazilian and Japanese," *Newcastle Daily Journal,* Jan. 7, 1910, 4, col. 5.

80. Hambloch, *British Consul,* 127.

81. Ibid., 127–28.

82. *Times* (London), September 11, 1871, as quoted in Dick Keys and Ken Smith, *Down Elswick Slipways* (Newcstle, UK: Newcastle City Libraries, 1996), 12.

83. David Bean, *Armstrong's Men: the Story of the Shop Stewards Movement in the Tyneside Works* (Newcastle, UK: Vicker Limited, 1967).

84. Doc. No. 1158, "Elswick Shipyard Reports Books Nos. 1 and 2, 1883–1913," Vickers Archive, Cambridge University Library.

85. Conley, *From Jack Tar to Union Jack,* 125.

86. Ibid., 9–11.

87. N. A. M. Rodger, *The Wooden World: An Anatomy of the Georgian Navy* (Annapolis, Md.: Naval Institute Press, 1986), 15.

88. Charles Butler, *On the Legality of Impressing Seamen,* 3rd ed., with additional notes "partly by Lord Sandwich,," reprinted in *The Pamphleteer,* vol. 23. Pam. XLV (London: AJ Velpy, 1824 [1777]), 226–87.

89. Ibid. 254–55.

90. Isaac Land, "Customs of the Sea: Flogging, Empire and the 'True British Seaman,' 1770 to 1870," *Interventions: The International Journal of Postcolonial Studies* 3, no. 2 (2001): 170–71.

91. Ibid., 177.

92. The Naval Discipline Act is the focus of Theodore Thring's *A Treatise on the Criminal Law of the Navy* (London: V. and R. Stevens and Sons, 1861). On the legislation and application of corporal punishment see Eugene Rasor's chapter "Discipline Regulations and Punishment" in *Reform in the Royal Navy: A Social History of the Lower Decks, 1850–1880* (Hamden, Conn.: Archon Books, 1976), 38–61, as well as chart 2, "Number of men flogged in the Royal Navy, 1830–65"; chart 3, "Floggings Per 1000 men in the Royal Navy, 1830–65"; and chart 4, "Average number of lashes per flogging in the Royal Navy, 1830–65," all of which appear in the appendix of Rasor's book. Additionally the suspension of corporal punishment did not apply to the caning or "birching" of boys and officer cadets under the age of eighteen. The admiralty saw the use of caning as an essential training tool wholly separate from punishment by the "cat-of-nine-tails." Ibid., 55–56.

93. Ibid., 55.

94. In a parallel policy to the introduction of the Brazilian apprenticeship companies, in 1853 the British navy formally
introduced the rating of "boy seaman"
for voluntary recruits between the ages
of fifteen and eighteen. For an overview
of British naval reforms see "Imperial
Challenges and the Modernisation of the
Fleet," in Conley, *From Jack Tar to Union
Jack*, 19–65.

95. The interview has been reproduced
in its entirety in Cândido, "Depoimento," 71.

96. Ibid., 75.

97. Ibid., 92.

98. Fogo's quote describing corporal
punishment opens the next chapter. He
also describes serving under Captain
Baptista da Neves, the captain of the
Minas Geraes who was killed in the opening moments of the revolt, as a regime of
terror. Fogo claimed that the captain had
more than one sailor punished with 1,000
lashes and once had a sailor lashed 1,300
times after he wounded a police officer.
"A Revolta na Armada," *O Estado de São
Paulo*, November 26, 1910, 4, col. 4

5. THE REVOLT OF THE LASH

1. This number, widely republished
as 250 lashes, has been criticized by some
historians. As it is exactly ten times the
legal number of lashes allowable by the
code, there has been some suggestion
among scholars more sympathetic to the
navy that it may have been a simple typo,
having shifted a decimal point. In endnote
22 in Martins, *A Revolta dos marinheiros,
1910*, he argues that the number 250 cited
in Morel, *A Revolta da Chibata*, must have
been an exaggeration, as such an application would "result in the death of the *element* punished. And Marcelino, who was
in the infirmary of the *Minas Gerais* [*sic*],
went to the hospital with Deputy Carlos
de Carvalho by foot" (italics added). In
the U.S. Office of Naval Intelligence,

"Brazilian Naval Revolt, 1910," Reg.
799, dated various, 1910–1911, National
Archives and Records Administration,
Washington, D.C. [Hereafter ONI,
"Brazilian Naval Revolt, 1910," Reg. 799].
In a personal letter written to Robert
Woods Bliss, the chargé d'affaires ad
interim by an unnamed officer of the
British Fourth Cruiser Squadron, which
was stationed in Guanabara Bay during
the revolt, the officer described details
of the revolt as they were told to him by
an English engineer who was serving
onboard the *Minas Geraes*. The engineer
told him that Menezes had been reported
by a sergeant for a slight offense, and in
retaliation "that night when the latter
was asleep he got busy with a razor and
slashed him badly about the face." He also
described the number of lashes applied in
punishment as 145, not 250. Overall, the
documents collected by the U.S. Office
of Naval Intelligence regarding the revolt
represent a valuable addition, as they collected several eyewitness accounts of the
revolts in November and December 1910,
as well as following up their repercussions.
Although they include information transmitted in the moment that in places proves
to be incorrect, many of the collected
primary documents add an objective view
in comparison with and in addition to
the published newspapers, Brazilian state
reports, and published historical narratives. They were never meant for public
use, and many of the documents offer
confidential and/or privileged opinions to
these events. They were in fact declassified
for public use only on May 3, 1972. I have
previously drawn on these documents
in the publication of "Brazil: The Revolt
of the Lash, 1910," which appeared in
*Naval Mutinies of the Twentieth Century:
An International Perspective*, ed. Bruce
Elleman and Christopher Bell (Portland,
Ore.: Frank Cass, 2003). The description

of Menezes's crime is supported by H. Pereira da Cunha; he describes Menezes as trying to smuggle alcohol on board the *Minas Geraes,* and seaman Souza reported him. In retribution, Menezes attacked him with a shaving razor. Cunha, *A Revolta na Esquadra Brasileira em Novembro e Dezembro de 1910,* 32–33. As for the number of lashes applied to Menezes, in both the interviews João Cândido gave, one with Edmar Morel and the above-cited MIS interview with Hélio Silva, he described the number of lashes applied as 250. Until more compelling evidence surfaces, I accept that number.

In the previously cited interview in the November 26, 1910, newspaper *O Estado de São Paulo,* Eurico Fogo also described serving under Captain Batista das Neves as a regime of terror.

Fogo claimed that the captain had more than once had sailors punished with 1,000 lashes and once had a sailor lashed 1,300 times after he wounded a police officer. "A Revolta na Armada" *O Estado de São Paulo,* November 26, 1910, 4, cols. 4–5.

2. Brazil, Congresso Nacional, *Annaes da Câmara dos Deputados,* 1910, 8:455. José Carlos de Carvalho is among the first to write about the Revolta da Chibata, in his *O Livro da Minha Vida: Na guerra, na paz e nas revoluções: 1847–1910,* vol. 1 (Rio de Janeiro: Typo do Jornal do Commercio, 1912).

3. The details of the revolt itself have been the subject of several modern Portuguese language works and one recent book in English. In the order of publication, they are H. Pereira da Cunha *A Revolta na Esquadra Brasileira em Novembro e Dezembro de 1910* (Rio de Janeiro: Imprensa Naval, 1953) [originally published in Revista Marítima Brasileira, Oct.–Dec. 1949]; Edmar Morel, *A Revolta da Chibata* (5th ed.) (São Paulo: Paz e

Terra, 2010); Mário Maestri Filho, *1910: A Revolta dos Marinheiros* (São Paulo: Global, 1982); Marcos A. da Silva, *Contra a Chibata* (São Paulo: Brasiliense, 1982); Mário Maestri Filho, *Cisnes negros: 1910: a revolta dos marinheiros contra a chibata* (São Paulo: Moderna, 1998); Hélio Leôncio Martins, *A Revolta dos Marinheiros, 1910* (São Paulo: Editora Nacional; Rio de Janeiro: Serviço de Documentação da Marinha, 1988); Fernando Granato, *O negro da chibata: o marinheiro que colocou a República na mira dos canhões* (Rio de Janeiro: Objetiva, 2000); Álvaro Pereira do Nascimento, *A ressaca da marujada: recrutamento e disciplina na Armada Imperial* (Rio de Janeiro: Presidência da República, Arquivo Nacional, 2001); *Cidadania, cor e disciplina na revolta dos marinheiros de 1910* (Rio de Janeiro: Mauad X: FAPERJ, 2008); and Joseph L. Love, *The Revolt of the Whip* (Stanford, Calif.: Stanford University Press, 2012). Additionally, there are two important dissertations on the revolt that have not yet been published. They are José Miguel Arias Neto, "Em Busca da Cidadania: Praças da Armada Nacional 1867–1910" [In search of citizenship: sailors/enlisted men in the national navy 1867–1910], PhD diss., Universidade de São Paulo, 2001 (*praças* was a colonial term for enlisted men, but in the context of the navy, it could just as well be sailors); and Sílvia Capanema P. de Almeida, "'Nous, marins, citoyens brésiliens et républicains': identités, modernité et mémoire de la révolte des matelots de 1910" [We are sailors and citizens of the republic of Brazil: identities, modernization and the record of the past in the Mutiny of 1910], PhD diss., l'École des Hautes Etudes en Sciences Sociales, 2009; both of these do important work locating the Revolta da Chibata as a struggle over the rights of citizenship rather than as a struggle over the rights of sailors.

4. It seems certain that the 2,379 number is too high, though exactly how much is hard to know. It is derived from H. Pereira da Cunha's study of the revolt first published in 1949, and Cunha based his figures on official naval records, which assume full crews on board ships. In fact, the dreadnoughts were constantly undermanned. In his 1912 autobiography Jose Carlos de Carvalho, the officer who negotiated the return of the ships to the government, stated that "the crews of the grand battleships should have been 800 or 900 men, but in fact neither exceeded a crew of 350 sailors." José Carlos de Carvalho, *O Livro da Minha Vida: Na guerra, na paz e nas revoluções: 1847–1910* (Rio de Janeiro: Typo do Jornal do Commercio, 1912), 1:320. A contemporary article that appeared in the January 7, 1911, edition of *Collier's* estimated the number of men involved as 1,500 (all of whom they described as "Negros"). The Brazilian navy collected a list of the names of sailors who were eventually excluded from naval service as a punishment for their active participation in the Revolta da Chibata, and there were 1,292 names included. "Relação das Praças Excluidas da Armada em Consequencia dos Movimentos de Novembro E Dezembro de 1910" (Rio de Janeiro: Imprensa Naval, 1912), 1–34. That number did not include the names of any of the leaders who were later put on trial, nor do I believe it included the names of the several hundred sailors shipped north to Acra on the *Satélite* or the sailors killed after their arrest in December 1910. (Both events are discussed in the next chapter). Based on all of that information, I think the number of active participants was likely somewhere between 1,500 and 2,000 sailors, though assuming a decent rate of

sympathy among sailors who were quickly removed from service during the revolt and thus could not join the reclamantes, the potential number of supporters may be close to that 2,400 number or even higher. I owe a debt to David S. Marshall for challenging me on my use of 2,379 participants in several previous publications.

5. Morel, *A Revolta da Chibata*, 81.

6. From an interview with Second Lieutenant Álvaro Alberto da Mota e Silva, quoted in Morel, *A Revolta da Chibata*, 82.

7. Martins, *A Revolta dos Marinheiros, 1910*, 33.

8. Ibid., 34.

9. Ibid.

10. In constructing this narrative, I have used the periodicals *O Correio da Manhã, Diário de Noticias, Estado de São Paulo, Jornal do Commercio*, the *New York Times*, and the *Times* (London), as well as the narratives written by Vice-Admiral Joaquim Marques Baptista de Leão in the *Relatorio da Marinha, 1910* (Rio de Janeiro: Imprensa Nacional, 1911), prepared for the new Brazilian president and José Carlos de Carvalho's autobiographical *O Livro da Minha Vida: Na guerra, na paz e nas revoluções: 1847–1910*, vol. 1 (Rio de Janeiro: Typo do Jornal do Commercio, 1912). As far as the sources agree on details, they will not be cited.

11. See "Os Maquinistas e os inferiores na sublevação," in Martins, *A Revolta dos Marineiros*, 67–70.

12. Hambloch, *British Consul*, 111. In an interesting claim, Hambloch discredits one of the most cited English language sources on the Revolta da Chibata, that of Sir James Bryce, author of *South American Observations and Impressions* (New York: MacMillan, 1914). He states that Bryce was departing Rio on the first day of the revolt, November 23. He was interested in events

in Rio but could not stay to witness the outcome. Hambloch describes a conversation that took place as Bryce left: "'Be sure and write me all you have been telling me,' he said when we parted; 'and let me know how it all ends.' I did so, and found the account in his book afterward. But I did not hear from him again," 110.

13. Martins, *A Revolta dos Marinheiros, 1910,* 43.

14. "Navios sem guarnições" (Ships without crews), *O Estado de São Paulo,* November 25, 1910, 3, col. 5.

15. The crews' abandonment of the *República, Floriano, Benjamin Constant, Primeiro de Março, Tiradentes, Tymbira,* and *Carlos Gomes* was described in the *Relatorio da Marinha, 1910,* 9, whereas Minister Leão's quote came from page 6 of that same document.

16. Curiously, this note did not mention the fourth ship that joined the revolt.

17. The president had little success blocking the publication of the rebel's messages; most were reprinted in local newspapers as the revolt went on.

18. Museu da Imagem e do Som do Rio de Janeiro, *João Cândido,* 78.

19. *Correio da Manha* (Rio de Janeiro), 1st ed., November 23, 1910, 1, and *Correio da Manha* (Rio de Janeiro), 2nd ed., November 23, 1910, 1.

20. "Mutineers Fire on Rio Janeiro: Dreadnoughts in Possession of Crews, Try to Enforce Demands for Better Conditions," *New York Times* November, 25, 1910, 1.

21. Ranajit Guha, "The Prose of Counter-Insurgency," in *Selected Subaltern Studies,* ed. Ranajit Guha and Gayatri Chakravorty Spivak (Oxford: Oxford University Press, 1988), 77.

22. Although Cunha's model of division between the city and the interior is among the best known in the historiography of Brazil's First Republic, it is often overstated, as he is quite sympathetic toward the backward *sertanejos* (people from the Northeastern interior) and is in places critical of the order and progress of the republican government. His argument is not as black and white as it is often presented. Euclides da Cunha, *Os Sertões: Campanhia de Canudos* (RJ: Maemmert, 1902), published in translation as *Rebellion in the Backlands,* trans. Samuel Putnam (Chicago: University of Chicago Press, 1944). On the civil war of the Contestado see Todd A. Diacon, *Millenarian Vision, Capitalist Reality: Brazil's Contestado Rebellion, 1912–1916* (Durham, N.C.: Duke University Press, 1991), and for the anti-vaccination riots of 1904 see Meade, *"Civilizing" Rio,* and Jeffrey D. Needell, "The *Revolta Contra Vacina* of 1904: The Revolt against "Modernization" in Belle-Époque Rio de Janeiro," *Hispanic American Historical Review* 67, no. 2 (May 1987): 233–69.

23. *Relatorio do Ministro da Marinha,* 1910, 10.

24. A copy of this handwritten document is available at the Acervo Edmar Morel, Divisão de Manuscritos da Fundação Biblioteca Nacional in Rio de Janeiro. Its image appears in Morel, *A Revolta da Chibata,* 98–99, and in Martins, *A Revolta dos Marinheiros, 1910,* 28–29.

25. Quoted by Martins, *A Revolta dos Marinheiros,* 22.

26. "Naval Mutiny: Brazilian Bluejackets Kill their Officers," *Times* (London), November 30, 1910, 4.

27. Ibid.

28. Lieutenant John S. Hammond (US military attaché), report no. 70, in ONI, "Brazilian Naval Revolt, 1910," Reg. 799, 5–6.

29. Ibid.

30. "Iconoclast Abroad," *Shipping Illustrated* 33 (December 31, 1910): 290.

31. As quoted in Morel, *A Revolta da Chibata*, 107.

32. "João Candido em S. Paulo," *O Combate*, December 11, 1919, 1. My thanks to James P. Woodard for sharing this citation with me. *Estado de São Paulo*, November 25, 1910, 2.

33. "The Naval Mutiny at Rio," *Times* (London), November 25, 1910, NARA.

34. Letter signed "B," N. 72, Dec. 8, 1910, in ONI, "Brazilian Naval Revolt, 1910," Register 799.

35. Enclosure I in 758, letter to U.S. secretary of state, from Robert Woods Bliss, the interim chargé d'affaires in Buenos Aires, Dec. 19, 1910, in U.S. ONI "Brazilian Naval Revolt, 1910," Register 799.

36. Formerly the state capital of Rio de Janeiro (the city of Rio was an independent federal district), Niterói is an independent city but serves as a part of metropolitan Rio de Janeiro. Today it is linked to Rio by the Rio–Niterói Bridge, established in 1974, but at the time one reached the capital by ferry or by private boat. *Correio da Manha* (Rio de Janeiro), 1st ed., November 23, 1910, 1.

37. Carneiro, "Revolta dos Marinheiros," *O Cruzeiro*, June 27, 1964, 110.

38. *Correio da Manhã*, November 23, 1910, 2nd ed., 1. On the surface it seemed that they had expanded their demands from simply halting the use of corporal punishment to doing so and raising their salaries. In fact, they has already circulated a manifesto that included five demands, so this was actually a reduction in their demands. That document is examined in detail below.

39. From table "População do Brazil por Estado (1872, 1890, 1900 e 1910)," Ministério da Agricultura, Industria e Commercio, Directoria Geral de Estatistica, *Territorio e População*, 252.

40. Though many newspapers described the crowds at the bay, the banner photograph atop the article titled "The Black Hand at the Helm of Brazil's Navy: Led by Two of Their Number, 1,500 Negro Sailors Forced the Government of Brazil to Yield to Their Demands" that appeared in *Coller's*, January 7, 1911, 19, was captioned "Crowds watching the mutinous fleet during a lull in the hostilities."

41. Presentation to Federal Congress by Federal Deputy for Rio Grande do Sul, José Carlos Carvalho, November 23, 1910, *Annães do Câmara, 8*, 456.

42. *Annães do Câmara, 8*, 454.

43. Martins, *A Revolta dos Marinheiros, 1910*, 53.

44. After leaving active duty, Vice-Almirante Hélio Leôncio Martins was a member of the Instituto de Geographia e História Naval Brasileira and produced a series of works on Brazilian naval history. His criticism of Carvalho's action during the revolt fits into a broad pattern of general hostility toward the statesman among Brazilian naval historians.

45. *Annães do Câmara 8*, 456.

46. Cunha, *A Revolta na Esquadra Brazileira*, 32.

47. "Que pedem os revoltosos?," *Diário de Notícias* (Rio de Janeiro), November 24, 1910, 1.

48. *Correio da Manhã*, November 26, 1910, 1; see also the lead article "Que pedem os revoltosos?" *Diário de Notícias* (Rio de Janeiro), November 24, 1910, 1.

49. *O Correio da Manhã*, November 26, 1910, 1.

50. John S. Hammond, "Mutiny of the Brazilian Sailors," 70, ONI, "Brazilian Naval Revolts, 1910," Reg. 799, 1.

51. Cunha, *A Revolta na Esquadra Brazileira*, 31.

52. Brazil, Congresso Nacional, Annaes do Senado Federal, *Sessões de 1 a 30 de Novembro de 1910*, vol. 5 (Rio de Janeiro, 1911) [hereafter Brazil, Annaes do Senado Federal (November 1–30, 1910)], 127.

53. Ibid., 136.

54. Ibid.

55. Ibid., 137.

56. Ibid., 147.

57. There was some legitimate concern among the officers about the loyalty of the crews of the modern *Cruzador-Torpedeiro* (torpedo boat) *Goyaz* (acquired from Yarrow in 1907) and that of the torpedo boats *Tamoyo* and *Timbira* (both acquired from German shipyards in 1896), and their crews were removed and replaced by officers. Their actions are described in the *Reletorio de 1910*, 6–9, and in "Navios não rebelados," in Martins, *A Revolta dos Marinheiros, 1910*, 41–51. For information on Brazilian ships, see J. R. Perrett, "Some notes on Warship Design and Construction by Sir W. G. Armstrong, Whitworth & Co. Ltd.," Vickers Archive, Doc. 811, Cambridge University Library, Department of Manuscripts and University Archives, Vickers Ltd: Records, MS Vickers. And Caminha, *História Administrativa do Brasil*, 36, "Anexo a ao capítulo VII, Relação dos navios da Armada Brasileira incorporados de 1890 a 1966," 292–313.

58. *Jornal do Comércio*, November 24, 1910, 3; Martins, *A Revolta dos Marinheiros 1910*, 61; and Cunha, *A Revolta na Esquadra Brazileira*, 34, 40.

59. Cunha, *A Revolta na Esquadra Brazileira*, 32.

60. *Relatorio do Ministro da Marinha, 1910*, 7.

61. Martins, *A Revolta dos Marinheiros, 1910*, 54.

62. *Relatorio de Ministro da Marinha, 1910*, 8–9.

63. "Mutiny of the Brazilian Sailors," by Lieutenant John S. Hammond, 3rd Field Artillery, American Military Attaché, Argentina, ONI, 4.

64. *Relatorio de Ministro da Marinha, 1910*, 12–13.

65. Morel, *A Revolta da Chibata*, 111.

66. *Relatorio de Ministro da Marinha, 1910*, 12–13.

67. Quoted in Morel, *A Revolta da Chibata*, 100.

68. Ibid., 101.

69. Ibid.

70. José Alves da Silva became the commander of the *Deodoro* during the uprising, and his description of the revolt is the basis for the description of the interaction on board during the final negotiation with the government. It was published clandestinely in 1934 as quoted by Dr. Adão Manuel Pereira Nunes [pseud. Benedito Paulo], *A Revolta de João Cândido* (Pelotas, 1934), 42.

71. Ibid., 43.

72. *A Revolta de João Cândido* (Pelotas, 1934), 48.

73. Ibid., 48–49.

6. BETRAYAL AND REVENGE

1. *O Pais*, Rio de Janeiro, November 26, 1910, 1.

2. Quoted by Martins, *A Revolta dos Marinheiros, 1910* 58.

3. Ibid. 58. It is interesting based on that statement that H. L. Martins would go on to question whether F. D. Martins wrote the initial manifesto dated November 22. He claims that was written by telegraph operator Ricardo de Freitas.

4. Marco Morel e Sílvia Capanema P. de Almeida, "O outro navegante: Novas informações sobre a revolta indicam uma segunda liderança, que colocou no papel as articulações dos marinheiros," *Revista*

de Historia da Biblioteca Nacional 5, no. 53 (Feb. 2010): 36.

5. This comes from a copy of the document translated into English and included within the following letter. ONI, "Irving B. Dudley to U.S. Secretary of State," Petrópolis, November 29, 1910, N°. 615, 3. The telegram was also published in *Jornal do Comércio*, November 25, 1910, 3 and *O Paiz*, November 25, 1910, 1. Irving Bedell Dudley (1861–1911) served as the U.S. ambassador to Brazil from 1907 to 1911; from 1897 to 1907, he had served as the U.S. ambassador to Peru.

6. Morel, *A Revolta da Chibata*, 119.

7. Quoted by Martins, *A Revolta dos Marinheiros*, 22.

8. In fact, H. L. Martins came to a similar, if more critical, conclusion. In his endnote 11 (243), he states that "the radiogram sent from the *Minas Gerais* [*sic*] was likely written by Deputy Carlos de Carvalhos." Martins, *A Revolta dos Marinheiros*, 243.

9. "Irving B. Dudley to U.S. Secretary of State," 5.

10. ONI, "Brazilian Naval Revolts, 1910," 6.

11. Morel, *A Revolta da Chibata*, 162.

12. ONI, "Brazilian Naval Revolts, 1910," 5.

13. Martins, *A Revolta dos Marinheiros*, 142.

14. Brazil, Congresso Nacional, Annaes do Senado Federal, *Sessões de 1 a 30 de Novembro de 1910*, vol. 5 (Rio de Janeiro, November 29, 1911) [hereafter Brazil, Annaes do Senado Federal (November 1–30, 1910)], 210–14.

15. Ibid. 216.

16. Ibid. 218.

17. *Relatorio da Marinha*, 1910, 21.

18. "Relação das Praças Excluidas da Armada em Consequencia dos Movimentos de Novembro E Dezembro de 1910" (Rio de Janeiro: Imprensa Naval, 1912).

19. Ibid., 10.

20. Martins, *A Revolta dos Marinheiros*, 150–51; Morel, *A Revolta da Chibata*, 148.

21. Museu da Imagem e do Som, *João Cândido*, 81.

22. ONI, "Revolt of the Naval Battalion (Marine Infantry) on Ihla das Cobras, Rio de Janeiro, December 9, 1910," 5.

23. Ibid.

24. Ibid., 3–5.

25. ONI, "Letter from Irving B. Dudley to the U.S. Secretary of State, 3.

26. A rumor had been circulating among the sailors that when the Government acted against the amnestied sailors, they would call in the army to arrest or attack the sailors. The Minister of the Navy described this revolt in his annual report to the President that year, *Relatorio da Marinha*, 1910, 16–17. Further details came from Martins, *A Revolta dos Marinheiros*, 164–65.

27. Martins, *A Revolta dos Marinheiros*, 165–66.

28. Ibid., 166.

29. The act of becoming someone tied to the past, an old fogey.

30. Martins, *A Revolta dos Marinheiros*, 155–60.

31. ONI, "Revolt of the Naval Battalion," 6.

32. According to ONI, "Revolt of the Naval Battalion," 6, the mutineers had been waiting for the *Minas Geraes* to join them in the revolt. When the ship began to fire on them, the rebels turned all the small arms they could on the *Minas Geraes*, which was anchored near the British Squadron, who found themselves caught up in the middle of this melee. In a descriptive letter to the U.S. secretary of state, an officer of the British Fourth Cruiser Squadron described the situation

as follows: "Things fly about our ships fairly thick at times, several bullets and pieces of shell have been picked up on board and one shell I saw strike the water close to the *Leviathan,* our flagship. . . . One bullet hit a thing on deck this morning within three yards of me – confound their imprudence!" ONI, "Brazilian Naval Revolt, 1910," Enclosure 1 in Document 758, December 19, Buenos Aires, 3.

33. Martins, *A Revolta dos Marinheiros,* 166–67.

34. ONI, "Letter from Irving B. Dudley to the U.S. Secretary of State," 3.

35. Morel, *A Revolta da Chibata,* 152.

36. ONI, "Letter from Irving B. Dudley to the U.S. Secretary of State," 5.

37. Brasil, Congresso, *Estado de Sitio: Acontecimentos de 14 de Novembro de 1904–Revolta dos Marinheiros 1910* (Rio de Janeiro: L'edition D'art, 1913), 252–53.

38. ONI, "Revolt of the Naval Battalion," 8.

39. Morel, *A Revolta da Chibata,* 155–56.

40. Marques, quoted in Morel, *A Revolta da Chibata,* 193; Martins, *A Revolta dos Marinheiros, 1910,* 190–93; and *O Estado de São Paulo,* January 14, 1911, 4.

41. Morel, *A Revolta da Chibata,* 195.

42. Ibid., 180–81; Paulo, *A Revolta de João Candido,* 62–63; *O Estado de São Paulo,* January 14, 1911, 4; *O Estado de São Paulo,* January 15, 1911, 3. Based on João Cândido's testimony, the number of sailors who entered the cell or cells has been inconsistent. In Cândido, "Memórias . . . ," 314–15, published in 1913, he claims that twenty-nine sailors entered two cells, sixteen in his, and only two survived. In the interview quoted in Morel, *A Revolta da Chibata,* 180–81, he states eighteen entered his cell and two survived, and this is the number accepted in most of the secondary scholarship. Finally, in his 1968 Cândido, "Depoimento," 83, he states that eighteen

men died and two survived, thus twenty men entered the cell. In Morel, *A Revolta da Chibata,* 194n1, the author attempts to explain the discrepancies, confirms that the number is in fact eighteen men who entered Cândido's cell, and credits the stress that Cândido was under while in the cell for the discrepancies.

43. Morel, *A Revolta da Chibata,* 181–82.

44. *Correio da Manhã,* January 17, 1911, 1.

45. Morel, *A Revolta da Chibata,* 182; Martins, *A Revolta dos Marinheiros, 1910,* 192.

46. Relatório of Captain Carlos P. Storry, March 5, 1911, reprinted in full in Morel, *A Revolta da Chibata,* 180–82.

47. Martins, *A Revolta dos Marinheiros, 1910,* 197. Of the numerous descriptions of events on the *Satélite,* Love's *The Revolt of the Whip,* 100–104, offers the clearest narrative and the best analysis of the sources.

48. Morel, *A Revolta da Chibata,* 179n1.

49. Love, *Revolt of the Whip,* 101.

50. Morel, *A Revolta da Chibata,* 179.

51. Relatório of Captain Carlos P. Storry, 181.

52. Ibid., 180–82.

53. On the topic of the Rondon's Commission, see Todd Diacon's *Stringing Together a Nation: Cândido Mariano da Silva Rondon and the Construction of a Modern Brazil, 1906–1930* (Durham, N.C.: Duke University Press, 2004).

54. Relatório of Captain Carlos P. Storry, 180–82.

55. Rui Barbosa, *Obras completas de Rui Barbosa: Discursos parlamentares* (Rio de Janeiro: Fundação Casa de Rui Barbosa, 1977), 38:23.

56. Barbosa's critiques of Fonseca and the naval minister are examined in Love, *The Revolt of the Whip,* 103, and Martins, *A Revolta dos Marinheiros, 1910,* 202.

57. Martins, *A Revolta dos Marinheiros, 1910,* 193. In fact, these confusions explain

some of the discrepancies that appear in Cândido, "Memórias . . . ," that were published in *Gazeta de Notícias* between December 31, 1911, and January 12, 1912. They were based on interviews done with Cándido during this time and they contain factual errors, such as that in the first installment, published December 31, 1911, he claimed to have been born in Argentina on June 24, 1882. This detail was corrected in the second installment. Based on such errors, some scholars questioned the legitimacy of these memoirs.

58. Martins, *A Revolta dos Marinheiros, 1910*, 192–93; Paulo, *A Revolta de João Candido*, 64. According to historian José Murilo de Carvalho, João Cândido spent a great deal of this time between Christmas 1910 and April 18, 1911, making intricate embroideries, which portrayed maritime scenes. Any sailor who entered the navy before its technological revolution began in 1904 had to understand knots and ropes of all types. Clearly João Cândido applied this knowledge to creating designs on facecloth-sized "canvases" as a hobby, though he kept this practice to himself. The works turned up in 1985 at the Museum of Regional Art in São Joao del Rei, where they had been donated by Antônio Manuel de Souza Guerra, a friend of João Cândido's. Jose Murilho de Carvalho, *Pontos e bordados: escritos de história e política* (Belo Horizonte: Ed. UFMG, 1998), 15–33.

59. For information on the 1906 dockworkers' strike see Maria Cecília Velasco e Cruz's "Puzzling Out Slave Origins in Rio de Janeiro Port Unionism: The 1906 Strike and the Sociedade de Resistência dos Trabalhadores em Trapiche e Café," *Hispanic American Historical Review* 86, no. 2 (May 2006): 205–45.

60. Martins, *A Revolta dos Marinheiros, 1910*, 199.

61. As quoted in Morel, *A Revolta da Chibata*, 211.

62. Proc. 565/1910, "Processo-crime em que João Cândido e outros são acusados de sublevação após anistia (Revolta da Chibata)," 3 vols., Supremo Tribunal Military, 1910–12.

7. CONCLUSION

1. "O Admirante Negro" (The Black Admiral); lyrics by João Bosco and Aldir Blanc.

2. *Relacão das Praças Excluidas da Armada.*

3. Meade, *"Civilizing" Rio*, and Kok, *Rio de Janeiro na época da Av. Central.*

4. Beattie, *The Tribute of Blood.*

5. Um Official da Armada [José Eduardo de Macedo Soares], *Política Versus Marinha*, 84.

6. Ibid., 85–86.

7. José Miguel Arias Neto, "Em Busca da Cidadania: Praças da Armada Nacional 1867–1910," PhD diss., Universidade de São Paulo, 2001.

8. Arthur Dias, *Nossa Marinha: notas sobre o renascimento da Marinha de Guerra do Brazil no quatriennio de 1906 a 1910* (Rio de Janeiro: Officinas Graphicas da Liga Maritima Brazileira, 1910), 232, as cited in Capanema P. de Almeida, "A modernização do material e do pessoal da Marinha nas vésperas da revolta dos marinheiros de 1910," 160.

9. Decreto 7124 de 24 de setembro de 1908, *Relatorio do Ministro da Marinha*, 1909, "Regulamento do corpo de marineiros nacionais" annex (Rio de Janeiro: Imprensa Nacional, 1910), 151.

10. Raymundo de Mello Furtado de Mendonça, *Introducion do Relatorio apresentado ao Sr. Ministro da Marinha pelo Contra Almirante Raymundo de Mello Furtado de Mendonça em Maio de 1911* (Rio de Janeiro: Papelaria Mendes, 1912), 24–25.

11. *Relatorio de Ministro da Marinha, 1910,* 23.

12. Ibid., 22–75.

13. Richard Hough, *The Big Battleship* (Penzance, UK: Periscope, 2003 [1966]); Scheina, *Latin America: A Naval History,* 135.

14. "The Mutiny in the Brazilian Navy, November 1910," December 8, 1910, No. 72 by "B" [presumed Lt. John S. Hammond, Military Attaché in Buenos Aires].

15. "The Revolt of the Naval Battalion (Marine Infantry) on the Ilha das Cobras, Rio de Janeiro. December 9, 1910," No. 76. by "B" [presumed Lt. John S. Hammond, Military Attaché in Buenos Aires].

16. Scheina, "World War I," in *Latin America: A Naval History,* 88–104.

17. Cândido, *Depoimento,* 85.

18. Ibid., 84–87.

Bibliography

ARCHIVES

AN	Arquivo Nacional, Rio de Janeiro
BM	Biblioteca da Marinha. Rio de Janeiro
BNL	British Newspaper Library, Colindale (North London)
CRB	Casa Rui Barbosa, Rio de Janeiro
IHGB	Arquivo do Instituto Histórico e Geográfico Brasileiro, Rio de Janeiro
LHC	Labour History Collection, Northumbria University Library, Newcastle
MIS	Museu da Imagem e do Som, Rio de Janeiro
NARA	National Archives and Records Administration, Washington, D.C.
SDM	Serviço de Documentação da Marinha (Arquivo Naval), Rio de Janeiro
TWA	Tyne and Wear Archives, Newcastle
VA	Vickers Archives, Cambridge University Library, Cambridge

PAPERS, LETTERS, AND OTHER
UNPUBLISHED COLLECTIONS

Armstrong Whitworth and Co. Ltd., Newcastle (Including WG Armstrong Mitchell and Co) "Boards and Committee Minutes," Board and Committee minute book, no. 2, 1903–09, No. 130/1267, TWA.

———. "Elswick shipyards, illustrations commemorating launches of Warships. Includes dimensions and armament details," 22 March 1898–28 April 1908. Doc. No. 450, TWA.

———. "Elswick papers, Letters" Books 11–19" Ref. No. 31/3595-3751, TWA.

———. "Letters and papers concerning orders from Brazil, 1877–May 1882," No. 31/5778-5875, TWA.

———. "Letters concerning Board affairs," October 1901–April 1913, 31/7923-7941. TWA.

———. "Letters concerning Board affairs," January 1903–October 1909, 31/4193-4235. TWA.

———. "Letters concerning Board affairs [Including papers concerning orders from Brazil, Portugal and Russia; also memoranda on Turkish and Balkan business and on armour plate production.]," March 1896–December 1912, No. 31/7595-7618 TWA.

———. "Letters from J.M. Falkner, Alfred Cochrane, etc.," February 1900–December 1910, No. 31/7038-7111. TWA.

———. "Poem 'The Armstrong Gun,' typed copy," No. 1027/359. TWA.

———. *"Ship photographs"* DF.CLR/8/1-24. TWA.

Armstrong, Whitworth and Co. Ltd., (W.G.) and (Sir W.G.), "A.R. Fairbairn's Unpublished History," Doc. 593, Cambridge University Library, Department of Manuscripts and University Archives, Vickers Ltd: Records, MS Vickers. VA.

———. "History 1886–1926," Document 590, Cambridge University Library, Department of Manuscripts and University Archives, Vickers Ltd: Records, MS Vickers. VA.

———. "Notes on launchings and fitting out: Ships nos. 289–385, 1902–1930," Doc. No. 1106, Cambridge University Library, Department of Manuscripts and University Archives, Vickers Ltd: Records, MS Vickers. VA.

———. "Register of Pricing, armaments, 1898–1908," Doc. No. 1144. Cambridge University Library, Department of Manuscripts and University Archives, Vickers Ltd: Records, MS Vickers. VA

———. "Ships built, 1873–1973," Doc. No. 1104, Cambridge University Library, Department of Manuscripts and University Archives, Vickers Ltd: Records, MS Vickers. VA.

———. "Ships built, 1873–1908," Doc. No. 1105, Cambridge University Library, Department of Manuscripts and University Archives, Vickers Ltd: Records, MS Vickers. VA.

———. "Ships built at Elswick and Walker 1883–1920," Doc. No. 811, Cambridge University Library, Department of

Manuscripts and University Archives, Vickers Ltd: Records, MS Vickers. VA.

Elwsick Works, "Early History of, by A Cochrane, 1909," Doc. No. 1170, Cambridge University Library, Department of Manuscripts and University Archives, Vickers Ltd: Records, MS Vickers. VA.

———. "History," Doc. No. 634, Cambridge University Library, Department of Manuscripts and University Archives, Vickers Ltd: Records, MS Vickers. VA.

———. "Ships' costs book 1897–1909," Doc. No. 1155, Cambridge University Library, Department of Manuscripts and University Archives, Vickers Ltd: Records, MS Vickers. VA.

———. "Shipyard Report Book Vol. 2 1897–1913," Doc. No. 1158, Cambridge University Library, Department of Manuscripts and University Archives, Vickers Ltd: Records, MS Vickers. VA.

———. "Warships launched 1883–1913," Doc. No. 639, Cambridge University Library, Department of Manuscripts and University Archives, Vickers Ltd: Records, MS Vickers. VA.

———. "Warships, press cuttings 1904–1911," Doc. No. 641, Cambridge University Library, Department of Manuscripts and University Archives, Vickers Ltd: Records, MS Vickers. VA.

"Da caderneta subsidiára do livro de socorros pertenecente ao Mirinheiro Nacional da 16ª Companha 1ª classe, no 85 João Cândido." In "Processo-crime em que João Cândido e outros são acusados de sublevação após anistia ("Revolta da Chibata)," 344–55. AN.

"Esboças de Codigos Penal e Disciplinar da Armas organisados pelo Dr. Clovis Bevilaqua, e outros documentos." Doc. No. 871618. AN.

Fundo Supremo Tribunal Militar e Justiça: Conselhos de Guerra da Marinha. Criminal court martial documents between 1860 and 1893. AN.

Gabinete de Identificação da Marinha, Marinheiros Nacionais, Livros 1–3, 1908. AM.

"Processo-crime em que João Cândido e outros são acusados de sublevação após anistia ("Revolta da Chibata)," Proc. 565/1910, 3 vols., Supremo Tribunal Militar, 1910–12, AN.

"Registro dos documentos remetidos no Arquivo Nacional. Relação dos autos de processos em conselho de Guerra existentes no Archivo da Marinha e que são nesta data remettidos ao Archivo Nacional" SDM

U.S. Office of Naval Intelligence. "Brazilian Naval Personnel, 1910–12, Extract from an Intelligence Report on Rio Janeiro [*sic*], Brazil, by Lieut. C.L. Hussey, Fleet Intelligence Officer, South Atlantic Squadron, November 24, 1904." Reg. 423, NARA.

———. "Irving Dudley to Secretary of State." Petrópolis. Nov. 29, 1910. No. 615. NARA.

———. "The Mutiny in the Brazilian Navy, November 1910." No. 72. by "B" [presumed Lt. John S. Hammond, Military Attaché in Buenos Aires], NARA.

———. "Mutiny of the Brazilian Sailors" no. 70. by Lt. John S. Hammond, 3rd Field Artillery, American Military Attaché, BA, Argentina, NARA.

———. Register 799, "Brazilian Naval Revolt, 1910" [Various sources and dates, 1910–1911]. NARA.

———. "The Revolt of the Naval Battalion (Marine Infantry) on the Ilha das Cobras, Rio de Janeiro. December 9, 1910," No. 76. by "B" [presumed Lt. John S. Hammond, Military Attaché in Buenos Aires], NARA.

Vickers Ltd., "Scott, J.D. "Vickers, A History" Doc. No. 1000, Cambridge University Library, Department of Manuscripts and University Archives, Vickers Ltd: Records, MS Vickers. VA.

PERIODICALS

Correio de Manhã, Rio de Janeiro
Diário de Notícias, Rio de Janeiro
Estado de São Paulo, São Paulo
Evening Chronicle, Newcastle
FonFon, Rio de Janeiro
Jornal do Commercio, Rio de Janeiro
New York Times, New York
Newcastle Daily Journal, Newcastle
Newcastle Weekly Chronicle, Newcastle
O Malho, Rio de Janeiro
O Pais, Rio de Janeiro
Revista Marítima Brasileira, Rio de Janeiro
The Times, London

PUBLISHED PRIMARY DOCUMENTS AND COLLECTIONS

Annexo ao Reletorio apresentado ao Presidente da República dos Estados Unidos do Brasil pelo Vice-Almirante Graduado Alexandrino Faria de Alencar em abril 1910. Rio de Janeiro: Imprensa Nacional, 1910.

Armstrong, Sir W.G. "Report on the Construction of Wrought-Iron Rifled Field Guns, Adapted for Elongated Projectiles." *The Industrial Resources of the District of the Three Northern Rivers, the Tyne, Wear and Tees, including The Report on the Local Manufactures, read before The British Association in 1863,* ed. W.G. Armstrong, I. Lowthian Bell, John Taylor and Dr. Richardson. 2nd ed., 309–16 Newcastle-Upon-Tyne: A. Reid, Printing Court Buildings, 1864.

Artigos de Guerra para manter na sua devida ordem o Serviço e Disciplina das

Minhas Esquadras e Armada Real. Lisboa: Imprensa Nacional, 1799.

Barbosa, Rui. *Obras Completas de Rui Barbosa, Discursos Parlamentares, 1910.* Vol. 37, Tomo 3. Rio de Janeiro: Ministerio da Educação e Cultura, 1971.

———. *Obras Completas de Rui Barbosa, Discursos Parlamentares, 1911.* Vol. 38, Tomo 1. Rio de Janeiro: Casa Rui Barbosa, 1977.

Brazil, Congresso Nacional. *Annaes da Camara dos Deputados, 1910.* Vol. 8. Rio de Janeiro: Imprensa Nacional, 1911.

Brazil, Congresso Nacional, *Annaes do Senado Federal,* Vols. 5 and 6. Rio de Janeiro: Imprensa Nacional, 1911.

Brazil, Congresso Nacional, *Estado de Sitio: Acontecimentos de 14 de Novembro de 1904–Revolta dos Marinheiros 1910.* Rio de Janeiro: L'edition D'art, 1913.

Caminha, Herick Marques. *História Administrativa do Brasil.* Vol. 15: *Organização e administração do Ministério da Marinha no Império.* Rio de Janeiro: Fundação Centro de Formação do Servidor Público, 1986.

———. *História Administrativa do Brasil.* Vol. 36: *Organização do Ministério da Marinha na República.* Rio de Janeiro: Fundação Centro de Formação do Servidor Público, 1989.

Código penal e disciplinar da Armada: Regulamento precessual e formulário de processo criminal military. Rio de Janeiro: Imprensa Nacional, 1914.

Collecção das Decisões do Governo do Império do Brasil de 1822. Rio de Janeiro: Imprensa Nacional, 1887.

Collecção das Decisões do Governo do Imperio do Brasil de 1833. Rio de Janeiro: Imprensa Nacional, 1908.

Collecção das Decisões do Governo do Império do Brasil de 1861. Tomo XXIV. Rio de Janeiro, Imprensa Nacional, 1862.

Collecção das Leis da República do Brasil. Rio de Janeiro: Imprensa Nacional, 1890–1912.

Collecção das Leis do Império do Brasil. Rio de Janeiro: Imprensa Nacional, 1830–1889.

Esboças de Codigos Penal e Disciplinar da Armas organisados pelo Dr. Clovis Bevilaqua, e outros documentos.

Estado de Sitio: Acontecimentos de 14 de Novembro de 1904 – Revolta dos Marinheiros 1910. Rio de Janeiro: L'edition D'art, 1913.

Gusmão, Chrysolito de. *Dereito penal militar, com annexos referentes a legeslação penal militar brasileiro.* Rio de Janeiro, 1915.

Instrucção para o recruta da marinha. Rio de Janeiro: Imprensa Naval, 1913.

Introducion do Relatorio apresentado ao Sr. Ministro da Marinha pelo Contra Almirante Raymundo de Mello Furtado de Mendonça em Maio de 1911. Rio de Janeiro: Papelaria Mendes, 1912.

Leis, decretos, etc: Códigos Penal e Disciplinar da Armada. Rio de Janeiro: Imprensa Naval, 1914.

Marques da Rocha, Francisco José. *Manual do marinheiros-fuzileiros.* Rio de Janeiro, 1908.

Ministério da Agricultura, Industria e Commercio, Directoria Geral de Estatistica. *Annuario Estatistico do Brazil 1908–1912.* Vol. 1: *Territorio e População.* Rio de Janeiro: Typographia da Estatistica, 1916.

Ministro da Marinha. *Subsídios para a História Marítima do Brasil.* Vols. 1–3. Rio de Janeiro: Imprensa Naval, 1938.

Oficio de Joaquim Francisco de Abreu. *Comandante da 1a Divisão de Evolucões, ao chefe de Esquadra da Armada, sôbre o castigo da chibata (reservado).* Rio de Janeiro: Janeiro, 1883.

Ordenença para o serviço da armada brasileira. Rio de Janeiro: Imprensa Naval, 1910.

Parecer da comissão de Marinha e Geurra do senado sobre o projeto de extinção do castigo corporal na armada. Rio de Janeiro, 1864.

Quartel General da Marinha. *Ordem[s] do Dia.* Rio de Janeiro, 1860–1911.

Regimentos provisional para o serviço e disciplina dos Navios da Armada Real. Rio de Janeiro, 1835.

Relacão das Praças Excluidas da Armada em Consequencia dos Movimentos de Novembro e Dezembro de 1910. Rio de Janeiro: Imprensa Naval, 1912.

Relatórios do Ministério da Marinha do 1833–34, 1859–1911. Rio de Janeiro, 1834–1835, 1860–1912.

Revolta do Batalhão Naval em fins de nevembro de 1910. Mandado de Intimação dos Reus que Tomaram parte nessa Revolta. Oferta do Sr. Evandro Santos. Rio de Janeiro, 1928.

Serviço de Documentação da Marinha. *História Naval Brasileira,* Vol. 5, Tomo 2. Rio de Janeiro: Imprensa Naval, 1985.

The South American Yearbook and Directory, 1915. London: Louis Cassier, 1915.

U.S. Department of State. *Papers Relating to the Foreign Relations of the United States, Transmitted to Congress, with the Annual Message of the President, December 3, 1889.* Washington D. C.: U.S. Government Printing Office, 1890.

MEMOIRS AND LITERATURE OF THE PERIOD

Andrada e Silva, José Bonifácio de. "Memoir addressed to the General Constituent and Legislative Assembly of the empire of Brazil on slavery," trans. William Walton. London, 1826.

Atchison, Charles. *A Winter Cruise in Summer Seas.* London: Sampson, Low, 1891.

Boiteux, Henrique. *Os Nossos almirantes.* Rio de Janeiro: Imprensa Naval, 1916.

Bomilcar, Álvaro. *O preconceito de raça no Brazil.* Rio de Janeiro: Typ. Aurora, 1916.

Bryce, James. *South American Observations and Impressions.* New York: MacMillan, 1914.

Caminha, Adolfo. *Bom-Crioulo.* New York: Luso-Brazilian Books, 2006 [1895].

———. *No país dos ianques.* Rio de Janeiro: Livraria Moderna, 1894.

Cândido Felisberto, João. "Depoimento" de João Cândido. In Museu da Imagem e do Som, *João Cândido, o almirante negro.* Rio de Janeiro: Gryphus, 1999, 65–101.

———. "Memórias de João Cândido o marinheiro." *Gazeta de Notícias,* Dec. 31, 1912–Jan. 12, 1913, 1; reprinted in Edmar Morel, *A Revolta da Chibata,* 5th ed. (São Paulo: Paz e Terra, 2010 [1959]), 290–319.

Carvalho, José Carlos de. *O Livro da Minha Vida: Na guerra, na paz e nas revoluções: 1847–1910.* Vol. 1. Rio de Janeiro: Typo do Jornal do Commercio, 1912.

Cunha, Euclides da. *Os Sertões: Campanhia de Canudos.* Rio de Janeiro: Maemmert, 1902.

Dias, Arthur. *Nossa Marinha.* Rio de Janeiro, 1910.

———. *O Problema Naval: Condições actuaes da marinha de guerra e seu papel nos destinos do paiz.* Rio de Janeiro: Officina da Estatística, 1899.

Freire, Felisbelo *História da Revolta de 6 de Setembro de 1893.* Rio de Janeiro: Cunha and Irmãos, 1896.

Graham, Maria. *Journal of a Voyage to Brazil and Residence There during Part of the Years 1821, 1822 and 1823.* London:

Longman, Hurst, Rees, Orme, Brown, and Green, 1824.

Hambloch, Ernest. *British Cônsul: Memories of Thirty Years' Service in Europe and Brazil.* London: George G. Harrap, 1938.

Jaceguay, Almirante Arthur Silveira da Matta. *De aspirante a almirante, 1860 a 1902, minha fé de ofício documentada, 1893 a 1900.* Rio de Janeiro: Brasiliana, 1906.

———. *De aspirante a almirante: minha fé de ofício documentada.* Vol. 2: *1870–1900.* 2nd ed. Rio de Janeiro: Serviço de Documentação Geral da Marinha, 1984.

———. *De aspirante a almirante 1860–1902, Minha fé de ofício documentada.* Vol. 5, *1895–1900* (Rio de Janeiro: Typographia Leuzinger, 1907).

Lambuth, David. "The Naval Comedy and Peace Policies in Brazil." *Independent* 69 (Dec. 1910): 1430–33.

Long, Edward. *A History of Jamaica.* Vol. 2. London: T. Lownes, 1774.

Peck, Annie S. *The South American Tour.* New York: George H. Doran, 1913.

Penalva, Gastão. *A Marinha do meu Tempo.* 2nd ed. Rio de Janeiro: Serviço de Documentação Geral da Marinha, 1983.

Pinto, J.C. Ferreiro. *As forças do mar desde a indepencia até aos nossos dias.* Rio de Janeiro, 1905.

Paulo, Benedito [Adão Pereira Nunes]. *A revolta de João Cândido.* Rio Grande do Sul: Pelotas, 1934.

Stephens, Henry. *South American Travels.* New York: Knickerbocker Press, 1915.

Tennyson D'Eyncourt, Sir Eustace H. W. *A Shipbuilders Yarn: The Record of a Naval Constructor.* London: Hutchinson, 1948.

Thring, Theodore. *A Treatise on the Criminal Law of the Navy.* London: V. and R. Stevens and Sons, 1861.

Um Official da Armada [José Eduardo de Macedo Soares]. *Política versus Marinha.* Rio de Janeiro: Livraria H. Garneir, n.d.

Weston Van Dyke, Harry. *Through South America.* New York: Thomas Y. Crowell, 1912.

Zahm, J. A. *Through South America's Southland.* New York: D. Appleton and Co., 1916.

SECONDARY SOURCES
AND THESES

Acerbi, Patricia. "Slave Legacies, Ambivalent Modernity: Street Commerce and the Transition to Free Labor in Rio de Janeiro, 1850–1925." PhD diss., New York University, 2010.

Adomo, Sam C. "The Broken Promise: Race, Health, and Justice in Rio de Janeiro, 1890–1940." PhD diss., University of New Mexico, 1983.

Albuquerque, Antonio Luiz Porto e. *Da Companhia de Guardas-Marinhas e sua Real Academia aÃ Escola Naval, 1782–1982.* Rio de Janeiro: Escola Naval, 1982.

Algranti, Leila Mezan. "O Feitor Ausente: Estudos Sobre a Escravidão Urbana no Rio de Janeiro." Master's thesis, Universidade de São Paulo, 1983.

Allen, Joan. *Joseph Cowen and Popular Radicalism on Tyneside.* Monmouth, Wales: Merlin Press, 2007.

Almeida Guillobel, Renato de. *Memórias.* Rio de Janeiro: Livraria F. Alves Editora, 1973.

Alves, Paulo. "A Verdade da Repressão: Práticas penais e outras estratégias na ordem republicana, 1890–1921." PhD diss., Universidade de São Paulo, 1990.

Amarel, Ignácio M. Azevedo. *Ensaio Sobre a Revolução Brasileira.* Rio de Janeiro: Imprensa Naval, 1963.

Andreski, Stanislav. *Military Organization and Society.* Berkeley: University of California Press, 1971.

Andrews, George Reid. *Blacks and Whites in São Paulo, 1888–1988.* Madison: University of Wisconsin Press, 1991.

Arias Neto, José Miguel. "Em Busca da Cidadania: Praças da Armada Nacional 1867–1910." PhD diss., Universidade de São Paulo, 2001.

———. "João Cândido 1910–1968: Arqueologia de um depoimento sobre a Revolta dos Marinheiros." *História Oral Revista da Associação Brasileira de Historia Oral* (São Paulo) 6 (2003): 159–83.

———. "Sob o signo do novo: O movimento dos marinheiros de 1910" *Revista Versões* 2, no. 2 (Jan.–June 2006): 9–28.

Araújo, Johny Santana de. "A construção do Poder Naval brasileiro no início do século XX: dos programas navais à grande guerra (1904–1917)," *Navigator* 1, no. 2 (Dec. 2005): 69–86.

Auerbach, Sascha. *Race, Law, and "The Chinese Puzzle" in Imperial Britain.* New York: Palgrave Macmillan, 2009.

Azevado, Célia Maria Marinho de. *Onda negra, Medo branco; o negro no imaginário das elites, Século XIX.* Rio de Janeiro: Paz e Terra, 1987.

Azevedo, Sânzio de. *Adolfo Caminha (Vida e obra).* Fortaleza: UFC Ediçoes, 1999.

Barata, Almirante Antão Alveres. "Revolta dos Marinheiros em 1910." *Revista Maritima Brasileira,* Feb. 1962.

Barbosa, Gen. Raymond Rodrigues. *História do Superior Tribunal Militar.* Rio de Janeiro: Impr. Nacional, 1952.

Barickman, B. J. "Persistence and Decline: Slave Labour and Sugar Production in the Bahian Reconcavo, 1850–1888." *Journal of Latin American Studies* 28, no. 3 (Oct. 1996): 581–633.

Barman, Roderick J. *Citizen Emperor: Pedro II and the Making of Brazil, 1825–91.* Stanford, Calif.: Stanford University Press, 1999.

Bastable, Marshall J. *Arms and the State: Sir William Armstrong and the Remaking of British Naval Power, 1854–1914.* Aldershot, UK: Ashgate, 2004.

Bastos, Paulo Cezar. *Superior Tribunal Militar: 173 anos de Historia.* Brásilia, 1981.

Bean, David. *Armstrong's Men: The Story of the Shop Stewards Movement in the Tyneside Works.* Newcastle: Vicker Limited, 1967.

Beattie, Peter M. "Adolfo Ferreira Caminha: Officer, Ardent Republican, and Naturalist Novelist." In *The Human Tradition in Modern Brazil,* ed. Peter M. Beattie, 89–106. Wilmington, Del.: SR Books, 2004.

———. "Conflicting Penile Codes: Modern Masculinity and Sodomy in the Brazilian Military, 1860–1916." In *Sex and Sexuality in Latin America,* ed. Daniel Balderston and Donna J. Guy, 65–85. New York: New York University Press, 1997.

———. "Conscription versus Penal Servitude: Army Reform's Influence on the Brazilian State's Management of Social Control, 1870–1930." *Journal of Social History* 32, no. 4 (Summer 1999): 847–78.

———. "The House, the Street, and the Barracks: Reform and Honorable Masculine Social Space in Brazil, 1864–1945." *Hispanic American Historical Review* 76, no. 3 (Aug. 1996): 439–473.

———. "Ser homem pobre, livre e honrado: a sodomia e os praças nas Forças Armadas brasileiras (1860–1930)." In *Nova História Militar Brasileira,* ed. Celso Castro, Vitor Izecksohn, and Hendrik Karaay. Rio de Janeiro: Editora FGV/Editora Bom Texto, 2004.

———. *The Tribute of Blood: Army, Honor, Race, and Nation in Brazil, 1864–1945.*

Durham, N.C.: Duke University Press, 2001.

Bethell, Leslie, ed. *Brazil: Empire and Republic, 1822–1930.* Cambridge, Mass.: Cambridge University Press, 1989.

Bieber Freitas, Judy. "Slavery and Social Life: Attempts to Reduce Free People to Slavery in the Sertao Mineiro, 1850–1871." *Journal of Latin American Studies* 26, no. 3 (Oct. 1994): 597–96.

Blackburn, Robin. *The Overthrow of Colonial Slavery.* London: Verso, 1988.

Blanchard, Peter. *Under the Flags of Freedom.* Pittsburgh, Pa.: University of Pittsburgh Press, 2008.

Bolster, Jeffrey W. *Black Jacks: African American Seamen in the Age of Sail.* Cambridge, Mass.: Harvard University Press, 1998.

Borges, Dain. "'Puffy, Ugly, Slothful and Inert': Degeneration in Brazilian Social Thought, 1880–1940." *Journal of Latin American Studies* 25, no. 2 (May 1993): 235–56.

Bretas, Marcos Luiz. *A Guerra das Ruas: Povo e Poliícia na Cidade do Rio de Janeiro.* Rio de Janeiro: Archivo Nacional, 1997.

———. "Slaves, Free Poor, and Policemen: Brazil." In *Crime History and Histories of Crime: Studies in the Historiography of Crime and Criminal Justice in Modern History,* ed. Clive Emsley and Louis A. Knafla. Westport, Conn.: Greenwood Press, 1996.

Brodie, Bernard. *Sea Power in the Machine Age.* Princeton, N.J.: Princeton University Press, 1941.

Brook, Peter. *Warships for Export: Armstrong Warships, 1867–1927.* Gravesend, Kent, UK: World Ship Society, 1999.

Brown, Christopher Leslie, and Philip D. Morgan, eds. *Arming Slaves: From Classical Times to the Modern Age.* New Haven, Conn.: Yale University Press, 2006.

Brown, Jacqueline Nassy. *Dropping Anchor, Setting Sail: Geographies of Race in Black Liverpool.* Princeton, N.J.: Princeton University Press, 2005.

Burton, Anthony. *The Rise and Fall of British Shipbuilding.* London: Constable, 1994.

Bush, M. L. *Serfdom and Slavery: Studies in Legal Bondage.* London: Longman, 1996.

Butler, Charles. *On the Legality of Impressing Seamen.* 3rd ed, with additional notes "partly by Lord Sandwich." Reprinted in *The Pamphleteer* 23. Pam. XLV (London: AJ Velpy, 1824 [1777]), 226–87.

Butler, Kim D. *Freedoms Given Freedoms Won: Afro-Brazilians in Post-Abolition Sao Paulo and Salvador.* New Brunswick, N.J.: Rutgers University Press, 1998.

Capanema P. de Almeida, Sílvia. "O Almirante Negro, glória a uma luta inglória." *Históriaviva* 27 (Jan. 2006): 74–80.

———. "A modernização do material e do pessoal da Marinha nas vésperas da revolta dos marujos de 1910: modelos e contradições." *Estudos Históricos* 23, no. 45 (Jan./June 2010): 147–69.

———. "'Nous, marins, citoyens brésiliens et républicains': identités, modernité et mémoire de la révolte des matelots de 1910" [We are sailors and citizens of the republic of Brazil: identities, modernization and the record of the past in the Mutiny of 1910]. PhD diss., l'École des Hautes Etudes en Sciences Sociales, 2009.

———. "Vidas de marinheiro no Brasil republicano: identidades, corpos e lideranças da revolta de 1910." *Antíteses* 3, n. esp. (Dec. 2010): 90–114.

Carew, Anthony. *The Lower Deck of the Royal Navy: 1900–1939.* Manchester, UK: Manchester University Press, 1981.

Carneiro, Glauco. "A Revolta dos Marinheiros." *O Cuzeiro,* June 27, 1964.

———. *História das Revoluções Brasileiras.* Vols. 1 and 2. Rio de Janeiro: Editora Record, 1965 and 1989.

Carone, Edgard. *A Primera República: Corpo E Alma do Brasil Difusão Européia do Livro.* São Paulo, 1973.

Carr, Barry. "Black Geordies." In *Geordies: Roots of Regionalism,* ed. Robert Colls and Bill Lancaster, 133–48 Newcastle, UK: Northumbria University Press, 2005.

Carvalho, Jose Murilho de. "As Forcas Armadas na Primeira República: O Poder Desestabilizador." In *História Geral da Civilização Brasileira, O Brasil Republicano,* book 3 of *Sociedade e Instituições,* ed. Boris Fausto. São Paulo: Bertrand Brasil, 1977.

———. *Os Bestializados: O Rio de Janeiro e a república que não foi.* 3rd ed. São Paulo: Companhia Das Letras, 2005.

———. *Pontos e bordados: escritos de história e política.* BH: Ed. UFMG, 1998.

Carvalho, Virgilio Antonio de. *Direito Penal Militar Brasileiro.* Rio de Janeiro: Bedeschi, 1940.

Castro, Celso, Vitor Izecksohn, and Hendrik Kraay. *Nova história militar brasileira.* Rio de Janeiro: FGV, 2004.

Chaves Junior, Edgard de Brito. *Legislação Penal Militar.* Rio de Janeiro: Forense, 2010.

Childs, Matt D. *The 1812 Aponte Rebellion in Cuba and the Struggle against Atlantic Slavery.* Chapel Hill: University of North Carolina Press, 2006

Collins, Sydney. *Coloured Minorities in Britain.* London: Lutterworth Press, 1957.

Conley, Mary. *From Jack Tar to Union Jack: Representing Naval Manhood in the British Empire: 1870–1918.* Manchester, UK: Manchester University Press, 2009.

Conniff, Michael L., and Frank D. McCann. *Modern Brazil: Elites and Masses in Historical Perspective.* Lincoln: University of Nebraska Press, 1989.

Conrad, Robert. *The Destruction of Brazilian Slavery.* Berkeley: University of California Press, 1972.

Conte-Helm, Marie. *Japan and the North East of England.* London: Athone Press, 1989.

Costa, Emilia Viotti da. *The Brazilian Empire: Myths and Histories.* Chapel Hill: University of North Carolina Press, 2000.

Cowell, Bainbridge, Jr. "Cityward Migration in the Nineteenth Century: The Case of Recife, Brazil." *Journal of Interamerican Studies and World Affairs* 17, no. 1 (Feb. 1975): 43–63.

Cunha, H. Pereira da. *A Revolta da Esquadra Brasileira em Novembro e Dezembro de 1910.* Rio de Janeiro: Imprensa Naval, 1953.

Cunha, Manuela Cameiro da. "Silences of the Law: Customary Law and Positive Law on the Manumission of Slaves in 19th Century Brazil." *History and Anthropology* 1, no. 2 (1985): 427–43.

Davis, David Brion. *The Problem of Slavery in the Age of Revolution, 1770–1823.* Ithaca, N.Y.: Cornell University Press, 1975.

Degler, Carl N. *Neither Black nor White: Slavery and Race Relations in Brazil and the United States.* New York: Macmillan, 1971.

Diacon, Todd A. *Millenarian Vision, Capitalist Reality: Brazil's Contestado Rebellion, 1912–1916.* Durham, N.C.: Duke University Press, 1991.

———. *Stringing Together a Nation: Candido Mariano Da Silva Rondon and the Construction of a Modern Brazil, 1906–1930.* Durham, N.C.: Duke University Press, 2004.

Dorwart, Jeffery M. *The Office of Naval Intelligence: The Birth of America's First Intelligence Agency, 1865–1918*. Washington, D.C.: Naval Institute Press, 1979.

Dougan, David. *The Great Gun Maker: The Life of Lord Armstrong*. Northumberland, UK: Sandhill Press, 1991 [1970].

Echeverri, Marcela. "Popular Royalists, Empire, and Politics in Southwestern New Granada, 1809–1819." *Hispanic American Historical Review* 91, no. 2 (May 2011): 237–69.

Eisenburg, Peter. "Abolishing Slavery: The Process on Pernambuco's Sugar Plantations." *Hispanic American Historical Review* 52, no. 4 (Nov. 1972): 580–97.

———. *The Sugar Industry in Pernambuco: Modernization without Change, 1840–1910*. Berkeley: University of California Press, 1974.

Elias, Norbert. "Studies in the Genesis of the Naval Profession." *British Journal of Sociology* 1, no. 4 (Dec. 1950): 291–309.

Fanon, Frantz. *The Wretched of the Earth: A Negro Psychoanalysts's Study of the Problems of Racism and Colonialism in the World Today*. New York: Grove Press, 1961.

Fernandes, Florestano. *The Negro in Brazilian Society*. New York: Atheneum Books, 1971.

Ferrer, Ada. *Insurgent Cuba: Race, Nation, and Revolution, 1868–1898*. Chapel Hill: University of North Carolina Press, 1999

Folarin, Shyllon O. *Black People in Britain, 1555–1833*. London: Oxford University Press, 1977.

Fontaine, Pierre-Micheel, ed. *Race, Class and Power in Brazil*. Los Angeles: University of California Press, 1985.

Foucault, Michel. *Discipline and Punish: The Birth of the Prison*. New York: Vintage Books, 1995 [1975].

Frank, Zephyr L., *Dutra's World: Wealth and Family in Nineteenth-Century Rio de Janeiro*. Albuquerque: University of New Mexico Press, 2004.

Freyre, Gilberto. *Order and Progress: Brazil from Monarchy to Republic*. New York: Knopf, 1970.

Fryer, Peter. *Staying Power: The History of Black People in Britain*. London: Pluto Press, 1984.

Galloway, J. H. "The Last Years of Slavery on the Sugar Plantations of Northeastern Brazil." *Hispanic American Historical Review* 51, no. 4 (Nov. 1971): 586–605.

Gilbert, Arthur N. "Buggery and the British Navy, 1700–1861." *Journal of Social History* 10, no. 1 (Autumn 1976): 72–98.

Gilroy, Paul. *Ain't No Black in the Union Jack: The Cultural Politics of Race and Nation*. Chicago: University of Chicago Press, 1987.

———. *The Black Atlantic: Modernity and Double Consciousness*. Cambridge, Mass.: Harvard University Press, 1993.

Goldin, Claudia Dale. *Urban Slavery in the American South: A Quantitative History*. Chicago: University of Chicago Press, 1976.

Goulart, José Alipio. *Da Palmatória ao Patíbulo: Castigos de Escravos no Brasil*. Rio de Janeiro: Conquista, 1971.

Graham, Richard. *Britain and the Onset of Modernization in Brazil, 1850–1914*. Cambridge: Cambridge University Press, 1972.

———. "Empire (1822–1889), 1850–1870." In *Brazil: Empire and Republic*, ed. Leslie Bethell. Cambridge, Mass.: Cambridge University Press, 1989.

———. "Free African Brazilians and the State in Slavery Times." In *Racial Politics in Contemporary Brazil*, ed. Michael Hanchard, 30–58. Durham, N.C.: Duke University Press, 1999.

———. *The Idea of Race in Latin America, 1870–1940*. Austin: University of Texas Press, 1990.

Graham, Sandra Lauderdale. *House and Street: The Domestic World of Servants and Masters in Nineteenth-Century Rio de Janeiro*. Cambridge: Cambridge University Press, 1988.

Granato, Fernando. *O Negro da Chibata: O marinheiro que colocou a República na mira dos canhões*. Rio de Janeiro: Editora Objetiva Ltda., 2000.

Green, James N. *Beyond Carnival: Male Homosexuality in Twentieth-Century Brazil*. Chicago: University of Chicago Press, 1999.

Greenhalg, Juvenal. *O Arsenal de Marinha do Rio de Janeiro na História: 1763–1822*. Rio de Janeiro: Instituto Brasileiro de Geografia e Estatística, 1951.

———. *O Arsenal de Marinha do Rio de Janeiro na História, 1822–1889*. Vol. 2. Rio de Janeiro: Arsenal de Marinha, 1965.

———. *Presiganga and Calabouços: prisões da Marinha no século XIX*. Rio de Janeiro: Serviço de Documentação da Marinha, 1998.

Guha, Ranajit. "The Prose of Counter-Insurgency," In *Selected Subaltern Studies*, ed.Ranajit Guha and Gayatri Chakravorty Spivak, 45–84. Oxford: Oxford University Press, 1988.

Hahner, June E. "The Brazilian Armed Forces and the Overthrow of the Monarchy: Another Perspective." *Americas* 26, no. 2 (October, 1969): 171–82.

———. *Poverty and Politics: The Urban Poor in Brazil, 1870–1920*. Albuquerque: University of New México, 1986.

Hearnshaw, F. J. C. *Sea-Power and Empire*. London: George G. Harrap, 1940.

Hobson, Rolf. *Imperialism at Sea: Naval Strategic Thought, the Ideology of Sea Power and the Tirpitz Plan, 1875–1914*. Boston: Brill Academic Press, 2002.

Hoetink, H. *Slavery and Race Relations in the Americas: Comparative Note on their Nature and Nexus*. New York: Harper and Row, 1973.

Holloway, Thomas H. "'A Healthy Terror': Police Repression of Capoeiras in Nineteenth-Century Rio de Janeiro." *Hispanic American Historical Review* 69, no. 4 (Nov. 1989): 637–76.

———. *Policing Rio de Janeiro: Repression and Resistance in a 19th-Century City*. Stanford, Calif.: Stanford University Press, 1993.

Holt, Thomas. *The Problem of Freedom: Race, Labor and Politics in Jamaica and Britain, 1832–1938*. Baltimore, Md.: Johns Hopkins University Press, 1992.

Hough, Richard. *The Big Battleship*. Penzance, UK: Periscope, 2003 [1966].

Howes, Robert. "Race and Transgressive Sexuality in Adolfo Caminha's "Bom-Crioulo." *Luso-Brazilian Review* 38, no. 1 (Summer 2001): 41–62.

Huggins, Martha Knisely. *From Slavery to Vagrancy in Brazil: Crime and Social Control in the Third World*. New Brunswick, N.J.: Rutgers University Press, 1985.

Johnson, Lyman L., and Sonya Lipsett-Rivera, eds. *The Faces of Honor*. Albuquerque: University of New Mexico Press, 1998.

Johnson, Walter. *Soul by Soul: Life Inside the Antebellum Slave Market*. Cambridge, Mass.: Harvard University Press, 1999.

Karasch, Mary C. *Slave Life in Rio de Janeiro 1808–1850*. Princeton, N.J.: Princeton University Press, 1987.

Keys, Dick, and Ken Smith. *Down Elswick Slipways: Armstrong's Ships and People, 1884–1918*. Newcastle: Newcastle City Libraries, 1996.

Kiple, Kenneth F. *Blacks in Colonial Cuba, 1774–1899.* Gainesville: University Presses of Florida, 1976.

Kok, Glória. *Rio de Janeiro na época da Av. Central.* São Paulo: Bei Comunicação, 2005.

Kraay, Hendrik. *Race, State, and Armed Forces in Independence-Era Brazil: Bahia (1790s–1840s).* Stanford, Calif.: Stanford University Press, 2004.

———. "Reconsidering Recruitment in Imperial Brazil." *Americas* 55, no. 1 (July 1998): 1–33.

———. "Slavery, Citizenship and Military Service in Brazil's Mobilization for the Paraguayan War." *Slavery and Abolition: A Journal of Slave and Post-Slave Studies* 18, no. 3 (1997): 228–56.

Lacombe, Américo Jacobina, Eduardo da Silva, and Francisco de Assis Barbosa, eds. *Rui Barbosa e a queima dos arquivos.* Rio de Janeiro: Fundaçafio Casa de Rui Barbosa, 1988.

Land, Isaac. "Customs of the Sea: Flogging, Empire, and the 'True British Seaman,' 1770 to 1870." *Interventions: The International Journal of Postcolonial Studies* 3, no. 2 (2001): 169–85.

———. *War, Nationalism, and the British Sailor, 1750–1850.* New York: Palgrave MacMillan, 2009.

Lima, Lana Lage da Gama, and Renato Pinto Venâncio. "O abandono de crianças negras no Rio de Janeiro." In *Historia da Criança no Brasil,* ed. Mary Del Priore. São Paulo: Contexto, 1996.

Livermore, Seward W. "Battleship Diplomacy in South America: 1905–1925." *Journal of Modern History* 16, no. 1 (March 1944): 31–48.

Lopes, Murilo Ribeiro. *Rui Barbosa e a Marinha.* Rio de Janeiro: Casa de Rui Barbosa, 1953.

Love, Joseph L. *The Revolt of the Whip.* Stanford, Calif.: Stanford University Press, 2012.

Maestri, Mário. *1910: A Revolta dos Marinheiros, Uma Saga Negra.* São Paulo: Global Ed., 1982.

———. *Cisnes negros: 1910: a revolta dos marinheiros contra a chibata.* São Paulo: Editora Moderna, 2000.

Maia, Prado. *A Marinha de Guerra do Brasil na Colônia e no império.* Rio de Janeiro, Livraria Editora Cátedra, 1975.

Malerba, Jurandir. "Sob o Verniz das Idéias: Liberalismo, escravidão e valores patriarcais no comentadores do Código Criminal do Império do Brasil, 1830–1888." Master's thesis, Universidade Federal Fluminense, 1992.

Marder, Arthur J. *The Anatomy of British Sea Power.* New York: Knopf, 1940.

Martins, Hélio Leôncio. "A revolta da Armada-1893." In *História naval brasileira.* Rio de Janeiro: Serviço de Documentação da Marinha, 1995.

———. *A Revolta dos Marinheiros, 1910.* São Paulo: Editora Nacional; Rio de Janeiro: Serviço de Documentação da Marinha, 1988.

Martins Filho, João Roberto. *A Marinha brasileira na era dos encouraçados, 1895–1910.* Rio de Janeiro: Editora FGV, 2010.

Matta, Roberto da. *A casa e a rua: Espaço cidadania, mulher, e morte no Brasil.* Rio de Janeiro: Ed. Guanabara, 1987.

Mattos, Marcelo Badaró. "Experiences in Common: Slavery and 'Freedom' in the Process of Rio de Janeiro's Working-Class Formation (1850–1910)." *International Review of Social History* 5 (Aug. 2010): 193–213.

———. "Vadios, Jogadores, Mendigos e Bêbados na Cidade do Rio de Janeiro do Início do Século." Master's thesis, Universidade Federal Fluminense, 1991.

Mattos, Hebe Maria. "Beyond Masters and Slaves: Subsistence Agriculture as a Survival Strategy in Brazil during the Second Half of the Nineteenth Century." In *The Abolition of Slavery and the Aftermath of Emancipation in Brazil*, ed. Rebecca J. Scott et al., 55–84. Durham, N.C.: Duke University Press, 1988.

———. *Das cores do silêncio: os significados da liberdade no sudeste escravista, Brasil século XIX*. Rio de Janeiro: Arquivo Nacional, 1995.

———. *Escravidão e cidadania no Brasil Monárquico*. Rio de Janeiro: Jorge Zahar Ed., 2000.

Mattoso, Katia M. de Queirós. *To Be a Slave in Brazil: 1550–1888*. New Brunswick, N.J.: Rutgers Univ. Press, 1979.

McCann, Frank. "The Nation in Arms: Obligatory Military Service during the Old Republic." In *Essays Concerning the Socioeconomic History of Brazil and Portuguese India*, ed. Dauril Alden and Warren Dean, 211–43. Gainesville: University Presses of Florida, 1977.

McDermott, Patrick Michael. *A History of the Brazilian Navy*. Master's thesis, University of South Carolina, 1968.

McKee, Christopher. *Sober Men and True: Sailor Lives in the Royal Navy, 1900–1945*. Cambridge, Mass.: Harvard University Press, 2002.

McKenzie, Peter. *W. G. Armstrong: The Life and Times of William George Armstrong, Baron Armstrong of Cragside*. Newcastle: Longhirst Press, 1983.

Meade, Teresa. *"Civilizing" Rio: Reform and Resistance in a Brazilian City 1889–1930*. University Park: Penn State Press, 1997.

Meznar, Joan E. "Orphans and the Transition from Slave to Free Labor in Northeast Brazil: The Case of Campina Grande, 1850–1888." *Journal of Social History* 27, no. 3 (Spring 1994): 499–515.

———. "The Ranks of the Poor: Military Service and Social Differentiation in Northeast Brazil, 1830–1875." *Hispanic American Historical Review* 72, no. 3 (Aug. 1992): 335–51.

Moraes, Paulo Ricardo de. *João Cândido*, Porto Alegre: tchê!/RBS, 1984.

Moran, Daniel, and Arthur Waldron, eds. *The People in Arms: Military Myth and National Mobilization Since the French Revolution*. Cambridge: Cambridge University Press, 2003.

Morel, Edmar. *A Revolta da Chibata*. 5th ed. São Paulo: Paz e Terra, 2010 [1959].

Morel, Marco, and Sílvia Capanema P. de Almeida. "O outro navegante: Novas informações sobre a revolta indicam uma segunda liderança, que colocou no papel as articulações dos marinheiros." *Revista de Historia da Biblioteca Nacional* 5, no. 53 (Feb. 2010). 36–41.

Morgan, Philip, and Sean Hawkins, eds. *Black Experience and the Empire*. London: Oxford University Press, 2004.

Morgan, Zachary R. "Brazil: The Revolt of the Lash, 1910." In *Naval Mutinies of the Twentieth Century: An International Perspective*, ed. Bruce Elleman and Christopher Bell. Portland, Ore.: Frank Cass, 2003.

———. "Legislating the Lash: Race and the Conflicting Modernities of Enlistment and Corporal Punishment in the Military of the Brazilian Empire." *Journal of Colonialism and Colonial History* 5, no. 2 (2004): n.p.

Motta, Roberto, ed. *Os Afro-brasilieros*. Recife: Fundação Joaquim Nabuco, Editora Massangana, 1982.

Muhammad, Khalil. *The Condemnation of Blackness*. Cambridge, Mass.: Harvard University Press, 2010.

Museu da Imagem e do Som. *João Cândido, o almirante negro*. Rio de Janeiro: Gryphus, 1999.

Nabuco, Joaquim. *Abolitionismo: The Brazilian Antislavery Struggle.* Urbana: University of Illinois Press, 1977.

Nascimento, Abdias do, and Elisa Larken Nascimento. *Africans in Brazil: A Pan-African Perspective.* Trenton, N.J.: Africa World Press, 1992.

Nascimento, Álvaro Pereira do. *A Ressaca da Marujada: Recrutamento e disciplina na Amrada Imperial.* Rio de Janeiro: Arquivo Nacional, 2001.

——. *Cidadania, cor e disciplina na revolta dos marinheiros de 1910.* Rio de Janeiro: Mauad X: FAPERJ, 2008.

——. "Entre o justo e o injusto: o castigo corporal na marinha de guerra." In *Direitos e Justiças no Brasil,* ed. Silvia Hunold Lara and Joseli Maria Nunes Mendonça, 267–303. Campinas, São Paulo: Editora da UNICAMP, 2006.

Needell, Jeffrey D. "The *Revolta Contra Vacina* of 1904: The Revolt against 'Modernization' in Belle-Époque Rio de Janeiro." *Hispanic American Historical Review* 67, no. 2 (May 1987): 233–69.

——. "Rio de Janeiro and Buenos Aires: Public Space and Public Consciousness in Fin-De-Siecle Latin America." *Comparative Studies in Society and History* 37, no. 3 (July 1995): 519–40.

Nowell-Smith, Simon. *Edwardian England, 1901–1914.* Oxford: Oxford University Press, 1964.

Patterson, Orlando. *Slavery and Social Death: A Comparative Study.* Cambridge, Mass.: Harvard University Press, 1982.

Pearce, Malcolm Lynn. "A Marinha Brasileira de 1900 a 1930." *Navigator: Subsídios Para História Marítima do Brasil,* no. 12 (Dec. 1975).

Rasor, Eugene L. *Reform in the Royal Navy: A Social History of the Lower Deck, 1850–1880.* Hamden, Conn.: Archon Books, 1976.

Rediker, Marcus. *Between the Devil and the Deep Blue Sea: Merchant Seamen, Pirates, and the Anglo-American Maritime World.* Cambridge, Mass.: Cambridge University Press, 1987.

Reid, Alastair J. *The Tide of Democracy: Shipyard Workers and Social Relations in Britain, 1870–1950.* Manchester, UK: Manchester University Press, 2010.

Reis, João José, *Slave Rebellion in Brazil.* Baltimore, Md.: Johns Hopkins University Press, 1995.

Renault, Delso. *A Vida Brasileira no Final do Século XIX.* Rio de Janeiro: José Olympio Editora, 1987.

Ribeiro, Carlos Antonio Costa. *Cor e Criminalidade: Estudo e Análise da Justiça no Rio de Janeiro (1900–1930).* Rio de Janeiro: Editoria UFRJ, 1995.

Robinson, Joe. *The Life and Times of Francie Nichol of South Shields.* 2nd ed. London: Futura Publications Limited, 1975.

Rodger, N. A. M. *The Wooden World: An Anatomy of the Georgian Navy.* Annapolis, Md.: Naval Institute Press, 1986.

Rouquie, Alain. *The Military and the State in Latin America.* Berkeley: University of California Press, 1982.

Russell-Wood, A.J.R. *The Black Man in Slavery and Freedom in Colonial Brazil.* New York: St. Martin's Press, 1982.

Salvatore, Ricardo, and Carlos Aguirre, eds. *The Birth of the Penitentiary in Latin America: Essays on Criminology, Prison Reform, and Social Control, 1830–1940.* Austin: University of Texas Press, 1996.

Scheina, Robert L. *Latin America: A Naval History, 1810–1987.* Annapolis, Md.: Naval Institute Press, 1987.

——. *Latin America's Wars.* Vol. 1: *The Age of the Caudillo, 1791–1899.* Dulles, Va.: Brassey's, 2003.

——. *Latin America's Wars.* Vol. 2: *The Age of the Professional Soldier, 1900–2001.* Dulles, Va.: Brassey's, 2003.

Schencking, J. Charles. *Making Waves: Politics, Propaganda, and the Emergence of the Imperial Japanese Navy, 1868–1922.* Stanford, Calif.: Stanford University Press, 2005.

Schwarcz, Lilia Moritz. *The Spectacle of the Races: Scientists, Institutions, and the Race Question in Brazil, 1870–1930.* Trans. Leland Guyer. New York: Hill and Wang, 1999.

Scott, J. D. *Vickers: A History.* London: Weidenfeld and Nicolson, 1962.

Scott, Rebecca J. "Defining the Boundaries of Freedom in the World of Cane: Cuba, Brazil, and Louisiana after Emancipation." *American Historical Review* 99, no. 1 (Feb. 1994): 70–102.

Silva, Marcos A. da. *Contra a chibata: marinheiros brasileiros em 1910.* São Paulo: Brasiliense, 1982.

Silveira, Almirante Balthasar da. *Pequenos Estudos Sôbre Grandes Administradores do Brasil.* Rio de Janeiro: Departamento Administrativo do Serviço Público, Serviço de Documentação, 1958.

Skidmore, Thomas E. *Black into White: Race and Nationality in Brazilian Thought.* 2nd ed. Durham, N.C.: Duke University Press, 1993 [1974].

———. "Racial Ideas and Social Policy in Brazil, 1870–1940." In *The Idea of Race in Latin America,* ed. Richard Graham. Austin: University of Texas Press, 1990.

———. "Workers and Soldiers: Urban Labor Movements and Elite Responses in Twentieth-Century Latin America." In *Elites, Masses and Modernization in Latin America,* ed. Virginia Bernhard. Austin: University of Texas Press, 1979.

Smallman, Shawn C. *Fear and Memory in the Brazilian Army and Society.* Chapel Hill: University of North Carolina Press, 2002.

Soares, Carlos Eugênio Líbane. *A capoeira escrava e outras tradições rebeldes no Rio de Janeiro: 1808–1850.* Campinas, Brazil: Editora da Unicamp, 2001.

Sousa, Jorge Prata de. *Escravidão ou morte: Os escravos brasileiros na Guerra do Paraguai.* Rio de Janeiro: Mauad, AD-ESA, 1996.

Stepan, Nancy. *The Hour of Eugenics: Race, Gender, and Nation in Latin America.* Ithaca, NY: Cornell University Press, 1991.

Tannenbaum, Frank. *Slave and Citizen.* Boston: Beacon Press, 1992 [1947].

Taylor, James L., ed. *A Portuguese-English Dictionary.* Stanford, Calif.: Stanford University Press, 1989.

Thompson, Vincent. *The Making of the African Diaspora in the Americas, 1441–1900.* New York: Longman, 1987.

Trouillot, Michel-Rolph. *Silencing the Past: Power and the Production of History.* Boston: Beacon Press, 1995.

Vale, Brian. "British Sailors and the Brazilian Navy, 1822–1850." *Mariner's Mirror* 80, no. 3 (Aug. 1994): 312–25.

———. *Independence or Death: British Sailors and Brazilian Independence, 1822–1825.* London: Tauris Academic Studies, 1996.

———. "Lord Cochrane in Brazil: The Naval War of Independence 1823." *Mariners Mirror* 57, no. 4 (1971): 415–42.

Velasco e Cruz, Maria Cecília. "Puzzling out Slave Origins in Rio de Janeiro Port Unionism: The 1906 Strike and the Sociedade de Resistência dos Trabalhadores em Trapiche e Café." *Hispanic American Historical Review* 86, no. 2 (May 2006): 205–45.

Vinson, Ben, III, and Matthew Restall. "Black Soldiers, Native Soldiers: Meanings of Military Service in the Spanish American Colonies." In Matthew Restall, *Beyond Black and Red: African-Native Relations in Colonial Latin America,*

15–52. Albuquerque: University of New Mexico Press, 2005.

Voelz, Peter M. *Slave and Soldier: The Military Impact of Blacks in the Colonial Americas.* New York: Routledge, 1993.

Wagner, Bryan. *Disturbing the Peace: Black Culture and the Police Power after Slavery.* Cambridge, Mass.: Harvard University Press, 2009.

Warren, Kenneth. *Armstrongs of Elswick: Growth in Engineering and Armaments to the Merger with Vickers.* London: MacMillan, 1989.

Wilson, Lt. A. W., R. A. *The Story of the Gun.* Woolrich, UK: Royal Artillery Institution, 1944.

Index

ZACHARY R. MORGAN is a fellow at the Hutchins Center for African and African American Research at Harvard University and has held faculty positions in the Departments of History at Boston College and William Paterson University.